A MATTER OF OPINION

66 **C**ome back with us now to those thrilling days of yesteryear," the announcer on the old *Lone Ranger* radio program would say. Come back, with this book, to those thrilling and not-so-thrilling days in the life of the only full-time Free Will Baptist evangelist over the last half of the last century. Back to the days when rural churches and homes to stay in weren't air conditioned. When revivals often ran two weeks, with services morning and evening. When the local church revival was the biggest event in the community and people came from all around. When the preacher brought his wife and kids with him and the church's pastor often didn't show up!

Bobby Jackson figured that God wanted him in that kind of ministry and never swerved, going wherever he was asked and for whatever they gave him. He was obligated, he said. His has been a unique and blessed ministry, and here's the story, without sugar coating. The highs and the lows and everything in between.

I've known him throughout, but it's not for that reason I recommend this book. I think you ought to read it because without what's here you won't know the whole story. You won't know where we've been, and you have to know that in order to plan where we're going. You'll laugh and you'll cry, and you'll get insight into the heart of a sharecropper's son who came to Jesus and did what he thought God wanted him to do. You'll be better for it.

– Dr. Robert Picirilli, retired professor and dean of Free Will Baptist Bible College, former Moderator of National Association of Free Will Baptists, general editor Randall House Commentary, Greek scholar and New Testament expositor.

The life's story of Bobby Jackson may be told on two levels. The first is personal – his own ministry of evangelism and all his experiences and stories. The other is as a mirror of 20th century Free Will Baptists. There's no one else who has seen, experienced, led, preached to, visited with, been abused by, converted, convicted, and analyzed FWB as he has. To those of us who lived through those years, this book is interesting reading; and to historians it is invaluable.

His account is virtually an oral history, and that format serves him well. I could hear his voice through the words on every page. He has a gifted speaking voice, pleasant and winsome to listen to, and hearing it through his written words is a pleasure.

I love this book. It's like jumping into his car and tagging along during a sixty-year road trip encompassing 2,000 revivals, 15,000 services, and a disproportionate number of misadventures. This is the unique story of a unique man during an unrepeatable era of American church life. The one statistic missing from the book is the number of people who found Christ during Bobby's ministry. Those calculations will only be made *Beyond*

the Stars. One thing's for sure–there'll never be another Bobby Jackson. I love him and Jane, and I stand in debt for their faithfulness in delivering a *Message that Matters.*
–Rob Morgan, prolific writer, published over 20 titles, including The Promise and Red Sea Rules, conference speaker, Bible Teacher, Senior Pastor Donelson Fellowship, Donelson, TN.

"Wow ... The story is fascinating, both on a personal and historical level.... I feel as though I took a trip through the recent history of Free Will Baptists."
–Eric Thomsen, writer, journalist, managing editor ONE magazine.

This one's a keeper! Wow, what a story. *Yesterday* belongs in every Free Will Baptist home. Evangelist Bobby Jackson takes readers by the hand and leads them through more than 50 years of laughter, revival meetings, and convention business sessions. The former moderator of the National Association of Free Will Baptists rolls out nearly six decades of denominational history, told like you've never heard it said until now. You don't want to miss this one.
–Jack Williams, Director of Communications Free Will Baptist Bible College, former editor of Contact magazine.

Evangelist Bobby Jackson presents a concise yet comprehensive summation of his years as an evangelist and denominational leader. Three perspectives surface in his book.
The first perspective is a *Heavenly Perspective.* Evangelist Jackson *Determined the Will of God, Did the Will of God* and *Delighted*

in the Will of God. His fidelity to God's call presents a challenge to every reader.

The second perspective is a *Human Perspective.* Evangelist Jackson's life exemplifies faithfulness, focus and fervency in his ministry. His life, labor and legacy serve as a model for others to emulate.

The third perspective is a *Historical Perspective.* The author conceptualizes with clarity, conciseness and comprehensiveness his life, labor and lessons. The reader comes to the conclusion that Bobby Jackson enjoyed his life and ministry. This book is quality work in style and substance, and reading it will be an enlightening, educational and enjoyable experience.
–Melvin Worthington, retired Executive Secretary of National Association of Free Will Baptists after 20 years service, conference speaker, co-pastor Liberty FWB Church, Ayden, NC.

I love to read an autobiography–especially when it is the life-story of someone I know. I have seldom read a more interesting one than this. To review the life story of Bobby and Jane has been exciting, thrilling, and amazing. I am shocked and very disappointed that they were paid so little for their outstanding ministry. They have truly been present-day missionaries for Christ and His Kingdom. Only eternity will reveal the results—souls saved, lives rededicated, those entering full-time Christian service, and especially the profound spiritual encouragement given to Christians all over America and elsewhere–including my wife and me.

I heartily recommend this book.
–Dr. Charles Thigpen, retired president of Free Will Baptist Bible College, former Moderator of National Association of Free

Will Baptists, past promotional secretary for Tennessee Free Will Baptists.

When my husband finished reading your book, I could not resist reading it, too. Not many college freshman English teachers live to read a book written by one of their students. Reading it was an enriching and rewarding experience!

I especially enjoyed your chapter about the Gospeliers! The creative way you chose to tell that part of the story was delightful.

From the literary viewpoint:

your style is much like having a conversation with you,

your description is vivid and excellent,

your humor adds much to your story.

–Mrs.Charles Thigpen, retired English and Speech professor.

"Yesterday" is a great read. I laughed and I cried as I reminisced with Bobby. Yesterday is a book that reminds us of where we came from and how we have evolved as a denomination through the eye of one who was there. It is hilarious, hard hitting, and historical. I love this book. It is a "Must Read."

–Carl E. Cheshier, former moderator National Association of Free Will Baptists, retired president of Hillsdale College, Moore, Oklahoma.

I have read and re-read your book and laughed and cried as you most brilliantly presented your life story.

–Dr. Alton Loveless, author, publisher, former CEO Randall House Publications, Nashville, Tennessee.

YESTERDAY 1953

Published by

BJEA

Other books by Bobby Jackson

Messages that Matter

Beyond the Stars

Awakening in the Wilderness

Six Steps to Successful Christian Living

All scripture quotations are from the King James Version

ISBN: 1470110504
ISBN 13: 9781470110505

YESTERDAY

MEMOIRS OF AN ITINERATE
EVANGELIST FROM 1950 to 2010

BOBBY JACKSON

TO

JANE

TABLE OF CONTENTS

ACKNOWLEDGMENTS

The one person without whom this project would have been impossible is Jane, my wife since 1953. She has transferred handwritten material from yellow pages into the computer, adding endings to words, interpreting stuff written between the lines or scribbled in the margins with arrows pointing every direction, completing unfinished sentences, and filling in left-out punctuation marks.

The only way I can think and write at the same time is in long hand, and most of the time the brain runs so far ahead of the hand that the hand skips over a lot of words in an effort to catch up. After the material is in the computer, I can add or delete a word here and there using the Columbus method – discover a key and land on it. Jane is the only person who can interpret those original first drafts.

Getting the memories on paper was not her only contribution. A vital part was recalling details beyond the reach of my recollection. At our age it takes both our brains to make one. We could not afford to get divorced; we each have only half a brain. The account of the memories is more accurate because she lived them with me.

Jane, thanks for the hours that became days and weeks at the computer, and for your compliments on the writing that encouraged me to continue, and most of all for living with me through the experiences that produced the memories.

Second only to Jane, Jack Williams had a unique part in putting these memories together. He has served as an unpaid editor of a sort, reading all the chapters, making good suggestions, correcting some things that needed correcting, and improving the material technically and practically.

Jack, thanks for taking time to read with detailed observation the various drafts of the manuscript, and giving your professional advice. You are good! Your prompt response amazed me... and all without pay. Remember, you get half the profit off the movie rights.

Dr. Robert Picirilli gave positive feedback after reading several sections of the manuscript, and along with James Earl Raper and Eugene Waddell helped to recover and clear up much of the Gospeliers' capers.

Pic, thanks for the memories of 60 years singing together, and for being my friend. Thanks to Raper and Waddell for being a vital part of my life. Without the three of you, there would be no Gospeliers chapter.

A very special thanks to Jean Picirilli Lewis, who grew up and became pianist for the quartet for over 30 years and whose professional proofreading expertise saved me from the embarrassment of many mistakes.

Good words have come from others who read some of the early drafts—Rob Morgan, Dr. Melvin Worthington, Dr. Matthew Pinson, and Dr. Charles Thigpen. Thank you for your encouragement.

An evangelist doesn't preach for people or churches. He preaches for preachers, and not all preachers, but a special circle of preachers. Each evangelist works with a group of pastors who are the source of his invitations for evangelistic meetings. More than 100, so many it would be impossible to name them, made up that circle with whom I worked for 60 years. In the busy decades between 1950 and 2000, the schedule stayed filled for two years, and we were always booking services three years ahead. Some of those pastors were permanently in the schedule for every two or three years, and I returned to their churches 12, 14, up to 17 times. Those men have been an essential part of the ministry from which these memories were made.

The seed for this book of memories was planted in 2000 by Dr. Jeff Gaskins, pastor of our church (Trinity Free Will Baptist Church) in Greenville, NC, at the time. The quarterly meeting was at the church and the pastor was responsible for the program. Jeff approached me requesting that I speak on the subject, *What Life Has Been as an Itinerate Evangelist for the Past 50 Years.* Preparing the material, I jotted down a few thoughts to give it some organization: places slept, people met, pulpits filled, pay received.

After speaking for 30 minutes, time was left for questions and discussions. Someone suggested, *That material should be written down, so generations to come will have an insight into life on the road as an evangelist during the years between 1950 and 2000.*

Others agreed, which was easy for them, since they didn't have to write it. Writing is difficult for me. Having neither the patience nor intelligence to be good at it, I hate it. But the aggravating thought kept nagging and pushing, and after 10 years has produced fruit. The soil in my brain is not as fertile as it once was. Seed sown there grows slowly, which explains the time involved in producing this manuscript.

Mark Twain said, "The difference between the right word and the almost right word is the difference between lightning and a lightning bug." Finding the right word is difficult and time-consuming when it is lost in a brain filled with the almost right.

The name of God is not on every page, but maybe a spiritual mind will recognize that He was involved through all of it. Whatever was for His glory, He alone knows and will evaluate my life accordingly.

I refuse to make reference to the words of Jesus from the cross, because there is nothing in the history of the universe, in time nor eternity, which bears any similarity to, nor can be compared with, the work that Christ completed when He died for our sins on a cross. But I do feel free to quote a notorious Roman governor, who lived at the same time: "What I have written, I have written."

INTRODUCTION

All of life is past tense except the moment that comes from the future at the speed of light and passes in a flash as the present on its way to the past. Memory goes into the past, pulls that moment back into the present, relives it as long and as many times as it pleases, giving it lingering quality in time. Memory, however, is subjective and selective, coloring and reshaping those moments. Beauty, and history, are in the eyes of the beholder.

Someone posed this question to Sir Winston Churchill concerning his administration and the big war, "How will history speak of you and this critical time of war?"

"History will be kind to me for I intend to write it." Winston Churchill, 1874-1965.

In autobiographical material the hero is too easily recognized. How can such an account be written without beginning every sentence and every paragraph with the first person singular personal pronoun? It could be done in third person. The suitcase which tagged along for 45 years could have written it, except it died before the story ended. Jane could have written parts of it, not all, since most of the time she traveled with me as a beautiful photograph in my mind, and a lover in my heart. That's not a good place from which to observe events. A penman with a foreign name could have disguised the hero for a few pages.

None of these wanted the job. So "*I*" wrote it.

The order of the story is topical, not chronological, although in some chapters there is a timeline. Each chapter is actually a story within itself. Specific dates and places were not drawn from the memory bank. At the time of their deposit a written record was made so as to balance the account. From June of 1955, three facts were jotted down – the date, the place, and the sermon. The Lord does much better at keeping up with the results. People, places, problems, pleasures were all filtered through the lens of memory, making them less absolute and much more subjective.

One day I looked into the crystal ball searching for tomorrow and what I saw was yesterday…or maybe it was tomorrow looking so much like yesterday that I didn't recognize it.

Here is part of what appeared from Yesterday.

DAY BEFORE YESTERDAY

Yesterday began with a conversion that changed the mind, the motives, the ambitions, the plans, the direction, the life of a seventeen-year-old boy in the beginning of his senior year in high school. What theologians call regeneration, a new birth. That seems an appropriate place to begin a biography which was totally formed by that experience with Christ Jesus, the Lord.

The Birthday

There is a preface. The day before yesterday began on Monday, December 14, 1931, in a three-room, shotgun, row house, in the Five Points section of Wilson, North Carolina, where a twenty-nine-year-old woman was laboring to give birth to a baby boy, fearing that she would lose him as she had two boys previously in the birthing process. Both were born dead or died so soon after birth that they were never named. She had buried them in little wooden handmade boxes in unmarked graves in the cornfield behind the house on her father's farm.

Dr. C. H. Rand was laboring with her in a desperate effort to deliver this one alive. When there appeared to be only one chance, with forceps in an almost semi-cesarean fashion and great force, he pulled the baby from the womb. He was alive. The joy of a living little boy in her arms anesthetized her to the pain and physical damage to her body for the moment. Her deep gratitude to the physician was stamped on the little fellow for life. She gave him the doctor's name – Bobby <u>Rand</u> Jackson.

Bessie Francis Mayo Jackson, age 29, and Joel J. Jackson, age 32, finally were the parents of a healthy, living son. What happens twice doesn't always happen three times. Now and then there is an exception to the rule.

Two and one-half years later she gave birth, extremely prematurely (weighed less than two pounds) to another boy who was kept alive, wrapped in blankets on the hearth before a fire in the fireplace in July – Billy, July 28, 1934. There were no incubators or hospital arrangements for the preemies of poor folks. She never bore another child.

In 1931, the world, the nation, the state, and the town of Wilson, were in the depths of the "Great Depression." Joel had worked at Hackney Body Company, making truck and school bus bodies 'til that ended, worked at carpentry 'til there was nothing to build or repair, drove an ice wagon door-to-door peddling ice by the nickel piece and coal by the bag 'til nobody had a nickel. A bag of coal was out of the question. He walked 25 miles from Wilson to Black Creek, Fremont, Pikeville, Goldsboro, seeking work on a farm or in a town and returned to Wilson without a job of any kind for any price.

"How do you remember the details of such an insignificant historical event?"

It seems like it was yesterday.

"But that was day before yesterday and the day before that."

The details are a little hard to find in a mind that was only three years old, so it has been necessary that a third person give the account. From 1935 my memory of events is much clearer, so I can tell the rest of the story.

Joel and Bessie Jackson 1920

Sharecroppers

In the fall of 1935, we were forced in desperation to move from Wilson to Wayne County between Fremont and Nahunta into the house with Daddy's father, Joseph G. Jackson, to help him till the farm he had rented for the next year. He had lost his farm in the financial failure of the banks. A farm valued in the tens of thousands of dollars sold for less than a thousand, and he was now a sharecropper.

Grandpa Jackson's rented place 1936

Tobacco curing barn

Tobacco Pack House

The frame tenant house stood on piers in an oak grove a hundred yards from the back door of Union Grove Free Will Baptist Church. Our family didn't attend church, but some teenage girls arranged for me to be in the Christmas play, Christmas of 1935.

At the end of the program Santa Claus appeared to distribute the stack of gifts under the tree. At four years old, I assumed that Santa was the source and the gifts were for everybody. Not knowing that all the packages had names written on them and were part of a gift exchange, I watched and waited anxiously for Santa to call my name and present me a gift. I didn't attend Sunday School. My name was not in the exchange drawing. The girls who invited me never thought about it. When all the gifts were gone, I stood empty handed. Santa Claus never called my name. He didn't even know me. A broken-hearted little boy wept. The girls quickly went to a nearby country store, bought a ten-cent bag of mixed hard Christmas candy, wrote my name on it, and pretended it came from Santa Claus.

I knew better and I didn't stop crying.

One year with Grandpa was all Mother could take, so we moved into a little dilapidated house, a mile behind Nahunta School up a path that was made into a dirt road by the state during that year–sharecroppers on our own. During tobacco harvest most of the barning help walked off the job on Daddy's day. Tobacco was burning in the July sun in the field. That day Mother looped 500 sticks, one week's cropping, enough to fill a 16 x 16 barn, single-handed, the work of three ordinary loopers in one day.

In the late fall of 1937, the family of four moved to a Hooks farm, a mile out of Fremont toward Kenly, to farm on halves during 1938. That winter I bought a pet, a kid goat, for a dollar, named him Billy and we fell in love with him. By the summer he had grown large enough to pull a wagon with one of us in it. Problem was, he would jump the fence, get out of his pasture, follow us everywhere or roam through the community. Daddy collared him, attached a chain, and fastened that to a tree to keep him penned. One weekend that summer we all left on Saturday, walked three or four miles to Aunt Minnie's, spent Saturday night, and returned home Sunday afternoon.

When Billy didn't call to us, nor run to the end of his chain to greet us, we assumed he had broken loose from the collar, jumped the fence, and attempted to follow us. Part of the assumption was right. He did try to follow us, had jumped the fence but had not broken loose from the collar, and was hanging on the outside of the fence, dead. When he jumped the fence, the chain was not long enough for his feet to reach the ground. He hanged himself. It was a sad funeral and we hoped he was as happy in Heaven as he had been on earth.

Two little boys had no way of knowing that in a few short months there would be another much more heartbreaking funeral as they said goodbye to their mother, who was killed in an automobile accident.

That fall Daddy and the landowner had a falling out over some tobacco that Daddy accused him of stealing. Knowing he was right, Daddy, who was usually an even-tempered person, became so angry he threatened to kill the landowner. Another tenant stopped him, calmed him, and brought him back to his senses. The Jacksons were forced to move immediately with nowhere to go, leaving their half of everything to the landlord.

It was too early in the fall for the game of fruit basket played by sharecroppers to begin. Most of them moved every year or two, not very far nor to any better circumstances. One difference between them and the serfs of Europe, serfs stayed with one owner on the same land. In the south, tenants were swapped and traded, one step above slavery. Between 1935 and 1940 we moved seven times, once every year, and twice one year.

Everything we owned could be loaded on two two-horse wagons and moved a few miles to a neighboring community and a different landowner of the same kind. Pigs, chickens, dogs, cats, all moved. My stepmother cut a little piece of fur off the cat's tail and buried it under the front steps of the new place to prevent the cat from going back home to the old place. It worked. What worked was the food out the back door not the fur under the front door. That's what kept the cat at the new house.

One tenant said they moved so often that when they went to get the chickens they would lie down and cross their legs, ready to be tied, knowing it was moving time. Our chickens weren't that cooperative. We had to catch and put them in coops.

The fall of 1938 was the year we moved twice. No farm for rent, no house was available except a three-room, shotgun, uninhabited place in the field behind John Mayo's, Mother's father, who owned a small farm and didn't lose it in the depression. We spent Christmas there, waiting for the tenant to move from the tiny piece of poor land that Rena, Mother's mother, had inherited from her father, George Waddell. In January, we took on the job of trying to produce a crop in sandy soil, infested with wild Bermuda grass, where corn grew four feet tall and produced nubbins. The grass, we dug out with a potato rake and burned. Daddy said it would come up again where the smoke settled on the other side of the field.

The Shotgun – Christmas, 1938

Mother's Death

Mother's body left Wilson in 1935, but her heart never joined it. Most Saturdays she followed her heart back to town. On Saturday morning, February 18, 1939, leaving Billy and me at Grandpa's house, for her younger sister, Lila, to watch over, she left with her brother Johnny and a friend for her weekly pilgrimage. She never came back. In an alcohol-related automobile accident in Dunn, North Carolina, she was killed. Her body was brought home to her father's house where it lay in a casket in the parlor. An uncle lifted me so I could see her. She looked like she was asleep. I touched her face, spoke to her, but she wouldn't wake up.

"Son, your mother's not asleep," he said. "Your mother's dead."

He took Billy and me for a walk through the field to the woods to get our minds off Mother, hoping that would help us stop crying. The funeral was conducted on the front porch, her body taken back to Wilson, and buried on the backside of the cemetery, near the water plant in an unmarked grave. Daddy didn't have money to purchase a grave nor pay for a funeral. He paid some by digging graves with a shovel for the undertaker. The man responsible for her death bought the grave.

When I was 21 and received my half of Mother's share from Grandpa's farm, I paid off the undertaker and bought a small tombstone to mark the body's resting place in the town where her heart never left. Daddy farmed the land, cooked the meals, washed and ironed the clothes, and tried to be mother and father to two boys, five and seven.

Billy and I spent Christmas 1939, with our grandparents, being told that when we came home after Christmas to Stantonsburg, North Carolina, where Daddy had hired out to milk 40 or 50 cows twice a day by hand at Doctor Crocker's Dairy Farm, we would have a new mother. She was to be a big secret and surprise. It was neither. We knew who she was, Mildred Gurley, a sixteen-year-old neighborhood girl with whom Daddy had been flirting all summer while her family helped on the farm.

When we arrived at the Dairy Farm, our suspicions were confirmed. Mildred was the new mother. The couple had gone to Dillon, South Carolina, where her age was no problem and our 40-year-old father had taken a sixteen-year-old wife. For one year Daddy milked cows from 2 a.m. to 7 a.m. and again from 2 p.m. until 7 p.m. That was enough.

Granny's Farm – Mother Died 1939

The Shack

That fall, 1940, we moved back to Wayne County, three miles out of Fremont toward Nahunta, down the road from that Union Grove Church, on one of many farms owned by a very wealthy landowner.

Half a mile off the road up a path in the edge of the woods was a three-room L-shaped shell of rotten weatherboarding, with a tin roof, cracked floors, broken windows, uninhabited and uninhabitable, dilapidated shack. There was no inside plumbing, no outside plumbing, no outhouse. (We didn't own any land but we had squatters' rights in the woods.) The heating system was a fireplace with the back out, a potbelly tin heater, and a wood-burning cook stove. Blocks of wood were used for steps to get in and out. Doors hung sideways off the hinges. Roof leaked, so did the floors. Some of the weatherboards had rotted so the wind could blow through making it air conditioned (same condition inside as out, summer and winter).

Some people cut a cat hole in the back door for the cat to go in and out. The shack didn't need a cat hole. There were a dozen holes in the bottom piece of rotten weatherboard where the cat and any other critter could go and come as he pleased. Kerosene lamps and lanterns lighted the place at night. The water system was an open, shallow, surface well from which to draw water with the help of a four-inch pulley, a chain, and a leaky bucket. Snow sifted in through cracks in the walls in winter. Rain ran in through holes in the roof in summer. The water that came in through the roof found its way out to the ground through the floor, without ever stopping to puddle. We moved the furniture around to keep it from getting wet in the process.

During the big snow in the winter of '42 four inches of snow accumulated around the water bucket on the side table against the wall in the kitchen, so that we had enough to make snow ice cream without having to go outside to get snow. With no screens for doors and windows, flies, ants, mosquitoes and bedbugs took up residence year round considering themselves the chief inhabitants.

Ants ran to and fro like settlers in a wagon train snaking their way across the desert in the southwest, along a winding trail from the woodpile to the house, under the house, up a block pillar, through a crack in the kitchen floor, across the floor, up a table leg, over the table to the biscuit plate or the sugar dish, and that's where the trail ended. We set the table legs in jar lids filled with water so the ants would have to swim the moat before they could get to the biscuit plate and sugar dish.

It's impossible to get ants out of granulated sugar, but when you put the sugar in the tea they'll float to the top and you can skim them off. I have eaten chocolate-covered ants, sugar-coated ants, and unflavored ants. Chocolate is my choice, and preferred by most people.

The bedbugs flourished in the cracks and crevices of old cotton mattresses, wood bedsteads and pine board walls. Those bloodsuckers came out of their hiding places in the dark of night and added to the sleepless misery of the summer heat. Light sent them scurrying to their refuge beyond the reach of boiling hot water or quicksilver. But when DDT came along, that got 'em. DDT may have polluted the entire universe, but it got rid of chinches.

Flies were everywhere. Reach for a piece of raisin pie and all the raisins flew away. It was sweet potato pie all the time.

The yard was hoed, not sowed and mowed. After the last weed and blade of grass were cleared off, the sandy yard was swept with a yard-broom of dogwood sprouts… clean, except for the mess made by chickens that evidently inherited no genetic traits from cats in the evolutionary process.

The yard had been cleaned and swept, except for a ten-foot strip in the back which separated the house from the woods and was grown up in grass and weeds knee-deep to a giraffe, a baby giraffe. From the woods through that tall grass, a four-foot long chicken snake found his way into the house, and in a pile of dirty clothes behind a chair in the corner of the bedroom, was quietly waiting for a mouse, until on wash day Mildred found him in an armful of dirty clothes. Without further discussion that ten foot strip had to be dug up and cleaned out.

The Shack 1941-1944

Grandpa's House

On Saturday morning, midsummer 1942, Daddy, Mildred and some of her family left early on a trip to the beach for a day of fun in the sun, fishing and swimming. Billy and I were left alone at home with orders to dig the weeds and grass from that miniature jungle behind the house, rake it into piles, carry it with a pitchfork to the woods, and sweep the ground clean, more than enough hard labor for two little boys in one day.

For two years we had been forbidden to go to see our grandparents, the Mayos. The last time we went Billy had bruises on his back from being beaten by the stepmother with a tobacco stick. When Aunt Minnie brought us home she threatened Mildred that if it happened again she would take up the fight. To make sure it didn't happen again we were not permitted to go to Grandpa's house ever anymore.

That Saturday morning, angry from being left behind to labor while the others went away to play, by the time their car reached the end of the path, turned down the road and disappeared, I said to Billy, "We're not going to stay here and work all day. We're going to Grandpa's house."

Four miles on sandy dirt roads, past familiar landmarks and houses of folks we knew, the route didn't seem long at all. We spent Saturday night, and Grandpa brought us home Sunday afternoon. Daddy appeared to be glad to see us. Mildred quietly stayed out of sight until Grandpa left. We knew one of the worst whippings of our lives was coming. She beat Billy first. He wouldn't cry nor beg. I cried and begged her to stop. She wouldn't stop because he wouldn't cry. She finally gave up. With a sadistic smirk, she said to me, "Now it's your turn."

I was already crying and pleading with her to stop, so my whipping was not as severe as Billy's. With her vengeance satisfied she ordered us to get behind the house and do the job we were left to do on Saturday. She cursed and swore, "That will be the last time you will ever go to that bitch's house." And it was.

Behind the house, out of sight and sound of Mildred, unable to see through the flow of blinding tears, we chopped frantically at the ground. Between sobs, in a subdued voice, I said to Billy, "Someday we'll be big and she'll never beat us anymore."

Five years later, when I was fifteen years old, that day came.

When I became a man I went back looking for Grandpa's house. It was gone. Harvey Lee, the baby boy with whom Billy and I played so many days, had died young with muscular dystrophy. Granny had died from damage done by diabetes, never realizing she had a sugar problem. Bob, the German Shepherd that grew from a pup frolicking with two little boys and remembered us that Saturday after over two years separation, had been shot and killed by someone who was afraid of him.

The old five-room house, made of fat heart pine, standing on piers two feet high, with an L-shaped front porch, a kitchen set apart in the back from the rest of the house, connected by a breezeway, had burned down, taking with it the two large oaks that shaded and cooled the front porch with a breeze on a hot summer afternoon, the cape jasmine and sweet betsy bushes which filled the night air with their tranquilizing fragrance floating lightly through the bedroom where two little boys slept, the front room at the end of the porch where my mother's body was displayed in a casket, and the porch from which her funeral was preached to a small crowd on a cold February day.

The fire started from a fifty-pound stand of hog lard near the kitchen stove, swiftly spread to the main house, and the fat pine exploded like a tinderbox sending billows of black smoke boiling upwards taking with it the entire life of an old man.

In its place was now a cracker box, four rooms sitting in the blazing sun, no trees, no flowers, no history, no memories, no character. Grandpa was totally blind and lived there with a niece who took care of him. We talked about what used to be, about the Lord, and his spiritual situation. He said that he had repented of his sins and found forgiveness from Jesus and had stopped cursing. Long ago when he married Rena he stopped drinking. His deepest remorse and regret was that he never went to church with Rena when she was alive. He was ready and anxious to die and go to be with her.

We prayed. I hugged him, said goodbye, and a short time later he died.

The house was on the same road, in the same community, on exactly the same spot of ground, but it wasn't Grandpa's house. There's some question about whether a man can go home again, but when a boy becomes a man he can never again go back to Grandpa's house. That Saturday when two little boys ran away was in reality the last trip to Grandpa's house. The punishment was severe but the experience was worth it.

We dug at the grass 'til dark, washed off part of the dirt in a wooden washtub, and slept. We were back with the bedbugs, mosquitoes, flies, snakes, and stepmother. For two more years that was our home.

The Merkersons

Half a mile from our house on the main road, there lived a black family, the Merkersons, sharecropping for the same landlord on the same tract of land. The landowner was too tight to furnish enough farm equipment, so both tenants were forced to use the one tobacco setter, one cotton planter, and one corn planter. That became a bone of contention seeing as how that family was not only uncooperative but belligerent and impossible to get along with. They kept the corn planter, refusing to share it, even though they weren't using it and had left it sitting in the middle of the field. Time for planting corn was almost past when Daddy approached the landowner with the problem.

"Go to their field. Get the idle planter and plant your corn," he said.

They met Daddy in the field. After a fuss, at the landowner's instruction, Daddy drove away with the planter.

After dark that night they fired a .22 rifle from their back porch at our house all night. Billy and I lay on the floor on a pallet in case they got lucky and a round came through a window. We were kept awake through the night by the crack of the rifle and the thud against the house of lead bullets from a gun with not enough power to pierce the pine weatherboards. Beside the shack was a tin-veneered tobacco packhouse. The lead ricocheted off that tin and whistled in the dark past the house into the woods. Like settlers in a stockade waiting for Indians to attack, we waited all night for them to come knocking on the door. They never came, and about daybreak the firing stopped.

The siege was over. Billy and I left for school. Daddy went back to the field to plant corn.

When we moved from the woods to the road, our houses were only a hundred yards apart on opposite sides of the road. One night in January, at our front door, there came a sound like a crying, whimpering, begging child. When Daddy went to the door it was not a child. A young, black woman with her clothing almost torn off, pushed past Daddy begging, "Mister, please help me. Those Mocassins gonna kill me. They're gonna kill me!"

She ran into the bedroom where the family was playing Setback, a card game. She crawled behind the baby's crib in the corner, crumbled to the floor in a helpless heap, shaking in fear and whimpering, "They're gonna kill me. They're gonna kill me."

Mildred fainted.

From the front door Daddy saw three of the Merkerson guys coming across the yard about ten feet from the front steps.

One of them said, "That's my wife in there and I'm going in to get her."

Daddy said, "No you're not. You're not coming in my house."

With that he reached over the door, took down Uncle Johnny's old rusty single-shot shotgun, pointed it in their direction and said, "There doesn't need to be any killing here tonight. But you're not coming in the house. I'll bring your wife out, but stop where you are. Don't take another step."

There was not a shell in the gun, not one in the house, and if there had been that rusty gun would have probably misfired. They didn't know that. They stopped.

Daddy went back in the house to fetch the girl, but she wasn't coming out.

"Please Mister, don't put me out. They'll kill me."

"He said that you're his wife. You must leave. You can't hide here in my house."

Screaming, she said, "No, No, I'm not going."

"If you don't get out of my house, I'm going to kill you. So the only decision you have to make is whether you want to die in here or out there."

Of course, he wasn't going to kill her. He picked her up bodily in his arms, and with her kicking and screaming and begging, carried her to the front porch and gave her to the three men. They dragged her across the road, back to their house.

When Daddy came in he said to Mildred's brother, Hugh, and me, "You boys had better go to Jake's house and call the sheriff. They may just kill that girl."

They certainly were capable. The year before at a Christmas party in the home of one of the Merkerson boy's in-laws, that boy had a razor and was chasing his wife's father. He had cut the old man pretty severely and would probably have killed him if he had caught him. The old man ran through the house and out the front door. In the meantime one of the old man's sons, brother-in-law to the Merkerson boy, was waiting on the front porch with a shotgun, and when that boy with the razor came through the door chasing the old man, the brother-in-law blew him almost in two. The boy fell into the yard, crawled under the porch, and two of the old man's sons dragged him from under the house, hit him back of the head with a shovel, and broke his neck. That's the account that was told and circulated through the community at the time. The wake and funeral were during Christmas holidays.

Hugh and I left immediately to go to the nearest telephone, a mile away at Jake Aycock's house. The sandy road turned to clay as it ran down a little hill, across a wood bridge, over a ten-foot-wide stream where Mildred caught bream two inches wide and smaller, fried them crisp, and we ate bones and all. Halfway to Jake's the road took a 90° turn around a graveyard that was five feet above the road, held back by a masonry wall of various sizes of native rocks, then ran straight uphill the last half mile. Hugh and I were on our way home, a hundred yards from the curve and cemetery, when the sound of boisterous laughter from beyond the curve reached us.

"That's them Merkersons coming up the road," Hugh said. "And if they see us they'll know we've been to call the law and we'll be in big trouble."

With that, he jumped a four-foot ditch and at high speed, took a shortcut home through a cotton patch behind the grave-yard. I jumped the ditch but was blocked by some loose garden wire at the edge of the field. The noisy group rounded the curve, and Hugh was right. The only thing left for me was to lie as close to the ground as a snake's belly under those cotton stalks in the moonlight and watch them pass within 15 feet of my hiding place. Frozen with fear from the inside out, my mouth was as dry as the dangling locks of cotton surrounding me. The moon apologized for leaving me so exposed. It couldn't find a cloud to get behind.

As they passed it was evident our fear for the young woman was unfounded. She was having a ball, laughing and partying with the men. Her dress was ripped apart, but she didn't seem to care.

They never saw me. The color of my face blended with the moonlight and made me invisible. When they were a safe distance up the road, I escaped from the wire and followed Hugh through the cotton field at a much slower pace.

The next day we were in the back field at the edge of the woods preparing plant beds where tiny tobacco seeds were sown in January, grew to seven inches by the last of April, and were transplanted in the field. A police car turned off the road and slowly made its way up the path around the barn across a plank bridge over a drainage ditch all the way to where we were working. The red light and insignia on the door identified the vehicle. It was a sheriff's car. He stopped at the end of the path, walked over to where we were at work, and said to my father, "Are you Mr. Jackson?"

"Yes Sir."

"Mr. Jackson, do you want to swear out a warrant for those Merkersons who tried to come into your house last night?"

"No Sir, I was just afraid they might really kill that girl."

"I came out last night, met them on the road. They're just hell-raisers, trouble-makers. Mr. Jackson, if they cross that road and try to force their way into your house again, you take your shotgun, shoot 'em, call the nigger undertaker to come and get 'em, and don't bother me with it."

And he got in his car and drove back to town.

That fall the Merkersons moved away and an older black couple, Uncle Roscoe and Aunt Laureen moved into that house across the road. It would be impossible to exaggerate the contrast. Our families became the best of friends, sharing vegetables from the gardens, harvesting tobacco and killing hogs together. They had no children. Aunt Laureen loved Billy and me as if we were hers. We laughed together and cried together. After one year we moved away, but they have often come to mind. When they grew too old to work and had nowhere to go, what became of them?

Our last two years in the three-room shack in the woods were a bit crowded. Daddy's brother, Johnny, totally crippled by paralyzing rheumatoid arthritis, left helpless by his wife who departed with their two children, and with nowhere to go, came to live with us in those two bedrooms and a kitchen. When he left, Mildred's grandmother Gurley, eighty-some, with no place to live took Johnny's spot. In the meantime, Nancy, Mildred's first baby, came to make it her permanent home. The family of five, along with anyone else that was homeless, for three years made the best of a bad situation.

The landlord, a small man, with a lot of money and energy, who went in a run like a Flannery O'Conner character, chasing his nose which was on the trail of something that was just beyond reach, owned four small tracts of land with four tenants. For the crop year of 1944, he cut the tenants to three, and that's when we moved from the shack a half mile down the path to a slight upgrade by the side of road. There was an extra bedroom, a well with a pump, an outhouse, and at some point during the two years REA (Rural Electrification Administration) came through and wired the house for electricity. With a bulb hanging from the ceiling in the middle of each room, there was bright, beautiful, unbelievable light.

Life was beginning to get better. One year we outsmarted the boll weevil, and made a bail of cotton (500 lbs.) per acre on five acres. Daddy paid me two cents per pound for all over 150 pounds I could pick in a day. Billy's quota was 100 pounds. We earned $14 and bought a used bicycle. Quinton, Mildred's second child, was born. Life was better. I was 13. Billy was 10.

After two years we moved again, one mile up the road toward Fremont to Jake Aycock's crossroads, beside Memorial Primitive Baptist Church, to farm with Jake for two years. During the previous five years Billy and I had walked that mile to catch the school bus at that crossroads. When we were late and missed the bus, we walked two and one-half more miles to school. Now it was only 200 yards to the bus.

The Last Fight

During tobacco harvest, 1947, a crisis, a bit of a civil war, a conflict that had been brewing for several years erupted. I was

15 years old, had been cropping tobacco all day after helping empty a barn beginning at 3:00 a.m., and helped hang a barn after coming from the field. I was tired and sitting on the back steps. Mildred ordered me to get wood for the cook stove from the woodpile and fill the wood box in the kitchen. I suggested that Nancy bring in enough to finish supper and I'd fill the box the next morning before going to the field. Mildred, with a how-dare-you-disobey-me-you-rebellious-wretch attitude, reached for a pole, ten feet long and an inch in diameter, used to whip mules from a cultivator plow seat, standing in the corner of the porch. With my back turned, I was not aware of her approach until I felt the blow across my bare back.

Before she could strike a second time I was on my feet, and in her face. Catching the pole in the middle of her stroke, snatching it from her hand, breaking it into four pieces, and throwing it at her feet, I said, "You have beat on me all of my life…not anymore…never again. If you ever lift a hand to hit me one more time, the next time the best man is going to win, and if I am physically able, I'm going to knock your teeth out."

She turned back into the kitchen and I left home. With only one pair of shorts and jeans covered with tobacco gum, no shoes, no shirt, I ran six miles to Mother's sister's house, arriving at Minnie and Brute's as they were finishing supper, asking for a place to sleep, and explaining why I left home.

The next day Minnie bought me a T-shirt and another pair of jeans. On Saturday Uncle Brute and I went to Fremont, met my father on the street, discussed the situation, and came to an understanding that if I would go back home and help harvest the crop there would be no more fights. Mildred had agreed "no more corporal punishment or physical fighting," and there never was. I returned home, lived there until graduating from High School in 1950, and she never again raised a hand to hit me. Many heated arguments, a lot of fussing and cussing, but no fights.

While at Jake's, Johnny came back to live with us. He had made the rounds to other brothers. They'd kicked him out. The County Home was filled. This time he stayed until he became so heavy Daddy couldn't lift him, which someone must do, from the chair to the bed, from the bed to a potty chair, every day. When Daddy could no longer pick him up, he was forced into the *poor folks* home, and remained there until he died.

The house was square, four rooms, no hall, front and back porches, ceiled inside, tin roof, no under-pinning, relatively comfortable for a tenant house, a bit crowded with six in the family, plus Johnny. For one of the two years we owned a cow named Betsy (All cows are named Betsy.), the cow of a lifetime, none before, none after.

In the eighth grade at Fremont School, I sang, accompanied by guitar, for my first performance before the class, to satisfy an assignment by Melba Martin, the teacher, who required every student to do something in front of those 30 classmates every week.

After seven years in school at Fremont a great change took place. The family moved to Pinkney, North Carolina, Wayne County, between Nahunta and Sasser's Mill on Highway 581. It was not exactly Pinkney, but about a mile down a dirt road, off 581, behind Pinkney Baptist Church, the Nahunta school district, on the Fleming farm, which Mr. Fleming managed for his wife, who inherited it from her father, one of the Morrises.

Together Again

In the middle of grade ten I left Fremont, returned to Nahunta where I had attended the last half of grade one and first half of grade two. Sharecroppers moved from one farm to another in December or January, so the children changed schools in the middle of the grade. My first day at Nahunta, I approached an old friend whom I had not seen for eight years, but with whom I had been very close when we were seven years old. Eugene Waddell was standing by a heat radiator, looking out a classroom window when I stepped up behind him and said, "I'm Bobby Jackson. We used to be friends."

"I haven't forgotten you," Gene said. And the fifteen-year-olds were back together as if time had stood still for eight years. Maybe it was in the blood. My mother and Eugene's father were first cousins. My grandmother and Eugene's grandfather were sister and brother. George Waddell was the common great-grandfather.

Gene was a fair guitar picker. I was a beginner. We spent hours together messing around with country music.

In the spring of 1948, the Home Economics teacher planning their Junior-Senior Banquet chose a Spanish theme and approached the two sophomores with a proposition. She'd heard we played guitars. "Could you perform Spanish music?" she asked.

"Sure. All we need is time to practice with the girls in the Home Ec department." We put together *South of the Border, My Adobe Hacienda, Mañana,* dressed in Mexican garb, and entertained at the banquet. I sang lead. Waddell sang harmony. We cracked a few funnies with me as the straight man, Waddell the comedian, and the response was beyond expectations. The following year when the senior class prepared to perform the senior play, they needed ten minutes between scenes to move furniture around on stage. The teacher in charge came again for assistance.

"Can you fellows step out in front of the curtain on stage and entertain the crowd for a few minutes while we rearrange the furniture backstage?"

"All we need is your class time for us to practice in the Home Ec department."

She agreed. We did. The response was great and exciting. Two or three songs, some corny jokes, and the crowd loved it.

By now Waddell and I were spending all our free time together, which wasn't much seeing as how each one was carrying a man's load on the farm, I on a tenant farm with my father, Gene on a small farm his father inherited from the grandfather. When Mr. Robert, Gene's dad, would loan us his 1938 Chevy, we went looking for girls. Never knowing when we'd get the car, it was impossible to make dates in advance, so we needed to get to the girl's house on Saturday or Sunday before the other guy. Most of the time, if we arrived first, we got the girl. In all of 1948 and 1949, summer, fall, winter, spring, in school or out, Gene and I were inseparable.

The summer of 1949 we spent running around together dating one of about three girls each, when possible, entertaining the thought now and then that someday by some miracle we might make it to Nashville, Tennessee, and find a place in the country music business. I was an Eddy Arnold, "easy-listening," George Morgan, "soft-sound," kind of soloist, and Waddell was a hilarious comedian.

Neither having any way of knowing that what was about to happen at the beginning of our senior year would land both of us in Nashville to sing one night in the Ryman Auditorium but under totally different circumstances.

Conversion

In the fall of 1949, Evangelist Oliver Greene was in Wilson in the big green tent. Waddell's parents had attended, making him aware of the meetings. On Saturday night, Mr. Robert loaned us the 1938 Chevy. No girls were expecting us. Gene suggested we go to Greene's revival. Motivated by curiosity, I agreed. There would be a big crowd including possibly some girls we knew from Kenly. It was standing-room-only except in the choir. Bennett Collins, Greene's brother-in-law, the song leader, insisted, "If you can sing, come to the choir." Then he became more desperate, "If you have ever sung at any time anywhere, please come and help us in the choir."

Gene looked at me, smiled and said, "Haven't we sung a few times?"

I said, "I believe we have." So, rather than stand for an hour or two, we took seats in the choir, about thirty feet from the preacher, and for the first time I was confronted with preaching. Greene was desperately trying to convince me that this life is not all there is, and beyond here there is a hereafter, and that Heaven and Hell do exist.

"He doesn't know what he's talking about," I kept telling myself. "He hasn't died. He doesn't know what there is over there."

Then a little voice inside would say, "You don't know either. You haven't been over there. Suppose he's right."

I didn't go forward, raise my hand for prayer nor make any outward response, but I couldn't silence that little voice warning me of the possibility that Hell might exist and I might go there.

Not being able to sleep, walking the floor 'til about midnight, finally standing at the foot of the bed, looking out the window into the shadows of a moonlit Saturday night in late September, 1949, I sincerely, honestly, wholeheartedly turned to God. Ignorant of Bible verses containing the plan of salvation, with no instruction about "how to," never having been led down the Romans Road, not knowing there was a Romans Road, not knowing there was a book of Romans, never being exposed to John 3:16, couldn't quote the Lord's Prayer nor the 23rd Psalm, I simply said, "Dear God, I'm ready to change sides in this war, and if you will accept me, I'll be on your side the rest of my life, and if you will forgive me, I'll swear off sinning, do right, and not sin anymore."

Some theologians suggest that God must have laughed, knowing human nature and the tendency to sin. But God knew the heart was sincere and the desire to do right and not continue to do wrong was genuine. Every person who turns to God turns from something. Paul said a central theme of his message was "repentance toward God and faith toward our Lord Jesus Christ." Repentance and faith are so dove-tailed together they are an inseparable part of the same mental and willful decision, which is a condition for receiving salvation.

A peace came to my heart knowing everything was right with God. Reconciliation had taken place, for God was already reconciled to me through the death of His Son. I was the one at war with God, so when I laid down my arms of rebellion, there was peace with God. My ignorance was evidence of the Bible truth that the problem between man and God is not a lack of knowledge.

Jesus didn't say, "You don't understand how to come to me."

He said, "You will not come to me, that ye might have life" (John 5:40).

That problem is in the will, not in the lack of knowledge.

Jesus said, "If any man will do his will, he shall know of the doctrine whether it be of God...." (John 7:17).

The eunuch from Ethiopia (Acts 8), Cornelius (Acts 10) and Saul of Tarsus (Acts 9) are all testimonies to the faithfulness of God to keep His promise, "Turn you at my reproof: behold I will pour out my spirit unto you, and I will make known my words unto you" (Proverbs 1:23). The reason men refuse to turn to God is not because they cannot. They will not.

Paul told the intellectuals and philosophers on Mars Hill in Athens, that God now "commands all men everywhere to repent"

(Acts 17:30). God does not command men to do what they cannot do and then send them to hell for not doing it. Anything that God asks of man, He provides grace to perform. No man born with one arm is going to hell for not working with two hands. The measure of a man's responsibility is equal to the degree of his freedom. Accountability is equal to performability.

Promises abound in the Bible that those who seek God with their whole heart find Him (Isaiah 55:6, Jeremiah 29:13). My testimony is the fruit of that fact. My ignorance and lack of understanding did not prevent God from hearing, responding, and coming into my heart and life.

Neither Gene nor I went forward that night at Greene's meeting. At home about midnight I gave my heart to God. The following week Gene settled the matter on another night.

A marvelous change began that night and continues to this day, but was more evident during that senior year in high school. The news of our conversion spread rapidly through the small country school and surrounding area. Singing, testifying, and speaking in churches took top priority in our schedule. Hundreds of young people responded with increasing crowds in rallies and evangelistic services.

Gradually my plans and ambitions turned 180° from medical school and becoming an MD, to the ministry. There was a struggle, watching the castles I had built crumble, telling God that in the practice of medicine I would make so much money I could send out fifty preachers, listening to Him say, "Not if all of them have your attitude. Whom are you going to send if everybody is in the sending business and nobody is willing to be the sent?"

Sometime during that year I gave up the struggle, told Him I'd go to Bible College and wherever His will opened doors, I'd try to go through them and preach His message.

First Sermon

Youth rallies were filling churches all over eastern North Carolina. Singing, directing testimony meetings, acting as master of ceremonies, spreading the word about those special nights kept me actively involved.

My first sermon (technically depending on the definition) was at Walnut Creek, near Goldsboro, at a Saturday night rally, the "Prodigal Son." Walking behind a cotton plow, behind a mare mule, I preached it to her a thousand times (more or less) before Saturday night, while she nodded her head in agreement. I must have covered that boy's life enough for a lifetime, because in 60 years I have not preached on the Prodigal Son again. Once I got that guy home, I hoped he had sense enough to stay there and not leave a second time.

Preacher Albert Rollins testifies that he was saved as a result of that sermon.

At graduation of that 1950 class at Nahunta, I prayed the invocation. Gene prayed the benediction. After the ceremony the little group, less than twenty, assembled privately for a prayer meeting to seek the Lord's guidance, protection, and blessings upon each of us as we separated from one another.

Eugene and I never separated. We landed in Nashville together.

Cash for College

Landed in Nashville, that is, after a summer of complications with the flight plans. There's no landing without a takeoff, no takeoff without a ticket, no ticket without money and no money for the son of a sharecropper without a miracle. From those who lived in similar circumstances during those days the question has arisen many times through the years, "How did you afford to go to college? Where did the money come from?"

During that summer, 1950, someone brought to my attention that there was a denominational loan fund available to ministerial students, the Anna Phillips Loan Fund managed by a lady in Winterville, North Carolina. Upon inquiring, I was told, "We have the money and would be more than happy to loan you $300. You will need, however, two property owners to co-sign the note with you."

That sounded easy enough. The landowner with whom we farmed was a deacon in my church. In fact, most of the land in the area was owned by members of the church which had licensed me for the ministry, and many of them were my friends. Obtaining two signatures would be a piece-of-cake. How naive can a kid be?

One after another my friends, the landowners, assured me of their support, complimented my decision to enter the ministry, bragged on my personal qualifications, encouraged me with confidence of my success, and ended by saying, "But I've always made it a practice to never sign anybody's note."

The summer was ending, college was beginning and one man Bagley Morris, husband of Mrs. Deanye, the lady who had the greatest influence in my life at the time, agreed to sign if I could find number two, who seemed to be so well hidden he was not to be found. A few days before departure time, a fellow rode up to my house on a motorcycle, called me from the field where I was working, and said, "I've brought good news. There's an old man, a lay preacher, who owns a store and little piece of land. He heard you were having a difficult time getting anybody to sign a note. He said to tell you that if nobody else would sign it, to come by his store and he'll put his name on it."

With that old man, Mr. Jap Overman's signature, three hundred-borrowed dollars, a little tin suitcase containing all of my belongings, except a two-year-old suit two sizes too small, I walked away from a sharecropper's home, a tenant farm, and headed for Nashville, Tennessee.

The most priceless possession I took along was the graduation gift from my father. His last words to me were, "You are a free man. You don't owe me anything. You go where you need to go. Do what you have to do. There's no obligation to ever look back. You have fulfilled your responsibility. I give you your freedom."

He had no money to buy anything. His net worth was somewhere below zero. But the value of his gift was beyond anything material. It could never be bought, and if it could, the landowner couldn't afford it for his son.

After one year in college, during the summer of 1951, I came home, worked for my dad on the farm during the day and preached at night in revivals almost every week. Love offerings in meetings were so generous by the end of the summer that I had accumulated enough money to pay back the $300 and to cover the cost of the next year in college, both semesters. When I walked into the lady's house in Winterville with the money, she said, "Oh, you don't owe it yet. You don't have to pay it back until you finish college and no interest will begin until you graduate."

"I'm returning the money today, and I'll try to never borrow anymore. I don't like begging for favors from rich men."

With the note marked PAID, the signatures of the two men were cut and mailed to them with a letter of appreciation for taking a chance on a sharecropper's kid. That was the last money I ever borrowed for consumer debt.

For the next four years in college, I preached during spring break, during Christmas holidays, took a week of cuts each semester to go away for services, preached meetings in and around Nashville, and filled each summer with revivals. The love offerings were sufficient to pay for college, buy a used Oldsmobile, marry a wife, have a baby boy, finish two degrees, and graduate in 1955 with $29 left over and "owing no man anything."

In answer to the question, "How did you pay your way through college?"

I literally preached my way through.

When Gene and I arrived at Free Will Baptist Bible College in Nashville, Tennessee, we began a quartet the first day, roomed together with Roy O'Donnell, in an eight-by-ten room in the Sword Building, and the rest of the story seems like it was only yesterday.

THE FIRST YEAR OF THE REST OF MY LIFE

Highlights from my four years at Free Will Baptist Bible College in Nashville show up at various places in this book of memories. Some are omitted. Some overlooked. Some forgotten. That's how the brain of an old man works.

Martha Jane Ketteman and I began dating a few weeks after I first saw her. Three school years later we tied an untieable knot, traveled in meetings during the summer of 1953, and came back for our senior year with Jane pregnant, along with several other women students who had married that summer.

By the second semester the girls were showing their expectations. The school authorities thought it best that they not attend classes, so Dr. Johnson taught systematic theology, a course required for graduation, privately in his office. The remaining requirements Jane finished by correspondence at a typewriter while caring for her new baby, Stephen, who was born during spring break. Within one year she received her Mrs., Mama, and B.A. degrees. We graduated in 1954.

The Year at BJU

The summer of 1954, with a baby in a bassinet, we were back on the road every week. That fall we arrived in Greenville, South Carolina, with everything we owned in a 4 x 4 U-Haul trailer with no place to unload it, and slept at the Rapers' apartment a few nights while I searched for a place to live. In the San Souci section of town, across Piney Mountain, five miles from the University, we rented one furnished room with a bathroom and access to a shared kitchen from a disgruntled old lady who took us in for one purpose, to shovel coal in the stoker furnace during the winter. When winter was over she asked us to move, since she no longer needed me to shovel coal. For the final two months of school we found a dingy, upstairs attic place with no air conditioning.

Enrolled at Bob Jones University in graduate school, I spent the nine months leaving home at 8:00 a.m., in classes and studying in the library until 5:00 p.m., and going out with the quartet on weekends.

Jane says that she spent the year learning to be alone. It was a hard lesson and she had no way of knowing that she would learn it again and again living alone with the two boys while I was away in meetings for eight and ten weeks at a time (The longest was three months.) without coming home. It would be more difficult for her to teach that lesson of aloneness to her two little boys.

When Philip was three he was excited about going to Heaven to play in Jesus' toy box, but when he found out that he couldn't go and come back, he wasn't so anxious to take the one-way trip. One night during their devotions he asked his mother, "Who in our family do you think will get to go to Heaven first?"

"Well, it will probably be your Daddy or me, because we'll grow old and you'll grow up to be a man. Then we will die and go up to Heaven, and you'll grow old and die, and come later. So, Daddy and I will probably go first."

She turned away to tuck Stephen in, and when she came back to Philip, his eyes were filled with tears as he looked up at her and said, "Mama, do you think Daddy might have already died and gone up to Heaven, 'cause he never comes home any more?"

At the time I thought it was dedication. Some folks thought it was foolishness.

Jane's impressions of the University were more negative than positive. One negative experience that lingers in her mind and upsets her to this day was when Stephen, who at eight months old, was crawling and discovered a bottle cap that had been filled with ant poison by our landlady. When Jane, who had no means of transportation, saw him with it in his mouth, she panicked and called the University trying to contact me to come home and get him to an emergency room so someone could pump his stomach before the poison was absorbed into his body. When she called, a very indifferent woman informed her that I was in class and could not be disturbed and the only thing she would do was to put a note in my mailbox.

Knowing nothing of the situation, I finished the day at school, came home late in the afternoon, to a worried, frustrated, weeping wife and poisoned baby. We rushed him to the hospital where they pumped his stomach several hours after her finding him with the poison container in his mouth.

What could have been a tragic day ended with a thankful mother, who had prayed for the Lord to take care of the situation when she was helpless to remedy it. The doctors thought that he had evidently not consumed enough of the poison to hurt, except for the discomfort of having his stomach pumped. That was relief to an angry young mother who desperately tried to get to her husband for what she thought was a poisoned baby, and the University not only didn't help, but showed total indifference and unconcern for her critical situation.

The next day I found the note in my mailbox.

The University allowed no children for services. No nursery was provided, and a babysitter was out of the question. In the entire year, Jane attended one Sunday vesper service. That was her only visit to the campus. Living off campus and being in graduate school, we were never involved in any of the social life of the University. Jane lived in one room with a little boy under a year old, afraid that he would make a noise and upset the grouchy landlady.

The year ended the last of May with the graduation. Based on the grades, and graduation exams, the professors recommended that I be admitted to the doctorate program to pursue the Ph.D. The revival schedule was filled for over a year and doors were opening in evangelism more rapidly than I could enter. I never answered a call to be an evangelist, but that was the field that was white and the laborers were few. In fact, in our denomination, the number was zero.

Had I planned to teach on a college level, I would have possibly continued the studies. But for the work in which I was involved, there seemed to be little benefit in chasing Greek and Hebrew prepositions for two more years.

So away we flew to Detroit, Michigan.

The Beginning

A life of full-time evangelism began June 5, 1955, in Highland Park Church, Detroit, Michigan. The days in school ended about June 1. The schedule was to begin in Detroit with Brother Charles Thigpen (He became a Doctor later.) on Sunday morning, June 5, 1955. He wrote me a gracious letter suggesting that we pack our car, drive to Charlotte, park it, and catch a plane to Ypsilanti, Detroit's airport, where he would meet us. This would not only make it easier traveling for us, but we would also be able to start the meeting on Friday night and get in two extra services. The answer was, "We would love to fly but my wings are a little weak."

Truth is, there was only $29.00 worth of feathers left in those wings. That wasn't bad. Five years of college, a wife, a baby, a 1951 Oldsmobile, and all were paid for, debt free, didn't owe anybody on earth a dime. There just wasn't much left over. He understood, took the hint, bought the tickets, sent them to us in Greenville, SC, and we flew from Charlotte to Detroit on an Eastern Super Constellation, with four gasoline propeller engines, twin tails, and a luxurious interior. It was a night flight and when the pilot fired those motors, flames spewed out of every piston's exhaust for twenty feet, and he quickly made an announcement on the speaker system to inform all of us first-timers that the plane wasn't on fire.

We flew from South Carolina to Michigan and back, drove to North Carolina for a meeting, and on to Miami for a revival at the First Free Will Baptist Church, Northwest 90th St., for 13 days, 14 services, two Sundays, in June, 1955.

Cookie and the Skunk

During that meeting we visited the Serpentarium where I learned that there are no hoop snakes that roll like a hoop with a poison stinger in the tail so powerful that if they stick it in a tree, the tree will die. There are no snakes that can run faster than a man, including black runners; more people die from shock when bitten by a snake than from the venom; and crocodiles are much more aggressive than alligators. The guide's demonstration was convincing. In an open pit several gators were dozing in the hot sun along with Cookie, a sleeping crocodile. While we watched, he tossed a frozen chicken toward a sleeping gator six feet from Cookie. The crocodile, in a flash, caught the chicken in mid-air before it hit the ground.

"If you dangle your arm over the side of this pit," the man said, "he'll hit it with the same speed without checking on what it is."

"There are a lot of alligator wrestlers," he said, "but no crocodile wrestlers. Well, there are a few, but they all have one arm! Young fellows hunt for rattlesnakes for us to use in our work."

Their work was in a lab where they took the venom from the snake, injected it in some form into a horse whose body built up antibodies to fight the venom, processed the horse's blood, and removed the antibodies to make a serum to inject people who were bitten by rattlesnakes.

"We buy the snakes by the pound. One day the boys came in with a suffocated skunk in a sack, threw that dead skunk into the gator pit, and Cookie, responding the same way he did to the chicken, swallowed that skunk. For a week he lay on that rock in the pit on his back, with his mouth open, groaning with a bellyache, smelling up the place with his bad breath."

One of the perks of living on the road was the opportunity to visit tourist sights in the area where we were in meetings. In Florida we visited Sea World, Silver Springs, Ross Allen Reptiles; in Georgia, the Okefenokee Swamp; in Asheville, North Carolina, the Biltmore Mansion, Grove Park Inn, and the Smokies; in Arlington, Virginia, the cemetery and tomb of the Unknown, and across the Potomac all the sights of Washington.

In Missouri, it was the little house of Harry Truman in Lamar, and the stomping grounds of Tom Sawyer in Hannibal; in Arizona, the Grand Canyon and Sonora Desert; in New Mexico, Carlsbad Caverns; in Colorado, the Rockies; in Wyoming, Yellowstone and Old Faithful; in California, Yosemite and Sequoia with the big trees; in San Francisco, the Golden Gate, Alcatraz, the waterfront and cable cars; in Hawaii, Honolulu, U.S.S. Arizona National Monument, Waikiki, Diamond Head, and Kauai, the island covered with enough sugar cane to sweeten the whole world; in Nova Scotia, Peggy's Cove; on Prince Edward Island, *Anne of Green Gables.*

In New York, north of Buffalo on the Niagara River, which connects Lake Erie with Lake Ontario and forms part of the U.S. boundary with Canada, are the notorious falls, which we stopped to visit when we drove from New Brunswick through Quebec to Windsor, Ontario.

While in a meeting in Buena Park, California, we stayed at a motel across the street from Knotts Berry Farm. We visited Disneyland before there was a Disney World. While in Dallas and Fort Worth, the boys went to Six Flags over Texas when it was the only Six Flags in the country. In 1955, the Serpentarium was the attraction in the Miami area.

There have been so many beautiful scenes in so many places, so long ago that the prints in memory's scrapbook have faded. One scene which will never fade, and will never be seen again by anyone, was after seeing all the sights in New York City with Stephen and Joel, our grandson, from the rooftop of the World Trade Center (the Twin Towers), we watched the sun go down over New Jersey and lights come on over Manhattan. A few years later while in Turin, Italy, we watched on television the Towers come down. A few days later, circling New York City to land, out the window of the plane we saw the smoke rising from the ruins.

In some cities it was not a tourist attraction. It was a processing plant. In Winter Haven, Florida, they processed oranges and grapefruit; in Wenatchee, Washington, apples; in Vermont, maple syrup; in Durham, North Carolina, cigarettes; in Emporia, Kansas, cows; in Pine Bluff, Arkansas, chickens; in Tarheel, North Carolina, hogs; in Detroit, Michigan, cars.

After the snakes in Miami, the next sight to see was the Okefenokee, four meetings down the road.

The meetings in Miami ended Sunday night, July 3. From there we drove to Rochelle, Georgia, started another on Monday, July 4, at Christian Hill; on to Vernon, Alabama, to do it over again the following Monday, July 11; from there to Smithville, Mississippi, Pearce's Chapel, July 17-24 (two services per day); left there after Sunday morning to begin at Fawn Grove Free Will Baptist, Fulton, Mississippi, twice a day, 24- 29. Four meetings after Miami, we landed in Folkston, Georgia, at Philadelphia Church.

The "we" in this story refers to Jane, my wife, our son, Stephen, fifteen months old, and me. For two summers and almost three years our home was a 1951 Oldsmobile. Well, we did move once from a 1951 Olds to a 1955. Stephen began traveling in a bassinet at two months old, grew to a porta-crib with legs that retracted, two retracted, two extended to fit into the back seat of the car, and outgrew that to a full-sized baby crib which had to be taken apart and reassembled every time we moved, and in some churches that was every day.

Land of the Trembling Earth

Philadelphia Free Will Baptist Church is situated at the edge of the Okefenokee Swamp, a name given by the Indians, meaning Land of the Trembling Earth, referring to the floating islands of mulch accumulated over the years, and thick enough for small trees and bushes to grow in it and tremble in the wind causing the mulched ground to shake. Located in southeastern Georgia and northeastern Florida, the swamp, 40 miles long, 30 miles wide, 700 square miles, almost 300,000 acres, is drained by the St. Mary's and Suwanee Rivers.

The white sand road that passed in front of the church narrowed as it entered the edge of the woods with meadows of palmetto bushes, large oaks, tall pines on either side and tracks in the sand where the legitimate inhabitants of this world had marked their domain, deer, wild turkeys, possums, large birds, bears, and countless snakes. Within the distance of a mile there were eight slick, crooked, winding evidences that a snake had dragged his belly across the top of the sand leaving a trail like a series of SSSs from the ditch on one side of the road to the other.

In Jane's mind they were all huge and had passed so recently nothing had crossed the track, so they were waiting at the road's edge for her to come close enough that one could hop from the ditch like a leopard and sink those fangs in her leg, bringing instant death. So she walked in the middle of the road that was too narrow for her safety, stopping to give close eye examination to every crooked stick in the ditch before she proceeded. To this day she's never been snake bit.

The Old Country Church

At the beginning of the woods, 100 yards off the road on the right, is a grove of old stately virgin long-leaf pines that have lived so long and grown so tall they can whisper to the fluffy white clouds floating by against a blue-on-blue summer sky, bowing their heads as the breezes whistle through their needles, like fingers passing through tangled hair when the strong winds blow, bowing from the waist low enough to notice what's happening on the earth around them, and what they see when they look down is a structure older than they are.

Tucked away under these pines is a wood frame, very old Primitive (Hard-shell) Baptist Church building. Dark gray, heart pine weather-beaten weatherboarding encloses the one room church, with openings cut for windows covered by wooden shutters, no glass panes. Wood piers hold it off the ground, and a tin roof keeps out the rain.

The one door is closed, but never locked, so curiosity opens it to look inside. The benches are heavy pine boards with peg legs, and along the floor in front of the benches every two feet through the one layer of pine boards, a three-inch hole has been cut, through which the men may spit their tobacco juice. On the other side of this segregated (male and female) congregation, are holes for the women to spit the overflow of their snuff.

Tobacco must not be considered a serious sin, because there are two holes on either side of the pulpit for the preacher to spit. Smoking may be a sin, but not chewing and dipping.

A dipper once said that smoking was wrong because, "It has to be a sin to burn up anything that tastes so good."

One day in another community in South Georgia, Jane got her foot in her mouth when she stumbled into a discussion of the tobacco question with the lady of the house where we were having lunch. Jane was helping with the dishes and the kitchen clean-up after the noon meal when the conversation drifted off into the area of the sinful lifestyle of the younger generation. The older woman was expressing her strong negative opinion.

"There's nothing more disgusting," she said, "than to see a young woman with a cigarette in her mouth, parading down the street, wearing a pair of shorts, and pushing a baby carriage."

"It's just as bad," Jane said, "to see an old lady with snuff running from the corners of her mouth, spitting in a can to keep the amber-colored stuff from dripping off her chin."

"Now snuff isn't so bad," the lady said defensively, "I use a little snuff myself sometimes."

With Jane, who is not an aggressive person, confrontations were rare. But you just don't spit in the wind, jerk Superman's cape, nor mess with a mama bear's cub. There was another minor collision the same year in the same part of the country when she and her hostess disagreed.

The lady of the house insisted that Jane take our baby, Stephen, to see an old woman in the community who could talk out fire, stop bleeding, take away warts, and cure thrush or trench mouth by rubbing the inside of a child's mouth with oak leaves, then blowing in the child's mouth.

In no uncertain terms, Jane told her, "I am not taking my baby to a witch doctor to blow his bad breath in my baby's mouth to cure anything!"

"It is bad enough for an adult to suffer because they have no faith," the lady said, "but it is much worse for a baby to have to suffer because of his mother's unbelief."

Jane swabbed Stephen's mouth with an antibacterial and glycerin solution. In a few days the thrush was gone.

There is no visible evidence on the floor that anyone has spit tobacco juice for some time. How many people attend or how often, no one seems to know. There is no electricity to the building, no lamps, no lanterns, which indicates the meetings must take place in daylight. Somebody thought, once a quarter on fourth Saturdays. From the appearance, there may be no service at all in the building anymore. Whether in use or not, the majestic old building will probably stand another hundred years, since the weather has done about all it can do to destroy it, the termites and bugs don't like the taste of the resin and turpentine, and the wood is now so hard that they can't get their teeth into it. The only danger is a bolt from the sky or a spark from anywhere and it would ignite like gunpowder in a tinder box, exploding in a cloud of smoke as black as midnight rising above those tall suffering pines, and it would be gone.

Philadelphia is not a city church, but in this community, compared with this church it is on Main Street.

Harry and the Bear

In the Okefenokee there are 25 or more islands of white sand scattered through the swamp. One of those islands is named for a family in the church, Chesser Island.

Brother Harry Chesser no longer lived on the island. He lived in the community not far from the church and invited us to supper at his house. The schedule for the week was two services at church, 10:30 a.m. and 8:00 p.m., two meals in two different homes, sleep a little, and do it again the next day. Some summers this routine continued for eight weeks without a break.

My first and last meal of bear meat was at the Chesser house. The bear was cooked in tomato sauce which dominated the flavor and was not much different from beef, maybe coarser and stringier. While eating the bear meat, I listened to stories of his life in the swamp and hunting escapades.

"My brother and I tracked a bear across the white sand, through thick underbrush, following broken limbs and trampled bushes into the marsh, down a tunnel formed by tall reeds that merged together overhead. As the reeds dropped lower and the tunnel became smaller, we first crawled on our hands and knees, and finally were snaking our way on our bellies through the reeds following that bear. The tunnel ended in the den of a she-bear with two cubs."

He paused, took a bite of bear, and we waited.

"The roar and the grin on her face as she stood full height with raised arms was not a sign of welcome to her house. An enraged she-bear protecting her cubs is a scary sight when you are within her reach, lying on your belly and held down by reeds. My brother was in front, nearest the bear. I was only inches behind. Each of us was dragging a shotgun."

Harry said, "I looked up and saw that angry bear standing over my brother. I managed to raise the shotgun just enough that when I pulled the trigger the load hit the bear in the heart. The roar slowly turned to a groan, her arms dropped, and she fell across my brother's legs."

"Brother Harry, did you eat that bear?"

"Yeah, it is better you eat the bear than the bear eat you. I'd rather eat a bear than to be eaten by one. We were young then and foolish," he said. "Hunted gators in the winter, sold the hides, and that little extra money helped make ends meet. In the spring we'd go back to farming."

Sometimes the bears would wander out of the swamp through the community, especially when there was fire in the swamp. Fires burned often and for long periods in the swamp when it was dry, consuming peat, mulch, and undergrowth.

At the home where we stayed for the week, on Christmas Eve of the previous year, they heard the dogs barking, went to investigate, shot and killed a 400 pound black bear on the front porch at the front door.

Wild turkeys, wildcats, deer, and opossums live here, including Pogo, Walt Kelly's comic strip possum, who spread his wisdom across the country in newspapers for many years and dropped this truth on all of us: "Yep, Son, we have met the enemy and he is us."

The Gator and the Hot Dog

The renowned inhabitant is the alligator. Years later, on a visit to the swamp (In 40 years, I returned to the church seven times for meetings.) Jane, the boys and Peanut, their little dachshund dog, were with me. We were walking down the road toward the visitor center and were greeted by the VIP of the swamp, a large gator that lay around the welcoming center most of the time, assuming the responsibility of seeing to it that none of the visitors who came to see an alligator went away disappointed.

Around the edge, just above the dark waters, his bulging eyes were always visible, sometimes his snout, maybe his back, and if you were really important he would come out of the water, crawl up the bank, and waddle across the grounds to greet you. He was coming to meet us, as if we were long-time friends and he was happy we came back to the swamp. Before we got close enough to shake hands, a caretaker said, "He sees that little dog and he's planning on a hot dog for lunch."

It is true that Peanut was a wiener dog, half a dog high, and a dog and a half long, but the guide said that it didn't make any difference about the shape or size. Dogs were his favorite food.

Good thing Peanut was on a leash, and when Jane picked him up and walked away down the road in the opposite direction, the disappointed gator slowly turned around and grudgingly made his way back to the black water, grumbling to himself, "Aw, shucks, it's chicken again."

When we toured the swamp in a small boat our guide and escort was a ten-foot gator who swam along beside the boat for five minutes or more waiting for a hand-out, thinking himself to be invisible, pretending we didn't see him, until the guy running the boat reached out with a foot, touched him gently between the eyes, and he quickly became invisible. A flap of that powerful tail splashed water on everybody in the boat, and he was gone, disappeared, and we never saw him again.

Evidently there was no danger in his attacking the boat. Alligators are not as ferocious or temperamental as crocodiles. We had learned that by observation at the Serpentarium near Miami.

A Pastor's Problem

The meetings we had in Philadelphia were well attended and folks responded. Services closed Sunday, August 6. That morning while Sunday School was in progress the pastor drove from Jacksonville, Florida, where he lived and worked, not knowing that meetings had been going on all week.

That was not so unusual in part-time churches with bi-vocational pastors who came one or two Sundays each month. Many times the evangelist led the singing, directed the service, took the offering, prayed the prayers, preached the sermon, dealt with those who came forward, took members in at the close of the meetings, baptized them, went on his way and never met the pastor.

The pastor learned about the meeting in progress from some men standing around under the trees in the churchyard waiting for Sunday School to end. He sent for a couple of deacons and asked them, "Who is preaching at 11:00, me or the evangelist?"

"It is our understanding that the evangelist is to preach," they explained.

That upset him terribly. In a huff he jumped in his car, slammed the door, and drove back to Jacksonville. We never met nor spoke. The incident was brought to my attention that afternoon.

After the closing Sunday night service we returned to a most gracious, friendly home where we had been lodging for the week, to sleep our last night before heading for Baxley, Georgia, the next day.

An Overwhelming Realization

At the end of 13 weeks of evangelistic meetings without a break, in seven states from Detroit, Michigan, to Miami, Florida, the summer of 1955 was coming to an end at Edgewood Free Will Baptist Church, Tarboro, North Carolina.

During the previous four summers, lingering always in the back of my mind was the anticipation of going back to college in September. The tough schedule with the mental and spiritual load of preaching every night ended with the rest and relaxation of college life. Not this time. A full schedule for September, October, November, December, and January was staring me in the face.

The overwhelming thought forced its way into my mind, landing like a load of bricks. There would be no back-to-college time off this year, or the next year, or the next. The weeks had become months, and months were looking like years.

The fall was booked in North Carolina, Georgia, and Mississippi. That winter, from the first of December to the first week in February was the cold, snowy time of some of the greatest, most fruitful meetings of my ministry in southern Illinois.

Beginning February 14, 1956, we were in meetings for twenty-seven weeks with only two breaks, Bible Conference in Nashville and the National Association in Huntington, West Virginia.

Dr. Bob Jones, Sr.'s Advice

During that stretch, April 18-29, I was in Arcadia, South Carolina with James Raper for 12 days, 14 services. Raper was pursuing his studies at Bob Jones University toward the B.D. and pastoring the church. I rode with him one day to school to visit old friends left over from the previous year and was sitting in the lobby of the administration building waiting for a professor to show up, when Dr. Bob Jones, Sr. came along. He stopped, offered extremely friendly greetings and asked "How are things going?"

I shook hands and introduced myself, "I'm Bobby Jackson. I am currently in full-time evangelistic meetings, mostly among Free Will Baptists. I finished a graduate degree here last year."

"Oh, I know you," he said. "You're one of Linton's boys from the school in Nashville – a Free Will Baptist." Linton was Dr. L. C. Johnson, president of Free Will Baptist Bible College in Nashville, and a graduate of Bob Jones University.

"Yes, Sir, you pretty well have me in place."

"Come with me to my office," he said. "We'll visit a while."

For an hour, as if the busy man had nothing else to do, we talked about revivals, evangelistic preaching, Free Will Baptists, and the potential for a full-time evangelist among them. During the conversation I asked, "What advice would you give a young evangelist to improve his delivery, make him more effective in the pulpit, and become a better preacher?"

"Read," he said, "Read and re-read over again and again the greatest evangelistic sermons in print, until you have saturated your mind and heart with them."

The logical follow-up question, "What sermons do you consider the greatest?"

With no hesitation, he said, "William Munsey. His sermons are the greatest I have ever read."

It added no weight to his opinion, but I heartedly agreed and had already come to the same conclusion. Two of my choice books were the volumes, *Sermons and Lectures* by William Munsey, which I had read through more than one time.

His second suggestion was, "Go and listen to the best preachers in evangelism today. Learn from them what you can about effective evangelistic preaching."

The hour passed as 15 minutes in psychological time. He appeared to be in no rush but I hesitated to occupy him any longer. He was the most approachable, open, friendly evangelist I ever met, and the experience made an indelible impression on my life and ministry.

I made a resolution to read one sermon every day and kept it for many years. My library is not filled with commentaries, but with over 200 volumes of mostly evangelistic sermons. Some of my favorites are Talmage, Biederwolf, Torrey, Moody, Sunday, Sam Jones, Finney, Truett, Graham, Bob Shuler, Havner, Rice, Oswald Smith, and still at the top of the list, with no rivals, remains William Munsey.

Near the top is a volume of *Bob Jones' Revival Sermons* which were preached to thousands in the Chicago Arena, May, 1946. He was one of the most moving, effective evangelists of his day, and one of the greatest storytellers that I have ever heard. When his imagination filled in details of the life of the Apostle Paul, or dramatized Lot's integration in the society of Sodom, he had the undivided attention of 3,000 people, held spellbound by his telling the stories.

By the way, in addition to the volumes of sermons, my two favorite books are *The Pursuit of God* by A. W. Tozer and *Mere Christianity* by C. S. Lewis. *The Cost of Discipleship* by Dietrich Bonhoeffer is also worth reading.

In 55 years I have been back to the University only two or three times, but that hour spent with Dr. Bob Jones, Sr., in his study is stored in the memory in a special place reserved for a few of life's most privileged experiences.

No End in Sight

The meetings in the spring of 1956 were in North Carolina, South Carolina, Georgia, Florida, and Arkansas. In 12 months there had been 35 meetings, 11 of them lasting ten days or two weeks. That was 47 of the 52 weeks of the first year on the road.

On the way to Mississippi for the last week of May, with 13 weeks without a break scheduled for June, July, and August, the realization struck like a bolt out of the blue, or a voice out of Heaven, "You have just finished the first year of the rest of your life."

And it was.

Three Travelers 1955

Hawkins Corner, NB, Canada 1963

THE JACKSONS SLEPT HERE

The singular became plural. One became two. Two became one. And through the magic mathematics of biological reproduction one plus one equaled four: Bobby, Jane, Stephen, and Philip, the little Jackson family around which all of these memories revolve. Here's how it started.

In the spring of 1950, Gene Waddell, my classmate and closest friend, and I attended Bible Conference at the college in Nashville, made plans to enroll there in the fall, followed through with those plans and landed on campus in September with around 100 others.

Among those others was a pretty little shy girl, Jane Ketteman, from Illinois, so much prettier than everyone else it was easy for my eye to pick her out, and at the get-acquainted gathering, I had to do a bit of maneuvering so as to wind up sitting beside her, but I wasn't fast enough, seeing as how my roommate, an upper classman, also had his eye on her and asked her to sit with him before the evening meal during the few minutes of chaperoned dating, and to go with him to church, date him on Sunday afternoon, and walk around the block, etc… regularly!

Before I knew what was happening, the powers that be, and some that weren't, were thinking of her as his girlfriend, and it wasn't kosher at the college to break that up and take another fellow's girl, but then I saw her first, sat beside her first, picked her out first, with more than a passing interest. Biding my time, waiting for the chance, flirting now and then in passing, and picking up good vibes in her response, the opportunity that knocks once and passes forever, came.

The choir in which both of us sang (The roommate didn't sing.) was to sing on Wednesday night in a local church. I was washing windows in the dining hall, which also housed the girl's dorm in the upper floors. She just happened to come down the stairs as I was passing by. When she reached the bottom step, a little spray of window washer got her attention. She stopped, laughed, turned, and there I was with the spray bottle in hand. Loitering between opposite sexes being outlawed, there was only a moment.

"Are you going to East Nashville tonight with Roy?" was the question.

"I don't know," was the answer, with a big smile.

I said, "Well, if you don't know, Roy must not know, and since nobody seems to know, why don't you go with me?"

She smiled, "Okay. I'll do that."

Now it was my unpleasant job to tell my roommate, who was unhappy with me for a few days, but later found a beautiful girl, who became his wife, and everybody lived happily ever after.

Her response led to almost three years of dating under Bible College rules (The rules had a purpose. Most couples changed partners more often than dancers at a square dance.) and to a wedding at the beginning of the summer of 1953.

What if she had said, "No" that afternoon? And she could have. A five-point Calvinist professor in graduate school, who was also a philosophical personalist, attempted to reconcile the two con-flicting views. Philosophical Personalism teaches that ultimate reality is a person. God is a person. Man is a person. For a year he desperately tried to harmonize Calvinism and Arminianism. He insisted that man, as a person, has a will which cannot be forced, but for the unconditionally elected God courts them like a man does a woman, and brings them to say "Yes." He would say, "You see, your wife thinks she freely chose you, but you brought her to that decision."

Then I would say, "Doc, could she have said 'No'? Is a man free to resist the Spirit of God, despise the grace of God? Or will God force him to say 'Yes'?"

In a similar discussion with a friend of mine in the mountains of North Carolina, he confronted me with, "But you know if God had not made you say 'Yes,' you never would have said 'Yes," and if He had not made me say 'Yes,' I never would have said 'Yes,' and would not have been saved."

"Dave," I said, "Do you suppose God wants all men to come to the knowledge of the truth, takes no pleasure in the death of the wicked, desires that every man turn to Him and live, not die in his sins, not desiring that men perish but that they repent?"

"Oh, I believe that," he said.

"Then I have a problem. If God desires the salvation of all men, and He made you get saved, and He made me get saved, why doesn't God make everybody get saved?"

"Well, you have to cooperate...."

"Now you've changed positions on me. Once you use the word cooperate, you make a man's relationship to God conditional. That is not cause and effect. That's influence and response."

Have you heard of the John Calvin Insurance Company? They pay no claims because they say everything that happens is an act of God!

That pretty little girl responded freely with a "Yes." She could have said, "No." She could have changed her mind during the past 50 years and said "No" at anytime, and sued for a divorce. She has continued to say "Yes" to this day, and has been a terrific wife and mother, making for a wonderful 58 years.

In the summer of 1952, revivals were taking most of my time when Rev. Clarence Bowen called with a problem. He was responsible to lead singing for the National League Convention (later became National Youth Conference) meeting in conjunction with the convening of the National Association of Free Will Baptists in Shawnee, Oklahoma. A mutual friend of ours had died and he was so close to the family he felt constrained to fulfill their request and conduct the funeral. Would I? Could I, go to Shawnee and fill his place?

The dates were open. The quartet with which I sang during the school year was finishing up in Newport News, Virginia, heading to Oklahoma. I was breaking away for the summer on my own to conduct revivals. Begging a ride, I met them in Newport News, to go to Shawnee and lead singing for that youth meeting.

We stopped in Nashville for a few hours for the others to rest, giving me a chance to see Jane, who was working in the college office during the summer. The two of us sat in a swing near the old dining hall building, not 50 feet from where she stood on that stair step and said "Yes" to the proposal for our first date, and in the dim lights, sitting closer than the rules allowed, we made wedding plans for the next May.

Under the circumstances, we got out of town that night over an hour behind schedule, reached Memphis about daybreak, and on to Shawnee.

During that Junior year, the quartet stayed very busy on the road most every weekend, four or five services on Sunday, driving all night Sunday night, and in class by 8:00 a.m. Monday. Sunday dating being impossible, the powers that be allowed us one hour during the week. For Christmas, that pretty little girl from Illinois received an unaffordable diamond, but who tells a man in love with a woman what's affordable?

Dean of the school desperately tried to convince some other couples they could not afford to get married that summer. He was not successful. People in love don't wait until they can afford it. If so, he would be in a wheel chair and she would be on crutches.

During spring break in April, 1953, with a little over $2,000 that I had inherited when I reached 21 years of age on December 14, 1952, being held in escrow at BB&T, Fremont, North Carolina, from my Grandpa Mayo, through my mother who had died in a car wreck in 1939, I went to Goldsboro to search for an automobile. Upon receiving that money, the first thing was to pay off Mother's funeral bill, which Daddy had never been able to pay. He paid some by digging graves, with a shovel, for the undertaker who applied that to the bill at $5.00 per grave.

The undertaker was somewhat surprised. Looking back 14 years he found the account of the debt. I paid him. The next thing to do was find a preacher friend in the monument business, purchase a small tombstone with the essential statistics engraved, try to find Mother's grave on the back side of the cemetery in Wilson, North Carolina, near the water plant, and mark it. Only two times had I visited the place since February 1939, but the caretaker with records and a map had no problem locating her grave.

That was really her money and she needed a marker and her funeral bill paid. With $1,600 left of the inheritance, I needed a car. A beautiful, two-toned green 1951 Super 88 Oldsmobile, like new, and with low mileage at Pate-Dawson Oldsmobile, was it. He knew I wanted that car, so $1,500 was his bottom price. After spring break, back in Nashville, that pretty little girl could see what she would be living in for the next few years, a 1951 Oldsmobile.

The college year ended Thursday morning, May 28, 1953. We were to drive to Illinois for a Saturday wedding, and according to the rules, the school would not allow Jane to ride with me, unchaperoned, to Illinois for our wedding. After much discussion and disagreement over practical principles, it was agreed that if Brother Miley, a professor at the college and participant in the wedding, would drive along with us, keeping us under surveillance, and the Mileys' little boy would ride with us in the car, Jane could make the trip home with me in my car for the wedding.

Friday was spent in preparation, decorating the little Webbs Prairie Free Will Baptist Church with homegrown white iris and roses (Webbs Prairie has now been closed, sold, and the building burned…we may not be married!), preparing for the reception, the wedding cake, and checking last-minute details. The groom waited.

Saturday must have been the hottest May 30th in the history of southern Illinois. At 2:00 o'clock, one in a double-breasted blue serge, wool suit, the other in a beautiful white organdy dress, made by her mother, with sweat dripping off their noses, they said, "I will and I do and I promise," and by 5:00 p.m. they were on their way to North Carolina to begin revival services at Reedy Branch Free Will Baptist Church, Winterville, North Carolina, on Monday night with Eugene Waddell, Robert Picirilli, and James Earl Raper – the Gospeliers Quartet.

Two became One May 30, 1953

The Long Journey Begins

The Wedding Night

Plans were for the first night of married life, honeymoon night, to be spent in a nice motel, The Coachman, in Paducah, Kentucky, about three hours down the road. Having given no thought to the fact that it was Memorial Day weekend and the beginning of summer vacations, no reservations were made, and two disappointed young people arrived at The Coachman with a NO VACANCY sign blinking in their faces, not only at The Coachman, but all over town. No rooms in Paducah, nothing left to do but keep driving. There was nothing all the way to Hopkinsville.

It was now very late, the wedding night was about to turn to morning when somewhere on Highway 41A, around Clarksville, Tennessee, on the right, a dim blinking neon sign pointed to "Patsy's Motor Court."

In desperation we stopped at a five-room fisherman's camp, woke the man, paid him, went to a room with a screen door, unlocked a weather-worn, splinter-covered wood door, walked into a 10 x 10 room with light bulb hanging from the ceiling on a cord, and a scuffed, torn, flowered linoleum partially covering the concrete floor. Against the wall was an iron bedstead with a cotton mattress on wire springs and a single-sized army blanket full of burned cigarette holes, over sheets made of No. 3 sandpaper, no place to hang clothes, a walk in - back out bathroom with a shower, no hot water. A fish camp, fishermen didn't need comfort or convenience, they came to fish.

With no other choice, we spent the first night of our lives together in that room, an omen of things to come, for not known to us, there would be many such nights.

Sunday morning, with over 400 miles ahead of them for the day, as the picture of Patsy's Motor Lodge gradually disappeared in the rearview mirror, leaving an image permanently printed in the memory, not knowing there would be so many more Patsy Places down the road, and they would spend a week in some of them, and grow old moving from one to another, the newlyweds headed east.

The day passed with reflections of the sun lowering in the western sky in the rearview mirror, when suddenly it was gone as we passed through the tunnel on Highway 70, on the east side of Asheville, NC, and upon exiting that shortcut through the mountain, immediately on the right appeared a beautiful, luxurious motel, The Mountaineer, with a weatherworn split-rail fence enclosing the grounds, and a neon mountain man watching over the place, inviting us to stop. So we did, and for $8.00 we rented a large, well-lighted, spacious room with two double beds (We needed only one.), instead of the one three-quarter bed at Patsy's.

Walking around the grounds in the cool mountain air, holding hands, waiting for sunset, we found our way to the restaurant for supper, sat at a booth with a small box next to the wall for inserting a nickel and remotely selecting a record from the juke box. Flipping through the possible songs, I stopped, pushed the nickel in the slot, mashed the button, and Les Paul and Mary Ford sang *I'm Sittin' on Top of the World.*

A beautiful bride, an almost new car, comfortable motel room, on the top of a mountain, three dear friends waiting for me the next night to begin revival, singing with them every night and preaching, the words seemed so fitting, "I'm sittin' on top of the world, just rolling along, singing a song…."

Bad Motels
We'd Rather Not

Patsy's was not the worst motel in which we ever spent a night. Note I did not say "slept." That record is held by a motel in Flomaton, Alabama.

When we arrived at the pastor's house and were greeted with, "Our house is small and a little crowded. We knew you folks would rather be in a motel."

We had no idea what he meant.

At that motel the screen door was unnecessary because of the big holes in the screen, no lock on the door nor windows, a 10 x 10 room with nothing on the floor of uneven broken concrete, on the bed a dirty old mattress that sagged in every direction, with no mattress pad, no evidence that the one little window had ever been washed, dirt everywhere and roaches, all in the summer heat of south Alabama. After one night, when a friend learned where we were staying, he said, "I know that place. It's terrible. Move to my house."

And we did.

A Leak in the Ceiling

In Nashville, Tennessee, it was a Holiday Inn, where the inner-spring mattress had been folded like a book and it's back broken, and water streaming into the bathroom through the ceiling from the bathroom overhead where evidently the commode had overflowed.

The Mole Hole

Recuperating from two weeks of the worst case of the flu that ever incapacitated me, we arrived in Arlington, Virginia, when I insisted on a motel room where I could rest during the day in order to preach at night. The pastor hesitated and said they couldn't afford it.

When I persisted that it was the only way I could fill the engagement, telling him that I would pay for the room, he found one on the edge of Arlington Cemetery, in a basement, down under a stairway, as dark as a dungeon, with little air circulation, and a difficult place to breathe. Someone had aptly written on the window, *Mole Hole.* Jane left the *Mole Hole* once a day to walk in the cemetery while I lay in bed trying to build up enough strength to preach every night.

Cabin – Not in Gloryland

East of Knoxville, Tennessee, on the south side of Highway 70, 50 years ago stood some cabins pretending to be a motel, but not fooling anybody, especially a body who lived there for a week, which we did in the end of August, making it a home away from home during a revival at Wooddale, 1962.

The buildings were concrete blocks not recently painted, with naked, uncovered, unpainted, gray concrete floors, no carpet, linoleum, tile, not even a throw rug. There are beds which sag from the weight upon them; others sag from their own weight. Those were the latter, one with a large meteor-like hole in the middle of the mattress where something had landed and exploded. The springs had sprung until there was no spring left, giving no support to the holey mattress. When two people laid on that broken down bed, the heavier, me, sank into a deep valley, bringing the lighter, Jane or one of the boys, rolling down a steep hill to land on top of the heavier. There was no sleeping on the beds. Pallets on the concrete floor were not soft, but more comfortable than the beds.

Some hotels are five-star. This was more like a dark stormy night with no stars. There are no negative superlatives to describe the place, bad to *worse, worser,* or *worsest* don't come close. On a scale of zero to minus 10, this was a 15.

We moved a table through a back door into a small backyard and in the shade of a tree I spent the week writing the material for *Beyond the Stars,* the book of sermons published in 1966.

The meetings ended Sunday night, September 2. Early Monday morning we called a truce in our fight with the cabin, neither winners nor losers, just leavers. We drove to Greenville to unload the car and Jane and the boys, after their having been on the road with me most of the summer, so Stephen could begin third grade, Jane and Philip could get home to that little stucco house on Summit Street, and I could go on to Elizabeth City, North Carolina for another meeting.

Dead Man Upstairs

It was 1:00 or 2:00 a.m. when a red light began flashing into the motel room in Columbia, South Carolina. Revolving at five-second intervals on top of the fire truck, it lighted the room in red, while right outside the window in the brightness of a search light, firemen, policemen, and a small group of curiosity seekers were talking loudly, disturbing everyone on the back side of the motel.

With the fear of fire in mind, after all, fire trucks don't usually show up at 1:00 in the morning delivering Girl Scout cookies, Jane went to the window, then to the door, cracked it open to speak to a fireman, "Should we evacuate this room?" she asked. "Where is the fire?"

"No need, Ma'am," he said. "No fire. A large man has died in the room directly above you and we've been called to help get him down."

We became part of the curious bystanders, watching the firemen raise a cherry picker bucket to the upstairs railing while some men removed a door, strapped the body flat and tight on the door, hooked that to the bucket lift, hoisted the body on the door over the handrail into the air and down to the bed of a truck, taking about an hour to complete the procedure.

The next morning the local newspaper reported that a truck driver, weighing nearly 600 pounds had been found dead by his fellow driver in the upstairs room of a local motel, with pictures of the firemen removing the body. No danger. Just excitement.

Wrestling

One Saturday afternoon in Inman, South Carolina, enjoying the quiet of a nap while Jane fiddled with her hands at something, cross-stitching, crocheting, knitting, crossword puzzles (Over the years she's done so many things to keep her mind and hands occupied.), the riotous sound of an hilarious party taking place in the room next door penetrated that thin wall, demanding our attention. Ladies laughing, talking, only two distinctly different voices, evidently it was not a crowd. Their voices came through loud and clear.

One would say, "Get him. Hit him. Look out, he's got something in his hand."

The other would join in, "He's choking him. That ref is blind. Can't he see? He poked him in both eyes. He's gonna hit him with that chair."

Sounded like wrestling, so we switched TV channels until we found the match. Sure enough, there it was, wrestling, with all those dirty tricks upsetting those ladies, producing the sounds that were reaching us through the walls. We watched and listened. Not to the TV sound, we turned that off and listened to the commentary coming from next door. For an hour they screamed, laughed, warned, and threatened, until finally their hero came out on top.

Happy and pleased, two ladies, one a housekeeper who cleaned rooms, made beds, swept floors, mopped bathrooms at the motel, the other, her friend who had dropped by for their regular Saturday afternoon visit and party, exited the room with the remainder of a Pepsi in one hand and a partially eaten Moon Pie in the other. They bade each other goodbye with the promise of "See you next week." As the visitor drove away the maid pushed her cart to the door of the next room to pick up where she left off cleaning bathrooms and making beds.

It is wonderful that for at least one hour, once a week, all the troubles of life with the load of responsibilities could be drowned out by the sound of laughter as they watched their favorite TV program – wrestling. Don't tell them it's fake. Who cares? Why add doubt about their heroes to all the other doubts that trouble them. Next Saturday we'd be gone, but they would be back, and so would "wrestling."

Sad Situation

When I was young before the years messed up my biological clock, if bedtime came at 2:00 a.m., eight hours later wake up time came at about 10:00 a.m., so 5:00 in the morning was the middle of the night.

During a television interview once, the lady asked me, "What is your daily routine?"

"The first thing I do every morning," I said, "is go to bed. You see, I sort of work second shift. I'm not a morning person. If the

Lord had intended for me to see the sun come up, He would have scheduled it later in the day."

Time has radically changed the routine. If there is a chemical in the brain that initiates that last four hours of sleep, it was depleted long, long ago. Four hours now, and then it's half-awake dreamland for another two or three.

In Charlotte, North Carolina, over 20 years ago, 5:00 a.m. was still in the middle of the night. A loud pounding on the door of that motel room shook me out of bed at that untimely hour. Who comes knocking with such urgency that time of day? Half-afraid and only half-awake, stumbling to the door, turning the knob, but not unlatching the chain, the break of day greeted me, and a young black woman who lifted her loose-fitting, pullover with nothing covering her underneath, said, "My name is Annie, and I'll be your girlfriend, if you want me to."

Shocked and shaking my head, "Annie, I don't want nor need anything you are giving away or selling."

As the door closed quickly and firmly and the lock clicked, she said, "Don't close the door, Mister. Wait a minute, don't shut the door."

She was persistent. She set in to knocking again loud enough to be heard all around the motel, saying, "Mister, please open the door. I won't hurt anything. I just want to be your girlfriend. Open the door, please."

Back at the door, through the crack with the chain hooked, I said, "Annie, if you don't go away, I'm going to call security or the police. So you really should move on," and closed the door again.

Now the knocking was at the door of the next room. Finding no takers, the knocking soon ceased and she was gone.

How desperate does a girl get to beg someone to allow her to sell herself, working motels at 5:00 in the morning?

Attic at Antioch

That first night at Patsy's Motor Court was preparation for later that summer in Bridgeton, North Carolina, Antioch Free Will Baptist Church, at Dan Gaskins mother's house. A widow lady with an unmarried son, living in a small farm house, unpainted, not underpinned, porch across the front, large kitchen with wood-burning stove and a huge round oak table with a lazy susan loaded with food, to turn from dish to dish and serve your plate.

With no extra bedrooms downstairs, Jane and I were sent up a narrow stairway to sleep under an A-frame tin roof with no insulation from the heat and no ventilation for fresh air. Closed inside that attic in the heat and humidity of August on the coast of North Carolina, everything in Jane's overnight case melted, including the lipstick which ran like water poured from the tube. At 2:00 a.m. it was still hot, 90° and 90% humidity.

In 1953, sweating was not an unusual experience for an evangelist anywhere in the South. In south Alabama, in August with no air conditioning, no window fans, finishing an evangelistic sermon preached with some enthusiasm, in a suit dripping wet, soaked through the lapels, the perforated shoes draining water through the holes and over the sides, leaving little puddles every place I stood for a moment, hair hanging in sweat trickling from the head across a tired face, making my way to the door of the church to shake hands with the folks leaving, I was the wet man. That's what a little girl affectionately called me.

The mother told me the story when I returned two years later. After the first meeting, every night in their family devotions they prayed for the church, their friends, members of the family, the pastor, and for preacher Bobby Jackson. When they finished, their little girl would say, "Mama, we forgot to pray for the wet man."

At first the Mama said, "Honey, who are you talking about? We've prayed for everybody. What wet man?"

"That man after church every night standing up front all soaking wet. You know, that wet man."

For two years, with the meetings long past, she knew that I must be preaching somewhere, so they continued praying for the "wet man."

At 2:00 a.m. lying motionless on a cotton mattress on the floor in a closed attic under a tin roof, dripping with perspiration the "wet man" and his new bride tried to sleep every night for a week.

Same Song, Second Verse

That bedroom in the attic was only a preview; the main feature came a few years later after we had two little boys. Wingate Hansley invited us for a meeting where he was starting a church in Wilmington, North Carolina, with no money, no building, few people, discouraging circumstances, having services in a front room in his house. With his family and the church occupying all the space, the only spot for the four of us was up a disappearing stairway into an unventilated attic with roof so low you couldn't stand up without bumping heads with the rafters.

Plywood was laid on the ceiling joists, mattresses were laid on the plywood, we lay on the mattresses, and the temperature in July was about yellowing heat in a tobacco barn, 100° to 110°. The stuff in Jane's overnight case had solidified only to melt again. For 12 nights the "wet man" with his wife and two boys slept in a sauna, while preaching in 13 services, July 3-13, 1960.

That summer heat was like Robert Service's poem, *The Cremation of Sam McGee*, who froze to death in the cold ice and snow, with his body carried by his friend until it was convenient to cremate it. As the fire rose around the corpse, he smiled in the flames and said, "It's the first time I've been warm since I left

Tennessee." It was an opportunity to get warm after a cold winter in Illinois.

The Ice Box

In the upstairs unheated bedroom of the Ketteman house, Jane's home in southern Illinois, in the winter of 1955/56, with the temperature -17° (that's below zero) right outside the window, and a sheet of ice covering the inside of the window, inside the room under enough quilts only a weight lifter could turn over, covered head and all, with a hole from the nose that led out from under the covers, like the breathing hole of a rabbit buried in the snow, to prevent suffocation and warm the air before it reached the respiratory system, we slept.

From 17° below to 110° above, the average temperature was great, but like the man with one foot in a bucket of ice water and the other foot in boiling water said, "Those extremes are what get you."

Ketteman Home, Ewing, Illinois

Jack and Mabel Ketteman

No Floor Space

Heat and cold aside, there have been some strange and uncomfortable sleeping places. The number of times after closing the bedroom door we have removed the mattress from weak or broken springs, laid it on the floor, slept on the floor, placed it back on the bed the next morning before opening the door, and the host never knew, is beyond remembering.

In Georgia, a little hitch showed up. The room was too small to place the mattress on the floor, and it was impossible for two adults to sleep on the bed, so Jane, in honor preferring her husband, attempted a palate made of quilts on a floor made of concrete. It didn't work. She couldn't get comfortable, much less sleep with that cement floor pressing against every bone in her body, so after the second night, when everyone was asleep she slipped into the den with a blanket and an alarm clock to wake her before the folks of the house awoke, to sleep on the couch and slip back into the bedroom about daybreak.

Suppose for some reason they were up during the night, caught her sleeping on the couch, and thought we'd had a fight. At breakfast, I explained the problem, "If you folks find my wife on the couch," I said, "we didn't have a fuss. The fact is two people can't sleep on that mattress and springs."

By then I was a bit perturbed. The son was sleeping alone on a very good mattress in the room next door. The lady was apologetic saying, "We have been planning to buy a new bedroom suite for that room."

"You don't need a bedroom suite. You simply need a mattress."

Jane slept on the couch. I slept on the bed. Neither of us has slept there since. That's the last time I was invited to their church for a meeting.

Bed Too Short, Crack Too Wide, and Hole Too Big

In Tulsa, Oklahoma, being alone and assigned to the unheated garage that had been made into a room of the parsonage, I was supposed to sleep on a fold-out couch, not a hide-a-bed, a fold-out. The back unhooked, dropped down, leaving a large crack in the middle, between the seat and the back. Part of the stuffing, having been torn out of both sides left a few lumpy islands. The arms became headboard and footboard, which limited the length to about five feet.

With a blanket packed in the crack down the middle, pillows stuffed in the holes, lying catawampus so that the head went beyond one arm and feet beyond the other, a six-foot man could fight that thing all night in the cold, but not sleep.

That was one of the many weeks there was some comfort in knowing Jane was at home in a good bed, the first item purchased when we finally stopped in 1960.

A Corpse Downstairs

In Andrews, South Carolina, 20 miles northwest of Georgetown, Victory Free Will Baptist was not much more than a mission, an effort to start a church in the small town. The local friendly undertaker graciously offered an upstairs furnished apartment at the funeral home for the visiting evangelist's hospitality arrangements during the week of revival meetings. Stove, refrigerator, television, a comfortable bed, all the essentials, made it a very good place to stay. I was enjoying the week, January 1984.

On Wednesday, the undertaker approached me with what he thought could be a problem.

"We have a lady corpse downstairs who will be spending the night. The reason we keep the apartment is because the law requires someone to sleep on the premises if there is a body here. So if you would rather not stay under these circumstances, one of us will spend the night. Will this be a problem?"

"Not for me, if it's alright with her. Have you checked with her on the matter? If she's content to sleep downstairs and not come up here, I'll be more than happy to stay up here and not go down there."

So we slept, each one in his and her assigned place not disturbing the other. If she stirred around downstairs I never heard her. I had a quiet evening after church before retiring and that was a good thing. If someone had come by after church to visit and broke that silence with footsteps coming up those creaking stairs that would have been a bad thing.

Having preached to a room full of caskets in Miami, I now could add to my funeral home experiences, sleeping with a corpse in Andrews, South Carolina.

Solitary Confinement

During the last 30 years some churches have begun providing "Prophet Chambers" for visiting evangelists. Some were very comfortable, bedroom, living room, kitchen, bath, fully furnished apartments.

On the other hand, some were more like dungeons for punishing false prophets. It could be a small bedroom, with no windows, one door in, no way out, varnish fumes strong from refinishing the floor in the gym above, no air circulation, dark as midnight day and night. Under the basketball court in the basement of the gym, at 2:00 in the afternoon the sound of a herd of horses galloping overhead made sleep and rest impossible and shook dust from the ceiling to alert all the allergies, swelling the sinuses, congesting the bronchials, infecting the larynx, and leaving a preacher so hoarse he could hardly talk above a whisper.

By the end of the week, my voice was gone, body exhausted, and another week under those conditions would have left me speechless.

When I arrived at the next town, after the first night laboring to preach, a nurse in the church scheduled me to see the doctor with whom she worked. He diagnosed a very serious allergy attack, began treatment, and by the end of that week my condition had improved greatly.

I was back in the church with the dungeon several times, but never again stayed in that cell of solitary confinement. Like Alcatraz it was no longer in use, only to be viewed by visitors as the torture chamber where prophets were once imprisoned and punished for preaching too loud and too long, where the volume of their sermons was lowered by laryngitis and the length was reduced by shortness of breath with bronchitis. Maybe preachers don't preach as loud and as long as they once did, so the dungeon is not needed anymore.

Where Thieves Break Through and Steal

Over the years there have been many prophet chambers in church buildings. John Gibbs approached me at a National Convention with, "Man you got me in trouble."

Not aware of any trouble I was responsible for where John and I were involved, in my ignorance I said, "Where? How? and How Much?"

He shared with me his stay in Fairfield, California. The sleeping provisions were in the church office on a hide-away couch. The first night with some fear and trembling due to the surroundings, while he was trying to get to sleep, with lights flashing, sirens blowing outside, there came a pounding on his door. When he opened it, there stood a threatening policeman, flashlight and handcuffs in hand, with plans to arrest John and take him away as an intruder who had broken into the church building, forcing John to call the pastor and confirm his story of being a visiting preacher conducting meetings.

The officer explained their anxiety. It seems there had been a shooting in the neighborhood (not exactly Mr. Rogers' neighborhood), maybe someone killed, and they were thinking the fleeing shooter could have broken into the church and was hiding there.

The next morning John told the pastor, "I'm not sleeping here another night. I'm going to a motel. I'll pay the bill. I'm just not staying here any longer."

"Well, Bobby Jackson slept in here all week. The place was robbed while he was here and he wasn't scared," the pastor said with a hearty laugh.

"So, I'm in trouble," John said, "and you got me into it. You stayed in that place all week?"

"Well, yes, and it was robbed," I said. "In that same room with the thin mattress removed from those crossbars and wire springs, and spread on the floor, it was rather comfortable. On those metal rods it was more like sleeping on railroad tracks.

"The sound of something overhead did arouse me about daybreak, but since I knew construction was still in progress on the building and the A-frame gable had not been closed in, thinking the workers certainly come to work early out here to miss the heat in the middle of the day, I decided to turn over, go back to sleep, let them work on the building without my help.

"When the pastor came about 9:00 a.m., he said, 'Did you hear anything during the night?'"

"Yeah," I said. "I heard the men working early this morning."

"Nobody was working. That was some guys who came into the attic through that open, unfinished gable, removed some ceiling tiles, dropped into the auditorium, stole our amplifier, microphones, speakers, some other stuff, and passed by your door carrying it out."

My door wasn't locked, and since I flew to California, no car was parked at the church and they didn't know anyone was in there, never opened the door to check, and I slept through it.

"John," I said, "we did have a good meeting. How did yours go?"

"Great," he said, "but I didn't sleep in that room during it."

That was in April, 1995. Jane and I were back again in 1996, 1997, and 2000, with the most comfortable, convenient, wonderful hospitality in the lovely home of Sam and Bobbie Hensley with the entire spacious upstairs for our living quarters.

During one of those meetings, Sam suggested we go into the city and act like tourists for a day … walk along the docks, eat seafood in one of the upscale restaurants on the wharf, tour Alcatraz, and take a fast drive down Lombard St. … a little excitement.

"Don't forget a sweater or jacket."

No chance. You make that mistake only once. In June, 1980, during a meeting at Sherwood Forest in El Sobrante, we made our first visit to San Francisco, and no one mentioned a coat. An icy 25 mph wind blowing in off the cold water of the north Pacific almost froze Jane. Not again … a sweater, coat, hooded jacket, Eskimo snowsuit … she'd wrap up in something.

The stroll was nice, seafood wonderful, skipped Lombard, tour of Alcatraz sold out for two weeks, so the only excitement left was the boat tour.

As we made our way west in the bay toward the notorious bridge, Sam, who never met a stranger and never passed up the opportunity to meet one, suggested we escape the crowd, find the bridge, see who was driving this thing, meet the pilot, whom we found to be a gracious friendly fellow who became especially interested when he learned I was from North Carolina. In his military service there had been some connection with Camp LeJeune, the marines at Jacksonville, or Fort Bragg and the 82nd airborne at Fayetteville.

As we chatted about North Carolina, he said, "Say, how would you like to drive this boat? Think you could keep her on course? See that buoy up ahead? Head for it and pass it on the left."

"I can do that."

So he stepped aside.

"Take the wheel."

Water was calm, weather clear, buoys very visible. Nothing complicated, we weren't trying to find our way across the Atlantic, navigating with the help of Betelgeuse from 300 light years away. We passed under and beyond the Golden Gate Bridge about 200 yards, made a 180 around the buoys, back under the bridge, headed toward the Rock, and before we reached Alcatraz, he took control.

"Good job, might need an assistant some day."

"Thanks for the experience."

I have now fished for Rock (really Cod, called Rock by locals because they live on the bottom in the rocks) under the bridge, ridden across it at sunrise in an old hippy van chugging along while I watched through a hole in the floor, the pavement pass under my feet and nervously wondered if I'd make it to the airport in time to catch the flight back to the East coast, and piloted a tour boat across the bay and under the bridge – pleasant memories of visits to California.

Scared Stiff

We have stayed in mobile homes, some comfortable, some extremely uncomfortable during these 50 years. In the church yard at Iola, Texas, Cross Free Will Baptist Church, was a very comfortable mobile home, residence of the previous pastor who had resigned and moved away, leaving the place available for us during the week of meetings.

It was dark when we arrived the first night. We moved in and unpacked. Jane was in the shower when I heard somebody walking on top of the trailer. The footsteps started at one end, made their way slowly to the other end and back, stopping for a moment. The silence around us in the dark woods and empty house trailer was deafening. Not a sound. Jane came out of the shower and we sat on the bed listening to those footsteps make another trip.

Somebody has slipped out here in the dark, and it was dark, so dark you could stick a finger out, pull it back and leave a hole in it, no outside lights in sight. They're pulling a prank, trying to scare us, I offered as an explanation, hoping that I was right. If they were trying to scare us, their purpose had been accomplished. We sat breathlessly quiet, listening for 30 minutes, psychological time, to someone walking around on top of that trailer.

My wife's courageous husband didn't go outside to investigate. If it were a prank, I didn't want them to know how scared we were; if not a prank, I didn't want them to know we were at all! We had no defense, not even a ball bat.

The footsteps stopped directly above a window, and in the light from the window, I watched a large cat leap off the top of the trailer onto a window air conditioning unit and to the ground, disappearing into the dark. The next morning at church we repeated the tale.

Someone said, "Yes, the former pastor owned a huge cat, could not catch him when they moved, and that cat hangs around the trailer looking for them."

"Man, I wish they would come and get him," I said. He never visited again during the entire week.

With the Chickens

Over 40 years ago south Mississippi was running a little behind most of the United States and was in no rush to catch up, new churches partially finished, some parts unpainted, and three years later still partially finished, and the same parts still unpainted. Life moved at a slow pace.

Jane, the boys and I spent a week in the home of a gracious schoolteacher, in August, unbearable heat, no air conditioning in a small room, with two double beds, and a window fan to pull the outside air in from a chicken house with 10,000 chickens about 20 feet from the window. The odor of the chickens mixed with the fine feathers and dust, filled the room night and day, making it difficult to breathe, almost suffocating. Suitcases went under the beds at night, on the beds during the day.

The man of the house laboring with emphysema, would stand on his head, feet up in a chair, head on the floor, to drain the fluid out of his lungs, coughing continually and gasping for breath, trying to live on air that contained more feathers and ammonia than oxygen. Dust, humidity, heat, chickens, strong odors, and sweat made it nearly impossible to sleep day or night. The boys tumbled restlessly on one bed, Jane and I on the other.

That was about the time Erma Bombeck wrote a book, *If Life is a Bowl of Cherries, What Am I Doing in the Pits?*

Jane said her book would be titled, *If the Road to Heaven is a Flowery Bed of Ease, What Am I Doing in Mississippi in August?* Needless to say, being from Illinois, her favorite part of the country never was the deep south, with the dirt, the filth, the trash along the roads, the heat, the bugs, gnats, roaches, laziness, unkempt houses, unkempt people, and her list continued…. The bugs sought revenge in South Carolina.

Battling the Bugs

It was not customary in a rural church in southeastern South Carolina, for an out-of-state evangelist to bring his wife and children with him for a week of revival meetings. As far as anyone knew it had never happened before. And as far as I know it has never happened since. At least this evangelist has never been invited back with or without his family.

Finding a place for them to sleep was not easy. Nobody was jumping at the opportunity to "put them up" or put up with them for a week. It was public knowledge that one family with a large frame farm house had two empty bedrooms, and when there seemed to be no other possibility those rooms were made available.

After the Monday night service, the man of the house gave me directions as to how to find his place, and disappeared. When we had shook all the hands in an effort to get acquainted, and with everyone else gone, we went searching for the house. When we found it, all the lights were off except one in the hall and in one of two adjoining bedrooms. The folks had already hurried off to bed. We were not unwelcome, just not welcomed. The two bedrooms with twelve-foot ceilings and large windows were left open for us, and lugging a week's luggage we quietly passed down the hall into those rooms, trying not to disturb anybody.

Jane prepared the boys for bed, led them to their bedroom to find their bed near the large open windows covered with black bugs that had been pulled through the screens of two raised windows by an attic exhaust fan. The bed was covered and more were coming. Jane closed the windows, shook the sheets, and remade the bed. We found a bathroom down the hall, used it only for the essentials so as not to wake anybody, came back to the room and the bugs had called in swarming reinforcements. They had covered the bed again. A second battle with the bugs and she tucked the boys in bed.

In the other bedroom with the light out, the bugs were not so bad. We closed the windows, didn't turn on the light, but by the time we lay down, here came the boys.

"Something is biting us. We can't go to sleep," in unison.

Jane went back to their room, pulled the light switch, and stood stunned by a bed covered with bugs. Could it be one of the plagues of Egypt? No way could the boys sleep in that bed full of bugs. Leaving the light on in that room, we brought the boys to our bedroom, closed the door, and the four of us tossed, tumbled, rolled, and slept a little in one bed, lying crossways which gave a little more room, except for the old man who was two feet too long. Two feet of his six-foot frame were hanging off the bed and went to sleep before he did. He woke the feet and sent them to get a chair, and set it beside the bed so they'd have a place to rest and not hang out all night.

With the door and windows closed, the attic exhaust fan had no exhaust. No bugs were being sucked in through the screens, but neither was any air, and it was midsummer in eastern South Carolina.

With four of us in one bed, I thought of the two little boys crowded in a small swing. One said to the other, "If one of us would get outta here, I'd have more room."

One night was enough. The next day we apologized for not spending the week, but since Carroll and Anna Lee Alexander, pastor at Westside in Johnsonville, had invited us to stay with them, and they were very good, close friends, we were moving to their place. We thanked them for their hospitality and on Tuesday night after church headed for Johnsonville. Those folks relieved of the responsibility, headed home, and wouldn't need to hurry off to bed before the evangelist and his family came in.

Being unwelcomed and unwanted is one thing. Battling biting bugs all night is something else. The two together will move you from one place to another.

No Place to Stay

The only situation more embarrassing and uncomfortable than a bad place to sleep is no place at all. At St. Mary's Church, Kenly, North Carolina, in the summer of 1954, Jane, Stephen, who was four months old, and I were in revival. Stephen became fussy and Jane thought it best to take him outside, since there were no nursery facilities, and outside there were mosquitoes, but she didn't want to disturb the service. While sitting in the car in the dark, unknown to a group of women who had exited the building at the end of the service, Jane heard their conversation.

"What are we going to do with that preacher?" one asked. "He has a wife and baby. We didn't know that."

"They can't stay at my place," one said.

"Well, I don't have room for a woman and a baby," added another.

"We just don't have any arrangements for them," they concluded.

By the time I reached the car, Jane was in tears.

"They don't want us here," she said. "Those women just made it clear. We are not welcomed and there's no place to go."

It is true there were no motels around and money was scarce had there been one. After everybody left, I said, "Well, we can always go to Miss Lillie Mae's at Stoney Creek."

She was the most gracious, generous, openhearted friend that a young preacher ever knew. At her place for two or three years we stored our things in boxes in her garage. In the spring, we stopped by to take out our summer clothes and box up the winter ones. In the fall we reversed the process. She had a bedroom with a great bed available anytime we needed it; Stephen slept in a bassinet. In addition she made the best biscuits this side of everywhere. They were small, thin, crusty, Ritz Cracker sized.

Joshing with her, I'd say, "Pass me a handful of those Ritz Crackers."

Around 11:00 p.m., knocking on her door, looking for a bed, we found open arms and "You know your bed is here for you anytime."

Sleeping there, driving back and forth, I preached to those gracious, friendly folks at the church for a week.

Money - But No Motel

For over 20 years the summers were all alike, only different directions. The day after Pitt County Schools closed, with the car packed for three months on the road, when the boys were young, with them asleep in the backseat, with the sun rising in the rearview mirror, not to return until the day school began again, the Jackson Four left Greenville. In the summer of 1963, we were in Alabama, Arkansas, and three weeks of August in Texas. Never, ever was a pastor not informed ahead of time that the family would be traveling together in the summer. If his meeting was during the months of June through August, he was always told that Jane and the boys would be with me.

The services in Dallas closed on Sunday night and were scheduled to begin at Trinity Church, Fort Worth, on Monday night, which meant we would drive from Dallas to Fort Worth on Monday afternoon. Finding the church and a public phone booth was easy enough. Calling the preacher, I said, "Preacher, we're at the church, where do we go from here?"

A moment of silence and then the shock, "We...who?"

"Me and my family. This is Bobby Jackson, scheduled to begin services tonight."

"Your family? We didn't know they were coming. There are no plans or arrangements for them. How many?"

"My wife and two boys."

The pastor had visited the services in Dallas, where the family was with me. Did he think I made a trip to North Carolina between Sunday night and Monday and took them home? If he was not informed ahead of time, that is the only preacher in over 50 years that didn't receive such information.

After a long, long silence, he finally said, "Well, come on to our house. There is nowhere else for you to go."

When we arrived, the wife met us at the door, and with a most belligerent attitude let my wife know in no uncertain terms that she and the boys were unwelcome, unwanted, and unprepared for, but if the four of us could stay in one bedroom, and she meant stay in the room, we could bring our stuff in, and he'd show us to the room. In the room with suitcases beside the bed, Jane sat on the bed in tears with two little unwanted boys.

"I need gas in the car," I said. "That will give me reason to go, and I'll get a motel room, pay for it ourselves and come back to get you and the boys as quickly as possible."

Leaving her sitting on the bed, her eyes filled with tears, her mind filled with uncertainty, I left to look for a room.

There was not a motel or hotel room available for any price between Fort Worth and Dallas seeing as how the Texas Cattleman's Convention was in town. One motel clerk suggested that I call the Chamber of Commerce, which I did, only to be told, "If there is one room in this town available before Thursday, I'm not aware of it."

The convention ended Wednesday. There would be plenty of rooms Thursday.

Nothing to do, but return to the preacher's house, go into that bedroom where a mother with two little boys waited to learn where we would sleep that night and take the bad news.

"There's not a bed available in town for any price, until Thursday night. Whether or not they want us here, if I'm to preach this meeting tonight, we're forced to stay in this bedroom. Maybe Thursday we can move out."

Using the bathroom only when necessary so as not to interfere with the pastor and his wife, dressing for church, skipping supper, we had eaten in the afternoon, we found our way back to church and I preached the meetings.

By Thursday, when we could have moved to a motel, the pastor had warmed a little toward the boys, who had not broken anything, dumped no drawers in the floor, torn no pillows off the couch, spilled nothing in the kitchen nor bathroom, wrecked nothing in his house, except their mother, who was a nervous wreck under the pressure that they would do something displeasing to the woman of the house. Stephen had been content to read encyclopedias about animals, while Philip played little competitive games in the bedroom floor. So the preacher insisted we stay all week, and took Stephen into the desert helping him catch a horny toad, which died in a box in the hot sun in the back window of the car on our way to Piney Woods Youth Camp in east Texas for the following week.

Maybe they overcame the shock of a man, wife, and two little boys whom they didn't know appearing at the door of their beautiful, well furnished house which was filled with trinkets that could be turned to trash by rambunctious children, when they decided after a day or two these boys would do no damage to their home. However, that is the only invitation that ever came from that preacher for a meeting.

Motel – But No Money

In Texas, with money but no motel rooms, four years before it had been Florida with motel rooms but no money.

We spent the month of August, 1959, in Texas. First Church, Dallas; Youth Camp, Piney Woods near Nacogdoches; Good Hope (better than Little Hope, which is in Alabama, both better than NO Hope), Henderson; Evergreen, Iola. We closed on Sunday night, August 30, and were scheduled to begin in Miami, Florida, on Sunday morning, September 6, continuing through two weeks, three Sundays, ending September 20. Six days in between made our 1,500 mile trip to Miami a leisure unhurried drive.

About day three we were taking our time down Highway 98 along Florida's northern gulf coast, stopping now and then to cool in the shade of a palm tree, listening to the ocean's breaking waves over white sand as far as the eye could see in both directions. At one such spot there was a tiny bath house where those passing through could change clothes in order to take a dip in the water. Confident the boys, Stephen, five, Philip, two, would enjoy wading in the surf, and with no one else in sight, plus some extra time, the decision was made for the four of us to relax and enjoy some relief from a hot, non-air-conditioned automobile.

We changed, leaving our clothes and valuables in the locked car, walked 50 yards across the hot, white sand to the cool waters of the gulf. Stephen splashed in with pleasure. Philip was terrified, crying and running from the smallest wave to his mama. Leaving Stephen and me at water's edge, she and Philip returned to the car, changed clothes in the bath house and came back along the beach, but not near the water.

We cut our time short, returned to the car to find that some-one had gotten into the car, forced open the glove compartment, removed all the money (over $200) from my billfold, leaving the open empty billfold lying on the front seat. There was no sign of forced entry so I assumed Jane forgot to lock the car when changing clothes. She suggested someone had a tool made for the purpose of opening locked car doors.

Arguing over how the thief entered the car was as pointless as the couple stranded on a deserted island by a thief who cut the rope with which their boat was tied. She said the rope was cut with scissors, he said it was a knife, she said scissors, he said …. Angry and exasperated he finally pushed her head under the water. As the bubbles came up, and her hand went down, she was making scissors with two fingers.

The money was gone. How and who were unanswerable questions. There was one possibility. About 100 yards down the beach was a guy pretending to be picking up trash. He was cleaning up. But there was no trash in his bag or on the beach. He wasn't picking up trash. He was picking pockets of folks who stopped to swim.

When he was approached about it, he said, "Oh! I haven't seen anybody. Nobody's been near your car."

"Somebody stole all my money while we were down at the water!"

"I'm so sorry," he said.

He wasn't sorry. He was glad. He'd had a pretty good day even if no one else stopped. He was cleaning up alright.

It was late afternoon. We were two nights and two more days from Miami. Credit cards were not widely used, bank cards didn't exist, ATM machines were unheard of. Money was the means of exchange for goods and services and we didn't have any! There was money in our bank account back in Greenville, and a bank statement had been forwarded to us in our mail, which would prove we had money in the bank, and someone would take a check. Wrong!

First stop was a motel, needed a place for a wife and two little boys to sleep. The motel owner/manager said, "No personal checks."

Explained to him how we came to be in such a predicament and that we were two days from Miami where I was to begin revival Sunday, showed him the bank statement with the balance, pled with the desperation of a beggar, to no avail.

"No checks, from nobody, under no circumstances."

"Do you know of a motel where I could find help?"

"No, sir, I'm afraid not."

And he walked back into his quarters, closing the door behind him.

Jane and the boys waited in the car for me to return with the sad news.

"No cash. No room. He wouldn't take a check nor offer any sympathy."

"What are we going to do?" Jane was worried about the boys. With a little fear in her voice and a tear on her cheek, 'Where are we going to sleep?'

"I don't really know. We can't drive straight through to Miami, don't have gas money, can't eat at a restaurant, and no motel will take a check."

We tried two more motels with the same response.

Searching in my brain for a solution, I finally said, "Well, I'll try to find a grocery store and see if we can buy food from them with a check." We found a supermarket. Loaded with my bank statement and family, I asked to speak to the manager. After explaining the entire miserable situation to him, begging again, I said, "Would you be so kind as to allow us to get some groceries to carry us for the next two days to Miami, and pay for them with a check?"

He smiled and said, "Preacher, you make that check for as much money as you need for motel, food, gasoline, and anything else to get you to Miami. I'll cash it. And if you want to buy anything in the store you go right ahead."

The name of that man and supermarket have long ago disappeared in an ocean of 10,000 names of people and places that cannot possibly be fished out, but the man and the experience are written in the memory in indelible ink, impossible to erase.

We made it to Miami. By the way, we didn't go back to that first motel to spend the night. From home, I wrote the supermarket manager a letter of gratitude and let him know we were safe at home.

There were extremes. All sleeping places were not in hot attics under tin roofs nor windowless dungeons in basements under gym floors. Some were luxurious, elaborate, and almost palatial. Still the good didn't make the bad better. The average was ideal. Again the extremes were the problem.

Up a Creek in a Cold Rain

The meetings in Tucson and Phoenix were over, ended July 23, 1968, with two weeks to see the sights, Grand Canyon, Yellowstone, Petrified Forest, Painted Desert, etc., before we were due to begin in Denver on July 7, for eight days. Roy Thomas, the Denver pastor, suggested that since we had a few days to relax, we should plan to be in Denver on Wednesday, the 2nd, preach for him Wednesday night, take his camper into the mountains, camp out two days, return Saturday and begin the meetings Sunday morning.

Camping is not my idea for resting, relaxing, recuperating, or recreation. Being in the woods for three years, 1941-1944, was enough camping for a lifetime. Those years were spent in a share-cropper's shell of a house with running water (when it rained, it ran in through the leaky tin roof and ran out through the cracks in the floor), natural air conditioning(same conditioning inside and outside year round), shared with all the native insects, flies, mosquitoes, bedbugs, ants, no plumbing inside nor out, three rooms and a path that didn't lead to an outhouse, but led into the woods where the occupants had squatters rights. Those years stripped camping of its glamour. There's nothing about lying on the cold ground at night zipped up in a straightjacket waiting for the rain that calls me to the wilderness to enjoy the fun.

The offer was gracious. It would be different. We'd be in the Rockies and maybe the boys would like it. So we arrived Wednesday afternoon, prepared for our little adventure, hooked the preacher's pop-up, Jack-In-The-Box tent on wheels, to his station wagon, since my car had no trailer hitch, loaded it with provisions for two days, plus hot dogs and marshmallows to roast over a campfire under clear, star-filled skies about two miles above sea level.

Wednesday night's service was encouraging and after a good night's sleep, early Thursday morning the little family of coura-geous campers headed west toward the tallest peaks, Mt. Evans and Pikes Peak. In about two hours we were in the mountains searching for a spot to make camp, and came upon a beautiful small green flat place between the road and a rippling creek of ice water from melted snow up in the mountains. Ideal, just room for the camper, station wagon and us, and the sound of that clear, cold water over the rocks would be a lullaby. We unfolded the Jack-In-The-Box and gathered a few limbs for a fire. The tem-perature had dropped about 20° from Denver. Camping wasn't so bad. We'd have two days of new experiences to remember.

Within an hour the sky changed from blue to gray, the wind began to blow, the rains came, the temperature dropped another 20° and bone-chilling cold wind, pouring rain, that must have started out as snow in the upper atmosphere, kept coming for the next two days and nights. Jane and the boys, wrapped in blankets, huddled up in that tent on wheels. Philip moved to the back of the station wagon and played games. The ice water in the creek began to rise, going up in speed and down in temperature.

On Friday during a short break in the rains, I gathered some wet sticks, rubbed a couple of dry ones together, and with a match and paper kindled a fire. In hooded sweatshirts and blankets we heated water for hot chocolate, roasted some marshmallows and a wiener or two.

Saturday morning with no let-up in the rain, we'd had enough, broke up our little camp, no need to worry about the campfire since it had been washed away, along with the excitement of camping, and came back into Denver.

"Why so early?" was the question.

"To escape the cold and the flood," was the answer.

Jane hadn't been warm for two days. The family has not actually been camping since. We've stayed at some camp facilities because that's what was provided, but never deliberately gone back into the woods for the fun of it.

The meetings in Denver ended July 14th. The little band of nomads wandered around in the west a few more days and headed east to begin services at Heads Free Will Baptist Church outside of Nashville, Tennessee, on July 22, 1968.

On a Lake with Loons and Mosquitoes

Five years earlier the family had lived in a cabin on a lake in northern Maine during meetings in New Limerick Free Will Baptist Church, Houlton, Maine, at the end of Interstate 95 North. In 1961, two years prior to our lake experience, I had meetings in the area and in that church: September 3-9, 1961 – New Limerick, September 10-13, 1961 – Linneus, Maine. September 16, 1961, was my first sermon in New Brunswick, Canada, at Stickney Primitive Baptist Church.

Thursday and Friday after closing in Linneus, Mack Owens, the pastor, suggested we go over to New Brunswick to investigate a small group of churches, descendents of the Free Will Baptist movement in the Maritime Provinces, doctrinally the same as Free Will Baptists, who after the merger of most of their churches in the early 1900s with the United Baptists of Canada, had reorganized, taken the name "Primitive," meaning "original" and no kin to the Calvinistic Primitives in the southern states. He had been told there was an older minister, named Hatfield, in Hartland who was the leader of the group.

We found Mr. Hatfield, who wasn't very happy to see us, introduced ourselves and asked about the churches.

"I have nothing to do with it anymore," was his disgruntled reply. "There is a man named Giberson, who lives down here in Bath. He runs things now."

"Where in Bath?"

"Second Street, parallel to the highway in the middle of the block. The only house with a 'grage' under it facing the street."

In Bath, we began searching for that house with a "grage," not knowing what one would look like if we found it. There was a house in the right spot, and a garage under it. The only difference was two syllables instead of one. There we found Philip Giberson, who was much more open and friendly than Hatfield. Philip requested that I preach for him at Stickney over the weekend and from that we became fast, enduring friends, and the doors of opportunity opened for evangelistic meetings in all those churches for the next 45 years.

During that 1961 visit, from Maine I finished up in Twin Mountain, New Hampshire, September 17-22; Littleton, 24-29; and on Saturday night, September 23, preached at a Youth For Christ rally in Orange, Vermont.

Most satisfying to any evangelist is to be invited back and we were, along with Jane and the boys for the month of June, 1963, Linneus, 3-9, and New Limerick, 10-15, and were staying in a cabin on a breathtaking, beautiful lake full of loons.

During the winter the lake had been filled with wiggle-tails under the ice which hatch out as little black mosquitoes in June, after the thaw. No competition in size with one Jane killed at a youth camp in west Texas. She slapped the mosquito on a man's back, before it could draw blood (The fellow would have needed a transfusion.), flattened the critter which had a wing-span of over an inch, and mounted him in the front of her Bible for exhibition.

In Maine, there were trillions of them, swarms that sang a bloodthirsty melody as they followed you to the outhouse, waited outside the door singing a requiem, chased you back to the cabin, and sent a few undercover agents inside to test your blood.

We went to town, bought hooded sweatshirts for the boys to protect them from the cold and mosquitoes. Water and wood must be retrieved from enemy territory and that was Daddy's job, so he could build a fire in a heater to keep warm, heat water, and cook. The loons sang to each other in monotonous unison all night. Wrapped head to toe with only the face exposed to the mosquitoes, Stephen and Philip ventured to the lake's edge to catch a glimpse of the looney-tune singers.

A day of grief and mourning for the family that week was the funeral of Uncle Wiggly, Stephen's tadpole that had travelled with us from its birth in the Tar River at home, had grown half-way to a frog, shed his tail and little legs were appearing. No one knows what happened, change of water, mosquito spray, or mosquitoes themselves killed him, counting on frog legs for their supper. Today, on a lake in Maine, there is a marker at the grave of Uncle Wiggly, the world's most widely travelled half-grown polliwog, frogpole.

Memories of the week are much more pleasant than the experience.

From that meeting we went back to Stickney, New Brunswick, June 16-23, and found great hospitality in Philip and Ursula Giberson's home. The boys became acquainted with Karl and Nancy, and the church was filled to overflowing every night for revival services.

In Littleton, New Hampshire, June 24-30, and Twin Mountain, July 2-7, then to Millville, New Brunswick, outback from Woodstock, at Hawkins Corner, July 8-15. We finished six weeks in the northeast and headed for Samantha, Alabama, Sulphur Springs, Free Will Baptist Church.

Fire from Heaven

The longest covered bridge in the world spans the beautiful St. John River, the Rhine of North America, at Hartland, New Brunswick. At the foot of the bridge on the Hartland side of the river tucked away among the fir and birch trees along the rocky bank is the Free Will Baptist campground, where the family lived for most of the summer in 1966.

On our way north we stopped for a week in Harrington, Maine, a little town on US Highway 1, in southeastern Maine, situated along the rocky coast on Pleasant Bay, to conduct meetings in the Baptist Church, June 12-19, 1966, then on to New Brunswick.

Holmesville, 20-26. Two weeks, June 26-July 6, United Baptist Church, Jacksontown, highest elevation point in Carleton County. From the front porch of the Frank Alexander home where we stayed, the view was beyond beautiful. Terraces of potato fields dropping layer after layer down to the river, beyond which the hills rose rapidly in forests of fir and spruce farther and farther away toward the outback, where the terrain flattened into more potato fields. On a clear day, the small mountains 20 miles east of Woodstock could be seen rising slightly above the dark woods against a blue sky. Fourteen days turned Jacksontown into a favorite spot and the Alexanders to dear, permanent, life-time friends.

For the four other meetings – Youth Camp, 7-17, Stickney, 17-24, Bristol, 24-31, Rosedale, 31-August 7, we lived at the camp in a cabin with all conveniences in common – bath house, kitchen, restrooms, etc., beds comfortable, but not the Waldorf.

The weather was cool, Man, cool. July 4th the temperature reached a sweltering 80° and Jane sat in the sun all day, trying to get warm, sympathizing with Sam McGee.

A heavy thunderstorm, sharp lightning, crashing thunder, and pouring rain hit the area one afternoon during teen camp. Services were in progress in the Tabernacle until the sound of beating rain drowned out the preacher, leaving everyone quietly waiting for the storm to pass, when lightning struck. The flash, the crack, the crashing sound of the delayed thunder, a few screams, and lights went out, and it was silent again. It hit something. The rains slacked, and some adults went outside to investigate.

The Jacksons' and Gibersons' cabins were side by side, only a few feet between them. In that space up against the Gibersons' cabin grew a tall fir tree 15 inches in diameter. The lightning hit that tree, splintered it from top to bottom and ran along an electric wire into the Giberson cabin, where Karl was lying on a bed underneath a ceiling light, reading a book. The 15,000,000 volts in that stroke of lightning, exploded along that electric wire every few inches, melted the light socket, and knocked the bulb from it onto the bed where Karl was reading.

Karl appeared in the door of the Jackson cabin, where Jane and Philip sat stunned with ears ringing, with a light bulb in his hand, eyes wide-open in shock, shaking like a leaf, saying, "Look! Look! Look what happened."

The tree turned into firewood and toothpicks, the electric wiring was destroyed, a mother and two little boys scared but physically unharmed. That was the extent of the damage. It could have been so much worse.

Looking at the splintered tree, the tale of the woodpecker came to mind. When he struck an old dead tree simultaneously with a bolt of lightning which exploded the tree, knocking the woodpecker 50 feet away, he shook off the shock, gained his composure, and said to himself, "Man! I don't know my own strength."

We finished the meetings in New Brunswick on August 7. Our next stop would be Ashland, Kentucky.

A Mansion on the Hilltop

In October, 1983, we had finished meetings in Cavanaugh, Fort Smith, Arkansas, on Sunday, the 30th, scheduled to begin in Poteau, Oklahoma, Monday, October 31, go through Sunday, November 6, and on to Tulsa for two weeks at Bixby and West Tulsa. As we drove into Poteau at the edge of town, on the right side of the road, on the highest hill in the area, overlooking green pastures rolling in natural contoured lines down to the road, lighted with flood lights, an English Tudor *castle* came into sight, leaving Jane nearly breathless.

"Look at that house!"

Unless you were blind, you had no choice. The house commanded attention. Everyone looked at that house. We drove past the cattle gate entrance that kept in the cows and allowed cars to pass into the lane that went winding up the hill through beautiful, landscaped grounds to the magnificent glowing house.

Jane laughed as we went by, and said, "That's where we'll be staying this week."

"Yes. And the U.S. president will probably attend the meetings along with the governor."

The parsonage was beside the church so there was no problem finding both and the pastor, who after brief pleasantries and welcoming us to town said, "You folks will be staying with one of the deacons this week in his home."

Nothing unusual so far, we often were housed in the home of a church member, especially if the pastor had a large family in a small manse.

"Follow me," he said. "I'll lead you to your sleeping quarters. There is time to unpack, dress for church, come back here, and we'll go out for dinner."

Like a very short funeral procession, the two cars left the church, down the street, turned back onto the same road out of town that brought us into town.

Jane's joke got funnier, "We're going back to that house on the hill. It's on this road."

We passed all the roads and streets that turned off and continued along the road. The house came into sight.

"See – we're still on the road to that house!"

"But the road goes beyond that house into the country and there's probably a gravel road and a path to a farm house in the woods."

As we drew near the entrance to the estate the pastor slowed down.

"We ARE going to that house!"

When the preacher put on his left turn signal, turned through the gate and continued slowly winding his way up the lane, Jane finally caught her breath and said, "There's nowhere else to turn. He's taking us to that house."

Sure enough, we spent the week with the most gracious, generous, friendly folks in that English castle, looking out over the city of Poteau.

We took our four mile exercise walk every day in the local cemetery. For entertainment Jane loves to read vital stuff on tombstones. She noticed one was the grave of the "World's Greatest Matador." The folks said he never fought a bull. His wife just wrote it on the stone after he died, for some reason that nobody knew but her.

All local business, economic, political, religious or otherwise was conducted in jam sessions at a small local restaurant. A case of botulism or salmonella in that food supply could have destroyed the town. One batch of bad chili could have slowed it down for a few days. The preacher and everybody else met there twice a day to visit and take care of the town's affairs.

Many weeks we spent in the valley, but for one week in Poteau, Oklahoma, we lived in a mansion on a hilltop

The Dream House

Stephen was in Rose High School playing trumpet in the band which was on its way to the Raleigh area. The bus was heading west on Highway 264, had passed through Wilson, and about seven miles west of town was approaching the intersection where 264 crosses over I-95. The bus driver's amplified voice called for everyone's attention.

"We're coming up on my dream house," he said. "On the left, take a look at that large beautiful place. When I get rich, that's my kind of house."

All the kids, with curious anticipation, turned heads left to behold a huge beautiful brick home. As they oo'd and ah'd,

Stephen shrugged and said to his friend seated beside him, "I lived in that house for two weeks."

"Yeah, and I slept in the Lincoln bedroom at the White House while visiting the president!" his friend replied.

"No joke, my Dad was in revival down the road, and we stayed in that house during the meetings. There's the church," he said, as they passed Milbourne Free Will Baptist Church on the right.

June 8-19, 1960, Stephen was six years old, Philip was three. Twelve days, 14 sermons, we were in the church, and living in that house, were entertained by that family. The house was actually two homes for two families, the wealthy father and mother who owned most of the land in the area, and the daughter with her family. It was the daughter who opened her home and heart, and provided a place for the evangelist with his family for 12 days and nights during the revival at her church.

Lee Chancey

The house was wood frame, hip tin roof, a long porch across the front with decorative molding and posts, a farm house and the home place of Brother Lee Chancey. It had been refurbished, refurnished, redecorated and was luxurious inside. Brother Lee had twin daughters. Those unfamiliar with the family could not distinguish one from the other. Madge had married into money in the northeast, her husband died; she came home and spent some of her money fixing up that house.

The room where we slept was in the front of the house with large windows that opened to the front porch. Through the front door into the hall, first door to the left led into the room filled with beautiful bird's eye maple furniture, plush wall to wall white carpet, two inches deep, comfortable mattress on a large bed. The remainder of the house was as well done, a modern kitchen, large spacious bathroom, and beautiful dining room.

Every room except Brother Lee's bedroom, Madge said that she had made an effort to fix that room. She put a gas heater in there, and her father said, "Get that lightning bug out of here. I'm freezing to death."

So he cut firewood and fired the little fireplace. In the small room with a linoleum covered floor, he slept on a small wrought iron bedstead with a cotton mattress and coil springs. The inside bathrooms were unnecessary. He ran water in a galvanized foot tub, took that to his room to do whatever bathing he did.

He was old, to a twenty-three-year-old he was very old, but probably not as old as in my memory, maybe in his seventies, had lived all his life in that community around the swamp, a large, huge, above-six-feet-tall and 300 pounds, giant of a man. In his younger days he had been a boxer; word was around that one of his sons who was large like his father went to the ring with some success.

All of this is to introduce to you an honest down-to-earth-straightforward-no-holds-barred, good man.

One afternoon during the meetings we returned to his house after the noon meal (dinner where I grew up, lunch in some circles), where I had stretched out on that comfortable bed in that lovely bedroom to take a nap, rest up before going out for another meal (supper where I grew up, dinner in some circles), and on to church. The window to the porch was raised, door to the hall opened, so a breeze blew across the bed, where I really wasn't eavesdropping, but lying there awake just happened to hear what was going on.

Brother Chancey was in that huge rocking chair on the porch and had been visiting with another old man, a friend in the community, and the friend was leaving. Brother Chancey followed him to the steps and said, "Say, why don't you come back tonight and go with us to the meeting?"

"Oh, I might just do that," he said, "who you got doing the preaching?"

"He's a young feller, just outta college. He works mighty hard, and talks mighty loud. He don't know too much, but he does the best he knows to do."

Honest and partially true. No twenty-three-year-old who hasn't been anywhere, seen anything, nor done many things knows much, in the mind of and compared with a seventy-five-year-old. He's just a dreamer on his way somewhere to do something. The partial truth is "does the best he knows to do." The Lord knows that in an absolute sense nobody has done that, including the young evangelist. The best I knew to do, not really, but I was busy.

From June to December, 1955, there were 20 series of meetings from Michigan to Miami; one in Nason, Illinois, ran 17 days with 19 services followed by one in Bakerville, Illinois, that started on December 25th, Christmas Day. Some of the most fruitful meetings of my ministry were in Illinois in December and January during one snowstorm after another, sub-zero temperatures, and the church houses filled every night.

"Talking mighty loud, working mighty hard" … and enjoying every day of it.

Grand Canyon

The purpose of the phone call was to introduce Paul Thompson, pastor of Heritage Church in Gilbert, Arizona, to a young man from the mission work in France, who was touring the United States by bus and had stopped over in Alabama for a few days before continuing on to Arizona. He visited our meeting in Fayette, August, 1996, and asked if I knew anyone in Phoenix. While on the phone Paul asked, "When are you coming to Arizona, take a week's vacation, and preach for me on Sunday?"

"I'm working on it. We'll get it together someday."

"No, we've been 'getting it together' for two or three years. We're going to get a date before I hang up."

The week ending February 23, went into the schedule for 1997.

Jane's sister, Catherine, had never toured the west, so she agreed to fly from St. Louis, meet us in Phoenix, and sightsee with Jane for a week. Paul met us at the airport, Monday, the 17th, with a wonderful set of plans for the week. With his Lincoln we drove to Flagstaff to spend two days and nights at the "BIG" canyon, where he had reserved two cabins on the rim. Jane and I had seen it before and before, but she never grows tired of watching the change of colors, shapes, and shadows, as the sun lights it from different angles. She has seen the sun come up, the sun go down, the moon come up, the moon go down over that great chasm, seen it at daybreak, at noon, at dusk, and in the dark, and could sit through all of that again with moving emotional response. My depth of appreciation is not near as deep as the canyon, nor hers. It's more in line with Will Rogers, who upon his first visit is reported to have said, "Now I know where I can throw my old razor blades."

We drove again through Sedona with its massive, various shapes of red and orange sandstone formations rising like so many figures in an abstract painting. We turned aside to see Montezuma's Castle, dwellings chiseled into the side of a rock mountain four or five stories high, accessible only with ladders. It was designed and inhabited by a tribe of cliff dwellers who disappeared centuries ago. Nobody knows why or where.

Paul insisted that the women should go to Mexico to buy leather and vanilla. So he took us through the desert, the fields of saguaro standing like stick men, through Tucson, to Nogales. Catherine will never forget that day, haggling over prices with street vendors and getting the lowest price for worthless stuff.

Saturday, February 22, Catherine flew back to St. Louis. Sunday, I preached, morning and evening. Monday Paul took us to the airport, gave me $1500 for the services, after having covered all the expenses for a week's vacation for three, testimony to the gracious, generous heart of a dear friend with whom I have enjoyed so many times of revival and fellowship, Paul Thompson.

Those two days in the cabin on the rim of the canyon were memorable for Catherine and Jane, and is one of Jane's favorite places where we have slept.

Red Hill

Leaving Asheville, North Carolina, on Highway 70 West, after passing through Marshall in Madison County, in about five miles Indian Grave Gap Road leaves 70 to the right, winds its way up the mountain, and tops out at Red Hill Free Will Baptist Church. Beside the church is a beautiful two bedroom, furnished parsonage, built by Howard Munsey with scrap and leftover logs from his log home business in Newport, Tennessee. In November, 1984, Howard invited us for revival, introduced us to the most wonderful congregation of friends and began a relationship that has continued for over 25 years, 13 revival meetings plus four additional weekends of preaching.

The various pastors have always lived in their own homes, so the parsonage is there, furnished and available for us anytime we wish. In the summer from the porch swing the view down the mountains with all the different shades of green, the shadows cast by the white fluffy clouds from a Carolina blue sky moving slowly from one hill to another, the tiny cars winding their way up the road deeper into the Smokies, brings relaxing relief from the fast-moving, busy, trouble-filled world beyond that valley. On a cool frosty morning life is good with a hot cup of coffee sitting at the large picture window, watching the mist and low hanging clouds fight with the warming sun for their existence.

Some mornings the sun wins, the clouds disappear. Sometimes it rains. Sometimes it snows large, beautiful, wet, heavy flakes hanging on the trees turning the sight from that window into a large Christmas card.

Jane and I have spent over 13 weeks there in these last 25 years in one of our favorite spots on the earth with some of our dearest, closest and most gracious, generous friends.

At the time of my prostate cancer surgery, only a few churches responded with a love offering. Red Hill was one.

That log house is one of the good places we have slept. Abe Lincoln didn't have it so bad after all.

Oh, by the way, if you miss Indian Grave Gap Road, and continue five more miles west on highway 70, there's a sharp curve, one of many between Asheville and Newport, not half as many as in the '50s, and on the right an ex-service station built of various sizes of smooth, round, beige, native rocks from the bed of the French Broad River. This forsaken looking place was one of a very few places to get off the road 50 years ago. Somewhere around there, there must be a spot where the grass has not grown for all these years, where Stephen emptied his stomach of the motion sickness generated by the thirty- mile roller coaster ride from Asheville to Hot Springs, every time we went west through the mountains, until we started giving him Dramamine. Then he slept through them.

John and Reppie's

The roar of a falling airplane, like a splash of cold water in the face, woke us and shook us out of bed. Stephen looking through two dirty panes of glass in the top half of a raised window confirmed the sound, "It's falling. That airplane is falling and it's going to hit this house."

The four of us, Stephen, Philip, Jane and I, silent and motionless, like a frozen frame in a horror movie, waited for the sound of a crash and an explosion that would indicate he missed the house and we'd live to tell about it. Flying on a level with and directly toward that window, the plane crossed the highway and a few seconds from the window, the pilot pulled back on the stick, and that single-engine, piston-powered, gasoline-fueled, propeller-driven, World War II fighter, lifted just enough to clear the house, shaking everything in it that wasn't already shaking, but failing in its attempt to suck off the tin roof.

We exhaled for the first time since we got out of bed, laid back on the two double beds to enjoy a moment of relief. The 10 x 10 room was full of beds. On each bed were four mattresses, stacked with quilts folded and stored in between them, which turned the surface of the top cotton mattress into a terrain of hills and valleys, lumps and holes. Our bodies would twist around the hills searching for a comfortable place to fall asleep in a valley. The boys climbed into one bed, Jane and I atop the other. The only sound was the window fan purring at low speed in the one window in the room, pulling in the cool, damp, early-morning air that would remain cool for another hour, but would be damp all day in 95° heat.

We laid there thinking how lucky we were that he missed the house while it soaked in that there was no crash, when the distant sound of that plane still flying floated through the air, entered the room and disturbed the silence. It was growing louder and closer. He was coming back to finish the job of snatching the roof off. Sure enough, louder and louder, until right down over the house he made another dive, in three or four minutes another and another. No more sleep that morning. Might as well climb down off the beds and begin to get ready for the morning service in the revival.

The wood frame house with asbestos siding veneer, tin roof, small front porch, four rooms, a hall, and a back porch, stood on piers on a hill of orange, sandy clay and rock, overlooking

Highway 43. A few feet from the front porch there was a forty-foot drop almost straight down where the front yard had been cut away to make room for the highway. Across the highway and below its elevation spread a green cotton field in full bloom with beautiful light purple and white flowers, home of a few families of boll weevils.

From the front porch a hallway passed two bedrooms on the left, a sitting room on the right, a door that led to the kitchen, and an exit to the back porch. In that front bedroom, the four of us slept during many revival meetings. With no closets, the only place to hang clothes was on a nail or two. The suitcases lived under the beds at night, on top of the beds during the day. The two double beds occupied the floor space of that ten- foot square room. In that room in the heat Jane dressed two little boys each morning for two church services and two meals in two different homes.

That morning the plane served as an alarm clock with no snooze button. So, clothed for breakfast and after a trip to the bathroom, which was a long narrow afterthought like a "lean-to" off the kitchen, we made our public appearance from the bedroom.

John was already in the sitting room dressed for church ... or work ... or any other occasion ... just plain dressed ... in every-day clothes, nothing fancy about John. Coughing and wheezing, fighting the war with emphysema he struggled for every breath. When the heat and heavy air made breathing almost impossible, John would go to a storm shelter, a small cave dug out in the side of the hill with concrete blocks laid across the front around an entrance door, where the air was cooler, lighter, and easier to breathe. At times he would lie with his body upon a chair, his head in the floor, almost upside down, to drain the fluid trapped in his lungs by those closed air sacs that wouldn't let the carbon dioxide out so the oxygen could get in.

John's favorite television program was wrestling on Saturday afternoon. The problem was that he would get so involved and excited he couldn't breathe. Reppie would have to take him to the emergency room at the hospital and get an oxygen treatment to get him over the wrestling match.

So the doctors told them, "No more wrestling. He can't watch it anymore. Unplug the television, whatever you have to do. He can't take it. Wrestling is out."

If my memory is doing its job, and sometimes it goofs off, John professed to get saved in the first series of meetings we had at Sulphur Springs Free Will Baptist Church, Samantha, Alabama. It was in a morning service. Reppie shouted that morning. She had lived with John for many years, prayed for him, and longed someday to see him change from such a hard, crude, rough man. After that morning there were some changes, but John was no longer young and a lot of the rough edges never did get smoothed out. He was opinionated, outspoken, and critical, especially of preachers. One of the reasons we continued to stay at John's house was to keep him from thinking preachers thought they were too good to live at his place.

One day John was discussing their pastor, who lived in Birmingham near his mother-in-law. The church had built a little parsonage across the road from the church, and was trying to get the preacher to move into that little house, so he would be in the community, but the preacher refused to make the move, for one reason or other.

John's observation was, "The pastor is a good man, and a very good preacher. He really has only one problem. He has to get his instructions from the Lord so indirectly. You see, God has to tell his mother-in-law, then she has to tell his wife, and then she has to tell the preacher what it is that God wants him to do."

That week at John's house was the week the spacecraft landed on the moon. John laughed in unbelief and ridicule, "Deceiving everybody," he said. "They ain't landed on no moon. They're making them pictures somewhere in the desert in Arizona. The moon is God's business. He ain't gonna let man go playing around with it."

Stephen tried with no success to explain it to John and decided if the man believes a circle is square, what difference does it make?

John called out as we went by, "You boys get in here and get some breakfast in you. That's how you get to be big, strong men."

Reppie was on the back porch soaking wet with sweat, drinking a cup of black, boiling coffee, fanning with a rolled up bonnet, rocking slowly, back and forth, resting from two hours of hot, hard labor in the garden located about 20 feet from the back door beyond the driveway, which came as a path off the highway from the south up a gradual incline through pine trees, passed behind the house, between the house and garden, in front of the cave storm shelter, and down the steep side of the hill back to the highway, a kind of circular drive, more like half a cucumber split lengthwise.

From the garden in July and August, Reppie gathered okra, yellow summer squash, butterbeans, tomatoes, cucumbers, and purple-hull peas. She shelled, cut, cooked, and packed them away in a freezer. This year she was filling the second freezer. The first was still full from last year, and the year before, and the year before that. Next year she'd need freezer number three. She had enough in store to feed all of Israel in case a seven-year famine struck Egypt.

Dressed in a loose-fitting long cotton dress, with little under it, a bibbed apron and a bonnet, she worked in the hot morning sun until church time. From the garden into the kitchen, she poured a cup of steaming black coffee from the percolating pot on the stove, sat for a short cool-down period in the rocker on the back porch, removed the bonnet, folded it into a fan, and drank that coffee hot enough to scald the mouth of an ordinary person.

In the afternoon, they sat in the shade of the large oak in the backyard, and shelled peas and butterbeans. Beside John's chair lay the large, beautiful, friendly, and obedient German Shepherd. A few cantaloupes and watermelons stacked around the roots of the oak were available for the mid-afternoon break.

At church Reppie sang bass in a women's quartet composed of four sisters, whose a cappella harmony would have been envied at any barbershop quartet convention.

After breakfast the four of us in the little bedroom dressed for a long day, morning service, a noon meal in a home, about six o'clock, another meal in another home, evening service and back to John and Reppie's. And so it went for several years and several meetings until room was available in the parsonage across the road from the church, after which we no longer spent the week at Reppie's house.

Sometime after we moved to the parsonage, John and Reppie decided to move to I-DEE-HOE where their children lived. Reppie was terribly unhappy in Idaho. The children attended a United Pentecostal, One-ness Church, with a band, drums, loud music, and emotional services, plus the exclusive theological position that they were the only people going to Heaven. Their futile effort to convince Reppie that she must be baptized by them, and receive what they claimed to have, only convinced her more that after many years of knowing the Lord she didn't need nor want what they had. When the preacher marched around the church strutting to the beat of the music, Reppie followed him making light of the whole ritual. Needless to say Reppie didn't fit in nor enjoy being in Ideehoe, so they came back to Alabama.

One of their boys was separated from his wife and alone in Idaho. John and Reppie moved a mobile home into their back-yard and moved him back home where Reppie could wash his clothes, cook his meals, and like every mother, take care of him. One morning when Reppie went to the trailer with his breakfast, she found him dead – suicide. The shock, the sight, the pressure was more than her mind could handle, and something snapped. Her mind never would acknowledge the reality of the situation. The ability to face facts left and never came back. She lost it.

She spent the last years of her life in a mental hospital. Some folks who knew her said that she was waiting for her boy to come home from school. "He'll be here when the school bus comes," she said.

The bus never came.

John's emphysema grew worse. The storm shelter and abstain-ing from TV wrestling wasn't enough to keep him breathing. He died in a rest home.

Oh, that World War II fighter was not really strafing the house. He was on a mission of genocide, ethnic-cleansing, deter-mined to exterminate from the face of the earth by dust-poison-ing every member of the boll weevil family, male and female, young and old, who lived in that cotton field across the highway – a crop duster.

North of Tuscaloosa on the west side of Highway 43 on a sandy clay hill, 30 feet above the road the little old frame house with the tin roof stands empty. The garden behind the house, left to its own resources is producing weeds and that's just as well. There's no one to pick peas and cut okra, no one sitting under the oak to shell them, no loyal German Shepherd asleep by the chair, no freezer to fill, no folks to feed, no need to prepare for winter. It is winter. The rocker sits motionless on the porch. Silence and stillness have settled over the hill. The crop duster doesn't fly anymore. Agricultural biologists accomplished his mission by developing sterile boll weevils, releasing them into the cotton field, and allowing the weevils to breed themselves out of existence.

The house sits alone on the hill, doors and windows shut like the eyes of a corpse waiting for someone to close the lid of the casket and hide from view the process of decay, lifeless, dead, awaiting burial, a testimony from a generation that has died, a witness to one that will, and a reminder to an old preacher of a couple of generous, good friends who called it home and shared it with a young evangelist, his wife, and two boys so many times during summer revival meetings.

Comforts of Home

There have been enough uncomfortable sleeping places to fill a hundred more pages. So many nights at two or three o'clock finding it impossible to sleep in such circumstances, I sat in the dark in a little pity party and said, "Lord, I need to sleep. I have to preach three times tomorrow. If I could rest, I'd do a better job."

Like the breath of a light breeze the soft voice whispered in the dark, "The foxes have holes, and the birds of the air have nests; but the Son of man hath not where to lay his head."

"Lord, I shouldn't have mentioned it. I'm just feeling lonesome and sorry for myself. I've always had some place to lay my head. Just help me to sleep. I do need to rest."

Now after 60 years and with fewer invitations I'm at home most of the time. Many nights when I lie down on the plush mattress on a clean comfortable king-size bed in a bedroom that's warm in the winter and cool in the summer, gratitude swells up inside, and my last words as I fall asleep are, "Lord, you didn't promise me this, but thanks for a house to live in out of the rain and cold…and a good bed. I appreciate it."

STOP THE SERMON

I n over 50 years, a few meetings have been missed, some almost missed, and one dismissed.

TRAVEL TROUBLES

Red Light in Rowland

In the 1950s, the main route between the cold, gray, dreary, wintry northeast and sunny, warm, green Florida was Highway 301, a spur that left U.S. #1 in Baltimore, taking a more eastern route south through Virginia, North Carolina, South Carolina, and reconnecting with its parent #1 in Folkston, GA. It ran through Richmond, Roanoke Rapids, Rocky Mount, Wilson, Smithfield, Fayetteville, Lumberton, and Rowland, North Carolina, a stone's throw from the South Carolina state line.

Rowland was a spot on the road with a stoplight that held up traffic for no reason except to satisfy the authorities by making every car stop as it passed through town. That light was responsible for one of the few revival services missed.

After Thursday night service at Bay Branch, Timmonsville, SC, I drove home to Greenville, NC, to get Jane and the boys for the weekend in the meeting. Five hours was long enough for the trip, had it not been spring break when every college kid from every university north of the Mason-Dixon goes to Daytona Beach. Five miles north of Rowland the traffic was stopped. After some time I spotted a pay phone, called the pastor, Jake Creech, assured him how I had a sermon prepared for that Friday night, and if he could send a helicopter and get me to the church, I'd be glad to preach it. There surely must be an accident. Two hours and five miles later, the accident was that stoplight, allowing four cars to go through between changes. The service was over when I arrived in Timmonsville.

Another Red Light in Rowland

Rowland was also where our friendly state highway patrol had the pleasure of giving me a ticket for driving 65 mph in a 55 mph speed zone. A meeting closed in Jacksonville, Florida, on Sunday night. Another was scheduled to begin Monday night at 8:00 in Oak Grove Free Will Baptist, on Highway 13 between Fayetteville and Goldsboro, which was easily possible for the trip, but with no time to spare.

Jane was collecting souvenir drinking glasses from various states, and we heard that *South of the Border* kept them in stock for all states. So for the only time in 60 years, in spite of the billboards with which I considered myself at war, and by never stopping I was winning, we stopped and bought several glasses, losing very little time. Back on Highway 301 heading north, somewhere around Lumberton, I stopped for gas. The attendant filled the tank (Those were the days when service stations cleaned the windshield, checked the oil, filled the gas tank and charged .30 per gallon for the gas.) but when I reached for my billfold, it was gone.

Memory kicked in like a mule. That billfold, with $200 in it, was lying by the cash register at *South of the Border* where I paid for those glasses. Embarrassed, aggravated, and worried, I explained to the gas man my predicament and he was very considerate, but then I don't suppose he could have taken the gas out of the car and put it back in his underground tank. Upon the promise to stop when I came back by from *South of the Border* and if I found my billfold and money, to pay him, if not, I'd mail him a check as soon as I got home, he agreed for me to leave.

Now in addition to the loss of money, driver's license, etc., there was over 100 extra miles forced into a day that had no room for 100 extra miles and Joshua wasn't available, so the sun kept moving.

Heading back south on 301 near Rowland, at the time I saw those electrical speed-timing cords across the road and glanced down, the needle on the speedometer of that Oldsmobile was steady at 95 mph. The brakes and tires were good. Skidding across the first cord I let off the brake about the time I hit the second. Out of the corner of my eye I saw the patrol car backed up in the woods, and gently taking my foot off the brake, pulled off the road and stopped, got out of the car in time to see him come screaming out of the woods, lights flashing, siren squalling, tires spinning. He pulled up behind me, shut down the noise and lights, got out of the car, and slowly walked to the rear of mine, where I was leaning against the trunk waiting for him.

Laughing uncontrollably he said, "Man, you sure have good brakes on that thing. You got it down to 65 mph. Let me see your driver's license."

"You're not going to believe this, but I'll tell you anyway," and I explained my situation. He believed me and was nice, friendly, and continuing to laugh as he wrote the ticket.

"After you get your license, as you come back you'll need to go into Rowland to the magistrate and pay him $17 for the 65 mph in a 55 mph speed zone. Don't worry about the license," he said.

He followed me to my car door, still laughing, "…and when you come back this way, remember I'll still be sitting in the woods."

Now, I've lost more time and must go into Rowland, find a magistrate, and lose more time and $17.

One bright spot in this tragedy, when I arrived at *South of the Border* and walked in, the lady at the cash register looked up and said, "I know what you're looking for."

She reached under the counter, took out my billfold which was already wrapped and addressed for mailing to me in Greenville with everything including over $200 still intact, and would not take a dollar for her honesty nor trouble, saying, "It is my job to look after the customers."

I stopped in Rowland and paid the magistrate. As I approached the speed trap, the electronic timers were still stretched across the road. I slowed to about 10 mph, creeping between them, and looked to my left into the woods. There sat the patrolman on the fender of his Ford, eating a slice of watermelon, still laughing. He gave me a friendly wave, which I returned with a smile, picked up speed, stopped at the gas station, paid the surprised owner for the gas, and continued at a little above the speed limit, trying to make it to the meeting, and arriving at the church at about 8:30.

The pastor, Norman Adams, was leading the last song, nervously putting together a sermon in his mind to fill in for the missing evangelist. I ran to the pulpit, and dressed in my traveling clothes preached II Chronicles 7:14, *Prescription for Revival*, Monday, March 19, 1956.

In the past 60 years millions have by-passed Rowland, North Carolina, on Interstate 95 and never noticed the exit sign. I know exactly where it is. The little town is located in the back corner of my mind, marked by two red lights, one hanging over Highway 301, the other flashing on the top of a patrol car.

Dropped a Diode

The weekend before Christmas, 1979, the Jacksons were on their way to Illinois, Jane for her annual pilgrimage to visit her parents, Philip and Sue to spend Christmas, and the old man to preach on Sunday. Late Friday afternoon on I-40 West, bypassing Statesville, NC, at 65 mph, demons abruptly pulled the cables from the battery, or so it seemed. Everything died. No lights. No horn. No radio. No engine. No power. Coasting into a rest area, the Cadillac slowed to a stop about 40 feet from a pay phone.

Within half an hour, the wrecker pulled in behind the Cadillac, a young man raised the hood, looked around with his flashlight and said, "Oh, I see the problem…no trouble at all… just a wire to the battery burned in two. I'll replace that and you can be on your way."

A cracking sound, a flash of fire, a small fireworks display, and his wire melted.

"Uh…oh…something's wrong," he said.

"Yeah, I think so!"

"There's a short somewhere in the system, and I don't know anything about that."

Both of us learned later that the wire was a fuse wire, meant to blow to prevent the car from catching fire.

The truck towed us into Statesville to his service station where two mechanics were waiting to solve the problem. They leaned over the fender so far their loose pants dropped below the crack of decency, looked the engine over and after about five minutes said, "We don't know what's wrong, maybe a short in the wiring system, lights, or something, and being Friday night before Christmas, there ain't no place open that we know of to help you."

Checked the family in a motel, went back to the station to sit 'til they closed at midnight hoping to find a solution.

About 11:30 a car drove up and one of the "mechanics" said, "Now, if that fellow ain't too drunk to walk, he can tell us what's wrong."

They explained the symptoms. He staggered with unsteady steps to the car, apologizing to the preacher, he said, "I guess I've already had too much of the Christmas spirits."

It was no time to argue over spirits, so I thanked him for trying to give me a hand.

He may have seen two or three alternators under that hood, but when one of them materialized and stopped moving around, he reached in, pulled the wire off, and said, "Now, put your wire back on the battery."

They did. It didn't explode.

"The short is in the alternator," he said. "It has dropped a diode."

"Dropped a what?"

"A diode: a vacuum tube with a cold anode and a heated cathode used as a rectifier of alternating current in an alternator."

No wonder it died, if it dropped one of those. That sounds worse than a myocardial infarction, and the red warning light never blinked to prepare us for the coming death.

Now we knew I needed an alternator, but at midnight, Friday before Christmas, it was impossible to find one and they were not sure of finding one on Saturday.

Back at the motel, I called my next door neighbor in Greenville, Jack Bryant, who worked at Cox Armature, woke him up and said, "Jack, I need a huge favor. I know you don't work on Saturday, especially the one before Christmas, but could you go to Cox's in the morning, get me an alternator, and put it on a bus for Statesville?"

"Be glad to," he said.

The next morning he called at ten and said, "Two of them are on the bus. Wasn't sure which would fit, so I'm sending two. The bus is scheduled to be in Statesville at 4:00 this afternoon."

The fellows at the station, which also served as the bus station in Statesville, were told that an alternator was on the way. This made the delivery simple with not a chance of messing up.

At about 4:15, Saturday afternoon, I returned to the station, confident everything was working out. The bus had come and gone and left NO package from Greenville for Jackson. No alternator. Back on the phone to Jack, he swore they were on the bus. Called Winston-Salem bus station where the package could have been left in changing buses. No package.

"Did you look on the bus?" I asked the guy at the station.

"That's not my job," he said.

"Did the driver check for a package?"

"He didn't get out of the bus."

"That package is still on that bus on its way to California. When it reaches Los Angeles, they'll send it back."

Now it's Saturday night and no place to find an alternator.

The station guys said that they had a friend in the used parts business. He owned a salvage yard, but he had been out of town, gone to get his daughter from college, and should be back sometime that night. They'd keep calling and checking.

Back to the motel with the disappointing news, we considered the possibility of spending Christmas in a motel in Statesville, NC.

At 10:00 p.m., the friend at the station called and said, "He's back in town. Said he has a 90 amp. That'll work if you don't use the heater for the back window. He'll bring it to us tomorrow morning and we'll put it on for you."

At noon on Sunday as I left the station, I said, "You fellows watch for that package for me from Greenville containing the alternators. It'll come back here after it turns around somewhere between here and the west coast. When I come through in two weeks from Illinois, I'll stop by, pick it up, and take the alternators back to Greenville, NC, so as not to have to pay for them."

The prophecy came to pass. On our way back, we checked at the station. There was the box with the two alternators.

"Oh yeah," they said. "It came in here on a bus about a week after Christmas."

We made it to Illinois in time for Christmas, but not the Sunday appointments. Missed them, couldn't make it, I dropped a diode.

Flat Tire

Soaked in sweat, dressed in a white shirt and tie, sitting on the bank beside a seldom travelled road with ten-inch-deep sand ruts lined with washboard ridges, watching the dust devils dance like miniature tornadoes in the heat, contemplating the flat tire that seemed to be welded to the hub by lug nuts which had been tightened with an air pressure wrench, is no place to spend a Sunday afternoon in south Georgia. It was already too late to make the two o'clock preaching appointment scheduled in a country church somewhere farther down that isolated road, and the question was, would I make it back to civilization in time for the evening service in town?

Changing a flat tire is not a complicated job. The spare was no problem. The jack worked perfectly. But breaking those lug nuts loose with a worthless, slightly curved, factory-supplied-original-equipment-no-torque lug wrench was beyond the realm of possibility. For 45 minutes I waited for somebody to come down that road from anywhere on the way to nowhere, which must be around here somewhere since I was already in the middle of it, hoping they would have a lug wrench. A woman stopped but the only tool she had was a copy of the useless one thrown in a Cadillac by General Motors.

Another 15 minutes and a friendly guy in a pickup stopped, provided a heavy duty wrench shaped like a large plus (+) sign, sturdy enough that a one-hundred-seventy-five-pound preacher could stand on it and bounce. Using that method the two of us broke loose those lug nuts which grudgingly lost the battle to the torque of that good wrench.

He helped change the tire, took no pay, bade me Godspeed, and went on his way. The service at the church would be over. No congregation waits on a preacher for an hour and a half, but it seemed only right to go try to find the church. A few miles down the road there it was, as empty as a premillenial sanctuary after the rapture, maybe more so, no one in sight. They gave up on the preacher and went home.

The first item of business when I returned to Greenville, NC, was to keep a vow that I made in the hot sun, frustrated with a flat tire, on that lonely road in Georgia. I went to the auto supply store and purchased the best cross-legged lug wrench money could buy. That wrench rode with me for many years and is now resting between two studs in the carport storage, retired, having been replaced by a road hazard, towing insurance policy and a cell phone.

Never missed another service because of a flat tire.

Up in the Air

"If you have time to spare go by air, otherwise catch a bus."

Einstein defined insanity as "doing the same thing over and over with the same results." By that definition anyone flying to keep appointments or meet a schedule must be insane. Everybody has his own stories, only the people and places change, the results are always the same.

Fog in Boston

Flying to Presque Isle, Maine, for meetings in New Brunswick, Canada, presents one big problem. The route goes through Boston for connecting flights. In November, fog from the North Atlantic spends every weekend in Boston. Its favorite place to stay is the airport where it sleeps on the runways from noon on Saturday until noon on Monday, with a *Do Not Disturb* sign hanging out.

The meetings in Bath were to begin Sunday morning. The flight was scheduled to arrive in Presque Isle at four o'clock Saturday afternoon. Sitting in Boston, waiting for the fog to lift, listening to the delay announcements every hour until *Cancelled* was finally posted, I called the pastor in Bath, told him I was grounded in Boston again, and scheduled out on a flight about noon Sunday. Missed two Sunday morning meetings, but made it for Sunday night.

Jane was with me on another occasion when the return schedule flipped upside down. The meetings in New Brunswick always closed on Sundays. Our flight was the early Monday morning flight out of Presque Isle. About an hour into the flight the captain in that confident reassuring voice broke the sleepy silence with, "Boston is under fog this morning. We're being diverted to Portland."

At Portland, we sat on the plane for two hours, knowing we had missed the connecting flight in Boston, realizing this would not be a good travel day. Loud and clear that familiar voice sounded again, "Folks, look out the window on your left. See that plane? If the fog lifts today that plane is going to Boston. We're going to Pittsburgh."

"We don't need to go to Boston. We want to go to Greenville," I said to Jane. "And we sure don't intend to sit here in Portland all day. We're going to Pittsburgh if I can get to that ticket counter."

With that, I ran into the terminal to get in line to keep our seats on the Pittsburgh plane. She sat, watched through the window while our luggage crawled out of the plane and disappeared into the terminal, and thought, "He didn't make it. We're stuck in Portland."

In 15 minutes she saw the luggage come out of the terminal, pass the Boston plane, and go back into the belly of the Pittsburgh plane. Breathing a sigh of relief, she kept her seat and said under her breath, "We'll at least get to Pittsburgh."

In the terminal with people pushing one another for space, things quieted a bit as a path opened for an older man, salt and pepper gray hair, pin-striped dark gray suit with a carnation in the lapel, the dignity of a mafia godfather with a handful of plane tickets, followed by eight or ten young men dressed in black pin-striped suits, white handkerchiefs in the jacket pockets, patent leather shoes, black straight hair slicked and combed tightly to the head. All cut from the same pattern, they could have been brothers. Following them were several carts of black leather luggage, like a scene from *The Godfather*. No one checked those violin cases to make sure they contained violins!

The older man handled the tickets and boarding passes. Jane watched that black leather luggage board our plane with some curiosity, which increased as those attached to the luggage took their seats near us for the flight to Pittsburgh, where upon deplaning the group disappeared. We never saw them again. We didn't go looking for them.

After re-routing, re-ticketing, waiting, running through the airport in Charlotte, we arrived in Greenville late that night about ten hours behind schedule.

Take a Bus

In the early 60's, before I learned about the fog spending the weekends in Boston, meetings were scheduled to begin on

Sunday morning in Littleton, New Hampshire. The flight plans were to connect in Boston with a small plane to Montpelier, Vermont, late Saturday afternoon. With nervous jitters, I listened to the delays and then the cancellations, rushed to the ticket counter to find some way to get out of Boston, only to learn there was nothing going north.

"Is there a train?"

"No trains any time."

"A plane to Manchester, Barre, anywhere?"

"Not on Saturday night in the fog."

"I'm scheduled to preach tomorrow morning in Littleton, New Hampshire. Is there no way out of here?"

"We'll book you out tomorrow afternoon."

"How does that get me there by 11:00 a.m.?"

"There's a bus, I think, that goes as far as White River Junction, about 100 miles south of Littleton."

"When does it leave?"

"Don't know."

"How do I get to the bus station?"

"Take a cab."

Before boarding the bus, I called the pastor. He agreed to meet me at White River Junction some time after midnight. There were only three bus riders and all three were off that cancelled flight to Montpelier. Had the flight not been fogged in there'd have been no one on the bus.

In the wee hours of Sunday morning I arrived in Littleton, making it one of those "almost" misses.

One Stop Light

On the route from Carolina to California, there was one stop light. That light was in Pittsburgh over a seat in the tail section of an aircraft parked 200 yards from the gate and it took over two hours to change from red to green.

Most of the trips to California have been with very little inconvenience, but when that flight gets off schedule, the mess-up is unbelievable. The worst travel day of my life must have been the flight to Oakland in February, 2003. Sitting on the plane for hours in Pittsburgh, I wrote the following account of that day:

Today began like any other with a Transcontinental flight planned. Rising at 4:30 a.m., I caught the early morning flight from the small-town airport in Greenville to the big city airport in Charlotte, where connections would be made to a non-stop flight to the west coast, trip travel time about seven hours. After an exaggerated, detailed, overkill examination of my luggage and me, remove shoes, remove belt, body search in more detail than an annual physical, thorough close examination of a nail clip to make sure it was not a terrorist's weapon, I was allowed to pass through security, board the little twin engine propjet and take off on time for the city.

Charlotte was fogged in so that our small plane couldn't land. After circling the field for over an hour, the pilot confessed to the delay and said, "We're running low on fuel and are heading for Tri-Cities." This was a landing strip at higher elevation that wasn't fogged in.

At Tri-Cities they refueled. We sat for another hour and a half on the plane waiting for the fog to clear in Charlotte and in the head of the flight attendant who didn't know how to advise anybody. I inquired about getting off the plane and finding some other way to Oakland, since the connection from Charlotte was long gone. She informed me that no one could leave the plane. Everyone must return to Charlotte where he came from and make plans from there.

Back in Charlotte over four hours late, I was re-routed to the northeast to catch a plane to the west. The plane to the northeast was two hours late. That would be no problem since the plane to California was three hours late.

In Pittsburgh, so late that I no longer counted the hours, all the passengers were boarded and settled in for the long, non-stop flight to the west.

The captain confidently announced, "Attendants, prepare for departure."

The plane backed away from the gate, moved about 200 yards, stopped, and the captain said, "It'll be a couple of minutes, Folks. There's a problem with an over-the-seat light in the tail section."

Fifteen minutes later he informed us that a mechanic was on his way to check out the light.

"Take only a few minutes," he said.

Yeah! What light was he referring to? How many over-the-seat lights are there? The only one I see is that little red one that says, *Please Turn off Electronic Devices* and *Fasten Seat Belt*. Evidently this plane cannot fly without that little light. It must be connected somehow to those two big jet engines which won't whine if that light don't shine.

The mechanic came, fiddled around for 15 minutes, said the problem was fixed, and left. The engines didn't start. We weren't moving.

In five minutes the captain said, "I've contacted the mechanic. He's gone to get a replacement part. That'll take about 30 minutes."

How long does it take a mechanic to find a light bulb?

Over an hour later, the mechanic showed up. He was in no hurry, may have eaten supper, stopped by the bar, and was more confused than the first time. He couldn't fix it. It was now after 8:00 p.m. of the same day that began at 4:30 a.m. with a schedule that was to have reached California at 11:00 a.m, west coast time.

The questions now were: Will we make the six-hour flight tonight? Will they de-plane us to a motel to sleep and try again tomorrow? Will they replace this equipment with another plane because they can't fix the light? I had already missed one preaching service and possibly a two-day minister's retreat. I should probably go back home. Not a chance. The only way to return home is to fly and I'm grounded in Pittsburgh because of a little light that still doesn't shine and the plane can't get off the ground. How did it fly in here with that light out? Those passengers never knew how dangerous it was flying and landing with that light not working.

Airlines are wondering why they're losing customers and money. And I sit here wondering why tribulation doesn't work patience. It's supposed to.

A second mechanic who was either smarter or more sober came an hour later, fixed the light, and about 10:00 p.m. we got in the air. Arrived in Oakland around 1:00 a.m. Pacific Time, 23 hours from the time I left home for a seven-hour journey.

Missed one service, but was so happy to reach California, I got off the plane singing, *This little light of mine, I'm gonna let it shine.*

Around the World

For the next trip to California, wisdom insisted that the schedule should be a direct flight from Raleigh-Durham, bypassing the small plane out of Greenville and the fog in Charlotte. Continental, with the best schedule and lowest fare, was the first choice out of RDU Saturday into Sacramento before noon.

Drove to Raleigh, parked the car, waited in line to check in, and the ticket agent greeted me with, "That flight has been cancelled. We have booked you out on a flight tomorrow morning."

"Not tomorrow morning! I have to preach tomorrow morning. I've got to get to Sacramento today. In the first place, you didn't inform me of the cancellation nor the change so I could make other arrangements. In the second place, I have driven 100 miles to the airport for this flight. In the third place, I'm neither on vacation nor a flexible schedule. I have an appointment to keep in Sacramento tomorrow morning. In the fourth place, the airline bears some responsibility for the mess I'm in."

She was very nice and tried to be helpful. She found a seat on another airline with an around-the-world schedule. We flew all over North America, didn't cross the Atlantic, stopped everywhere once, some places twice, changed planes and airlines a few times, and landed in Sacramento, without my luggage, around midnight over 12 hours late. On such a hectic day the luggage never keeps up, always lags about a day behind.

One fellow checking in at RDU for NY asked the baggage handler to check his luggage to Miami.

"I can't do that," he said, "with you going to New York."

"You did last week."

At least I made it in time to preach Sunday. Just another one of the "almost" misses.

HEALTH HAZARDS

Canceling meetings or cutting them short has not been a habit over the past 60 years, not necessarily the result of dedication to the Lord, but the inner commitment to doing what I said I would do, keeping my word, obligation, which may be more pride than piety. Only the Lord can analyze all the reasons why we do what we do. That's why He's the Judge.

When the boys were young and we were pressed to an inconvenience, Philip would ask, "Why do we have to?"

Stephen would answer, "We're obligated."

That may not be very spiritual, but we did it anyway.

Home Sick and Homesick

Two times over the years meetings have been closed early, aborted, stopped before the end.

The year was 1965. The Church was in Illinois. The meetings were planned from Wednesday through two Sundays, 12 days, 14 sermons. The first six services had been fruitless, no interest, no one concerned. Tuesday morning of the second week our pastor in Greenville called.

"Bobby," he said, "Jane is very sick. She and the boys have been at our house for the past two nights. Tomorrow she may go to the hospital for surgery. She doesn't know I'm calling you. But I think you need to come home."

The weight of the decision was heavy. I told the pastor that I was considering the matter. He made no comment.

Leaving the meeting wasn't easy. In 1957, when Philip was born, a window of five days was left open to be with Jane in Illinois. The meeting in Florida closed May 5, I drove to Illinois. The doctor had calculated Philip would come that week, but he wasn't that anxious to leave his warm secure world for this cold uncertain one, so he refused to turn from a posterior position. In a large city an obstetrician would probably have taken him Caesarean, but in a small town, a family physician allowed the pregnancy to continue for two weeks, at the end of which, with much labor and great difficulty, Jane gave birth alone with her baby.

I had six weeks of meetings booked in North Carolina, Alabama, and Mississippi, beginning May 12, and didn't think I could cancel them. The meeting in Pine Level, North Carolina, ended June 23, and having not seen her, the baby or Stephen in five weeks, I drove to Illinois for a few days before going on to Northport, Alabama. Maybe it was the foolishness of youth. I cried a lot during those five weeks. The week Philip was born and the week before, in two meetings, there were 100 decisions, over 50 each week.

Daddy sees Philip first time

Philip's first birthday
Daddy missed most celebrations

A few years later the meetings were in Oklahoma, we had moved to North Carolina. Stephen was in first grade and Philip was three years old. Stephen became very sick and was hospitalized with pneumonia. Our pastor, Robert Crawford, and family cared for Philip while Jane stayed with Stephen in the hospital. That time Jane never told me of the problem until the crisis was over for fear it would worry me and that might hinder the meetings.

So the decision to close the meeting in Illinois was difficult. After a couple of hours I said to the pastor, "Preacher, I'm closing the meeting tonight. Could you get someone to take me to the airport in St. Louis tomorrow morning? I need to go home."

With little sympathy, he agreed.

That night I explained to the congregation, who didn't seem to care one way or the other. The next morning they transported me to St. Louis and with no love offering or pay for the meetings, I flew away. A few days later a check for $100 came in the mail, out of which I subtracted the plane tickets and wound up with a minus, another indication of the interest, or lack of, in the meetings.

Jane's problem was an ovarian cyst, which seemed to be difficult for the doctors to diagnose. She has always felt bad that I came home. I have no regrets. There had been four days at home in 12 weeks and nine weeks scheduled ahead with no break. It was time to go home.

Jane was home sick. I was homesick.

Thorns in the Flesh
"A Cute" Hernia

In July, 1968, an acute hernia developed in about two weeks' time. Dr. Robert Sadler in Nashville said it should be fixed immediately to prevent intestinal strangulation. I was in a meeting in Columbia, Tennessee.

"If it is so urgent, when can you fix it?" I asked.

"As soon as you can get to it," he said.

"I'll close this meeting Sunday night. Can you do the surgery on Monday?"

"Monday morning, we'll fix it," he said.

He did. It felt as if he had sewed my knee to my abdomen. I just couldn't straighten that leg for a few days.

"When can I go back to preaching?"

"You shouldn't lift anything for a month. After that not over 20 pounds for another couple of weeks."

The meeting in Columbia closed August 4. The surgery was the 5th. Two meetings were cancelled, one in Hopkinsville, Kentucky, the other at Pleasant View, Tennessee. We remained in Nashville for a week to recuperate and have the stitches removed. Jane drove us to North Carolina, where I rested another week, then was able to fly to Dothan, Alabama, to begin a meeting with John Edwards on August 18, with the understanding that he had to carry my suitcases, since I wasn't to be lifting things for a while.

Prostate Cancer

In the spring of 1994, with a typical preacher problem, congested chest, bronchitis, laryngitis, occupational hazards, I went to the family doctor.

"When have you had a physical?"

"Never, as far as I know."

"You need one."

A few days later he called and said, "I think I found a few blood cells in that urine sample. You need to check with a urologist. Have you ever had a PSA?"

"Never heard of it."

They found no blood cells, but the PSA was seven, about twice as high as normal.

Ten biopsies found no cancer cells. A year later, PSA was 14, more biopsies with no cancer cells. Six months later the PSA was 18.4. Now the doctor was ready to take the gland out. A final blood analysis separating the bound and free fell heavy on the side of cancer.

"I can't find it," he said, "but I know it's there."

"Sounds to me like you just enjoy taking out prostate glands."

"Well, I am better at that than anything else I do."

"So, when can you do it?"

"Friday morning."

It was Monday. I was to begin a meeting that night at Ruth's Chapel, in New Bern, North Carolina. It was scheduled to go through Sunday.

"You need to check in Thursday for the preparation necessary for the surgery early Friday morning," he said.

On Monday night, an explanation was given to the pastor, Dennis Wiggs, who was very concerned and understanding. The people likewise, assured me of their prayers and agreed that it was the right decision.

The surgery on Friday found a very aggressive cancer. Grading the aggressiveness of the cancer on the Gleason scale of 1-10, the higher the number the more aggressive, it was a nine.

"Doctor, what do you think would have happened if we hadn't found it and removed the gland?" I asked.

"You would have lived about three years."

The surgery was January 19, 1996. Three meetings were cancelled in California, and I began in Jacksonville, North Carolina, at Cardinal Village on February 18.

Five years later the PSA, which is to remain at 0.0 without the gland, rose to 0.3. Thirty-five radiation treatments of the area, where the gland had been, brought it back to 0.0 where it has remained for the past ten years. During the radiation I preached revivals, drove home after services, had radiation at 7:00 a.m., and went back to preach that night.

That is the two times that meetings have been closed before closing time, ended before the end, finished unfinished, shut down ahead of schedule, cut short.

A couple of meetings were postponed and rescheduled in Illinois when my tonsils were removed and some of the septum in the nose chiseled away. Other than that, a few snowstorms, a hurricane or two, and that will sum up the number of meetings, missed, cancelled, or cut short, during 60 years. The Lord has been good. My health has been good. The health of Jane and the boys has been good. The pastors and people have been good. If I had to do it all over again there'd be a few changes…not many. There were long, difficult months away from home, Jane and the boys, but at the time there appeared to be no other way to *do the work of an evangelist.*

PEOPLE PROBLEMS

Little PEOPLE
Service Dismissed

Highway 301 works its way across South Carolina from Dillon to Florence, Manning, Summerton, Santee, Orangeburg, Bamberg, and a few other "bergs," goes into Georgia 30 miles north of Sylvania, on through Statesboro, Claxton, Glennville, Ludowici (speed trap capitol of the world), Jesup, and near the Florida line reconnects with Highway 1 at a little spot called Folkston, the marriage capitol of Georgia.

In the 50's, one left Folkston, southwest toward Okefenokee, on a road of white sand with large ancient oaks on either side reaching out to one another over the road, touching branches like gnarled fingers on aged hands, with Spanish moss hanging like tangled locks of gray hair from hoary heads. They had outlived all the humans, gathering wisdom over the years, which they would gladly pass on to this generation, but no one was interested enough to stop and listen, so they whispered it to one another. One day they would pass away and be replaced with cultivated pines that would never live long enough to be wise. But in 1950, they stood, with their arms reaching together over the road creating a tree tunnel of dark shade and shadows through which to drive. A beautiful and unique experience.

A small frame building stood near the edge of the swamp on the right side of the road, on a little hill of white sand, in the midst of small scrub oaks growing in soil that was too poor to grow the giants. The only thing raised on that hill was a fuss now and then in the little church, Philadelphia Free Will Baptist.

You got it! Philadelphia Church is not in Philadelphia, it is in southeast Georgia.

It was 1955, my first revival in the Church, although I had been there with the Gospeliers Quartet a time or two in the previous five years. There were two services each day, Monday through Friday and Sunday, with one on Saturday.

The only time in over 50 years that a service was lost completely to disturbances was a night in that meeting. It all began easy enough. After I had been preaching about ten minutes, a little three-year-old girl broke loose from her ten-year-old sister on the back row, came halfway down the aisle and sat down. She sat slapping the floor with two church fans, the kind with the Good Shepherd and 23rd Psalm on one side and a funeral home advertisement on the other, made of material heavy enough with a flat wooden handle, it could be used to stir the air in a steaming hot house full of people. The folks smiled as the cute little girl entertained them.

When she grew weary of that she came down to the front, went over to the piano, slapped the bench with her fans and watched me preach.

From the piano she came over to the pulpit, and stood looking up at me, as if to say, "You fool, don't you see me. Look down here."

So I stopped and said to the little sister on the back row, "Will you come and get her so I can continue preaching?"

The three-year-old saw her coming and took off running. She chased her around the front of the church to the entertainment of the congregation, finally catching her, and with her kicking and screaming took her to the back pew.

All the commotion and screaming woke up a little fellow who was stretched out asleep on the front pew. When he rolled over, he fell in the floor with a thud and now he was hollering for Mama, who came running from the midst of the crowd, picked him up, and departed out a side door, leaving everyone wondering if he was critically injured. That woke another one sleeping on the front pew across the church, which brought another mother running to take care of him.

By then, 30 minutes was past, and I had nobody's attention, but being young and foolish I thought I would try again. In about five minutes the mother with the first child returned through the side door, across the front, down the aisle to her seat, and all along the way stopped to explain that the child was not hurt. When she settled in, the second one came back with her child still sniffling and crying.

In the meantime the three-year-old had torn loose from her sister in the back, and that chase was on again. Forty-five minutes of my time was gone, and nobody was listening. The story of Belshazzar was over, and if a preacher can't keep attention with that story he might as well quit.

So I said, "Folks, let's end this with a prayer. Come back tomorrow night and we'll start over."

All kinds of living things have disturbed evangelistic services. Most often it is little human beings.

Cowboys and Indians

Closed a revival in Eastern North Carolina and flew to Mobile, Alabama, to start over again in Buckatunna, Mississippi. The pastor met me at the airport, drove about 50 miles northwest on Highway 45, crossed the Mississippi state line, and found Buckatunna 10 miles into Mississippi. Across the tracks (There may have been no tracks, but if there had been, we would have crossed them.), up a narrow street in the edge of the woods, we found the little building, arriving just in time for service.

The congregation was a crowd of seven (I didn't leave a 'ty' off. Not seventy. *Seven,* the number after six.), and one of them was a four-year-old little boy playing cowboys and Indians, running around the church, shooting at me over the back of the pews while I was trying to preach.

I stopped and said to his mother, "The next time he comes around will you catch him and hold him. I can't compete with him. I don't even have a gun."

That upset her, so she caught him, snatched him up, stomped out, slammed the door, didn't come back, and there were five left.

And that's not the smallest crowd I ever preached to. That record is Dublin, Georgia, in a mission beginning in a storefront where on Sunday morning there were three, counting the pastor and me. The largest local church attendance was Bethel Free Will Baptist, Kinston, North Carolina, when on the closing Sunday night we had over 1,100. My dear, close friend, David Paramore, was the pastor. The most people I ever preached to in an evangelistic service was the opening Sunday afternoon of a cooperative meeting in Johnson City, Tennessee, in Freedom Hall, about 3,000.

So it is evident I have never set any records in evangelistic meetings. However disturbances in services have nothing to do with the size of the crowd.

Most of the time, it is children. Billy Sunday said, "At invitation time if the devil couldn't break it up any other way, he'd pinch a baby and make it cry."

People get offended if you comment about their crying babies. So usually, I don't say anything to keep from getting caught like one preacher who after a baby had cried for some time, the mother started out with the child, and the preacher, thinking he would relieve her of some embarrassment said, "Lady, never mind. Your baby's not bothering me."

She looked back over her shoulder and said, "No, but you're bothering my baby."

A variety of other critters have shown up, interfering in services, at the time frustrating, in retrospect funny, but most of the time the problem has been people.

BIG PEOPLE
Knitting Party

In California a woman came every night, brought her knitting to occupy her mind so as not to pay attention to anything the preacher said, sat beside her physician-husband, second row from the front, and knitted through the entire service. Her ears were open but her mind was closed. Every five minutes she would hug and kiss her husband as if she had not seen him for sometime, distracting him from listening, which he appeared to be desperately trying to do, give the preacher a heavy sigh of disgust, and go back to her knitting. Halfway through the service she would take an intermission, leave her seat, parade down the aisle, go outside for a five-minute break and smoke a cigarette, return to her seat, kiss her husband, whom she hadn't seen for a while and go back to her knitting.

This annoying ritual continued all week. On the closing night, at the door, she spoke for the first time to the evangelist. "You're a manipulator," she said, "and I'm too intelligent to be manipulated."

"You're not only intelligent," I said, "you are absolutely, without any doubt, the rudest person I have ever met."

She was a psychologist.

Out-a-Here

She was a visitor, her first night in the meeting, sitting near the front, next to an aisle. As the sermon progressed she became more fidgety and conspicuously uncomfortable. Discussing the relationship between husband and wife, it was inevitable the question of who is the head would come up. Jane says that I always spend more time on "wives obey your husband" than I do "husbands love your wives as Christ loved the church."

Maybe so. Most of us would rather read those passages written to others about how they should treat us than the other way around.

When the note sounded that he's the king and she's the queen, that woman could sit still no longer. She jumped up, snatched her coat from the back of the seat, threw it over her shoulder, shook her head with that red hair flying and said, "I'm getting out-a-here. I don't have to put up with that stuff."

She surely didn't. From her size and temperament she could go bear-hunting with a switch. She didn't have to take anything from anybody.

After she slammed the door, a quick-witted comeback from Winston Churchill came to mind. I said, "Folks, it's a good thing I'm not married to her. If I were her husband she'd probably put poison in my coffee....and if she were my wife, I'd gladly drink it."

Smoking Break

Before the days of refrigerated air, August meetings in south Georgia were in open churches, so the hot, humid air from the outside could circulate, mixing with the hot, humid air on the inside being stirred with hand fans.

Sunday morning the doors and windows were open, the house was full of people fanning and I was sweating and preaching. The subject was *Doing the Will of God,* from Romans 12:1-2, the negative side, separation from the world. I was chasing a rabbit through the tobacco patch, giving reasons why Christians should not smoke cigarettes.

An agitated deacon, to register his disagreement and display his defiance, rose near the front, stalked down the aisle, out the door, around the building to a window near the pulpit, in sight of most of the congregation, lit a cigarette, leaned against an oak tree, puffed and blew the smoke through the window at me while I continued the preaching.

I finished the sermon, finished the meetings, and finished my ministry in that particular church.

Maybe he didn't die with lung cancer nor heart disease nor any other premature death caused by tobacco.

Immovable Objects

The extent to which some people will go to get attention, to be seen and heard in church, sometimes approaches the unbelievable. The meeting began on Monday night and so did the problem. At the end of the song service and before the sermon the choir came down and sat with the congregation...all except two older women, who remained in the choir directly behind the preacher, laughed and talked loud enough to be disturbing all during the sermon.

After service I mentioned the matter to the pastor who said, "I can't get them to come down. They sit there every service and visit with one another. I've learned to just go on and preach."

The second night they were so loud that I couldn't concentrate. It was really bothering me. After service I approached the two and said, "Ladies, you would be doing me a great favor if you'd come down with the choir and sit in the audience. I can't keep my mind on the sermon. If the Lord's trying to say something to me I can't hear him for the static."

They kept talking with no comment.

The third night, the choir came down and there they sat, perched on the same roost. The pastor introduced me. At the pulpit, I stopped, turned to the women and said, "Ladies, I'm not going to preach until you come down and sit out front."

They smiled in defiance and kept their seats, that old immovable object and irresistible force problem.

I said, "I'm serious. I'm not preaching with the two of you sitting behind me talking."

What would I have done, if they had called my bluff?

It was no bluff. I was prepared to turn the service back to the pastor for him to preach, pray, dismiss, whatever.

Deafening silence so loud you could hear it fell over the congregation. Everything stopped for a long pause. Huffing and puffing, they didn't blow the house in, but they slowly descended the choir loft, took seats at the end of a pew near the wall. At a lower volume in a less conspicuous place, they continued talking, fussing about being asked to move down from their choir seats to the level of everybody else. The audience exhaled a sigh of relief, letting the air out of an inflated situation before someone could stick a pin in it. They came and sat in the congregation for the remaining services, which ended on Sunday night. What they did after that I have never known. I never asked. No one ever told me, and no one ever invited me back to that church. That was one of those three-in-one meetings, the first, the last, and the only.

"Give 'em Hell"

Victory Free Will Baptist Church in Kansas City, Missouri, was so near the street only a sidewalk came between them. The building was old style architecture, with a small auditorium. The wooden theater seats in a fan arrangement would seat maybe 150. It was 1971, and our meeting was May 3-9, Monday through Sunday night. Lawrence Thompson, the pastor, was a very close and good friend who was later killed with two other preachers in the crash of a private plane returning from a Bible seminar and conference.

For the weekend, a full-time gospel trio with a great sound furnished the music. They had an Assembly of God background. The leader said that he was considering getting off the road, taking a church to pastor, and insisted that when he did he wanted me to come and preach at his church the same material that I had preached at Victory. Later he called from Edina, Missouri. I accepted his invitation and it opened the door for a cooperative meeting in the little town located in extreme northeast Missouri.

On Saturday night at Victory with a good attendance I was about half through a sermon on Belshazzar, when in the front door, which opened directly onto the sidewalk, staggered a man off the street. He closed the door, leaned against the wall for a moment to secure his footing, stood for a while in the back of the church, made his way slowly and deliberately to a back seat next to an aisle, and quietly sat down, not disturbing, but visible to those on the other side of the fanned seats, and only 40 feet from the pulpit. He shifted his position in the seat several times, fidgeting, trying to stay awake and not getting the sermon at all.

After about ten minutes, he got out of his seat, walked back to the vestibule, had everyone's attention wondering what he would do, turned, waved goodbye to me, and said, "Give 'em hell, Preacher...give 'em hell!" He walked out the door, closed it, and like Melchizedek, nobody knew where he came from nor where he went.

His concept of hell is not that different from the general public and they're not drunk. Hell is something one person gives to another when he's "telling him off."

Saved His Soul, Lost His Teeth

As he shook hands at the church door after the Sunday morning service, a broad grin spread across his face lifting the lip and bringing into view the upper front teeth, he hesitated a moment and said, "You remember these?" calling attention to those teeth.

"How could anybody forget? Everybody remembers those teeth. Some things happen only once in a lifetime, and with such shocking impact, indelible images are printed in the brain."

It was March 19, 1961, Sunday night, the final service of a week-long, very fruitful revival meeting in White Oak Free Will Baptist Church, Bladenboro, North Carolina. Brother Walter Jernigan, who had served churches for many years in South Carolina, had semi-retired, returned to Bladen County, North Carolina, his original home area, and was pastoring White Oak. Many more will remember Wade, Walter's son, whose ministry as a pastor, evangelist, missionary, church planter, was more widespread than his father's, especially in the west.

The church was filled to capacity every night, and that closing night was packed. After the altar call for salvation, the pastor extended an invitation for church membership, "opening the doors of the church." More than 20 responded, mostly middle and upper teens. They lined up at the front of the church, from one side all the way across to the other. In the middle of the line, facing the congregation was a tall, slender guy, about 17, joining the church as a candidate for baptism along with the others.

It was hot in that building, a large crowd with everyone creating the heat of a 25 watt light bulb. The oxygen content of the air was low. The tension from the pressure of standing in front of the congregation was high. The young fellow's mind sought some relief. It blacked out. He fainted. Some people, when they faint, relax, collapse, knees buckle, and they crumble to the floor in a heap, like a skyscraper brought down by well-placed explosives planted by a demolition crew. Not this guy. He froze standing up, stiff as a board, and fell face forward like a tree. The first thing to hit the floor was his mouth, and teeth and blood went everywhere. The men rushed to his rescue, packed his mouth to stop the bleeding, gathered some teeth just in case they could be saved, and sped away with him to a doctor.

Now here he was almost 50 years later, smiling at me at the church door, reminding me that he not only joined, was baptized, but was still in the church. I've been back 11 times for revivals since 1961, and he's always there.

With that bridge holding those replacements, nobody notices much, except those who remember how he brought the invitation that Sunday night to a sudden, shocking close.

Jane's Pretty Dress

Summer storms could cause some inconveniences in the days before refrigerated air, when doors and windows were all open to prevent suffocation in a house packed with people sweating and fanning. REA (Rural Electrification Administration) had strung wire all over rural America, but sometimes it was so inefficient that ten drops of rain or a dog visiting a light pole could put the lights out.

The little church building in Maury, North Carolina, wood frame, tin roof, on piers, not underpinned, capacity of 75 including the small balcony which was probably a carryover from the days when black slaves stood in that balcony attending church with their owners who sat on the main floor, men on one side, women on the other, three distinct segregated classes. Every night during this week in the summer of 1952, there was standing room only in this little building. The hayloft balcony, the main floor, the aisles, foyer, around the pulpit and around the potbellied heater, the church filled to capacity. It was summer, the heater was unnecessary, but nobody had bothered to remove it. So people in chairs sat right beside it.

Jane, my sweetheart, had ridden a bus all the way from Nashville with Geraldine Gay (Waid), who was from eastern North Carolina. Jane had come to church wearing a pretty pale yellow cotton dress, so as to remind her boyfriend preacher he need not be looking around at other girls. The only place for them to sit was in chairs by that heater. All during the service, thunder and lightning from far away crept closer and closer, warning of the storm that was coming.

Near the end of the service, at invitation time, the time when most disturbances hit, the storm struck. Deafening down-pouring rain pounded the tin roof. Sharp lightning cracked around us. The lights went out. Wind shook that little building, trying desperately to remove it from the piers. Silence fell over the crowd waiting for a catastrophe. When the rain and thunder quieted enough for my voice to be heard over the storm, I suggested someone get candles or flashlights. When the worst was passed I invited anyone interested in becoming a Christian to meet me in the back corner of the building. Seventeen people came and professed salvation.

When Jane moved from the darkness into light, she was horrified to see her beautiful yellow dress covered in soot. The wind had blown down that stove chimney, and the heater had sneezed black ashes and soot all over her. She was so beautiful I never noticed the soot-covered dress. I had not seen her in two months. The next summer in 1953, we were married on Memorial Day, May 30.

Often the lights went out during meetings but that was the least of the disturbances. Children were more frequent and more of a problem. There were no nurseries in those days. There was nowhere for the mothers to go but outside, try to convince the child to behave and come back in church. Through all the years and thousands of services, the only one completely abandoned to disturbing children was that one in Philadelphia at Folkston.

A Congregation of Caskets

A meeting in Miami in the summer of 1955 was a unique experience. It began on Tuesday night. It took two days to drive down, and ended two weeks later on Sunday morning. That middle Sunday, June 26, plans were made to telecast the Sunday morning service live from the church, sponsored by a local funeral home, which was telecasting various church services every Sunday morning. Saturday night after service the TV crews showed up to set two large cameras on elevated platforms in the back corners of the auditorium. The pastor, his wife and a few others frantically worked to decorate the church to make the best possible impression on the TV audience the next day.

A serious disagreement developed between the pastor and his wife about some arrangement, causing her to leave terribly upset. When the work was done and the pastor and I went to the parsonage, she was in the bedroom with the door locked. He slept on the couch. I slept in the guest room.

Sunday morning attitudes were improved and the service went very well, no bobbles, no hitches. The sermon was on the *Crucifixion of Jesus*. We were just finishing lunch when the phone rang. The funeral home asked for me, "Do you have that message in print?" the man asked. "We are having so many requests for it we need to make copies to mail out."

"No, Sir," I said. "None of my sermons are in print. Well, at least not with my name on them."

This was years before videotaping, and audiotaping was reel-to-reel.

"Well, could you write it out?" he asked.

"In a day? No sir. I really don't have the time."

He hung up. In a few minutes he called back.

"Say, could you come down to our place and preach it on a tape, so our stenographers could take it off, type it up, and make copies?"

"I possibly could do that," I said, not knowing what I was getting into.

The next morning, Bible in hand, I showed up at the funeral home to accommodate them. The funeral director led me into a room full of caskets, closed the lid on one, set the recorder on top of the coffin, handed me a mike and said, "When you have finished, turn off the tape recorder."

He walked quietly out and closed the door.

Now I have preached in dead churches to lifeless unresponsive congregations, but never anything like that. The silence was deafening, only the click of the recorder and the sound of the turning tape. That's just as well. A whispered "amen" from inside one of those caskets would have hit the pause button on that recorder and there would have been a long intermission before that sermon was finished. It may not have stopped the sermon, but it would have interrupted until the wits got back together from wherever they had been scattered by that unexpected voice from an empty coffin, . . . and the preacher got back from the restroom.

The honest effort to duplicate the Sunday morning delivery of the sermon was partially successful, which didn't matter anyway. The sermon was never heard from again and since a copy was promised to me, it is a safe assumption that no copies were ever made. Some stenographer gave up when she came to "crucifixion was the most shameful, painful, excruciating death that Roman ingenuity could devise."

House on Fire

Tucked away under the red clay hills of northwest Alabama is a strip of coal 18 or 20 inches thick, visible and accessible at the surface. Men, small in stature, but large in courage, cut 20 inch openings into the hillside, deeper and deeper into the belly of the mountain, extracting the black gold as they went, crawling into the darkness, working on their back and bellies, mining by hand that narrow vein of coal, a hard way to make a living. A local bi-vocational pastor, with whom we had several revival meetings, was one of those men. He was about five feet tall, short arms, short muscular legs on the torso of an overgrown midget, or an undergrown man.

Some of the coal was changed to coke. In the '40s and '50s in many local communities there were small coke furnaces, like concrete igloos with a hole in the top where the smoke from smoldering coal covered with sand to prevent it from flaming could find its way out while the heat removed certain chemicals from the coal, turning it into coke. In 1971, the process had moved from little local furnaces to a large plant operation handling train carloads of coal in huge furnaces. But the concrete igloos still dotted the landscape giving their name to certain roads and communities. There were the Old Furnace Road, the Furnace Hill, and so Liberty Free Will Baptist Church was known to some locals as "Furnace."

August 2-8, 1971, Jane, the boys and I, were there in a week's revival services, morning and evening. We arrived Monday afternoon so there was no Monday morning service. At the 10:00 a.m. Tuesday service, I informed the congregation of about 20 people that I would be speaking every morning from Psalm 126:6 on *The Formula for Fruit Bearing.*

Jane, Stephen, who was 17, and Philip, who was 14, were sitting in the back third of the 20 listeners. On the pew in front of them was an older couple, whose mates had died and they had recently married. Newlywed was written all over them. She was as close as possible without being inside his shirt, with that "woman-in-love look" as she straightened his collar and smoothed the hair on the back of his head. In his lap was a large family Bible, and when I announced the text, he set out to find it. In short order, he went through the whole Bible but somehow missed Psalms, so she offered her assistance. He pushed her hands off the Bible, put them back in her lap, and in no uncertain terms let her know he didn't need her help. He was neither helpless nor ignorant. He could find it himself.

Back through the big Bible again, and someone must have taken out the Psalms. That book had hid itself between Job and Proverbs and he couldn't find it. She offered help. He refused again, frustrated and a bit disgusted with her know-it-all attitude.

By then, I was halfway through the first message on the first requirement for fruitfulness, the "goeth."

Jane and the boys watched the battle between him, his helpful wife, and the lost book in his Bible, refusing to look at one another for fear the pent-up humor of it would explode.

In desperation, he thought of the table of contents in the front of the big Bible, found that, and began at Genesis. They watched his lips move as he read each book, "Gen-e-sis, Ex-o-dus, Le-vit-i-cus," down the line until he reached Psalms. Sliding his finger across the page from Psalms, he found a page number. He had solved his problem. He knew now where it was. Following the page numbers, he slowly turned pages through the first 18 books of the Bible, and there it was — the Book of Psalms. When he punched his wife in the ribs with his elbow, got her undivided attention, and with a broad grin of success pointed to the Book of Psalms, Jane and the boys almost lost it. He had found the book without her help and I was almost finished with the message, so he didn't need to find the 126th. At least, not for that morning, maybe he'd get there on Wednesday, and by Thursday he'd get to verse six.

YESTERDAY

Aside from the fun of watching them in church, they were a gracious, friendly, generous old couple. The man gave Philip a Jews' harp, an act that did at the time bring into question the generosity of the gift. It brought to mind Mark Twain's tale of the traveling salesman who gave a whistle to each of Brigham Young's children and they nearly whistled him to death. By the time Philip learned to play a tune, I feared he would break out all of his front teeth and the dental bill would far exceed the revival offering.

The couple invited all of us for supper one evening. When we arrived, she was sitting on the porch crying and he was fussing. While preparing the meal, she left a pan of grease on the stove, went out of the kitchen, forgot it, and was reminded when the smoke began boiling from the house. The grease caught fire, burned a hole through the cabinets and ceiling into the attic and set fire to the rafters. They had extinguished the flames, leaving the kitchen covered with smoke and greasy smut. She was heartbroken and he was mad. Jane and the pastor's wife calmed her down, told her not to worry and that they would help her clean up the kitchen. We would eat supper with her anyway. At least the food wasn't burned – only the house.

In Wheeling, West Virginia, October '89, it was the food. Jane and I arrived Saturday night to begin meetings Sunday morning through Friday night. Sunday morning the busy, thrifty, pastor's wife planned for all of us to have dinner at the parsonage. She prepared the vegetables, side dishes, and basted a nice turkey, leaving him in the oven with the thermostat and timer set to cook while we were in church. After church, and I honestly didn't preach much beyond twelve o'clock, we were in no rush since we didn't have to wait in a long line at a restaurant, and there was a delicious turkey dinner waiting for us at the pastor's house. The smell reached us in the driveway before the smoke.

"Smells like something burning," Jane said.

Then we saw the smoke seeping out through all the cracks around the kitchen door.

"The house is on fire," we all added in a choral response.

When the preacher opened the door, greasy dark smoke came boiling out to greet him. He quickly located the source, the stove, the oven, turned the heat off, opened the oven door in time to see a few small tongues of yellow flames licking the last bit of fat and flesh from the large breastbone of that turkey and spitting the ashes, with those of all the meat and smaller bones they had already consumed, into the bottom of a twisted roasting bag melted in the intense heat. The oven thermostat had stuck and turned that oven into a turkey crematory.

While Jane and the pastor's wife cleaned up the kitchen, opened all the windows and doors, cranked up every fan they could find, and sprayed air freshener everywhere, the pastor went to a local fast food chicken house and bought dinner already cooked.

With the old couple, the food was edible, only the house had a hole burned through the ceiling. The women washed the dishes, the table, the chairs, and we sat down to a delicious Alabama summer garden-fresh meal of fried okra, crowder peas, potatoes, tomatoes, yellow squash and fried chicken.

We were sitting at the table in the midst of the meal when Jane looked up through the hole in the ceiling and with some alarm said, "That rafter is on fire! It's still burning up there."

There was no flame, but red burning coals were shining from the rafters on fire.

The old man looked up from his food, turned his eyes toward the hole in the ceiling, and said, "Yeah, I know it. And when I git through eatin', I'm gonna git the water hose and git up there and put it out."

With that he went back to his supper.

The 45 minutes he spent searching for Psalm 126 didn't stop the service nor hinder the preacher, but it occupied the attention of Jane and the boys and those around him, and slowed things down a bit.

CRITTER CRISIS

Bat

In Sulphur Springs Church, Samantha, Alabama, on a hot night in July before the days of air conditioning, with all the doors and windows open and a house filled with people, a bat came to church. Everyone has heard, "blind as a bat," and that they are guided by sonar. Those stupid creatures are not only blind, that sonar doesn't work except at close range. With him darting and fluttering through the crowd at a low altitude, within six inches of women's heads, while they shrieked and tried to get under the pews, I stopped preaching and said to Olan Kuykendall, "Olan, turn out the lights and maybe he'll find his way out."

That's definitely not the solution. That was the wrong thing to say. With the lights out, no one knew where the thing was and with one voice, they shrieked, "Turn the lights on!"

The bat didn't find his way out. When the lights came on he was still having fun scaring all the women and creating general havoc in church.

Olan said, "I'll get him," whereupon he got a broom and took his stance at the back of the building.

I said, "Olan, you can't hit that bat. His sonar will zero in on that broom."

The second time the bat circled around that vicinity of the church, Olan took one swing and evidently this one had defective sonar. He hit the bat. The bat hit the floor, and I said, "Folks, sign that man up with the Yankees. They'll pay him $100,000 a year to swing a bat."

Blackbird

In Hilltop Church, Fuquay, NC, it was a starling, an oversized blackbird. The sanctuary was constructed with laminated beams, and from the floor to the ridge row was 40 feet. All through the song service on Sunday morning that bird was flying around in the top of the auditorium, out of reach, except with a shotgun and that didn't seem practical. No one, including the bird, knew how nor where he came in, or how nor where he could get out. At least he seemed desperate to get out, but couldn't remember where he came in.

On the platform waiting for my place on the program, I was watching that bird like everyone else, and wondering, "How am I going to get anybody's attention with a sermon, when that bird is so much more entertaining?"

Neither the song leader nor the pastor acknowledged the bird's presence, pretending he was not up there or hoping he'd disappear, drop dead, or find his way out.

If the Lord feeds and cares for sparrows, He surely is acquainted with blackbirds, and maybe He has some say-so about other areas of their lives like where they fly, roost, eat, sleep, etc. Out of desperation I breathed a little prayer and said, "Lord, can you do something about that bird?"

And believe it or not, about a minute before I came to the pulpit, I watched the bird crawl behind a light fixture in the very top of that building and he never came out. When service was over and the crowd dispersed, that bird had not reappeared. He has never been seen since.

Mouse

In Decatur, Alabama, it was one of those services when the preacher is aware that everyone sees something he doesn't see

and knows something he doesn't know. The people were looking past me at something behind me, and every few minutes
there was a collective smile and a whisper or two. It wasn't serious enough for me to stop for an explanation, and then it could
be something about my appearance or movements, like my fly
being unzipped, which I wouldn't want to know until the meeting was over.

As soon as the "amen" was said, several folks rushed to me,
with a question for which they knew I'd like an answer, "I guess
you were wondering what everybody was looking at during your
sermon?"

"Well, I am a little curious. I was aware that something had
everybody's attention."

"Behind you there was a mouse that came from under the
organ, took his time and ran slowly across the platform to
the piano. In about five minutes he decided he liked it better
under the organ, so he came from under the piano, crossed
the stage back to the organ. In another five minutes he must
have realized that he left something under the piano so he
went back across behind you to get it. Evidently he found what
he went after and went back to the organ. He crossed that platform behind you four or five times back and forth while you
were preaching."

We didn't trust the Lord to take care of the mouse. That night
the pastor set a mousetrap under the organ and the little fellow
was in it the next morning. Gone to mouse heaven or wherever
dead mice go, and with no funeral.

Dog

In Jacksontown, New Brunswick, Canada, it was a dog, a Border
Collie. The sermon was half over, when from the vestibule,
through an open door into the auditorium, down the aisle
toward the pulpit came a beautiful black and white Border

Collie. I paused for a moment, acknowledged his presence and said, "Well, where did you come from?"

One of the men ushered him out so quickly he did not have time to answer my question. The dog was not that happy about leaving as he was put out through the front door. The man closed the door; made sure the latch was caught, and went back to his seat just in time for the dog to come again from the vestibule into the church.

I said, "Well, here you are again. You are determined to attend church tonight."

Everyone laughed, including the man who patiently took the dog back to the front door and outside.

By the time that man reached his seat and sat down, here came the dog, trotting down the aisle.

This time I said, "Well, here you are again, and again, and again. Tie him up, put him in a room, and find out where he is coming in!"

It was getting hilarious.

So the man put the dog outside, followed him around the church, found a basement window half-open, through which that dog jumped into the basement, up the stairs and back in church, before the man could get to the front door. The man closed the window and put the dog outside, with no way for him to get back in. The crowd finished their laughter and I finished the sermon.

Snake

There have been bees, wasps, dogs, cats, mice, children, but the most unusual was at Youth Camp in South Carolina. August 8-20, 1960. The services were in an open tabernacle, nothing more than a large shelter, with overhead roof and rafters not closed in with any ceilings. It was teenage camp with 75 to 100 attending and for once everybody was paying attention to a sermon on *The Crucifixion of Jesus.*

Looking another way I didn't see what happened. There was a dull thud like the sound of a twenty-pound bag of flour dropped on the floor, a shrieking scream, and I turned in time to see a hysterical little sixteen-year-old girl climbing over the back of a pew. The others were clearing out a space around her at a speed just under the speed of light. All of them were looking at the floor, dancing like Indians on the warpath, like they were walking through a cow pasture trying not to step in something. Crawling from under where her feet had been was a three-foot-long black snake. The first thought was that some teenage boy brought the snake in and threw him into her lap, but then I noticed all of them were climbing over the pews.

Scattered and screaming, a dozen kids were saying that the snake fell out of the overhead rafters, missing the girl's lap and landing on her feet. If you don't think that broke up church, you should have been there. One of the preachers caught the snake by the tail, killed it, took it to the woods and hung it on a tree. Stephen wrote a poem to commemorate the occasion. The symbolism was too significant to be coincidental. The snake dropped in, was killed, and hung on a tree in the middle of a sermon on, "As Moses lifted up the serpent in the wilderness, even so must the Son of Man be lifted up," to die for the sins of the world.

My comment was, "Well, folks I have had the evil spirits, fallen angels, and demons try to break up a lot of revival services, but this is the only night the devil ever came in person."

Conclusion

Dr. R. G. Lee, a prince of preachers among Southern Baptists, was preaching his classic, famous sermon on Ahab and Jezebel, *Payday Someday,* to a congregation held spellbound by his vivid, moving, presentation. The pin-dropping silence spoke loudly that they were hanging on every word. At a most tense moment, he stopped, for what appeared to be a dramatic pause, until he said to a little boy on the front seat, "Son, stop playing with that coat. It's bothering me." And without missing a word, he went back to the sermon.

Every public speaker battles distractions now and then while trying to keep the attention of an audience and deliver a message. With preachers it seems more "now" than "then." A book could be filled with such illustrations. One chapter is enough.

HUMOR IS A FUNNY THING

There is a "...time to laugh" (Ecclesiastes 3:4). "A merry heart maketh a cheerful countenance: but by sorrow of the heart the spirit is broken" (Proverbs 15:13).

"...he that is of a merry heart hath a continual feast" (Proverbs 15:15).

"A merry heart doeth good like a medicine..." (Proverbs 17:22).

Humor is a funny thing. By its very nature humor self-destructs, and that gives it medicinal value. Problems which have grown far beyond their serious importance create emotional distress, mental anguish, physical troubles, even heart attacks. If those problems become genuinely humorous, really funny, they vaporize, vanish, and disappear. That's good medicine.

When that which you stew over becomes humorous there's nothing there to stew over.

An article in *The Daily Reflector*, Greenville, North Carolina's local paper, dated October 18, 2009, taken from the *Connecticut Post*, Darien, Connecticut, written by Maud Purcell, listed eight scientifically proven physical, mental, and emotional health benefits of humor:

Relieves pain

Strengthens the immune system

Decreases stress

Lowers blood pressure

Lightens the burden of troubles

Helps overcome fear

Helps take self less seriously

Stimulates creativity

A group of scientists have found a family of pain-suppressing chemicals in the brain called *endorphins*, "morphine within." Some psychologists believe that a burst of laughter releases some endorphins, bringing a soothing balm to quiet nerve cells and relieve pain to some degree. That burst of laughter, along with an aspirin, may actually relieve that headache.

Humor is also good medicine for the terrible disease of strife and dissension in relationships. It is impossible to think a man is really funny and hate him at the same time. If you are on the outs with somebody, nothing he says or does is actually humorous. If the issue that created the strife becomes funny, it vanishes into frivolity, and how can you hate each other over something that's so frivolous. If you like a guy, his jokes are hilarious. If you dislike him, even the jokes are disgusting. Watch a girl's response to a boy's funny stuff and you'll know whether she likes him or not.

Humor is effective as a tool of communication. Nothing breaks down barriers of opposition between a speaker and his audience faster than a sense of humor. Humor holds attention, makes the speaker a likeable fellow, easy to identify with, opens the mind to give a sympathetic ear to what's being said, and gives the mind a moment to relax from thinking on the serious, so as to consider the serious more thoughtfully afterwards.

Humor disarms disagreeable audiences, diffuses disputes between persons, and destroys devastating, distressing, deadly diseases, mental and physical, in the lives of individuals by its self-destructive nature, evaporating the problem. Like the morning mist or steam from the kettle, the difficult dilemma disappears.

A merry heart and laughter really is good medicine. Love may make the world go around, but a sense of humor keeps you from jumping off. This analysis of humor is not to justify its use in the ministry nor explain the reason for this chapter. Sixty years of preaching, over 2000 evangelistic meetings, 15,000 services, and ten years presiding at a National Convention has done that.

A young pastor asked, "Do you have all those funny stories in a book?"

"Not a book that I've written, nor a book that I've read. Not all of them, none of them are in any book in my library."

The stories are really to be told, not read, so they have piled up over the years in the brain from listening, not reading. Telling them is easy. Writing them is difficult. Many times the humor is in the timing, the voice inflection, the accent, all impossible to put in print. Most of them are so old the source has long ago disappeared in the crowd of people in my past, and if I could remember where I heard the story, I would not know where the man who told it to me heard it. None of them are original with me. They were told by somebody, sometime, somewhere.

"Well, if you ever write a book of funny stories, I want a copy," he said.

With his request in mind the decision was made, not to write a book, but one chapter. Who knows? Someone may laugh and prevent a heart attack.

This may not be the way it was, but it's how I heard it!

Preachers, lawyers and doctors are great sources for funny stories. Since I know more preachers than lawyers or doctors, and since I am one, the joke's on us.

PREACHER TALES
Wrong Man

The emcee introduced the speaker as the man who had made a million dollars in oil in California. Taking the podium the speaker said, "Well, it really wasn't California, it was Pennsylvania...and it wasn't oil, it was coal...and it wasn't a million dollars, it was two hundred thousand...and it wasn't me, it was my brother.....and he didn't make it, he lost it!"

Sounds like preachers introducing each other.

Most Embarrassing Introduction

It was a large church, and the pastor, in an effort to honor me, insisted that I wear a paper crown, a ridiculous robe, and ride in a royal litter which was sitting on two poles, hoisted on the shoulders of four men, who carried me down one side of the church across the back, up the other side, delivering me to the podium like a king riding on the shoulders of his subjects. Jane, embarrassed to tears, wanted to crawl under a pew.

When I reached the pulpit, I said, "Folks, I'm really embarrassed, but I shouldn't be. Jesus rode into Jerusalem on the back of one. I've just been carried around the church on the shoulders of four."

Don't Tell 'em

The first night of evangelistic services the crowd was very, very small. The visiting preacher came to the pulpit, looked back at the pastor and said, "Did you tell these folks that I was coming?"

"No," he said, "but I'm going to find out who did."

Poor Preacher

As he was leaving church, one little fellow shook the preacher's hand and said, "Preacher, when I get big, I'm going to make a whole lot of money and give all of it to you."

"Well, that's generous," responded the preacher. "But why do you want to give me so much money?"

"My daddy says you're the poorest preacher he's ever heard."

....

When the meetings were over the evangelist said that they invited him to come back. They told him the day and the month. He was just waiting on the year. They said it would be a cold day in July.

He's Gone

Many people, including preachers, look better going than coming. A man called a law office and asked for Mr. Bloomberg.

The secretary said, "Mr. Bloomberg is dead."

Next day same guy called again.

"I told you yesterday that Mr. Bloomberg has died," reported the agitated secretary.

Fourteen days in a row this same fellow called.

On the fourteenth day, the secretary called another lawyer to the phone and said, "Convince this guy that Bloomberg is dead."

He took the phone and said, "Sir, Mr. Bloomberg has died, departed this life, deceased, dead, – gone. He will not be back anymore. Do you understand that?"

"Yeah, I understand it."

"Then why do you keep calling every day?"

"I just love to hear it," he said.

When some preachers resign, the phone may ring for a month, just to hear a secretary say, "He's gone. He won't be back anymore."

....

A country preacher came to the pulpit to resign and said, "Folks, Jesus led me here when I came and now Jesus is leading me to leave."

The choir stood and sang *What a Friend We Have in Jesus.*

Who Cuts the Grass?

The new pastor called the church board together to discuss hiring someone to mow the grass. One of the deacons said, "Preacher, our former pastor always cut the grass himself."

"I know it," he said, "and I've talked to him about it, and he says he's not going to do it anymore."

Three Envelopes

When the older preacher resigned the church, he left the new preacher some advice in three sealed envelopes, numbered one, two, and three, with the suggestion that when he got in trouble he should open them in numerical order. Before long a situation developed that he couldn't handle so he opened envelope number one. It said, "Blame it on me, the former pastor. I've moved on so it will cause me no problem. Just say it is my fault."

He did. It worked.

Time passed and a second problem arose. He opened envelope number two. It said, "Blame it on the devil. Folks always believe that. It gets them around personal responsibility."

He did. It worked again.

By and by a third conflict erupted. He opened envelope number three.

It said, "Prepare three envelopes."

Church Splits and Splinters

Shipwrecked on a deserted island, the castaway thought he was alone, until walking along the beach he met a long-haired-bearded guy. Surprised, he greeted him with, "Where did you come from? How long have you been here?"

"Oh, I've been on this island for 20 years."

The resident then took the newcomer through a wooded area into an opening with three or four buildings.

"What is that large building?" asked the visitor.

"That's my house…built it with my own hands. The little one is a shed."

"The one on the left, what's that?"

"My church," he said. "That's my church."

"The one on the other side of the house looks a lot like the church."

"Oh, that was my church before we split."

New Harmony

There is a church down the road with a peculiar name for a Baptist Church, *Harmony*. On the opposite side, a quarter-mile down the same road, there is a *New Harmony Baptist Church*. They maintained harmony by each group making its own music.

How Cold?

Some churches are colder than a Canadian winter, and that's cold. How cold is it?

Somebody saw a lawyer with both hands in his own pockets.

A beagle was seen running across a field with a set of jumper cables in his mouth planning to jump start a rabbit.

A tapping on the back door at six o'clock in the morning turned out to be the thermometer trying to get in out of the weather.

At bedtime a fellow cracked the door to let the dog out. The dog looked at him and said, "I think I can wait 'til morning."

Good for Nothing

The good active church members were dying off too rapidly. The concerned pastor went to the Lord to plead his case, "Lord," he said, "You're taking my best people. I need them here for a while to help build a church. Now, if you need some in Heaven, I can give you a list of names."

The Lord said, "I don't want them either."

Out of Gear

Now and then a speaker's thoughts are tumbling around in his brain and they stumble out of his mouth in a disorderly fashion.

A Baptist pastor in middle Tennessee had one of those unbelievably busy endless Sundays. At 4:00 a.m. his phone rang and one of his deacons had been rushed to the hospital seriously sick. He dressed, hurried to the hospital to see the sick deacon and left the hospital just in time to make it to Sunday school. The superintendent didn't show, so he had to be in charge of the Sunday school. The adult teacher wasn't there, so he had to teach the Sunday school lesson. Then he had the Sunday morning sermon. That afternoon he had a funeral and a rehearsal for a wedding, then a youth meeting, the Sunday evening sermon, and at the end of that a baptismal service.

He was standing in the baptistery with a lady to baptize her, had been running since 4:00 a.m. and with his brain all muddled and mind in a whirl, he said, "And now my sister, in the name of the Father, and the Son, and the Holy Spirit, I pronounce you man and wife."

Looking for Jesus

The baptizing was over and the preacher was inviting others to come, be baptized and find Jesus. He sounded so urgent and persistent, this fellow, about three-sheets-in-the-wind, waded out into the river.

The preacher put him under, brought him up and said, "Did you find Jesus?"

"No sir, I didn't."

Down he went again, a little longer this time, came up, and the preacher repeated, "Did you find Jesus?"

"Nope, I didn't find Him."

Third time the preacher held him under so long that he almost drowned. Came up, gasping for breath.

"Did you find...?"

The fellow stopped him and said, "Are you sure this is where he fell in?"

Some folks are looking for Jesus in all the wrong places. If you don't find Him before you go under the water, you won't find Him under it anywhere.

Not Really Glad

A politician went to a penitentiary to deliver a speech to the prisoners. In his introductory remarks, perambulating around trying to make contact with his audience and break down the barriers of a very chilly reception, he said, "It is certainly good to be here with all of you fine inmates."

Realizing his mistake immediately, they were not his inmates. He wasn't one of them. He said, "No, I mean it's good to be here in the midst of all you good citizens."

Not exactly, prisoners are not necessarily good citizens. Some of them cannot even vote. Their citizenship is suspended for a while.

So he backed up sputtering and stammering, and came stumbling through a third time, "Well, what I'm trying to say is – I'm just glad to see so many of you in here."

Wake Me When It's Over

The drowsiest hour in the week must be from 11:00 to 12:00 Sunday mornings. Why is it that a man at 3:00 a.m. in a dark, quiet bedroom, lying on a king-sized mattress, with Egyptian cotton sheets and a down comforter can't sleep? The same man at

11:00 o'clock in a lighted noisy church, sitting on an uncomfortable pew with somebody talking to him, can't stay awake.

John Gamble, an evangelist, told, in 1951 or '52, at FWBBC, of one fellow who fought it, struggled with it, tried to stay awake, until he just quit trying, laid his head over on the back of a pew in front of him and went to sleep. As he went to sleep, he stuck his arm out to the side and he had a note pinned on his coat sleeve. The guy sitting beside him leaned over to read the note and this is what it said:

> *Now I lay me down to sleep.*
> *The sermon's long and the subject's deep*
> *If he should stop before I wake,*
> *Please give my arm a gentle shake.*

Some sermons are long, others seem long. Einstein said time is relative and to prove his point, suggested that one minute sitting beside a beautiful girl with an arm around her, and one minute sitting on a red hot stove are two different lengths of time. Too often the sermon minute is more like the last than the first. Some preachers are like Beckett's old woman in the rocking chair. They don't know when to stop.

Wear a Watch

A man took his grandfather clock to the local horologist to get it running again. A few days later he stopped by to check on the progress and to his surprise, it was fixed. It was only a couple of blocks from his house and he had walked down to see about it. He decided that it was not very heavy and only a short distance up the street. So if the clock smith would help him get it on his back, he could easily carry it home.

They strapped it to his back, and he was slowly making his way along the edge of the street, when this country boy from way back somewhere came along in his pickup truck. The sight turned his attention from the road. He swerved toward the fellow with the clock, and ran him into the ditch. The boy stopped, came back to make sure the guy wasn't hurt, and watched him climb out of the ditch with that clock still strapped to his back.

The clock bearer, in anger, said, "Why don't you look where you're going?"

The boy said, "Why don't you wear a watch like everybody else?" *Eugene Waddell at Chimney Rock, NC*

Preachers wear watches like everybody else. They just don't look at them. Most preachers don't mind someone in the congregation looking at a watch, but when the guy starts shaking it like he thinks it's stopped, that unnerves the preacher a bit.

··········

One preacher always timed his sermons with a lifesaver in his mouth. When it melted, he knew it was time to stop. One Sunday he got a button!

Cut the Sermon

The pastor was shaking hands at the door when a lady noticed a tiny piece of tissue stuck to his face.

"What happened to your face?" she asked.

"I was shaving, had my mind on my sermon, and I cut my face."

"Next Sunday," she said, "keep your mind on your face and cut your sermon."

··········

And then sometimes the subject is deep, so deep that people drown in the deep water of incomprehension. A fellow in the back of the church called out to the speaker, "Talk louder, Preacher, I can't hear you."

A guy down front said, "I can and I'll change seats with you."

··········

Some sermons are better slept through. Time passes faster.

Two churchmen were discussing their pastors. One asked the other, "What color are your pastor's eyes?"

"I never have thought about it," he said, "I don't really know. In fact, I never have seen his eyes. When he prays he closes his eyes. When he preaches, I close mine."

....

One pastor asked another, "Do you ever talk in your sleep?"

"No," he said, "but between 11:00 and 12:00 on Sunday morning. I talk in other people's sleep."

Need to Stand Up

A friend came out of a dull drowsy service, met me at the door, shook hands and said, "You know, right in the middle of that sermon I had an uncontrollable urge to stand up."

Thinking maybe it was a leg cramp or some other physical problem, I asked, "What's the trouble, Bruce?"

"I need to prove to myself that I can sleep standing up," he said.

To most listeners the Sunday morning sermon is like the sound of soft rain on a tin roof.

....

One preacher promised his congregation if they would stay awake, pay close attention and not go to sleep, he would try to do for them as Elizabeth Taylor said to her seventh husband, "I won't keep you long."

Refreshed

Leaving the Sunday morning service, a lady smiled as she shook the preacher's hand and said, "Pastor, I feel so refreshed."

Accepting the comment as a compliment, the pastor responded, "I'm happy you found the sermon refreshing."

"Oh, it wasn't the sermon," she said, "I always feel refreshed when I wake up from my nap."

Ride That Horse

An evangelist, Jack Lassiter, after being introduced in our home church, by the pastor, Bobby Parker, who was his long-time friend, gave this account of their exciting day. It was the year the National Convention met in Fort Worth, Texas, *Cow Town, U.S.A.* The pastor was making plans to attend and decided it would be appropriate to play like a cowboy for a week, the evangelist said.

"He had bought himself a Stetson hat, $500 pair of boots, a big belt buckle, and was trying to walk bow-legged," said the evangelist, exaggerating. "And this afternoon we were riding around and saw this horse.

'Stop the car,' insisted the pastor, 'I believe I can ride that horse and I need to practice.'

"So we stopped. He got on that horse and the horse started moving up and down, picking up speed. When the horse was going up, he was going down, when he was coming up, the horse was going down. Like a cantankerous church member, that horse wouldn't cooperate. He slipped out of the saddle, fell off that horse, got a foot hung in a stirrup and was hanging on for dear life.

"Folks, he might have been killed, if the manager of K-Mart hadn't rushed out and unplugged that thing!"

No need to pretend to be something you're not, nor try to display ability you don't have.

Parable of a Preacher

Life is difficult for some preachers. An extra biblical parable illustrates. Jesus was walking down a road and came upon a man, sitting beside the road, crying.

"What's the problem?" Jesus asked.

"I'm blind. I can't see," replied the man.

Jesus touched his eyes and the man went on his way rejoicing.

Jesus came upon another man, waiting by the road, weeping.

"What's wrong?" He asked. "What's your trouble?"

"I'm crippled. My legs are twisted. I can't walk."

Jesus touched his legs and healed them. The man ran away rejoicing.

Jesus came upon a third man, who was sitting by the road, crying.

"Friend, what is your problem?" He asked.

"I'm a Baptist preacher," he said.

Jesus sat down and cried with him.

....

"Who do you love the most, me or the children?" asked the amorous preacher of his wife.

She looked straight at him and said, "You're no blood kin to me."

Not Much of a Preacher

On the way to a meeting the young preacher proposed to his girlfriend, only to be turned down with the comment, "I'll never marry a preacher."

On their way home after the sermon, he refused to take that first no as final and brought the question up again. This time she said yes.

"I thought you said that you never would marry a preacher?"

"After hearing you preach," she said, "I've decided you're not enough preacher to hurt."

....

Some preachers don't eat a meal before service. It hinders their preaching. They can't preach very well, they say.

After such a preacher's sermon, a little boy said to him, "Preacher, you might as well have gone ahead and 'et."

How to Become a Preacher

"How do you become a preacher?" an ambitious young man asked an old evangelist.

"Well, in addition to knowing what to say you must learn to say it effectively. You need to develop good pronunciation, good diction, elocution, clarity, volume, and learn to speak fluently. The Greek orator, Demosthenes, is said to have learned by shouting over the sound of the ocean waves with a mouth full of pebbles. Use marbles instead. Fill your mouth with marbles; learn to speak in spite of the difficulty. As you practice each day remove one marble. And when you have lost all your marbles ....."

PHYSICAL PROBLEMS

In response to his son's question, one father was explaining that the names of the men on the bronze plaque in the church vestibule were names of those who had died in service.

The boy's second question was, "Morning service or evening service?"

Testing...Testing...

A preacher was testing his wife's hearing as she stood at the kitchen sink washing dishes with her back to him. From some distance he said, "Can you hear me?"

No response.

He came closer and a little louder, "Can you hear me?"

No response.

Much closer and much louder, he said, "Can you hear...?"

"For the third time, YES!" Loud and clear.

Jane says my deafness is her problem, not mine. She has to repeat everything three times and louder every time.

S...S...Selling B...B...Bibles

He couldn't hold a job because his stuttering handicapped communicating. When he saw a fellow selling Bibles, he thought, "I'd like to do that."

The area manager tried to convince him there was no way he could sell, but gave in to his persistency, and let him have a

Bible, knowing it was hopeless. In 30 minutes he came back for another. In an hour he had sold ten.

The manager stunned in disbelief, asked, "How are you selling those Bibles?"

"W-w-w-well, I just wa-wa-wa-walk up to the d-ooor, O-o-open the B-bi-bible and say, 'Woo-woo-would yyyy-you-you-you like to b-b-b-buy this booooook, or woooold you-you-you rather I r-r-r-read it to you?"

Coughing

In San Francisco, the city built on all those hills, a hearse with a casket and a corpse sped down a steep hill, reached the bottom, and began the incline up another when it hit a bump. The back door flew open, casket bounced out, rolled down the hill, across a sidewalk, through the open doors of a drugstore, down the aisle, hit the counter. The lid flew open, the guy sat up and said, "You got anything to stop this coffin/coughing?"

I didn't see any of that, just heard about it.

Memory

When I finally got it all together, I forgot where I put it.

Dementia/Alzheimers

A neurological authority on Alzheimers suggested how to distinguish between that and dementia. He said if you forget your friend's name that's no serious problem. Everybody does that. But if you forget that it's your friend, that's Alzheimers. When you go to the refrigerator and forget what you're after, that's a common problem. When you forget what the refrigerator does, that's Alzheimers.

That's encouraging. I at least remember what the refrigerator does. If you leave the door open in winter, it warms the house.

Little Old Lady

Two little old ladies were driving across town. The driver ran a red light. The passenger got a little nervous. She ran the second red light. Now the passenger was really nervous. When she ran the third red light the passenger said, "Susie, you've gone through three red lights!"

"Oh, my!" she said, "Am I driving?"

Memory Pills

A preacher, discussing his memory problem with another, said, "Man, I've got some new memory pills, and they have done worlds of good for my memory."

His friend said, "My memory is bad too. I need some of that stuff. What is it?"

"Oh, they're little …little round white things …in a brown…. Oh, what's the name of that flower that's red, has thorns, and smells good?"

"A rose?"

"Yeah…."

"Rose," looking back over his shoulder, toward his wife, "what's the name of those little white pills…?"

Which Way?

An example of mountain humor, a lost salesman stopped to ask directions from an old man standing by the side of the road at his mailbox, "How do you get to Asheville?"

"Most of the time my son-in-law takes me."

··········

In rural eastern South Carolina, a traveler asked a stranger for help in finding an address.

"You go about two miles straight down this road and you'll see a white house on the right, with a red pickup truck in the driveway and a Collie dog in the back of the truck. You turn left, right there."

"Suppose when I get there, the truck and the dog aren't there?"

"Turn left anyhow," he said.

....

One fisherman called to the other across the river, "How do I get to the other side?" he asked.

"Are you crazy? You're on the other side," came the reply.

No Problem

A woman took an old photo of her grandfather to a photographer to have it restored. "Can you take this faded picture and bring it back to life?" she asked.

"Yes, I can do that."

"Well, in the picture he's wearing a hat and my grandfather almost never wore a hat. When you redo the picture could you remove the hat?"

"I think I can do that."

"That's wonderful. Let me know when it's ready."

As she was leaving the photographer happened to think of a bit of needed information and called to her, "Oh, by the way, on which side did he part his hair?"

"You can see that when you take his hat off," she said, and went on her way.

Money Matters

The twenty-dollar bill and one-dollar bill were discussing the story of their lives. Twenty-dollar bill bragged about all the exotic places he'd visited, luxury cruises he'd taken, five-star hotels he'd slept in, exclusive golf courses he'd played.

Little one-dollar bill said, "I've had the most boring existence. All my life it's been nothing but go to church, go to church, go to church."

....

One preacher said, "If money talks, my congregation never speaks above a whisper."

Poor Deacons

In order to raise the church budget and knowing where everyone sat, the pastor wired certain pews with electricity controlled by a button at the pulpit. When he asked for $50 pledges, he hit a particular button, the charge in the pew made some jump up and he counted them before they could sit down. The $100 button brought a rise out of some more. He counted them. When he hit the $500 button, he electrocuted four deacons sitting on the front seat.

A Lot-o-Bull

An old man who seldom attended church was sitting second row from the front. When the offering plate passed he dropped in a $100 bill. Everybody was aware that something had happened, so he stood and gave a testimony of explanation.

"This morning," he said, "I went out to separate the bull from the cows. That bull pinned me in a corner, pushed me to the ground, was about to trample me to death, and I promised the Lord, if He'd save me from that mad bull, I'd serve Him the rest of my life!"

He sat down.

A little old lady in the back of the congregation rose and said, "Preacher, I make a motion that we take up an offering, buy that bull, and turn him loose in this church."

....

The baby swallowed a dime, the mother said, "Call 911."

The father said, "Call the preacher, he can get money out of anybody."

....

Which is worse, a singing preacher or a preaching singer? When some preachers sing it is evident they should stick to preaching. One church advertised for a new pastor. Only two qualifications were absolute requirements, he must not sing solos, nor have been to the Holy Land.

If a preacher doesn't do anything really well, he learns to do a little bit of everything, so over the years, I've sung a little and preached a lot. Some folks probably feel sorry for me when they hear me preach and they say, "Can you do anything else?" So I try singing.

IN THE EYES OF THE BEHOLDER

Beauty is only skin deep, but ugly goes all the way to the bone.

"Sing, Honey"

If after hearing me preach for three or four nights they continue insisting that I sing, it brings to mind the boy who married the girl because she had such a beautiful voice and sang so pretty, but she was rather homely, really she was actually ugly.

She was like the girl the fellow described as a two-bagger. He said, "That means you not only put a bag over her head, you put a bag over your head in case her bag breaks."

She could sing pretty. The morning after they were married the night before, he looked over at her with the hair all twisted up in curlers, the face all covered with putty to fill in the cracks, shook his head and sighed, "Sing, Honey, Sing!"

Some folks feel sorry for me when I preach so they say, "Sing, or do something, magic, karate, tricks…whatever."

....

Maybe she just wasn't a beautiful baby and retrogressed from there. One guy said that he was so ugly when he was born, his father asked the doctor, "Is it a boy or girl?"

The doctor said, "No."

Get change back

A couple asked the preacher to perform their wedding cere-mony. After he agreed the young man thought it wise to inquire about the cost.

"How much do you charge?" he asked the preacher.

"Oh, just pay me according to how beautiful you think she is."

Being a poor boy with very little money, he handed a ten dol-lar bill to the preacher who folded it and stuck it in his pocket.

At the end of the ceremony when the groom lifted the veil to kiss the bride, the preacher whispered, "Remind me to give you back your change."

Killing Squirrels

She was uglier than the man who went squirrel hunting without a gun. He uglied them to death. A doubter came through the community and questioned the man's reputation. So they went to the woods to prove his ability. There they found a tall tree with a squirrel sitting on a limb. The ugly man looked at the squirrel. It keeled over dead, dropping to the ground with a thud.

"Unbelievable," said the convinced doubter, "I've never seen nor heard of anything like that before. Have you ever known anyone else who could do that?"

"Oh yeah," said the old man, "My wife can do it, but she had to stop. She was tearing 'em up too bad."

The Beauty Machine

An old man from the hills of Tennesee had never been to a big city until he took a trip to Nashville. He stood amazed in the lobby of a large fancy hotel and for the first time in his life saw an elevator. He watched the door open and an old lady, stooped, gray, wrinkled and decrepit, slowly enter that elevator. The door closed, and in about one minute, that door opened, and the most beautiful young woman you have ever seen came stepping out of that elevator.

He turned to his boy and said, "Son, go get your mama. We're going to run her through that machine."

All of us would look better if we could find that machine.

··········

A fellow asked his wife, "Honey, why did God make you so beautiful, but so dumb?"

"He made me beautiful so you would love me," she said, "and He made me dumb so I would love you."

··········

A young woman came to her pastor and said, "I have a terrible problem with the sin of pride, because every time I look in the mirror, I think of how beautiful I am."

The pastor said, "Well, Honey, that's not a sin….that's just a mistake."

Paying for Her Sins

A pastor, Lonnie Graves, introducing an evangelist, me, who had been in meetings with him for 18 consecutive years, indicating an enduring friendship, began with this tale:

"I dreamed last night that I died and was trying to get into Heaven," he said. "When Saint Peter met me at the gate, he said, 'You may come in, but on one condition. You have not paid for all your sins, some are still on the books. To settle the account you must escort this woman around Heaven for the first 1,000 years.'

"I took one look and couldn't believe my eyes. Ugly isn't the word. Homely wouldn't touch her. The resurrection hadn't helped her at all.

"But I decided that it was better than not getting into Heaven. So I agreed to be her escort for a thousand years.

"We hadn't gone three blocks before we met this evangelist and the most beautiful woman in all of Heaven on his arm. I was upset. I went back to Saint Peter and said, 'Something's wrong. I know I'm not perfect and all that, but that evangelist is not that much better than I am. How come he gets to walk around Heaven with that lovely woman and I'm stuck with this creature?'"

"'Well,'" Saint Peter said. "'That beautiful woman has to pay for her sins too.'"

The great and wonderful truth is that nobody in Heaven has to pay for his sins, nor do penance to satisfy God. Jesus has paid the sin debt in full when He died upon the cross. The only condition for forgiveness is repentance toward God and faith (trust) in the Lord Jesus Christ. That's what Paul told the Ephesian elders at Miletus that he had preached to them and all those in Asia Minor.

MOTHER-IN-LAW FABLES

Behind every successful man, there is a surprised mother-in-law.

....

The mother-in-law had been living with them for ten months, and finally went home. The son-in-law called her on the phone and said, "Mom, it's so miserable here without you; it's as if you had never left."

....

A fellow told his neighbor that for his mother-in-law's fiftieth birthday he bought her a ticket to Hawaii.

"Now, what are you going to do for her sixtieth?" he was asked.

"I'm going to send her a ticket to come back."

Can of Peaches

An older lady accused of shoplifting stood before the judge.

"What did you steal?" he asked.

"A can of peaches."

"Why?"

"I was hungry."

"Did you eat them?"

"Yes."

"How many were there?"

"Six," she said.

"Alright, I am giving you six days in jail, one day for each one of those peaches."

A little shy, intimidated son-in-law stood in the back of the courtroom and said, "Judge, may I say something?"

"Yes."

"She also stole a can of peas."

He wanted her to go away for a long time.

Mixed Emotions

Not everyone is happy when the preacher leaves. Some are sad, and some are somewhere in between glad and sad. Some laugh, others cry. Some have mixed emotions, laughing and crying, like the young man watching his mother-in-law drive his new automobile off the top of a cliff, rejoicing and weeping all at the same time.

He loved the mother-in-law like the young fellow whose mother-in-law died. At the funeral, he was standing beside the casket viewing the corpse, broke down in tears and started weeping. His wife put her arm around him and said, "Well, Honey, you did love Mama a little bit, didn't you?"

"I thought I saw her move," he said.

In A Hurry

The patrolman chased a guy at high speed above 100 mph, and finally got him stopped. The guy met the patrolman at the patrol car, which had pulled in behind him with lights flashing, and said, "You see that woman in the front seat of my car?"

"Yes."

"That's my wife. You see that one in the back seat?"

"Sure."

"That's my mother-in-law. She's been living with us for six months. This morning they had a falling out and I'm trying to get her home before they can make up."

He didn't give him a ticket, gave him an escort.

A Long Fifty Years

At their fiftieth wedding anniversary, the old man was sitting sort of smiling. A friend said, "You must be thinking about how wonderful these 50 years have been."

"Well, not exactly," he said. "I was actually thinking about how it all started. You see, her mother caught the two of us together and threatened me that if I didn't marry her, she would send me to prison for 50 years. And I was just thinking, if I had taken prison, today I'd be a free man."

....

One fellow testifying about his years of married life said, "The Lord gave me a good woman. We lived together 20 happy years and the Lord took her. Then he gave me a second one, and she was a wonderful wife and companion for 15 years and the Lord took her. Now He has given me a third one and we've been together for two years, and the Lord can have her anytime He wants her."

PRESSURE POINTS

A man will do what he thinks he cannot do if he is under pressure.

Doing Fine

The opposing lawyer was cross-questioning the witness about his injuries in an accident.

"Did you not tell the patrolman that you were fine and had no problems?"

"Well, you see I was pulling the trailer with my horse in it behind my pickup, and we came to this…"

"I didn't ask for the history of your life. Just answer my question, yes or no. Did you tell the patrolman you had no problems?"

"We came to this stop light and …"

"Yes or No?"

"I need to explain this, your Honor."

"Oh, let him tell his story," the judge said.

"…We came to this light," the witness continued, "I had the green. This other fellow ran a red light, and hit us so hard, he knocked my horse out of the trailer and me out of the truck.

"This patrolman looked down at my injured horse, called to me and said, 'This poor horse ain't gonna make it. I'm going to put him out of his misery.' He shot him…two times…and came walking up to me with that gun still in his hand and said, 'How are you doing?'"

Fell in a Grave

This guy coming home late one night took a shortcut across the field, through a local graveyard where a grave had been dug and left uncovered in preparation for a burial the next day. In the dark, he stumbled and fell in that open hole in the ground. He jumped, stretched, attempted to climb out, but it was so deep and in the dark he couldn't see how to get out. Unafraid, he settled down in the corner of the grave, knowing that with the coming of daylight, he'd figure a way out. He relaxed and fell off to sleep.

In the deep, dark hours of the night, this other fellow who had been coon hunting, following the dogs, chasing a coon across the field through that same graveyard, stumbled and fell in that same hole in the ground. He was jumping and trying to climb out, and in his floundering around, he woke this other fellow up.

That first guy raised up over in the corner of the grave, laid a hand on the shoulder of the second and said, "Buddy, you can't get out of here."

But he did!

Kiss a Mule

An old prospector in southwest Texas had been panning for gold for days with no luck. Tired, weary, dusty, dirty, and disgusted, he staggered into a little Texas town in the days of the early west. A half-drunk cowboy strutted out of a saloon, laughed at the old man and said, "Old Man, you know how to dance?" and began firing that six gun at the old man's feet.

The old man jumped up and down to miss the bullets and flying rocks while the cowboy had a big laugh and a "Ha! Ha!", stuck his gun back in the holster and turned to walk away, not having noticed that in the meantime that old man had walked around to the other side of his mule, taken a double-barrel shotgun, and when that boy turned around he found himself facing that shotgun aimed at his belt buckle with both hammers pulled back and the old man's finger nervously twitching on the trigger.

The old prospector spit his tobacco juice at the young man's feet, and with a grin, said, "Son, have you ever kissed a mule?"

"Well, no Sir," he said, "but I've always wanted to."

Not too Fast

A young man applying for a job as a deputy sheriff went for the interview. In the interview the sheriff asked him, "Who shot Abraham Lincoln?"

"I don't really know," he answered.

"Go home and think about it. We'll continue this tomorrow."

When he arrived home, his wife inquired about the interview. "How did it go?"

"Great," he said, "I've as good as got the job. They've already put me on a murder case."

She Got the Job

The CIA was in the market for an assassin and was testing candidates. A man came in and the CIA agent handed him a revolver and said, "Your wife is in the next room. Take this gun, go in there and shoot her."

"I can't do that," he said, and walked out.

Another came in. Same proposition, "Take this gun, go into that room and kill your wife."

The fellow took the gun, went into the room, stayed about a minute, came out, and said, "I just can't go through with it, can't do it."

"You don't get the job," replied the agent.

A woman came in, facing the same requirements for the job. The agent gave her the gun. She went into the room. There were the sounds of chairs breaking, tables crashing, like a storm inside that room.

She finally came out, handed him the gun, and said, "You didn't tell me that thing was loaded with blanks. I had to take a chair and beat him to death."

She got the job.

She Didn't Want To

A scout master was preparing the little fellows in his Cub Scout troup for a badge of some kind. To receive the badge each of them was required to do a good deed.

He got them together to question them for the badge and asked the first one, "Have you done your good deed?"

"Yes Sir."

"What did you do?"

"I helped a little old lady across the street."

"That'll work, I guess," the master said, and he asked the second one, "Have you done your good deed?"

"Yes Sir, I helped him help that little old lady across the street."

"Maybe that will count."

He then asked the third one the same question.

"Oh yeah, I helped them help that little old lady across the street."

When the fourth one started, "Yeah, I helped them...."

"Now, wait a minute, Fellows," he said, "It doesn't take four guys to help one little old lady across the street."

"It does, if she don't want to go," he said.

··········

It takes a lot of work to get a guy who doesn't "want to go" to go to church, and equally as much to keep those going who are supposed to "want to go." Keeping folks in church is like loading a wheelbarrow with bullfrogs. Sleep on it. You'll get it.

GOLF-A FOUR LETTER WORD

On The Ball

A beginning golfer, not even amateur, decided to try his hand at hitting a golf ball. He set the tee, placed the ball, adjusted his stance, took a practice swing, addressed the ball and from a long backswing, took his eye off the ball, missed it, and hit an ant hill beside the ball, spattering that ant hill and scattering ants everywhere, most of them dead.

Not to be defeated, he took aim a second time with the same result, hit the same ant hill, killing more of them.

The third time he hit that ant hill, he had killed all the little ants but two. With the wind whirling and sand flying, one of those little ants looked at the other one, blinked his eyes, and said, "Buddy, if we're going to stay alive, we'd better get on the ball."

It takes time, dedication, and commitment to become a good golfer. Those who follow the sport know very well.

Drag John

One such golfer went out early in the morning to play a round. He finished as the sun was going down. When he came to the clubhouse exhausted, a friend asked, "How many holes did you play?"

"Oh, just 18," he said.

"Only 18 and you've been out there all day? What on earth took you so long?"

"On the second hole this morning, John had a heart attack and died, and all day it's been, hit the ball and drag John…hit the ball and drag John…."

Wedding's Off

A young man was standing on the first tee, waiting his turn to tee off, when a limousine sped up, stopped, a young woman dressed in her bridal gown rushed up to him and said, "They're waiting at the church, wondering what has happened to you."

"I said 'IF IT RAINED.'"

Bad Grip

Two fellows took their wives for a round of golf…a foursome. The women were standing on the ladies' tee on the right side of the fairway. When the first guy teed off, he hit a bad slice. The ball hit his wife in the side of her head knocking her unconscious. The men ran over to where she lay on the ground – out cold. The friend looked at the husband and said, "What are you going to do about it?"

"I'm going to change my grip," he said. "I'm going to turn my hands this way."

Commitment and dedication are necessary ingredients for success in any field.

BIBLE STORIES
Milking Bears

At a leadership conference in Nashville, Millard Sasser told this story.

A mountain preacher, or he may have been from the flat country, couldn't read very well and his understanding of what he read was often a misunderstanding. He was reading the passage in Genesis 22 about Abraham's brother, Nahor, and his family. The verse says, "...these eight Milcah did bear to Nahor, Abraham's brother" (Genesis 22:23). He came up with "these eight milk-a-de-bear for Nahor."

"Now I don't know much about milking bears," he said. "But I think there's a good sermon in that verse."

"You see, the first thing it takes to milk a bear is conviction. You've got to really believe that bear needs milking. 'Cause bears don't give much milk and there ain't no market for it, and besides that, the job ain't easy. If you ain't convinced that this bear's gotta be milked, you ain't goin' to all that trouble.

"The second thing it takes is consecration. It's going to cost you something. 'Cause you gotta face the jaws, the paws, and the claws. Milking bears ain't no pushover job. If you ain't willing to pay the price you won't milk no bear!

"The third thing it takes is cooperation. I reckon it does say it took eight men to milk that bear. Ain't no one man can milk a bear by hisself. He needs a whole bunch of help. It takes at least eight good men to milk any average size bear."

He misunderstood the text, but it is a good sermon. In fact, it is so good I used his outline in the sermon I preached at the National Convention in 1985, as the essentials for *Realizing our Potential.* Whether you're milking bears, planning a union evangelistic meeting, or involved in a work of any sort, these are the elements necessary for success.

Wrong Ark

One preacher read about the construction of the ark by Noah in Genesis, chapter 6, and said, "I have no problem with Noah building that thing, 450 feet long, 75 feet wide, and 45 feet tall, with the window around the top; after all he had 120 years to work on it. What I have never been able to figure out is how the children of Israel carried that thing on their shoulders all over the land of Canaan."

A Modern Version

A little boy, after a junior Sunday school class, came home to face his dad's question, "What did you learn today in Sunday school?"

"Learned about Moses and the children of Israel escaping from Egypt by crossing the Red Sea," he answered.

"And how did it happen?" the follow-up question.

"Well, you see, they really came up against it. Their escape route was blocked, the Red Sea was in front of them, and the armies of Egypt were in hot pursuit. So Moses called for air support and a helicopter gunship showed up. He radioed for artillery bombardment and those shells began to fall on the Egyptian army. Then he called the army engineers who came and laid down a pontoon bridge across the Red Sea, and after the children of Israel crossed the bridge, they blew it up with the Egyptian army on it, and destroyed them in the sea."

"Now, back up," his father said. "Start that over. Are you sure that's what your teacher said?"

"Well, not exactly. But if I told it like she told it, you wouldn't believe a word of it."

What God Looks Like

The five-year-old was on the floor under the table busy drawing things. "What are you doing?" inquired his mother.

"I'm drawing a picture of God," he said.

"Oh, you can't do that. Nobody knows what God looks like."

He said, "They will in a minute."

Wrong Joshua

A judge looked down at the defendant and said, "Joshua, is that your name?"

"Yes Sir."

"Are you the Joshua that made the sun stand still?" asked the judge.

"No Sir. I is the Joshua that made the moonshine."

A BOY'S EYE VIEW

When I was a child, I spake as a child, I understood as a child, I thought as a child…(I Corinthians 13:1).

When the father finished picking up the toys left scattered in the den by his little boy, he said that he had found a new application of Paul's statement, *"…when I became a man I put away childish things."*

....

Mama had cooked his favorite pie. He'd eaten three pieces and was begging for the fourth. "No more pie," she said.

"Please…one more little, tiny piece…"

"If you eat one more piece of pie, you'll burst wide open."

With a sparkle in his eye he said, "Mama, you just pass the pie and get out of the way."

....

With another little guy it was cake. Having eaten all the supper he could hold, he announced his abated appetite, "I'm full up to my neck."

"Too bad," said his mother, "I have baked a cake."

"What do you think I saved my neck for?"

The Flight to Egypt

There's the one that drew the nativity scene with an airplane and a little fat man prominent in the picture. When the teacher asked about these unusual parts of the picture, he explained that the fat man was "round John Virgin" and the plane was Mary, Joseph, and the Babe on their flight to Egypt.

He also thought that when the shepherds came and found Mary and Joseph and the Babe lying in the manger, it must have been a little crowded.

The Bicycle

A nine-year-old wanted a bicycle with no possible way of obtaining one, no money to buy it, and was afraid to steal it. Someone suggested, "Why don't you write Jesus a letter and ask Him for one?"

As a last resort, in his desperation, he decided to try that. He began the letter: Dear Jesus, I've been a good boy and …. He stopped and thought, no, that won't work. He knows better than that.

He tore that letter up, began again: Dear Jesus, I've tried to do right most of the time … stopped again. He knows everything in the world. I'm not going to fool Him. This isn't going to work.

He decided to go down the street to the church and ask a preacher about it. As he went into the vestibule of a Catholic church, he noticed a small statue of Mary in the corner. He took the statue while nobody was watching, ran home, hid it in his closet under some old clothes, and went back to write his letter:

Dear Jesus, he began, I've gotcha Mama.

Too bad, God can't be blackmailed, bribed, hired, bought off, nor obligated.

Big Trouble

Two little brothers in a Christian school were in trouble all the time over their mischief. Exasperated, the teacher sent them to the principal's office for discipline. While the older brother went in to face the judge, the younger sat in the secretary's office watching the fish swim around in the tank.

The principal approached the problem with a serious question, "Son, tell me. Where is God?"

"I don't know," was his answer.

"Well, you go home. Think about it. Come back tomorrow and we'll talk about it."

The little guy left and as they walked down the hall, his little brother asked, "What happened? What'd he say?"

"Little Brother, we're in big trouble this time. They've lost God and think we had something to do with it."

Lost His Dog

A boy stood on a street corner with a dog for sale.

"How much?" asked a neighbor.

"$500."

"You'll never get that. He ain't worth it," he called back over his shoulder as he passed on down the street.

The next day that same neighbor came by and the dog was gone.

"Did you sell the dog?"

"Yeah, I sold him."

"You didn't get $500."

"Yep, I did. I had to sell him on credit. By the way, what's a steward in the Methodist Church?"

"Oh, that's about the same as a deacon in a Baptist Church."

"Uh oh, I've lost my dog."

....

Another little guy wanted $500 for his dog, was told he'd never get it and after the sale a man asked him if he got his $500.

"Oh yeah," he said, "I had to take two $250 cats on a trade-in."

Keep Pulling that Rope

The preacher bought an old lawn mower from a little boy and was trying to crank it. He worked and struggled with it to no avail. It just wouldn't start.

"What do you do to start this thing?" he asked the boy who was silently watching.

"You gotta cuss it first," he said.

"Son, I stopped cursing years ago."

"You keep pulling that rope. It'll come back to you."

Discipline and self control are more difficult under certain circumstances.

SPOONERISMS

The father of all tang tonglers was Professor William A. Spooner (1844-1930) of Oxford University in England. His reputation of repeatedly, accidentally switching the first syllable of words and forming different words was so widespread that a new word was added to the English dictionary identifying the practice as 'Spoonerisms.'

He told an absentee student, "You hissed my mistery class." At the conclusion of a wedding, "It is kistomary to cuss the bride." He supposedly had two favorite songs, *God Save the Weasel* and *Pop Goes the Queen*. He was a Baptist minister and very intelligent, so the problem became a sign of intelligence, not idiocy.

Most speakers at one time or another have tangled the words, confusing the audience, who roared with laughter, looking at each other with a *what-was-that-he-said* expression.

··········

The nervous usher was given the responsibility of asking a lady to move from a seat reserved for someone else. He approached with fearful jitters and said, "Mardon me padam, this pie is occupewed. May I sew you to another sheet?"

··········

Fear may be a contributing factor between the brain and the tongue. A fellow who was held up on the street, scared almost to death, came running up to a policeman and said, "Occifer, Occifer, I was siding on the standwalk, cigging on a big smogar, and up walked a gun with a man on it, that said, 'Hand over your brains, Buddy, or I'll blow your money out!'"

··········

A tramp in New York City stumbled into the back door of a theatre looking for a job. He was given a bit part in a play, and was supposed to run out on the stage and say, "I thought I heard a pistol shot. Who fired that shot?"

When he ran on the stage the lights blinded him, the crowd stunned him. He stood speechless for a moment, and said, "I thought I heard a shistol pot, a shostol pit, who shired that pot? – Oh shoot, I'm fired."

Prinderella

Over 40 years ago, at Youth Camp in South Carolina, Benny Turner entertained the junior campers with a William Spooner version of Cinderella, and it was hilarious. All of us kids laughed to tears and no question in my mind, I was going to memorize that thing. That night on a bunk in a cabin, I put together most of it. The next week he repeated it to the teenagers, and that second time all the blank spots fell into place. Never having read it, nor seen it written, it will surely lose something in print. It is made for telling, not reading – for the ear, not the eye:

Once upon a time in a coreign fountry there lived a geautiful birl named Prinderella. She lived with her mugly other and two sad blisters. In that same coreign fountry there lived a pransom hince. One day the pransom hince decided he'd have a bancy fall, and Prinderella's mugly other and two sad blisters went out and bought some dancy fresses and went to the bancy fall. But Prinderella couldn't go, 'cause all she had to wear were rirty dags.

So while the mugly other and sad blisters went to the bancy fall, Prinderella stayed home. She was just citting home srying, citting there srying when suddenly her mairy godfother appeared and touched her with her wagic mand. There suddenly appeared a cig boach and hix sorses. So Prinderella went to the bancy fall.

When she arrived, the pransom hince met her at the door 'cause he'd been watching through a widden hindow as she got out of that cig boach with the hix sorses. They nanced all dight, just nanced all dight. And while they were nancing all dight he lell in fove with Prinderella. They always lall in fove in these tairy fales! He was about to quop the prestion when suddenly the mlock struck cidnight and Prinderella staced down the rairs and when she reached the stottom bep, she slopped her dripper.

The next day that pransom hince went all through his coreign fountry looking for that geautiful birl that had slopped her dripper. When he came to Prinderella's house, he tried it on her mugly other and it fid'nt dit. He tried it on her two sad blisters and it fid'nt dit. But when he tried it on Prinderella, it fid dit, and they were mappily harried and lived heppily aver efter.

This has served as a wonderful attention-getter, and mind opener to tell young people a true Cinderella story. The King of Heaven sent His Son, the Prince of Life, into this world. That Prince came and chose a bride from among the poor, ragged, outcast, unloved, unwanted beggars of humanity. He chose her (the spiritual church) to unite Himself with her and take her with Him into His Father's Kingdom, to reign with Him forever. This Prince received the poor, the lame, the helpless, the thieves, the harlots, the prostitutes, the tax collectors, the social and religious outcasts and said to the arrogant, pious, proud, religious devotees, that these outcasts "go into the kingdom ahead of you."

This is no fairy tale. This is a real love story. The Cinderellas of this world who come by faith are united with the Prince of Heaven, the Lord Jesus.

NO LAUGHING MATTER

...and that's not funny.

There is a time to laugh. There is also a time when laughter is impossible. The self-destructive nature of humor makes it impossible for a man's deep, real, inner relationship with God to be humorous lest that relationship disappear. When Sarah laughed in her unbelief at the announcement that she would bear a son in her old age, the promise to her was meaningless, vaporized into thin air.

Many years later as Abraham made his way up the mountain to kill Isaac, there was no humor in the experience.

Humor may cause the serious to vanish into frivolity. Laugh at that which poses itself to be serious, but it really isn't. The experience and relationship with God is life's most serious matter, never to be laughed at. That is not, and cannot ever be, funny.

BROTHER MODERATOR

After finishing a meeting in Midland, Texas, in the summer of 1965, Jane, the boys, and I drove to Monterrey, Mexico to visit with missionary Arthur Billows, preach in some of the Free Will Baptist churches, do a little sightseeing, and relax for a few days. While there, a phone call came from a pastor friend in Norfolk, Virginia.

"Are you going to the National?" was the question.

"Hadn't planned to. We are in Monterrey enjoying some time off."

"You need to come. It's important. W. S. Mooneyham is giving up the moderator's job, and a group of pastors want to place your name in nomination. We think you can be elected and could fill a need in the denomination."

"Having given no thought to such a matter, I will think about it, and if you fellows have prayed about it and are convinced I should be there, we'll cut this time short in Mexico and plan to attend."

The National Association was meeting in Raleigh, North Carolina, so we headed in that direction.

The Election

At the convention the group met, we talked, and I agreed if it were the Lord's will and the delegates elected me I would serve to the best of my ability.

Democrats and Republicans could learn something about political maneuvering from a religious convention. It was immediately evident that those in charge had other plans for a moderator, so my nomination would come from the floor, not the nominating committee appointed by the present moderator. Furthermore, the powers-that-be picked up on the possibility of such a nomination, and "W. S." was smarter than the group. His nominating committee nominated Wayne Smith from North Carolina for assistant moderator, which would be elected before the moderator in the order of electing general officers, with the confidence that the convention would not elect both moderator and assistant from the same state, specifically North Carolina.

Time came to elect officers at the close of the business session. Dr. Robert Picirilli was serving as clerk and was nominated for reelection, highly praised by W. S. as the most knowledgeable, efficient assistant in expediting the procedures in a parliamentary fashion, and was elected unanimously. The assistant moderator was elected with no opposition. The committee placed in nomination for moderator O. T. Dixon, a fine pastor/evangelist from the Ozarks of Missouri and Arkansas. From the floor someone nominated Bobby Jackson, who immediately stood and withdrew his name, and placed instead the name of Dr. Robert Picirilli for moderator. Picirilli consented to serve if elected. With all the qualifications attributed to him by the moderator, the assembly elected Picirilli, who gave six years of exceptional service presiding at the National Convention.

Six years later, when Picirilli had fished that stream out and decided to pass the gavel, Dr. J. D. O'Donnell was assistant moderator. This time the nominating committee appointed by Picirilli placed my name in nomination for moderator. When election time rolled around, Richard Cordell nominated Dr. O'Donnell from the floor, noting and rightly so, that he had served as assistant and was in line for promotion to be the presiding officer. The assembly agreed and elected Dr. O'Donnell as moderator. This meant giving up his position as assistant moderator, to which he had just been reelected, leaving that office open.

Someone from the floor nominated me for assistant moderator, the majority agreed, and I was elected.

Need a testimony to the openness of the National Convention? Try this. Three general officers, two moderators and one assistant elected from nominations from the floor instead of those nominated by the nominating committee.

Executive Committee

Elected assistant moderator in 1971, as such, I served on the Executive Committee of the General Board for the next six years. The committee met twice each year. In December they met to plan the program for the next convention, decide on a general theme with subtopics for speakers, select preachers, attempting to spread the privilege and responsibility around among the vast variety that make up the denomination, giving preference to those who had never preached to the National body, leaving the committee open for criticism, seeing as how it was impossible to define what good preaching was.

In 1970, a motion came to the floor to instruct the program committee to select two speakers with college education and two without and all must be Free Will Baptists. The next year a motion was presented that no person speak, nor preside at the convention more than once until everyone had been given an equal opportunity. The delegates decided not to put such restrictions on the committee. Both motions lost.

In July, on Friday and Saturday before the convention they met to consider any matters referred to the committee by the General Board or Convention, make a decision, and prepare their report.

During the convention proceedings the assistant modera- · tor sat on the platform in a conspicuous place waiting for his moment in the spotlight to display his extraordinary knowledge of parliamentary procedure by presiding over the final item of business, taking the vote on the reelection of the moderator.

In 1973, a proposal from the General Board passed that the Executive Committee of the General Board be composed of the general officers plus six other members elected from the board by the National Association, three members elected each year from those whose terms begin that year to serve for two-year terms. Prior to this, the committee consisted of officers plus four members elected by the board. Changing this procedure opened the Executive Committee to the entire assembly to some degree decentralizing the selection of the committee and enlarging it to nine members.

During those years, however, there was enough controversy to keep life on the committee from ever being dull.

Modesty, standards, dress, and hair length for youth participation were on the agenda regularly. A resolution from the floor in 1973 that ladies refrain from wearing to the services of the National Association slacks, pant suits, and other apparel that pertains to a man. It was debated, amended, and lost.

Christian School Mandate

The *Christian School Mandate* surfaced at the convention in 1976. It had been circulating below the surface for sometime. The controversial position simply stated was that God's command to His people to teach their children included boycotting public schools and sending them to a Christian school. Failure to do this was disobeying God. It would naturally follow that those who taught in public schools were disobedient, along with those who attended secular universities for graduate degrees.

The resolution was amended to insert the word "some" before every reference to public schools, and to add a fourth resolve: "That we encourage our people who remain in public schools to be involved in the program and direction of our schools, to call our people back to God, striving to elect public officials who are Christian." Adoption of this amended resolution was evidence that most of the people were not ready to take the "mandate" position on the matter, so the controversy continued with Free Will Baptist Bible College caught up in it, since most of the educational department didn't embrace the "mandate."

At the time, one pastor of that persuasion assured me that everything anyone needed to know could be learned from the Bible at a Christian school.

That depends upon what one needs to know. One cannot learn from the Bible nor from a typical Christian school how to take out an infected appendix before it ruptures. Maybe man doesn't need to know that energy equals mass times the speed of light squared. Most of the knowledge of this physical universe is outside the Bible, and most Christian schools have not yet reached that level of academic instruction, someday maybe. So if a student pursues studies in medicine, he'll likely be forced to go to a school that doesn't profess to be Christian.

Years later that preacher approached me at a conference and simply said, "You were right."

More years later, long after my time of service to the Association had passed, a fellow preacher came to me with the question, "Are you the national evangelist who said that Dann Patrick didn't know anything about literature?"

"I don't think so. Dann and I have never discussed literature. We've never talked about the subject."

"I was just wondering," he said, "if you were the one he had in mind that day at Fuquay when he held up a book and said, 'I don't care what a national evangelist said about Dann Patrick not knowing anything about literature! I know this is trash.'"

I don't remember ever discussing literature, nor any particular book, nor writer, with Dann.

Some more time passed and when the matter would come to mind, I racked my brain trying to figure it out. Memory kept searching that hard drive until one day it found the material, cleared it up, and moved it to the waste basket.

In 1980, when Richard Cordell was not reelected to the Bible College board, although he was eligible to serve another six-year term, a phone call came after the Convention from Richard, who was in revival with Frank Davenport, Faith Church, Goldsboro, NC, asking me to meet him at Bum's Restaurant, Ayden, NC, at 2:00 p.m. for coffee and fellowship. Richard was a good friend. He had used me for revival meetings in all the churches he pastored.

Knowing the get-together was not for coffee only, but to discuss denominational problems, I was glad for the opportunity. Richard, Frank Davenport, Richard Hendrix, Frank's assistant pastor, and I met and spent most of the afternoon in honest discussion and sometimes friendly disagreement.

"Won't you agree that the Bible College promoted a political campaign to get me off that board?" Richard asked.

"I don't honestly know. No one from the college ever came to me with the proposal to get you off the board. Your friends approached me with the idea that they wanted you on the board. No one from the college ever mentioned it. If however, you looked around when the vote was taken, you must have noticed that those from the college didn't vote for you. Evidently, they didn't want you on the board."

"If I had stayed on that board there would have been a house cleaning in the teaching staff and administration. Some of those teachers need to be fired. Ken Riggs is an educational liberal. Mary Ruth Wisehart is liberal."

"Now, Richard, I don't know anything about education, never studied various educational philosophies, never taught a class in high school nor college, but if I wanted to discuss education with all of its controversial ideas, I'd probably go talk to Ken Riggs. He has a doctorate in the field and has spent his life in it, and probably knows more about education than you or I either one.

"And if I wanted to learn something about literature, since I'm not very widely read in that area, I'd probably go to Mary Ruth, who has a doctorate in that field and has spent her life reading and teaching, and probably knows more about literature than you or I or Dann Patrick."

Why Dann's name came into that mix, nobody knows, other than he was an outspoken advocate of the mandate position, Richard's close friend, and a part of the five-man majority on the nine-man board that, according to Richard, was planning the house cleaning.

When this little get-together at Bum's Restaurant came back to mind, the cloud lifted, and the smoke cleared. The basis for Dann's comment, if he made the comment, might have been that conversation. Someone could have told Dann that I said he knew nothing about literature. What I said was that Mary Ruth knew more than Dann or I about literature, classifying myself along with Dann somewhere below the more advanced scholars. The reference was more general than personal. No effort has ever been made to clear up the misunderstanding. Such an effort would probably leave the matter more clouded and make it worse. That sleeping dog has been left lying.

Having not heard the comment, and not knowing the point of reference, this assumption is as close as I could get to an answer. If Dann made the reference, he knows whom he had in mind and the source of his information.

Therefore, in answer to the man's question, I should have said, "I don't know. The only person who knows what was in Dann's mind is Dann. Go ask him."

This is simply a testimony that the "Christian School Mandate" was a problem for the college.

Inspiration Position

The *King James Only* issue had not yet become a very widespread controversy. In 1976, delegates adopted a resolution that:

Whereas many modern translations cause confusion, and are not reliable and trustworthy, we urge our people to use the King James Version of the Bible in public services.

This matter would later become more of a problem among evangelicals and fundamentalists.

The next year a very strong statement on inspiration and inerrancy was adopted and included in the treatise, with the general understanding that the position was in reference to original manuscripts, and not a translation, although that question never came up.

A resolution to recommend not ordaining divorced and remarried men passed in 1976.

Elected Moderator

In Detroit, in 1977, Dr. J. D. O'Donnell stepped down after six years as moderator and, as was done in 1971, the assistant moderator was moved into the moderator's position. Melvin Worthington was elected assistant.

In expressing appreciation for the confidence of the body and promising to preside fairly and to the best of my ability over the convention, in jest I prophesied a true prophecy.

"You folks have delivered me from one of the 'woes' warnings of Jesus, "Woe unto you when all men speak well of you..." (Luke 6:26). Referees are necessary, but they don't win popularity trophies. The middle of the road is a dangerous place.

Two qualifications make for a good moderator, a thorough detailed knowledge of the constitution and by-laws under which the organization functions, and faithfully observing the general rules of parliamentary procedure when presiding over the conducting of business.

After more than 15 years, that college course in *Parliamentary Law,* taught by Dr. Laverne Miley, had some purpose other than two hours credit on an English Minor, fulfilling the requirements for entering graduate school with no undergraduate deficiencies. Those five basic principles in that textbook on *Parliamentary Law* by Hall and Sturgis are the foundation upon which the structure of motions and rules are built:

1. Only one subject may claim the attention of the assembly at one time. Individuals have a one-track mind and it requires effort to keep it on track.

2. Each proposition presented for consideration is entitled to full and free debate. All sides have a right to be heard.

3. Every member has rights equal to those of every other member. This is democracy in a country or an assembly.

4. The will of the majority must be carried out, and the rights of the minority must be preserved. As in a democracy so it is in an assembly, a member, in return for his privilege of voting agrees to abide by and carry out the decision made by the majority. The minority always has a right to be heard on every proposition.

5. The personality and desires of each member should be merged into the larger unit of the organization. When an

individual attempting to carry out his own ideas and wishes opposes the desires of others without considering the best interest of the assembly as a whole, it creates discord and difficulty for the assembly to function. When an individual acts as a member of a group, he should act with that group in the way decided by majority. He is a part of a team and should use his ability to execute the maneuvers of the team as a unit, not in a way to make himself a star. (*Textbook on Parliamentary Law*, by Alta B. Hall and Alice F. Sturgis, copyright, 1923 by the MacMillan Company, NY)

Number five is the most difficult to achieve but absolutely necessary if the organization is to continue without division and complete disintegration.

A "Liberal" Among Us

In Kansas City, in 1978, first year as moderator, number five was tested. News had reached North Carolina that there was a pastor in Texas who was known to be a theological liberal, and some of the North Carolina brethren could not bear the thought of being in an organization with that preacher. Since the National Association of Free Will Baptists is an association of associations and as such has no disciplinary authority over preachers nor local churches, the only action possible to rid itself of a preacher would be to deal with the state association, of which the local association is a member, of which the local church is a member, of which the preacher is a member.

That state association was Texas. And since seating of the delegates is the first item of business, the controversy opened the convention. A recommendation came from the North Carolina State Association that the Texas State delegates not be seated. The General Board's recommendation that the delegates be seated and the Credentials Committee look into the matter and report to them at the 1979 meeting was adopted. The Credentials Committee met with the Texas delegation and North Carolina brethren until 2:00 a.m. attempting to solve the problem to the satisfaction of both.

The Texans explained that the matter was in the hands of a local association. They were not aware of all the details, but assured the North Carolina brethren the matter would be resolved before the next National. They were not sure of the man's theology. It had been reported that he said that the Bible was not the objective Word of God lying on the table, but became the Word of God when subjectively applied by the Spirit in the life of the individual, which sounded more like some form of Neo-orthodoxy than classical liberalism. Waiting a year to deal with it didn't satisfy some of the brethren.

One of them suggested, "We're killing snakes and that's dangerous and not easy. Snakes don't want to die."

"Preacher," I said, "if there's a snake in the middle of Manhattan, you can drop an atomic bomb on him and that will sure kill the snake. But you'll do a lot less damage if you can kill him with a hoe. We're dropping H-Bombs on mosquitoes."

The personal promise from each one of the men from Texas that he would see to it that the one in question would be examined for doctrinal heresy and properly dealt with in his local church and association within the next year, satisfied the North Carolina brethren who agreed to drop their objection to seating Texas delegates. The meeting ended in the wee hours of the morning. We all slept three or four hours, the Credentials Committee reported to the convention Wednesday afternoon that the charges against Texas were unfounded and the matter was settled.

Scouting

The recommendation from the General Board to combine the Church Training Service (CTS) with the Sunday School (SS) under one board and department was adopted.

The CTS board recommended scouting as an activity churches could use in their youth programs. In the heated discussion, objection was raised because some Boy Scout leaders had been found to be homosexual. It was explained that the program was to be patterned after the Southern Baptist scouting, not the Boy Scouts. Some of the objectors wanted nothing to do with Southern Baptists.

In the heat of the debate in a spontaneous outburst, came one of those never-to-be-forgotten quotes that everyone, including the speaker wants to forget, "I'd rather be associated with a pervert than a Southern Baptist." Laughter indicated that no one took him seriously. Those who remember laugh even louder now. His sons are ministering in Southern Baptist churches, and it didn't break up the family.

So the matter was killed by a motion to table.

Electing Executive Secretary

In Charlotte, in 1979, Rufus Coffey resigned as Executive Secretary. Melvin Worthington was nominated by the nominating committee and elected in a close race with a nominee that was nominated from the floor. The General Board proposed that the entire procedure be changed and the Executive Committee serve as a search and nominating committee, with the convention voting on that candidate with no nominations from the floor. If voted down the committee would bring another candidate, and when elected his term of service be indefinite with a ninety day notice of resignation. After much discussion the recommendation lost by a motion to table even though this procedure was commonly used by churches in securing pastors.

A motion was adopted to refer the matter to the Executive Committee for further study and report back in 1980. That report recommending the time of service to be an indefinite period was adopted the next year.

This was the second time an effort to change election procedure had failed. In 1974 and 1975, the fear of centralized authority and misunderstanding shot it down. However, years later when the time came to find another Executive Secretary, people saw the reason and the wisdom, and changed the procedure.

Meet Every Two Years

Every now and then talk circulated about changing the National to every two years. In 1979, after a lot of whereases the resolution came up again that the Association convene on a two-year basis and the General Board handle any business in the non-convening years.

If every pastor, missionary, department head, and delegate had paid his own way out of pocket, the suggestion may have at least got off the ground for discussion. However, since for most, it was an all-expense-paid affair, the question not only never got off the ground, it never moved to the runway, never left the terminal, never started the engine, DOA, voted down with little discussion.

At election time Melvin Worthington moved to Executive Secretary and Eugene Waddell replaced him as assistant moderator.

At the semi-annual meeting of the Executive Committee in December, the new Executive Secretary's first item of business was the provision in the Treatise to pay the moderator's way to the convention.

Melvin suggested, "It says 'to' the convention, not 'from.'"

The men thought he was being facetious, responding with a little laughter, but when he appeared to be serious, it became hilarious. A one-way ticket? Where was he to go at the end of the convention? That comp room wasn't available for six months. He could hitchhike, thumb, or jog. The self-destructive element of humor kicked in, vaporizing any disagreement. When the committee explained to Melvin that it had always been under-stood that "way to" meant pay his traveling expenses to attend the National Convention, he agreed, seeing as how he was on an unlimited expense account every day to everywhere and back, plus the provision of a department car.

Traditionally, every ten years at the turn of the decade the convention landed on the West Coast. In 1980, it was Anaheim, California.

Among other business, the charter for the Free Will Baptist Foundation was approved, a committee was appointed to make plans for the Golden Anniversary in Nashville in 1985, resolution passed to clean up TV, and on Thursday morning, a resolution was presented from the floor that the standards code concern-ing hair, dress, etc., be applied to the entire national convention. Motion to amend to apply it to program personalities, including ushers and musicians, and after much discussion, disagreement and different positions the matter was tabled.

Atlantic Canada Association

Three representatives from the Primitive Baptist Denomination, New Brunswick, Canada, met with the Executive Committee and the General Board. A letter was read from this group officially requesting affiliation with the National Association of Free Will Baptists, and thus becoming the Atlantic Canada Association of Free Will Baptists.

We recommended the acceptance of this association into the fellowship of the National Association of Free Will Baptists as the Atlantic Canada Association of Free Will Baptists.

This item, number one, from the General Board was adopted in 1981, and many of my friends in New Brunswick, whom I had known, preached to, and fellowshipped with for 20 years were now a part of the Free Will Baptist denomination.

Eugene Waddell accepted the responsibility of Associate Director of the Foreign Missions Department, leaving the office of assistant moderator open to which Ralph Hampton was elected.

The most encouraging and exciting business of the convention in 1981 was welcoming my New Brunswick friends into the Free Will Baptist family.

Wine

The wine controversy started at the college in Nashville, travelled across town to the Foreign Missions Department, took flight over the Atlantic to mission fields in Spain and France, caught a return flight to the U.S., and landed on the floor of the National Convention in Fort Worth, Texas, in 1982.

A sincere student with no ulterior motive asked Leroy Forlines, a professor at the Bible College, an honest question, "Was wine in the Bible fermented, especially in the New Testament, more specifically in John 2? Was there alcohol in the wine Jesus made at the wedding in Cana?"

"Wine in the Bible was evidently fermented," he said. But that did not change his position of total abstinence. He made it clear that based upon principles given in the Bible to direct our lives, he practiced and taught total abstinence.

That answer was funneled at the speed of light, by some student in the class who heard it, to an element of the denomination already at war with the school over Christian education, "standards," and ministerial leadership philosophy, who had raised the "mandate" flag which didn't fly very high, because there was too much sympathy for public schools throughout the denomination. The standards flag left so much to the application of the principles of modesty that it was difficult to identify, and it was taken down and raised again over and over, changing color and design each time.

Word began to circulate among the college critics that this wine issue was something to hang them with, a flag that would fly, a red cape of alcohol to be waved before the bull of total abstinence. They were confident there would be an uprising when people learned that a professor at the college believed Jesus was a bootlegger and a drunkard.

The fermentation professor met with leaders of the grape juice group hoping to explain his position on the difference between that wine and modern wines and that he believed in total abstinence, and to bring them to a place of toleration, if not agreement. He left the meeting thinking he had accomplished his purpose, being told by some that they could live with his position. Then he heard that word was being spread that he believed Jesus was a bootlegger.

Like a contagious disease, the virus spread rapidly to the Foreign Missions Department. From there a strong west wind carried it across the Atlantic with the first infection appearing in Spain, where a senior missionary scheduled to conduct a wedding for one of the young men in his church, reneged upon learning that wine would be served by the bride's family at the wedding supper in another location after the ceremony. He not only backed out, but ordered a younger, more recently arrived couple to have nothing to do with the wedding. The wife-half of the younger couple was on program to sing in the wedding and they thought it best to keep the commitment, so she sang, making them guilty of two sins. They not only compromised on the wine issue, they disobeyed the senior missionary who immediately insisted that they be fired and returned to the states.

The director of the department refused, and the board supported his position, making every effort to resolve the conflict by going to the field and attempting to work out a compromise that would bring harmony to the work in Spain. By the time the matter reached the National body there were those who pushed to replace the board and fire the director.

When the National did not go along with that demand, the older missionary resigned and one of his friends on the National floor left this bit of wisdom, "The only thing that works under a board is a worm."

It is interesting that some of the same fellows were convinced that the Bible College Board, which they controlled, had the authority to fire professors teaching at the college.

The senior missionary returned to Spain under different sponsorship. The younger couple continued to work there under the Missions Board.

From Spain to France, with accusations coming that some missionaries in France were weak on enforcing the total abstinence position of the Church Covenant, giving rise to a group of "Covenant Contenders" who met several times to promote their position against drinking wine, or fellowshipping with those who do.

Interesting again, when the National settled its position by reaffirming the Covenant statement concerning the use of intoxicating beverages, that didn't satisfy the "Covenant Contenders" who came back with a resolution to fire every employee and board member who believed Jesus made or drank wine.

During the heat of the debate, the brother of the young missionary in Spain asked one of the contentious contenders or conscientious contenders (depending on your point of view), "This is not a question of whether Jesus made fermented wine. The question is, Did Jesus attend a wedding where fermented wine was being served?"

The evident answer stuck in the throat of the questionee. The questioner is still waiting for the answer.

The structure of the National made it necessary and inevitable that the controversy must be settled by the voting delegation of the Association. Various boards are elected by the Association and charged with overseeing certain ministries. Their reported decisions and budgets are subject to the approval of the body, and may be rescinded by that body. Whatever those boards decided as to hiring and firing could be called into question. It would be very unusual, but had the college board of trustees voted five to four to fire a professor, the National could vote to rescind that action and reinstate him.

The matter reached the General Board in letters from California, North Carolina, Virginia, New Mexico, South Carolina, Alabama, and others which were referred to the Resolutions Committee. The committee presented a resolution that a seven-man study commission of people representing various viewpoints be appointed and report their findings and recommendations to the 1983 session. The resolution lost by being tabled.

A second resolution was presented that pressured the body to settle the issue without delay. After long and heated debate, with many efforts to amend by changing words and phrases, a motion was made to amend by substitution, offering another resolution to replace the one before the body.

That was the day a superior parliamentarian from the west called the moderator out of order for allowing two motions to be discussed at one time. I drew him a picture. The main motion being A, a motion to amend by substituting B for A is one motion including A and B, one to be substituted for the other. The reason both are included in the motion and open for debate is, if the amendment is adopted A is defeated and replaced by B, which then becomes the main motion. The assembly is deciding which of these, A or B, it prefers, so the pros and cons of both must be open to debate.

He never saw it. Nothing to be frustrated about, I'm perfectly willing for him to go on believing the moderator was out of order. When a man looks at a circle and says it's square, draw three or four more circles for him. If he continues to see squares, don't get frustrated by attempting to change his mind. He'll go on seeing squares. His will is affecting his perception. The world will go on turning. Let him live and die believing a circle is square. But don't hire him to teach geometry. That was part of the wine problem, pasteurizing wine before Louis Pasteur (1822-1895).

The substitute motion:

Whereas these concerns have evoked various state and/or local groups to pass resolutions of concerns sent to this body, and

Whereas, all the parties involved in the wine issue have declared their belief in teetotalism and wholly condemn the use of any form of alcoholic beverages, and

Whereas, to attempt to agree on the interpretation of all scriptural references to wine would only lead to divisiveness, and

Whereas, all parties involved in the wine issue believe that Jesus Christ was absolutely sinless:

Be it therefore resolved that this body re-commit itself to the statement on alcoholic beverages found in our church covenant, and that such statement be accepted as an adequate answer to our concerns on the wine issue.

Be it further resolved that since the drinking of alcoholic beverages is one of our nation's greatest problems and since it is a most sensitive issue among Free Will Baptists, that any and all who speak and/or teach on the subject take such sensitivity into account and be cautious accordingly.

A motion to table lost. A motion to recess passed, and on Thursday morning the motion to amend by substitution was passed and the resolution as amended was adopted, becoming the official position of the National Association on the wine issue.

They also voted to combine the minutes and directory into one volume.

The war of the wine fermented for another year like new wine in old wineskins breaking out in various places, popping a cork now and then, working its way to the surface again in Columbus, Ohio, in 1983 with this resolution from the grape juice brethren:

Whereas, there is a doctrine believed by some Free Will Baptists that Jesus made/drank/gave to others wine which had alcohol content, and

Whereas, it is not the intent of this resolution to attack those who believe this doctrine or his or her conviction on this subject since it is their right to believe what they wish, and

Whereas, the doctrine does do violence to the doctrine of the principle of the Holiness of God, and also violates the scripture that forbids the use of wine with alcohol content, and

Whereas, it has not been established which doctrine that the majority of Free Will Baptists believe, namely: Jesus DID or DID NOT make/drink/or give to others wine with alcohol content.

Therefore BE IT RESOLVED that this body vote to establish which doctrine they will hold to be Biblical. BE IT FURTHER RESOLVED that if this body by majority vote establishes that it DOES NOT believe the doctrine to be Biblical that Jesus made/drank/or gave to others wine with alcohol content, then those that believe that he did who hold positions as teachers in our college or are board members resign or be dismissed.

An objection to consideration of the resolution was sustained by 80% of the body. Voting not to consider the resolution was evidence that the previous year's statement was their final word on the subject.

Neither convinced nor content, on Thursday a motion was introduced from the floor that the body adopt the statement that, *Jesus did not make, drink, or give to others to drink wine with alcoholic content.* Motion tabled.

A motion was made to reconsider the objection to consideration. An objection to consideration was raised to the motion to reconsider. Objection was sustained.

A motion was made that, *Employees of the Association be forbidden to write or print any material on the wine issue.* Motion tabled.

A motion was made that, *a study committee consisting of co-chairmen Leroy Forlines and Richard Cordell and eight men appointed by the chair from the National Association of Free Will Baptists study this issue and endeavor to develop a workable statement to be presented at the 1984 session that will bring harmony to our fellowship.*

A motion to amend by substituting, *that we encourage the aggrieved parties to get together on their own and see if they can settle their differences on the wine issue.* Motion to amend carried. Motion as amended was adopted.

The moderator was given a standing ovation for his fairness in this meeting.

Motion to adjourn carried without a dissenting vote!

In 1982, anticipating the wine controversy, Romans 14 was the moderator's message. "The kingdom of God is not meat or drink but righteousness and peace (verse 17). For meat destroy not the work of God (verse 20)." Critics thought it was poor timing. Nothing seemed more fitting at the time.

After two years of trying to turn the wine in John 2 back into water, we gave up, put a lid on it, corked it, and sealed it. The National Association refused to analyze the wine in the New Testament, and closed the bottle. The battle was over. Nobody won.

Some Observations

The Bible lesson on the plagues in Egypt in Exodus was enlightening. The free steak was delicious. The fellowship was enjoyable. Seated at the head of the table was the retired college professor, outstanding English Bible teacher, best-loved among Independent Baptists and well-known among Free Will Baptists. My place was at his immediate left.

In the course of conversation he asked "Are you folks having any trouble with the *King James Only* people?" looking at me and meaning Free Will Baptists. He evidently was.

In answering someone's question in open class he had said that no translation was considered inerrant nor infallible and that the King James was a translation, resulting in an immediate challenge to a debate on the subject. When he refused to debate in a classroom format, a large part of his class marched out in anger, an exodus, and never came back.

"No," I said. "Preacher, it takes three or four years for issues to drift into our neck of the woods and find us. We'll likely have the problem down the road. Our problem right now is the wine in John 2."

The response caught me off guard. His emotional reply was, "I can tell you for certain that Jesus never made anything that would turn my brother into an alcoholic and drunkard."

It was totally subjective, unscriptural, unreasonable, undeniable, unbiological, untheological, and undebatable.

There may be some question about the alcoholic content of the wine miraculously made from water at the wedding in Cana. But there is no question that if Jesus made the natural laws which govern this physical universe, the law of gravity, law of centrifugal force, law of inertia, law of photosynthesis, law of fermentation, He has made a lot of grape juice into wine with alcoholic content since that wedding. However, He didn't make the teacher's brother a drunkard. Jesus made the law of gravity so we could function on the surface of this planet without being flung off into space, but He didn't make the man jump from the Golden Gate Bridge and commit suicide.

My mother was killed by a drunken driver in 1939 and that has nothing whatsoever to do with the content of wine in the Bible.

No, I didn't mention any of this to the professor. The conversation turned back to the King James. We could discuss that more objectively.

However, the former could be dragged into a discussion of the latter. Many of the grape juice brethren were also *King James Only*, which introduces an interesting scenario. If the King James is preserved in absolute accuracy and contains no errors, there is no need to look into the Greek at the word for wine, nor make a study of the Hebrew terms for strong drink. The English version is word for word true. Go get an English dictionary and look up the word "wine." Looking for a classic oxymoron? Try non-alcoholic wine.

In the midst of the wine debate the question was posed to one of the most spiritual-minded, theologically, Biblically, and scientifically qualified men among us. His response was that he wished he could say New Testament wine was not fermented, but he couldn't say that. He probably expressed the position of many others whose hearts were so set against alcoholic beverages, because of the physical, social, mental, moral misery their use and abuse have caused in the world since the days of Noah, that they wished the wine in certain parts of the Bible were non-alcoholic, but intellectual honesty prevented them from saying that.

In October 1982, I was with Sam Truett at West Calvary Free Will Baptist Church in Smithfield, NC. Sam rose early one morning, went to his study, and from his well-stocked library photocopied John 2 from about 20 commentaries. By the time I was ready for breakfast, he appeared in the kitchen with this armful of material. All the expositors, except one, agreed that the wine was fermented and that one took no clear position.

Maybe that's where the National stood, leaving the matter of interpretation to scholars and individuals, not willing to be forced into deciding the alcoholic content of wine in the Bible.

That war being over, 1984 in Little Rock was relatively peaceful. Some brethren in Tidewater, Virginia, were being sued by a minister whose credentials had been revoked. A motion to deny exhibit space to any person involved in such litigation was batted around and then tabled. The association adopted a resolution that the body go on record as disapproving any action contrary to the Biblical injunction in I Corinthians 6:1-8, which forbids a brother to take another brother to court. After the previous two years that was a walk in the park.

Preparations were underway for a big year in 1985, the Golden Anniversary, the Year of Jubilee.

Floyd Wolfenbarger

Was it only May? The heat in the shade of the carport felt like North Carolina in July. Shaded from the sun, but not the steaming humidity, Jane and I were scraping, sanding, smearing paint remover, scraping some more, and sweating, refinishing furniture from her farm home in Illinois, brought to North Carolina in December after her dad and mom sold the farm and moved into Benton.

The phone rang, and I recognized David Joslin's voice, "Bobby," he said, "Floyd is dead. He died about 7:40 this morning."

For a moment stunned into speechless silence, then loud enough for Jane to hear me, I said, "Floyd Wolfenbarger is dead!"

"You have just lost a very good friend," she almost whispered.

David was Arkansas' promotional director. Floyd was a pastor in Russellville.

I knew he was going for intestinal bypass surgery to help him fight diabetes, but I thought that was rather routine. There was some problem and the doctors had to go in a second time. Unaware to any of them was his allergy to the anesthesia. That is what killed him. Later we learned that it is called "malignant hyperthermia." Floyd probably received the genetic allergy from his father's side. His temperature rose above 108° and the medical profession couldn't save him. The reason for the second surgery was a pinhole leakage in the intestines which set up a critical infection, gangrene, blood poisoning. He was 36 years old.

Floyd and I first met in Kansas City, Missouri, in May, 1969, when I was with Jim McAllister at Central Free Will Baptist in revival. He was a twenty-year-old student. I was an old man of 37 who had been in full-time evangelism for 15 years, but we sure liked each other. A friendship began and grew closer for the next 15 years and ended for the time being with David's phone call.

In Springfield, Ohio, at the First Free Will Baptist Church I was with him, October, 1977. Then he moved to Russellville, Arkansas. Jane and I were there in two meetings, March, 1981 and April, 1984. One night after church as we watched TV, the closed caption went crazy, letters all jumbled. Floyd knelt in front of the set and said, "Hey, you're messing up. You got your fingers on the wrong keys. We can't read the stuff."

He waited a moment, nothing cleared up. He looked back at us and said, "There's nobody back there. I don't believe there's anybody back there!"

Two months before he died, we were in Greenbriar, Arkansas, 55 miles from Russellville. He drove more than 100 miles every night, Monday, Tuesday, Thursday, and Friday, to listen to the same old sermons he had heard before and compliment them again. The battle with full-blown diabetes and his weight had reached a critical point. We spent an entire day together, eating lunch, talking, and walking around the mall. He told me that the doctors said the only solution was intestinal bypass. We were forced to cut the walk. Weak, dripping with perspiration and trembling, he went back to the car. His blood sugar had dropped extremely low.

While he was on the Executive Committee and I was moderator, if the two of us arrived early we would get together and talk about Tolstoy, Dostoyevsky, Brothers Karamazov, Soren Kierkegaard, Bonhoeffer, or C. S. Lewis. That is, he would do most of the talking. I'd listen and now and then offer my insignificant opinion. He was so widely read in so many fields that the conversations were always interesting and enlightening.

One day he said, "In one of these confusing business sessions, I'm going to rise on the floor and make a motion to reconsider and have entered on the minutes."

"And I'm going to ask you if you voted with the prevailing side on the motion to be reconsidered."

"And when you say 'no,' I'm going to call you out of order."

We laughed.

Throughout the denomination others had begun to recognize Floyd's ability as a preacher and his vast storehouse of knowledge. He had spoken at the Bible Conference at Free Will Baptist Bible College in Nashville, at many other state and national gatherings, held offices and served at several levels, and in the Executive Committee meeting in December, 1984, was chosen to speak at the Wednesday night service to climax the Jubilee Celebration of the National Association.

Now Floyd was dead two months before his opportunity to challenge a denomination at its fiftieth anniversary.

A few days later, Melvin Worthington called, "I have polled the Executive Committee and it is unanimous for you to take Floyd's place on Wednesday night."

"I have said that as long as I am on the program committee, I will not preach at the National Association. It doesn't seem right choosing yourself as a speaker."

"You haven't chosen yourself. The fellows on the committee have given you a responsibility. One suggested you would be Floyd's choice, if he had a vote."

"Then I'll do the best I can. I can't fill Floyd's place, but I'll pray, prepare, and by the Lord's help, preach."

"Realizing our Potential" seemed simple and easy when assigned to Floyd. Suddenly it became very complicated and difficult.

Developing the thought produced two sub-topics from the closely related definitions of realize, one subjective, one objective. Realize–to understand fully, to apprehend. We must understand what our potential is. Realize–to bring to concrete form, to achieve. We must plan to bring that potential to reality.

While contemplating that second thought and considering obstacles to reaching our potential, walls we build that make it impossible to minister to various groups was at the top of the list of hindrances. Educational, economical, cultural, racial walls, all of them are built by pride.

Jane brought a glass of tea. I shut down the mower, sat in the swing under our grapevine cooling for a minute before finishing the backyard, preached one point of the sermon to her, and said, "Do you suppose fundamental preachers have a problem with pride?"

She gave me that 'are-you-kidding' look.

"All these preachers pursuing spurious, easy, honorary doctors' degrees are like a gospel quartet trying to get a bus," I said.

Her laugh signaled not only agreement but also her being impressed with the comparison, and into the sermon it went.

Jubilee Convention

On Tuesday at the National the grapevine was circulating that some preachers were being awarded doctors' degrees at the convention. No one had ever done that before, nor since. The thought came to mind, should I strike the comment about doctors' degrees? When it was put into the sermon six weeks earlier, no one in particular was in my mind, certainly no one receiving a degree at the convention.

The thought and the simile were left in the sermon. I did not know then and do not know now who received degrees that Wednesday night.

The most critical letters came from preachers who were not at the convention, didn't hear the sermon in person nor on tape, and have probably never read the printed version.

Why would degrees be awarded at that time and place? Such degrees are usually given during commencement on the campus of the institution. After several years of thinking, this possible conclusion continues coming to mind. It was an "in your face" expression by an Independent school in conflict and competition with a Free Will Baptist college, owned and operated by the National Association of Free Will Baptists at whose convention, and during the program, they would have their honorary degrees exhibition.

When accused of being jealous because I don't have a doctor's degree, I have the satisfaction of knowing I turned one down, and the pride for refusing it is probably a greater sin than those who pursue such, if it were not for the fact that the institution was so insignificant, there's nothing to be proud of in turning it down.

Other than that bit of criticism the Wednesday night service was well received.

The moderator's message for that fiftieth Anniversary was the Year of Jubilee, "After seven Sabbaths of years, seven times seven years, forty and nine years, ye shall hallow the fiftieth year, and proclaim liberty throughout all the land" (Leviticus 25:8-24). The civil and religious activities included:

Release of Prisoners
Restoration of Property
Rest from Planting
Reverence for the Provider
Righteousness toward People
Reason for Practices

Paul told the Colossians that all the Sabbath days were a shadow of things to come, but the body is Christ (Colossians 2:16-17). Those civil observances were only shadows. The spiritual reality is provided for us in Him. Sound the trumpet. Christ is our Jubilee.

A brief history of the 50 years, the minutes of the 1985 convention, and the three sermons, *Remembering the Past* by L. C. Johnson, *Reviewing the Present* by Alton E. Loveless, and *Realizing Our Potential* by Bobby Jackson were published in 1988 by the Free Will Baptist Historical Commission in *The Fifty-Year Record of the National Association of Free Will Baptists,* edited by Mary Wisehart.

The convention adopted the typical resolutions. Rolla Smith retired as director of the Foreign Missions Department. Eugene Waddell replaced him. We adjourned to begin the first year of the second 50 in 1986, in Tulsa, Oklahoma, having set a new attendance record of 8,340 registered for the three conventions, and appoved budgets totaling over $11,000,000.

Final Two Years

After the excitement of the previous five years, 1986 and 1987 were rather peaceful, an eye in the midst of the storm, a temporary truce, nothing earthshaking. The Management Committee was authorized to look into relocating the National offices at no additional cost to the Association, and report to the Executive Committee and General Board. The end result being the offices were relocated but not without additional cost, to the surprise of nobody.

In Birmingham, Alabama, in 1957, in a hotel ballroom with undergirding pillars scattered through 1,600 registered delegates, I preached Jesus' commission to fruitfulness from John 15.

Dr. Charles Thigpen was moderator. W. S. Mooneyham was Executive Secretary. He insisted that I write out the message and give him a copy beforehand, which I never did. Instead, he was furnished a very detailed script, but with the understanding that I would not be reading it in the pulpit. W. S. was an outstanding journalist and through his effort the sermon received a great review in the local paper, with the heading, *Young evangelist, Billy Graham of the Free Will Baptists,* a compliment or a curse according to where one stood on the Graham issue of cooperative evangelism.

Thirty years later, presiding over my tenth and final convention, I was back in Birmingham. The experience was unforgettable. The privilege and joy of serving the Association for 16 years, almost one-third of its life, six as assistant moderator, ten as moderator, would always be a part of the ministry that I would look back upon with some sense of satisfaction.

In 1987, there were resolutions against AT&T for pornography, and to boycott Holiday Inn because of adult movies. Both were tabled.

Resolutions were passed against adultery, fornication, infidelity, homosexuality, promiscuity, and distributing birth control devices which seem to encourage immoral behavior.

If passing resolutions would produce morality, we have passed enough to purify the world which seems to be more impure than ever. We continue speaking out, but nobody's listening.

At the end of the session Ralph Hampton was moved from Assistant Moderator to the chair. Carl Cheshire was elected Assistant Moderator. My tenure was finished.

The battles weren't over. More skirmishes were around the bend.

Basketball Uniforms

The next year at the conclusion of the Bible College report a motion was made from the floor that the body rescind the action of the Free Will Baptist Bible College Board of Trustees concerning wearing regulation basketball uniforms and forbid the wearing of the uniforms. After long and heated debate about wearing shorts, immodesty, uniforms and related apparel, the motion passed. The board's action was rescinded and the boys were not allowed to wear basketball uniforms.

The following year, 1989, this resolution came before the body.

Whereas, the Board of Trustees of Free Will Baptist Bible College recommended in 1988 that the boys basketball team (Flames) be allowed to wear regulation uniforms when playing basketball, and

Whereas, we believe the nine men composing the Board of Trustees are men of integrity and spiritual discernment with the best interest of our college in mind, and

Whereas, practically all other Christian Schools and Bible Colleges play basketball and other sports in approved regulation uniforms,

Therefore be it resolved that we refer this matter back to the Bible College Board of Trustees to be handled at their discretion and that this body abide by this decision.

Motions to amend and motions to postpone in an effort to defeat the resolution failed.

Motion to amend by substitution passed and the body adopted the resolution to rescind its previous action on this matter and give our Bible College Board of Trustees full approval, thus allowing our Bible College basketball team to play ball in regular regulation uniforms.

For two years we spent hours arguing over basketball uniforms, yet approved over $10,000,000 in budgets each year with little or no discussion. It's easy to be neutral presiding over that kind of debate.

To borrow and adapt a thought from Louis L'Amour, *some men hide the desire to fight behind the mask of a cause, motivated not by dedication to the cause, but by love of the fight.*

Our battle is with the world, the flesh, and the devil. Paul never meant for us to put on the whole armor of God and go out and fight with each other. In the National Association of Free Will Baptists we're all on the same side. So be it.

Presiding at the Jubilee 1985

REALIZING OUR POTENTIAL[*]

The morning that David Joslin called me, when Floyd died, I turned to my wife with a lump in my throat and a tear in my eye and said, "Floyd is dead."

And she said, "You just lost one of the best friends that you had in the world."

She was right. He had just driven all the way to Conway, Arkansas, to sit on an uncomfortable bench and listen to me preach for three nights—the same old sermons he'd heard me preach before. So when Melvin stuck me with this job, I sort of said to Floyd, "If you were such a good friend, what are you doing in Heaven and leaving me with your place on Wednesday night?" I expect he's smiling about it.

---

[*] This sermon was preached on Wednesday evening, July 24, 1985, at the Golden Anniversary, Jubilee year, of the National Association of Free Will Baptists convening in Nashville, Tennessee. It was transcribed from audio and edited by Dr. Mary Wisehart, and first published in *The Fifty-Year Record of the National Association of Free Will Baptists* by the Historical Commission, in 1988. It is used here by permission with some additional editing, such as adding headings to make for easier reading.

The burden that I carry for tonight is for three things. First, that God would enlarge our generosity and loose us from our stingy purse strings and create in us the kind of stewardship that would give to God sacrificially—not out of our abundance, but out of that which costs us something. That somehow God could do something in our hearts that would increase our devotion to Him and therefore enlarge our giving to Him.

The second thing I desire is that this service will encourage those who've grown weary in the work of God to reenlist whole-heartedly in the service of the Lord.

My third concern is that among our young people we may have those who will enlist in the service of the Lord Jesus. If we are to realize any potential in this denomination, there must be somebody to follow those of us who are growing old.

It troubled me a little bit to see a number of our young people checking out and going home today, knowing that they would not even be in this service tonight. We have thousands of young people who attend the youth conference. But there's not a thousand students in all of our colleges added together. What has become of the thousands that come to youth conferences that dwindle into hundreds that go to all of our colleges combined, and out of those hundreds, just tens who give themselves to God? We are losing thousands. Unless something happens in our midst to stir the hearts and souls of young people to enlist themselves in the service of Jesus Christ, we will have no potential for the future.

So, to that end I want us to pray that God will speak to us tonight about our concern and generosity, encourage those that are discouraged, and that the Spirit of God will move in our midst upon the hearts of those that need to give themselves to the Lord.

The subject assigned for tonight is, *Realizing the Potential.* I noted that the word realize has two closely related definitions.

In one sense, it means to think vividly, clearly, and with such imagination that the thought becomes reality in the mind. That is the sense in which, when you get out and start back to the hotel tonight, and climb that third hill, you will suddenly realize that it's a long way from here to the Hyatt. Another closely related definition is to accomplish. Now that's to put thinking into practice and bring it to a reality outside of the mind. As you climb that last hill the body is putting into practice what the mind already knows. It really is a long way to the Hyatt.

Concept – Becoming Aware

First, then, we should think and try to evaluate the potential of our movement and our denomination. Let me illustrate. If the Washington Redskins (Dallas fans may insert Cowboys.) are considering drafting a football player, they will take all of his physical, mental, and emotional attributes—positive and negative—and feed them into a computer. The physical includes his weight, height, size, speed, and movement. The mental means whether he's able to understand and remember 200 offensive plays or not, his ability to understand that particular team and the game of football. The emotional attributes include his aggressiveness, even his anger. Now when they feed all these facts in, the computer organizes them into a concept of the potential of that player. The coach now realizes the prospective player's potential. When the player plays to that potential in the game, the potential becomes actual concrete reality.

Jesus suggested that it is wise, before you go to war or before you start to build a house, to sit down and evaluate what your potential is. One businessman in our city was quoted as saying that the difference between a successful organization and one that's unsuccessful is that the people in a successful organization determine who they are, where they are, where they're going, and how to get there.

It is worth our while to try to evaluate ourselves and determine who we are, where we are, and where we are going. And then the last part is how to get there.

Physical Assets and Liabilities
What We Have
Property

First, then, let's evaluate our assets and try to offset them with our liabilities. That's the way you would do it if you were evaluating the potential of a company or organization, and that's the way I want us to do it tonight. We can start with physical, or tangible, assets. Thirty-five years ago, when I started in the Free Will Baptist ministry, we did not have much. I'm talking about buildings, starting with local church buildings that are now larger, more comfortable, better located, more of them, and air conditioned where you used to preach with the gnats and the sweat. We also have state offices, national offices, colleges, and other properties. We have many physical assets that we did not have 35 years ago.

Even so, there are some things on the liability side of our physical assets. For one thing, many of these churches have over-built. It may be a testimony to some pastor's ego that a building can seat 1,500 people and has 300 rattling around in it, therefore increasing the overhead and expense, using money that could have been used to build a church in Brazil.

For another thing, we have built churches unnecessarily simply because people couldn't get along with each other. One faction leaves a church that costs $600,000 and can take care of 800 people. Down the street, another half mile, they build a new church for $600,000 that can take care of 500 more people. If you put the two congregations together you'd have 300 people. How completely unnecessary! And in my town, I think some of that has gone on. We have seven Free Will Baptists churches in my town. I mean that's how many we had when I left; I don't know how many there'll be when I get back. When you go to a town and see 15 churches in a little town, it does not necessarily mean that they are spiritual; it may mean they can't get along with each other.

Another liability in this area occurs when people misunderstand and identify the church with the building. We begin to think that because you have a building, you have a church. Nothing can be farther from the truth. You can go to a new city. You can float a bond program. You can build a building for $200,000 and you can leave and say, "We've got a church in that city." Not necessarily. You've got a building. The building and the church are two different things. Don't confuse the building with the church.

Personnel

Now, as part of our tangible assets and liabilities we can include personnel. Dr. Johnson mentioned last night we probably have more preachers, more missionaries, better trained, than we have ever had in the history of this National Association. I agree. We do have more personnel than we had at one time, and that certainly is an asset.

But we need to be aware of liabilities in this matter, too. For example, we must not think that training necessarily guarantees effectiveness and fruitfulness. Sometimes a fellow goes to Bible College, gets his degree, gets out, and nothing happens, so he says, "Something went wrong. I didn't get enough training."

He goes back and spends two more years and gets out and still nothing happens; and he says, "I still didn't get enough training."

So he goes off to a conference on evangelism and soul winning, gets excited, comes home, and nothing happens, and he says, "I still don't have it." Even with our training we may not necessarily be effective and fruitful in the task that God has given us.

Furthermore, even with the personnel we have, we still do not have enough personnel. The field is still white and the laborers are still few and there are still spots that we have nobody trained to fill. The Christian schools have desperate problems getting qualified teachers and leaders. If you are trying to add someone to your staff in a church, you have difficulty getting someone. There are not enough preachers to fill the places where the needs are, so while we have more we still have to pray, "Dear Lord, the field is white and the laborers are few." We need more personnel than we now have.

Pay

Now, while we're evaluating tangible things, we can talk about pay. I'll use that word in order to have alliteration. It's true that our budgets are larger. Our income is greater, we receive more money, we spend more money, and there's more money available to be spent in the work of God. And that is a definite asset—money and its proper use to get the Gospel out.

But there's a liability here, too. Even with the increase of the money we still have not developed an effective stewardship program that will meet the financial needs of the work of God.

On the local level, there are many churches that have not to this day accepted the responsibility for a full-time paid ministry. I would venture to say that most of our pastors are subsidized by a working wife or by a second job. It would be interesting to know how many pastors in our entire denomination are meeting all their material needs solely by what the church pays them, with no subsidy to that income. We haven't yet accepted the responsibility of a full-time, educated, paid pastor, much less evangelists.

People wonder why we have no more evangelists. I can relieve you of wondering. Ask me about the miles, the expenses, and the offerings—if you're wondering why there's not a long line applying for my job! We have not accepted the responsibility of full-time evangelists because we have not accepted the responsibility of full-time pastors. And that is a liability. Southern Baptists got a hundred- years' jump on us in taking the responsibility for a full-time, educated, paid ministry.

Mental Assets and Liabilities
What We Believe

The Bible is True

Now, let's talk about the mental assets. First, what we believe about the Bible is a positive asset for us. While Southern Baptists may be discussing and debating and arguing about the infallibility of the Scriptures, it's interesting that—far as I know—there is not one among us who does not believe in an infallible, inerrant Bible. Several years ago, when the National Convention adopted that strong statement on inspiration about the infallibility and inerrancy of the Scriptures, even in matters of history and science, there was not one single negative vote, not one single negative voice in the debate.

Now, we may argue about what the Bible means. We may argue about the application. We may argue about its principles. We may argue and divide over issues like modesty or separation or a dozen others, but we are not arguing about whether or not the Bible is true. And I think it is an asset that we still believe in an infallible, inerrant Bible, inspired of God, that charts for us the direction and the program that we should follow in this world.

But even here, there is a liability that we need to watch for. Our favorite verse on inspiration, 2 Timothy 3:16, says all Scripture is given by inspiration of God and is profitable for doctrine, for reproof, for correction unto righteousness. I fear that it's possible to believe in an infallible, inerrant Scripture without permitting that Scripture to do for us what God intended it for: to correct us when we do wrong and turn us from sin and bring us to practice righteousness. Believing in an infallible Bible, without permitting that Bible to reprove you when you sin, correct you when you're wrong, and bring you to practice righteousness, leaves the Bible powerless and fruitless in our lives. It's not enough that you believe what it says; you are to put it into practice and live by it.

I was reading that verse in 2 Timothy, getting ready for this, and decided to read the entire third chapter and stumbled over an interesting paradox. You remember that Brother Ralph Hampton read this today. The first few verses of that third chapter, just before the verses about the perilous times shall come. *For men shall be lovers of their own selves, covetous, boasters, proud, blasphemers, disobedient to parents, unthankful, unholy, without natural affection, truce breakers, false accusers, incontinent, fierce, despisers of those that are good, traitors, heady, high-minded, lovers of pleasure more than lovers of God;* and verse 5 is what stopped me, stunned me for a moment.

When I read this, my first thought was that those were the characteristics of the unregenerate, heathen world in which we live. But then I noticed that Paul said this particular group would be *holding, or having, a form of godliness.* The word translated "form" is used one other time in the New Testament, in Romans 2, where Paul describes Jews who teach the law and don't live by the law. In verse 20 he says that they have *a form of knowledge and of the truth,* and so I realized that those weren't irreligious heathen, those were religious people.

That's true here in 2 Timothy, too; they have *a form of godliness.* They aren't heathen at all. Then I thought, "It's the liberals. They're the ones Paul is talking about, because they have a ritual without reality." But then I read G. Campbell Morgan and he said that Paul is describing conservative religious people.

So I asked myself, "Is it possible to have an ungodly fundamentalist?"

You say, "Well, it all depends on the context."

So I looked at the context. Paul says they were *lovers of themselves,* and I said, "Have I ever known a fundamentalist who loved himself, whose favorite note in the musical scale is me, me, me?"

Lovers of money?: "Have I ever known a fundamentalist who got sidetracked by money, fell in love with and sought to pursue money?" Now, don't go misquoting me: I didn't say that all fundamentalists are ungodly. Some of the most godly people in this country are fundamentalists. But what shocked me was realizing that not all fundamentalists would necessarily be godly, that there could be those holding to the form and the truth and the knowledge but not having the power of God in their lives to produce the godliness.

By the way, there is really nothing wrong with money. If it falls into a man's hands while he's on the road of the will of God in service and sacrifice, the money will be legitimate and he will use it right. It's when he turns aside to pursue the money because he loves it, that it gets to be a problem.

Paul said, *Boasters.* Did you ever know a fundamentalist who boasted and bragged? There are some, and it's usually about two things. He'll either boast about what he has done because his church is the biggest in the world, or he'll boast about what he knows because of his theological training and education. While I'm at it, let me throw this in: I honestly don't know any group of people that run any faster than fundamental preachers pursuing easy, spurious, honorary doctors' degrees. Some fundamentalists pursue a doctor's degree like a gospel quartet trying to get a bus. A preacher without a doctorate is like a quartet without a bus.

Or, have you ever seen one that was *proud*? That's the next word. Then comes the word *blasphemer*s. You say, "A fundamentalist couldn't be those he described as blasphemers."

That's interesting. Both here and in Romans 2, Paul accused those he described as blasphemers. Which is the greatest blasphemer against God—the atheist who steps out in a storm and looks up at the clouds and curses God and the lightning? Or the man who says he believes there is a God, but in his works denies that God, who through ritual and testimony in the church speaks the name of God insincerely without the knowledge of God? If there are degrees of blasphemy, which is the greater blasphemer?

Now, did you ever know one that wasn't very loving? That's in verse 3: *without natural affection*. It means unloving: not having a loving spirit or attitude.

Trucebreakers: The New American Standard translates that *irreconcilable*. The reason they're called trucebreakers is they're at war, and you'll never get a truce with them because they won't be reconciled. Did you ever know any fundamentalists who fight all the time and are irreconcilable?

False accusers: I wonder if there's ever been a fundamentalist that accused another fundamentalist falsely.

Incontinent: That word simply means without self control, flying off the handle, no control over their temper.

Fierce: That's brutal and cruel. Did you ever know any cruel, brutal fundamentalist?

*Traitor*s: That word could be translated *treacherous*.

You see, the liability in all this is we may believe that the Bible is the infallible, inerrant word of God, having an orthodox head but a heterodox heart, being ungodly although we believe the Bible to be true. That's a liability.

Salvation is Conditional

Now another one of the things which we believe, that is an asset, is what we believe about God and man and the relationship between the two. If any group of people should have as an asset their doctrinal position concerning the relationship between man and God, it certainly should be Free Will Baptists. Now I could understand if the Calvinists had no missionary program or Sunday schools. If you believe that some are unconditionally elected and the unconditionally elected will be saved by the Lord whether they want to be saved or not, then what's the purpose of having a missionary program? What's the purpose of having Sunday school?

But Free Will Baptists do not believe that. We believe that the relationship between man and God depends upon a condition, and man must meet the condition of repentance and faith to come into the right relationship with God. So, if any group of people ever had a doctrine that should encourage them in evangelism, missions, and soul winning it should be Free Will Baptists, who believe that one's relationship with God depends upon meeting the condition.

Edification is Necessary

Oh, and if anybody believed in edification and follow-up and teaching and training, it should be Free Will Baptists, because we not only believe that salvation begins conditionally, we believe that it continues conditionally. That makes edification necessary.

We agree with the Apostle Paul who said to the Galatians: "I am laboring as travailing with labor pains, like a woman who would give birth to a child. But the labor pain that I now have is that Christ may be formed in you." See, Paul carried the same kind of burden and passion and labor pains for those that professed to know Christ, that He would be formed in them, as he did that they would be born to begin with. He must not have thought, just because you take a man down the Romans Road, that he's just as sure of Heaven as if he were already there.

We don't either. You are not as sure of Heaven as if you were already there. And neither is anybody else. If a man's relationship to God is conditional, as we believe, then of all the denominations on this earth that should have a program of edification and teaching and training, it ought to be Free Will Baptists. That is one of our assets.

The liability part of that is that sometimes we don't really believe the freedom that we express in our theology. We practice the same kind of evangelism as the Calvinists, who give everybody instant Heaven—like instant grits and instant tea and instant coffee. That's the easy way. And if we're not careful, we'll work with people as though we also have the concept that once we've led them to the Lord they are sure of Heaven. And if we do, we don't really believe anymore what we say we believe, that the conditional relationship between a man and God continues as long as he lives upon this earth.

Another asset, in this realm of the things which we believe, is what we believe about the church. We believe that the church is an organization, an organism, of people who have responsibilities to God as individuals, and that this responsibility cannot be overridden by any other organization whether it be a church or a pastor. There is a special amount of freedom and democracy involved in our concept of the individual and his relationship to a local church and their relationship to one another.

Dr. Johnson mentioned, last night, that we're living in a day when the emphasis is on individual freedom and independence. If there's any group of people who do not believe in a totalitarian religion, whether it's in this country or some other country, certainly it should be Free Will Baptists.

That kind of freedom should flourish in a society that also believes in freedom. I think one of the reasons that Baptists have done well in this country, from the very beginning, is because they have the most open, free, religious organization of any religious system. That makes it difficult for a totalitarian system to grow and flourish in this country where religious systems are that free. It's an asset that we believe in individual responsibility, in individual freedom, and that ours is not a totalitarian system.

We do not have a bureaucracy at the top that gives orders to people down at the bottom, and we also don't have individuals at the bottom that order others around. Augustus Strong was probably right when he said that every Baptist preacher has within him an undeveloped pope. Some of us have difficulty keeping that pope from developing, but the truth is that not one of us—preacher or layman—lords it over any other one of us.

Now the liability in this is that as long as you have that kind of freedom, you're going to have disagreements. You're going to have arguments. You're going to have dissension and divisions. Personally, I'd rather have the dissension and divisions, and have the freedom, than to have totalitarianism and not have the dissension and the division. We have to learn how to live with our differences.

Spiritual Assets and Liabilities
What We Need

Quickly, now, let's evaluate our spiritual assets and liabilities. The number one spiritual asset we have is the power of the precious, personal Holy Spirit who moves in the midst of men and has a ministry in our minds and hearts. The charismatics do not have the Holy Spirit cornered on this earth. In fact, He is present and active and powerful and working to do three things in our lives.

Power to Witness

First, if you permit Him, He will make you an effective, courageous, powerful witness. The Bible says, *You shall receive power after that the Holy Ghost is come upon you, and you shall be witnesses unto me both in Jerusalem and in all Judea and to the uttermost part of the earth.* We have as an asset the fact that the Holy Spirit can take your life and turn it into an effective, powerful witness for God upon the earth.

The liability side of that is this: You also have the power as a free person to resist Him, to refuse to submit and yield to Him; and therefore you may not be a good witness. It's simply a matter of allowing Him to perform His ministry in your heart.

Power to Overcome Sin

Second, He is present in our lives to empower us to overcome sin. As you read the 8th chapter of Romans, you will recognize that those who possess the Spirit of God are led by the Spirit of God. And, by the way, these are the only ones in Romans 8 that Paul said are the sons of God. Now, if you are a son of God, you do possess the Spirit of God, and you are led by the Spirit of God; then according to Romans 8, you will not follow the flesh, but you will walk after the Spirit. And those who walk after the Spirit and not after the flesh have the power of the Spirit in their lives to overcome sin.

The liability, here, is that we may excuse sin, make alibis for sin. We live like the Calvinists, who justify sinning by separating the believers' two natures, and say, "Well, nobody's perfect."

Why do you smile when you say that? Why are you so happy because nobody's perfect? Does it make you feel better about your own imperfections?

You say, "Well, you aren't perfect either."

I know it and it aggravates me to death.

We have a tendency to say, "Well, every man sins."

That's true, but you can't justify or excuse your sin by blaming it on everybody else, or Adam, or human nature, or the old nature, or your circumstances, or environment. God has provided the power to overcome sin in your life and there's no excuse for you to continue in sin.

Power to Produce Fruit

Third, the work of the Holy Spirit is also to produce *the fruit of the Spirit* in our lives. Read Galatians 5 and look around you; better yet, look inside you and see how much of the fruit of the Spirit—love, joy, peace, longsuffering, meekness, patience, goodness, faith, temperance—you can find. Then look again and see how much strife, dissension, sectarianism, or division you find, as the works of the flesh.

What amazes me is the number of us that can make the fruit of the Spirit sound bad and the works of the flesh sound good. Have you ever noticed that if a man preaches on *love* he may be a liberal because loving people is supposed to be bad? Somehow love is supposed to be bad if you love everybody. Now, hating things and people is supposed to be good because you're standing for what's right when you hate certain things and people. Hatred suddenly becomes good and love becomes bad.

Or consider what we do with *meekness*: that means having no backbone, being yellow, without courage. Strife and dissension and fighting are good, because that shows you've got courage. Even *peace* is bad because you've got to sacrifice purity if you have peace. But war must be good because being at war proves you're standing up for purity.

Isn't it interesting how easy it is to make the fruit of the Spirit sound bad and the works of the flesh sound good? Some night when you can sit down long enough to meditate and read it, just go back and read Galatians 5 and see how much of the fruit of the Spirit you find in your life and in the life of our denomination, and how much of the works of the flesh.

Concrete – Becoming Hard Reality

But I must leave the evaluation of our potential, with its assets and liabilities, and hurry on to the last part of this message, and that is how to get where we are going, how to realize our potential. In the evaluation there are more pluses than minuses. We have more things going for us than we do against us. I'm happy for us to be where we are.

As you weigh it we do have potential among us.

Now, the next question is: How do we put it to best use? How do we perform to the maximum of that potential?

Millard Sasser, two or three years ago at a Leadership Conference, told about this preacher who was reading through Genesis 22. His comprehension wasn't too good, and when he came to the verse about Abraham's brother, Nahor, and his wife, Milcah, he got it all tangled up.

The verse says, "These eight (meaning eight sons) did Milcah bare for Nahor."

He said, "I don't know much about milking bears, but I think I could get a good sermon on that."

So, he just analyzed the text and he said, "Now the first thing it would take to milk a bear is conviction, 'cause you'd have to really believe that bear needed milking, since there ain't no market for bear's milk and bears don't give much milk and there's going to be a lot of obstacles."

Then he said, "Now the second thing it would take to milk a bear is consecration, 'cause you've got to face the jaws and the paws and the claws. You'd have to be dedicated to the job because if you weren't, you wouldn't go through all that trouble.

"Now," he said, "the third thing that you're going to have to have to milk that bear is cooperation." He said, "It would take at least eight men to milk a bear. There ain't no one man alive who can milk a bear by hisself."

Now, when trying to think of how we're going to accomplish the task God has put before us, I don't know of anything better than what that fellow said it would take to milk a bear.

Conviction

We're certainly going to have to have some deep settled convictions in our hearts about certain things. We need to be absolutely convinced in the first place that men need saving, and I mean all men—rich, poor, educated, ignorant, black, yellow, white, all men on this earth.

And then we have to be convinced that they are worth saving. If they are poor, shabby, dirty, bus kids they are worth saving. If they are ignorant Amazons in Brazil, they are worth saving. If they are black, they are worth saving.

Next, we've got to be convinced that God is willing that they be saved, that, from God's standpoint, He is not willing that any should perish, but that all men should come to repentance. It is the will of God that every man on the earth be saved.

Then we must be convinced that God will save every man who meets the condition. And if we can get this settled in our hearts, then we will spend our lives confronting men with the gospel of the grace of God that they need saving, that salvation is possible, and that they must meet the condition; then God will save them.

Cooperation

It will also take cooperation. There's a job to do for God. When Jesus sent out the seventy, He sent them two by two. Some things one person can't do, two people can do. When the man sick of palsy was brought to Jesus, four friends brought him and took him up on the roof. Evidently there are some things two people can't do that four people can do. When Gideon set out to accomplish that for which God had called him, he finally narrowed it down to 300. There are some things 300 can do that four can't do.

Every pastor loves to see cooperation in his local church. If he would just practice the same cooperation with the pastor in the neighboring local church, that would be wonderful. But he doesn't do that; he wants them to cooperate with him on a one-way trip.

All the way from that local pastor and the neighboring church to the National Association, one note we keep hearing over and over, from the laity on the field, is: Why don't the departments in Nashville stop fussing and fighting and learn to cooperate with one another? Why is the Home Mission Board in competition with the Foreign? Why is the Bible College in competition with both boards?

Aren't we all in the same business? Isn't the Bible College a part of the missions program, not only because they train missionaries but also because many of them are called while they're still in school at the Bible College? Isn't the missions program a part of the Bible College's arm of extension? That's where the students go to minister for God when they leave and send more back to the school.

It is extremely difficult to explain to the layman out there who looks around and says, "I just don't understand why people can't get along when they're leaders in the denomination." God has a job for us. If we ever do it, we're going to have to learn to cooperate.

Consecration

This brings me to the climax of the message. The greatest requirement is going to be consecration, dedication. Now I'm talking about the kind of dedication that the Apostle Paul had, that Dr. Picirilli told us about yesterday morning.

The kind of dedication seen in Acts 20, when Agabus said to Paul, "You're going to Jerusalem and they're going to bind your hands and put you in prison and we won't ever see you anymore."

Paul simply looked at him and the others and he said, "I'm ready to go to Jerusalem to be bound or to die. I have only one life's ambition—to finish the task of the ministry of the Gospel of the grace of God that's laid upon me. I count not my life dear to myself."

They followed him to the boat. They fell on his neck and kissed him. He left all of them weeping. The reason they wept was the last thing he said: "You will never see my face anymore."

Sure enough, they put him in prison, which ended with his martyrdom and execution.

That's what he had said to Timothy: "I fought the fight and my race is run, but somebody needs to take up the race and find his place in the ministry and get in."

Yesterday morning, as Brother Connie Cariker was closing his message he alluded to one of the outstanding incidents in the history of the state of Texas. It provides a clear illustration of the kind of dedication that is necessary if we are to reach the potential that God has for us.

It was the winter of 1835 and '36. The citizens of Texas grew weary under the government of Mexico and decided to wage a war of independence. The Texans took the city of San Antonio. They left 140-150 men, all volunteers, under the leadership of Lt. Col. William Travis, the officer in charge, to guard the city of San Antonio. On February 23, with 4,000 to 6,000 Mexicans in an army, Antonio Lopez, of Santa Ana, attacked the city and surprised the Texans. They had not expected the attack. They retreated to a Spanish colonial mission, called the Alamo, and turned it into a fort.

Colonel Travis sent out a call for relief and some 25 or 30 more men from Gonzales made it through the Mexican lines and came to their relief. A few days before the siege started, David Crockett, with some riflemen from Tennessee, had joined them. The number in the Alamo was now 182 men. The Mexican troops assaulted them for nine days, one assault after another. Three times the waves of those assaults were turned back.

On the night of March 3, Colonel Travis called together all the men except those who had to stand sentry duty. He explained to them the situation. No relief was coming. It was impossible to withstand the continuing assaults of the masses of that Mexican army. Their ammunition was running out. He explained why they should hold that fort as long as possible, so as to give Sam Houston time to recruit and organize an army of Texans, and also to weaken the army of Santa Ana so that it would have to be reorganized.

Then he said, "I'll need to know who I can count on when the end finally comes."

They understood what the end was, because with every assault of that Mexican army, the bugler had blown the Spanish charge, *The Assassin*, which means: Take no prisoners, leave nobody alive, kill all of those in the fort. He took the sword and in the dirt he drew a line. He stepped across the line and said, "I want everyone who can be counted on in the end to follow me across the line."

David Crockett was one of the first. Immediately his men from Tennessee followed him and stepped across the line. Some hesitated, thoughtfully waiting; some stepped across quickly.

Jim Bowie had been brought to the meeting because of his influence with men that he had led. He had been wounded and was on a stretcher. He looked across the line at the other men and said, "Boys, I can't make it by myself, but I'd appreciate it if you'd give me a hand." When they lifted the stretcher and moved him across the line, the remainder of the men followed him and stepped across the line—all except one. Julius Rose, a mercenary from Napoleon's army in Europe, slipped quickly over the wall and disappeared outside in the dark. He was the one person who lived to tell the story of the challenge of that night.

Three days later, early on the morning of March 9, the Mexicans overran the Alamo. They killed all the men but six. Santa Ana commanded that these six be shot. There was left an officer's wife, named Mrs. Dickinson, and her baby and a nurse and a black boy. Then he commanded that the bodies of all 181 be piled in a stack in the street and burned and that all their bones be buried in a common grave.

But that wasn't the end. On April 21, after Sam Houston had time to recruit an army of Texans, they caught the Mexicans in the city of San Jacinto during their afternoon siesta, routed the army, captured Santa Ana, and the next morning forced him to sign a treaty for the independence of the state of Texas.

Most historians who tell of the death of those 181 men will tell you that they did not die because they loved the state of Texas. They didn't die for freedom. They didn't die for the independence of the state of Texas. Those men died for one reason: they were dedicated to three leaders. Some of those men died for Col. William Travis. Some of them died out of dedication to David Crockett. Others died with Jim Bowie.

The truth is men don't usually die for causes or principles. And tonight I am not here to ask you to dedicate your life to foreign missions. Or to the Free Will Baptist denomination. Or to home missions. There is, in this building tonight, a Person, a wonderful loving, sacrificing, caring Leader who is our precious Lord. He's the One that draws the line and looks back over His shoulder with a tear in His eye and a nail print in His hand and says, "Follow Me." Don't enlist your life for missions or the Free Will Baptists, but for the Lord Jesus.

Thirty-five years ago as a seventeen-year-old boy, one Saturday night about midnight, I didn't know then what I know now, and I didn't understand then what I understand now. I heard the voice of the Lord calling and saying, "Come follow Me." I didn't know the Romans' Road. I didn't even know there was a book of Romans. I stood at the foot of my bed, looked out the window at the dark, and I said, "Lord, I want to be on your side. That's all I know to say. As long as I live, I just want to be on your side."

There have been a lot of times in these 35 years that I've repeated that and reminded myself. But those of us who are in the work now won't last forever. Who's going to fill the place when I no longer hold 46 meetings a year and some young man's got to kiss his wife and babies good-bye, and go and stay gone for two months? Who's going to India to take Carlisle Hanna's place? Paul Ketteman lived on the road all these years and now with cancer, how long? Who's going to go on the road? Connie Cariker has heart problems; how long will he continue? Who's going to fill his place when Connie dies? Floyd Wolfenbarger's already gone.

The same Lord whispers tonight throughout this auditorium, and tonight He's drawn a line and He says, "Will you commit yourself, will you step across that line and say, 'I give my life to the Lord Jesus'?"

Some of you who committed yourself years ago have grown weary. There have been times you wanted out and you sort of asked for a discharge. You need to reenlist. You don't need out.

Will you say to the Lord tonight? "It's me and I've come to reenlist. I'll step across the line. Until the last battle's fought, and the war is over, the victory's won, and I can stand on the banks of the river of life, get an honorable discharge, and hear You say, 'Well done, good and faithful servant.'"

Tonight, will you honestly, simply, and sincerely commit yourself to the Lord Jesus, to live or die? Will you just look up at Him and say, "Lord, it's me. I just want to be on your side."

O God, when the tears are dried and we leave this place, we pray that there will be commitments and decisions made that will be permanent and lasting, decisions that will change the lives of people so that they will follow the precious Lord Jesus Himself.

OUT OF ORDER

This seems to be the most appropriate point at which to explain why being from eastern North Carolina, I cast my lot in membership and ministry with the National Association of Free Will Baptists rather than the North Carolina Convention of Original Free Will Baptists.

A Crack

In the early '50s a crack was appearing between the old established, entrenched leadership and the young zealous Bible College trained preachers, who returned to eastern Carolina with a confrontational style of evangelism, preaching repentance, saving faith, conversion, regeneration by the new birth, assurance of salvation, a Bible that in the original languages was inerrant even when it spoke of science and history, heaven with gold in it, hell with fire in it, and a lifestyle for Christians that distinguished them from the world. They were against smoking tobacco, social drinking, immodest dress, mixed swimming (male and female), bikini bathing suits, dancing, Hollywood movies, and the list goes on. Most were not members of the Masonic Lodge, had no plans to join, and some preached against it.

In contrast, the older ministers who controlled the movement were non-confrontational, invited people to make a profession of faith, join the church, and be baptized. Some thought no one could be sure of salvation. Many were devoted active members of the Lodge. Services were more formal with more ritual, and non-evangelistic.

People were responding to the young who were attracting large crowds with more professions, more growth, more full-time churches, and creating more conflict.

At a youth rally on a Saturday night, I preached a simple sermon on the *New Birth* to a packed house. Many responded to the invitation, after which the pastor commented that I would never be allowed to preach in that pulpit again because the sermon left some of his best members thinking they weren't *born again*. And I never did.

One of those older ministers, who was not particularly fond of evangelists, offered his opinion, "The problem is, you are young, zealous, enthusiastic, and energetic, but you will grow older, mature, and get over it."

Grow older? Yes. Mature? Questionable. Get over it? Not yet, and it has been about 60 years of full-time evangelistic preaching.

A Crevice

The crack continued to expand during the decade. The eastern North Carolina establishment began to lose ground and influence in the National Association. Some of their men were not reelected to boards, specifically the Bible College board, so they began their own liberal arts college, evidence of their disagreement with the school in Nashville.

At one convention the North Carolina member of the nominating committee brought back a minority report, nominating a

North Carolinian for moderator. The majority nomination was from another state. The two were placed before the convention. The North Carolina minority candidate lost. The day before that election the fellow from North Carolina approached me about being designated as the National Evangelist.

"Would you folks solicit meetings for me?" I asked.

"Well, no," he said.

"Would you underwrite the ministry financially?"

"Well, no."

"What would you do?"

"You would have the honor and recognition as the National Evangelist."

"That's not necessary. And anything further might involve control, so let's leave it as is."

"If I become moderator," he said, "we could give you that position."

That cleared the smoke away. He was running for moderator of the convention.

Most of the young preachers from Bible College were not supporters of North Carolina's liberal arts school, which had become Mt. Olive College, Mt. Olive, North Carolina. There were unanswered questions about their views concerning inspiration of the scriptures, theology (whether it was conservative, neo-orthodox, liberal, or a mixture of all of the above), biology, evolution, lifestyles, etc.

When one of the more radical of the young took a hard stand against the school with the backing of the majority of his congregation, a minority in the church contacted the conference leadership to come in, recognize the minority as the true Free Will Baptist Church, expel the pastor along with the majority and take control of the property.

That was the case that landed in court to determine who had right to the property and gave rise to the conflicting positions of congregational and connectional church government. The conference officials insisted that historically Free Will Baptists had practiced a form of government by which the conference was the final voice of authority and exercised control over preachers and churches in times of disagreements.

At the trial I was on the stand as a witness for the congregational position. The connectional attorney asked me, "Did you not understand when you were ordained that the conference had authority over you as a minister?"

"No Sir. That was not my understanding."

"Why did you think otherwise?"

I slipped my ordination certificate from my coat pocket, handed it to him, and said, "Read that."

When he came to the second paragraph this is what he read, silently of course. He preferred that the court not hear it.

This Certificate of Ordination shall be in full force and effect for life or during the maintenance of sound doctrine and good moral character. It shall be subject to recall or annulment by a council of at least three ordained ministers called by the church to which he belongs, and upon official demand by said church, he is hereby under solemn promise to deliver this certificate.

He was stunned and silent for a moment. The word 'conference' was nowhere on the certificate. The local church, Union Grove, appears as the church of membership, but nothing is said of which conference that church is a member.

When his voice returned he muttered under his breath, "You're an evangelist so yours is different. I have no further questions."

Being an evangelist had nothing to do with it. The certificate was issued August 30, 1952, and was standard for men being ordained at that time. The word 'conference' was added sometime later in an effort to tighten the control by those controlling the conference over nonconforming preachers.

The trial ended with the Judge ordering the two sides to get together on an equitable division of the property, concluding that the issue could never be settled in the court. The two sides divided buildings and land, settling that case, and since neither side won, the conference was slow to sue anymore churches for their property.

A Chasm

By the end of the decade in the early '60s the crack had become a chasm, a great gulf fixed. The established leadership could not fail to see that the young in influence, outreach, and numbers were growing faster than the old. Their churches were going full-time, becoming the largest in the state, and new ones were popping up all around. In ten more years they would probably be in control. So the established leadership pushed the matter to the breaking point.

The decision was made to force all the preachers to sign a pledge to support all state institutions in order to be seated as a minister at the conference, knowing that most of the young would not sign such a pledge which included Mt. Olive College, especially since the conditions for their ordination were moral and doctrinal, not institutional support. Since the requirement for being a delegate was signing the pledge, the only delegates allowed to enter discussion or vote would be their supporters.

The Central Conference met at the Greenville Free Will Baptist Church, Greenville, North Carolina, where I held membership, and Robert Crawford was the pastor. When I attempted to register as a minister, but refused to sign the pledge, I was excluded, until Brother Crawford appointed me as a delegate from the church. Church delegates weren't forced to sign the pledge.

When I stood to speak on the floor, the moderator said, "You're out of order. You're not a delegate. Sit down."

He assumed that along with many others I had not signed the card and could not be a delegate.

Raising my delegate's badge, I said, "Brother Moderator, I'm a delegate from this local church. May I speak?"

"No Sir. Sit down. You're still out of order."

The stacked delegation that day voted to annul the ordination of all those ministers who refused to sign the pledge.

When I showed my ordination certificate to Brother Robert Crawford, my pastor, he read it and said, "The only institution that can revoke this certificate is the local church to which you belong. You're a member of this church and it has not voted to recall this certificate. Keep it. You are still ordained."

The certificate is in my possession today. Issued to me August 30, 1952, signed by Fred A. Rivenbark, James A. Evans, and F. B. Cherry, and subject to recall by the church to which I belong, which at the present is Unity Free Will Baptist, Greenville, North Carolina.

When a leadership-controlled conference, stacked by disenfranchising legitimate delegates annuls the credentials of scores of ministers for illegitimate reasons that have nothing to do with morals or doctrine, those preachers don't silently vanish into thin air. They organize another conference. They resurrected and reconstituted the old "General Conference," adopted the statement of Faith and Practice issued in England in the early 1600s by Baptists believing in the general provision in the atonement which was both Arminian and congregational, took many of the churches into that conference and continued their ministry.

A few years later that conference was divided into three or four district associations which came together forming the North Carolina State Association of Free Will Baptists, sent delegates who were seated in the National Association of Free Will Baptists which had already taken a stand for congregational church government by declaring vacant the offices filled by anyone who had signed the statement believing in connectional government, and elected someone else to serve in the position.

Like an iceberg broken apart by a deep fracture the two groups drifted in opposite directions. There had been previous battles between the National Association and this group in North Carolina. The North Carolina group fought the National having its own Sunday School Department, writing, printing, and marketing Sunday school materials, insisting that the National continue using the non-affiliated Free Will Baptist Press in Ayden, North Carolina. That break with the Press displeased the North Carolina brethren.

There was dissatisfaction with the college in Nashville, so they began their own. Their influence and leadership in the National convention was fading. Some of the North Carolina leadership was more than ready to withdraw from the National organization, so the final division may have been inevitable.

My fellowship and ministry has been primarily in the National, overlapping now and then in revivals in several State Convention churches.

Some Observations

The division was not over the form of church government. More practical issues came between the two groups – confrontational evangelistic preaching, lifestyles, applying Biblical principles of separation, defining worldliness, educational philosophy. Connectional church government was a product of the entrenched leadership to control churches and preachers.

The southern movement of Free Will Baptists historically was more congregational than the northern movement. Otherwise, how would so many local churches have been lost to the Particular Baptists in colonial days, the Campbellites in the mid-1800s and the tongues movement in the early part of the 1900s? If the conferences had authority over local churches and the property, how did those churches leave the denomination and take the property with them? Up until 1952, according to my ordination certificate, the local church had the authority to recall that certificate. Control was the issue, not government.

Could the division have been prevented?

Maybe. Maybe not. If more level heads had prevailed among the young and the disagreements had come ten years later, and a fair representation had been allowed in denominational meetings, the young would have been older and could have been the majority. Those in control, realizing that possibility, would not have waited ten years when they were no longer in control, to push the issue. It was to their advantage to force a showdown while they controlled the conference. If there had been no division, the leadership of Free Will Baptists in North Carolina would have undergone a great change. The separation may have been unavoidable if those in control favored it in order to stay in control.

Questions with no answers:

Many of the men involved in putting together the National Association were Masons. Did this lodge brotherhood assist them in overcoming differences and settling disagreements? Did that make it easier to get along with one another? For the first 25 years those same men were very active in the Association. During times of dissension, strife, and division did that brotherhood serve as an adhesive helping to hold them together?

After 25 years, leadership in the National, including the college, had changed. Most of the new generation were not lodge members. Did that make it more difficult to settle issues of disagreement?

Did lodge membership play any part in creating the unspannable chasm in North Carolina? Most of the young 'radicals' were outside the brotherhood. An interesting footnote – two preachers whose credentials were never revoked, who were given letters in good standing as they left the North Carolina group and identified with the National, were both Masons.

Such questions could only come from a critical, suspicious mind without enough curiosity to seek answers, or enough concern to care.

Will the two ever get back together? Ever is a long time. Who can say? But not in my lifetime, in a hundred years maybe, if the world continues, and all those involved have been dead long enough to have been forgotten, positions, people, religious movements have changed, and another generation decides they have more in common than contrary, they may at least come to treat each other in a civil manner and find some grounds for fellowship. The problem with prophesying is that the future depends upon decisions that will be made by those who live in it. Predicting those decisions, yet to be made by human beings with free wills, is impossible.

Several Nashville-trained preachers are pastors in some of the North Carolina Convention churches. Revival invitations come more often. Last year I was in meetings in four of those churches, and spoke at a Bible Conference at the institute in Pine Level, North Carolina. After all, it's been almost 50 years now, since we were not allowed a seat in the Central Conference. There were no hard feelings then or now. The decision to work in the National and spend my life in an evangelistic ministry has been satisfying and to some degree fruitful. It was the right choice.

Certificate of Ordination

This Certifies That the bearer, *Bobby Rand Jackson*

of the town of *Fremont*, county of *Wayne*

state of *N. C.*, a regular member of the *Union Grove*

Free Will Baptist Church

in said county, has this day been publicly set apart to the work of the GOSPEL MINISTRY by prayer and the laying on of hands, according to the usage of the Free Will Baptist denomination, and is hereby authorized to preach the Gospel and administer its ordinances wherever God in His providence may call him.

This Certificate of Ordination shall be in full force and effect for life or during the maintenance of sound doctrine and good moral character. It shall be subject to recall or annullment by a council of at least three ordained ministers called by the Church to which he belongs, and upon official demand by said Church, he is hereby placed under solemn promise to deliver this Certificate.

ORDAINING COUNCIL: Address:

Rev. *Fred A. Rivenbark*   *109 Spring Rd. Dunham, N. C.*

Rev. *James A. Evans*   *1103 S. Tarbers St. Wilson N.C.*

Rev. *F. B. Cherry*   *Ayden, N. C.*

Date *Aug. 30, 1952*

For though I preach the gospel, I have nothing to glory of; for necessity is laid upon me; yea, woe is me, if I preach not the gospel! 1 Cor. 9:16.

Preach the word; be instant in season, out of season; reprove, rebuke, exhort, with all long suffering and doctrine. II. Tim. 4:2.

Study to show thyself approved unto God, a workman that needeth not to be ashamed, rightly dividing the word of truth. II. Tim. 2:15.

Take heed unto thyself and unto the doctrine and continue in them for in doing this thou shalt both save thyself and them that hear thee. I. Tim. 4:16.

Go ye therefore, and teach all nations, baptizing them in the name of the Father, and of the Son, and of the Holy Ghost: teaching them to observe all things whatsoever I have commanded you; and lo, I am with you alway, even unto the end of the world. Matt. 28:19, 20.

Ordination Certificate 1952

TOGETHER

Cooperative evangelism, mass evangelism, union meeting – a group of churches of the same denomination or different denominations coming together to promote with finances, workers, and attendance, a coordinated evangelistic effort to reach out to a city, town or community with the saving Gospel message of Jesus Christ. It may be by personal canvassing and visitation, but most often it is in special evangelistic services with an evangelist preaching.

THE POSTULATE

Grounds for such efforts are biblical. During those times of great spiritual revival and evangelistic outreach, there was togetherness. Before Elijah called fire down from heaven, he said to Ahab "...send, and gather to me all Israel unto Mount Carmel... So Ahab sent unto all the children of Israel and gathered the prophets together unto Mount Carmel, and Elijah came unto all the people, and said, 'How long halt ye between two opinions? If the Lord be God, follow him: but if Baal, then follow him'" (I Kings 18:19-21).

The great revival during the days of the good king Hezekiah began, "and there assembled at Jerusalem much people...a very great congregation." (II Chronicles 30:13).

In the eighteenth year of King Josiah, he sent, "and they gathered unto him all of the elders of Judah and of Jerusalem. And the king went up into the house of the Lord, and all the men of Judah and all the inhabitants of Jerusalem with him, and the priests, and the prophets, and all the people, both small and great: and he read in their ears all the words of the book of the covenant..." (II Kings 23:1, 2).

The post-exilic revivals under Ezra and Nehemiah add more evidence. "Now when Ezra had prayed and when he had confessed, weeping and casting himself down before the house of God, there assembled unto him out of Israel a very great congregation of men and women and children...." (Ezra 10:1).

"And all the people gathered themselves together as one man into the street that was before the water gate ... and he read in the book of the law of Moses ... and the ears of all the people were attentive unto the book of the law" (Nehemiah 8:1-3).

The New Testament Church, as recorded in the Book of Acts, with the least possible means, in the shortest period of time reached thousands with the gospel message and brought them into the kingdom.

"...they were all with one accord in one place" (Acts 2:1).

"And all that believed were together: and had all things" (Acts 2:44).

Selfishness raised its head. Ananias and Sapphira, lying over a land sale, and the Grecian and Hebrew widows arguing over the daily distribution, made their communal arrangement short-lived, but the togetherness and fellowship continued.

Someone defined fellowship as, "two fellows in the same ship" to which another added, "paddling in the same direction and not beating each other over the head with the paddles."

Paul's admonition concerning strife, division, harmony and unity certainly suggests that Christians agreeing on the basic fundamentals should be able to cooperate with each other.

"...endeavoring to keep the unity of the Spirit in the bond of peace. There is one body, one Spirit, ...one hope, one Lord, one faith, one baptism, one God and Father of all ...." (Ephesians 4:3-6).

"...till we all come in the unity of the faith, and of the knowledge of the Son of God...." (verse 13).

"...the whole body fitly joined together..." (verse 16), with every part working effectually.

To the Corinthians he said, "Now, I beseech you, brethren, by the name of our Lord Jesus Christ...that there be no divisions among you; but that ye be perfectly joined together in the same mind..." (I Corinthians 1:10).

"We then as workers together with him, beseech you...." (II Corinthians 6:1).

"...being knit together in love"(Colossians 2:2). The whole body is "knit together" (verse 19).

This unity in the body is not union. Two cats with tails tied together is union not unity. A couple may be united in marriage with no unity. It is not uniformity which is paraded on the outside. It is not unison with everyone sounding the same note and some of those flat and no harmony. It is a spiritual living organism with each part functioning in harmony with all the other parts to furnish nourishment and strength for the health of the whole.

This without question should make possible some degree of cooperation in evangelistic endeavors.

Add to this the fact that the biblical mission of the church is to perpetually evangelize every generation 'til the end of the age, and with six billion on the earth today the enormity of the task presupposes working together.

The ministry of the great revivalists and evangelists of the past 300 years has reached beyond the bounds of any one church or denomination. In England and New England in the 1700s it was the Wesleys and Whitefield.

George Whitefield (1714-1770) met John Wesley (1703-1791) at meetings of the "Holy Club," a small group started by Charles, John's brother, in Oxford University. They became good friends and after a mission trip to Georgia, Whitefield joined Wesley in preaching throughout New England. Whitefield broke with Wesley over doctrine and became a Calvinist. Wesley was Arminian. For a short time their relationship was strained, but they agreed to disagree on some doctrinal points and the friendship was renewed for life.

It has been told that after Whitefield's funeral someone asked Wesley, "Do you think you'll see Whitefield in Heaven?"

"No, not likely," he paused, "he'll probably be so close to the throne and I'll be so far away, I'll not be able to see him."

Charles Finney (1792-1875) was a lawyer and Presbyterian, a Congregationalist preacher whose theology so crossed with the Calvinists they called him a heretic, but the masses by the thousands were attracted to his meetings and when he invited them to come forward to the "anxious bench" to seek the Lord, thousands of them responded. His ministry was boundless.

Dwight L. Moody (1837-1899), shoe salesman turned evangelist. In great mass cooperative meetings a million heard him preach. When asked about coming to a town, he'd say, "Get the preachers together."

In a question and answer forum someone asked, "Why don't you preach more about baptism?"

"That's none of your business," he replied.

Billy Sunday (1862-1935), converted baseball player, became an evangelist who was supposed to have preached to 100,000,000 people with over 1,000,000 converts. He was a Presbyterian minister whose ministry went far beyond any denomination.

As the writer of Hebrews said, time and space would fail me to tell of all the evangelists whose ministries have been characterized by working together.

Sam Jones, the Methodist from the South, whose language was considered vulgar by some, but so was Sunday's, was asked by a rather sectarian critic, "Why don't you hop on the Catholics?"

He said, "When I finish with the Methodists, its bedtime."

Mordecai Ham, Bob Jones, John Rice, Eddie Martin – there are so many.

In the fall of '49, Fred Rivenbark and some more pastors in Wilson, North Carolina, invited and convinced Oliver Greene to bring his big green tent to town. Those pastors and churches promoted and cooperated in evangelistic services which drew three or four thousand people each night, crowded under and around the big tent with standing room only. A small part of the fruit of that mass evangelism effort was the conversion of Bobby Jackson, who has now been an evangelist for over 60 years.

No, he hasn't been forgotten. It goes without saying that the outstanding leader of mass evangelism and cooperative meetings in our day is Billy Graham. The facts and figures of that ministry's outreach go beyond my knowledge to calculate.

The questions of his cooperation going beyond the limits of legitimacy and tolerance continue to be batted around. The Lord will settle all of that when He tests every man's work in that fire at the judgment seat.

It remains true that there are some genuine, biblical grounds for working together in evangelism, reaching out to this generation with the good news that Jesus Christ came and died to save sinners.

THE POTENTIAL

The greater the outreach, the greater the potential is for reaching the unsaved and for widespread revival among God's people. On Mount Carmel when the fire fell, "And when all the people saw it, they fell on their faces: and they said, The Lord, he is the God; the Lord, he is the God" (I Kings 18:39).

The revival in Hezekiah's day began in Jerusalem with that very great congregation and spread through all of Judah, Benjamin, Ephraim, and Manasseh, "...all that were present went out to the cities of Judah, brake the images in pieces, and cut down the groves, and threw down the high places and the altars...until they had utterly destroyed them all. ...then every man returned to his own city" (II Chronicles 31:1).

Under the influence of the Word of God, hearing and understanding it, in the days of Ezra and Nehemiah, the people of Israel individually and collectively fasted, prayed, confessed their sins, repented, made a covenant, and worshipped the Lord their God (Nehemiah 9:1).

That sweeping movement in Acts started in Jerusalem with 3,000 converted in one day. Soon it was 5,000 men, and then the number of disciples *multiplied in Jerusalem greatly*. By chapter nine it is *all the churches throughout all of Judea and Galilee and Samaria... were multiplied.* In chapter 11, those that were scattered abroad by the persecution that arose from the stoning of Stephen travelled as far as Phenice and Cyprus and Antioch preaching the word to none but unto the Jews only. Some of them came from Cyprus and spoke to the Greeks, preaching the Lord Jesus.

The far-reaching effects and fruitfulness of the great mass meetings of Wesley, Whitefield, Finney, Moody, Torrey, Sunday, Graham may be documented by reading the biographies of the men and their ministries. Even then the facts and the figures fail to measure the impact of those revivals and evangelistic campaigns. The stories of individuals whose lives were changed, young men who entered the ministry, and missionaries who are now on fields around the world, are hidden away in the statistics.

An example, under the influence of D. L. Moody, J. Wilbur Chapman became an evangelist, Billy Sunday was influenced by Chapman, Mordecai Ham was saved in Sunday's revivals, Billy Graham came to Christ under the preaching of Mordecai Ham.

The revival that moved through eastern North Carolina in 1949-1955, resulting in hundreds being saved and dozens going into Christian ministry, began in the mass meetings of Oliver Greene under the big green tent.

The outreach of a successful cooperative evangelistic campaign is so much greater than one local church that the potential is inevitably greater.

Outreach determines potential. What determines outreach?

People. The extent of such meetings is enlarged or reduced by the number of people and churches cooperating, and their degree of commitment to the meetings. When people work together the sum of the whole is greater than the total of its parts.

The wise man said, "Two are better than one: because they have a good reward for their labour" (Ecclesiastes 4:9). Two produce more together than the total of each working separately.

"For if they fall, the one will lift up his fellow: but woe to him that is alone when he falleth...." (verse 10). On the battlefield a soldier needs a buddy so he'll not be left wounded to die.

"Again, if two lie together, then they have heat: but how can one be warm alone?" (verse 11). Togetherness prevents hypothermia.

"And if one prevail against him, two shall withstand him; and a threefold cord is not quickly broken" (verse 12). The strength of two fighters together is greater than the total of each alone, so also the cord is stronger than the total strength of the three separate strands.

There is strength in numbers. The four friends who brought the palsied man to Jesus in Mark 2 testify of what can be done together. It may be that either of those men alone could have carried the sick man to Jesus. No one knows how much he weighed or exactly how far it was. However, forcing their way through that crowd, carrying that guy up an outside stairway onto the roof, clearing away a top layer of hardened clay, breaking up the baked clay shingles, making a hole in the supporting base large enough to let the man pass through, and then holding the ropes and letting him down easy into the room, appears to be an impossible task for one man. Four men did it.

There are some lost men that no one man including the pastor will ever be able to bring to Jesus. A group of men working together could more likely do it.

In a well-planned campaign, there is the assembling of a choir, musicians, special singers, etc., ushers, trained and ready to do their job, personal workers to assist those who respond to the invitation, prayer groups meeting in homes and public places, and so many people involved that the outreach is enlarged and the potential increased.

Publicity. Beginning months ahead of time to saturate the town or community with the news that meetings which will benefit everybody are coming, lays the groundwork for the outreach. If advertisement didn't get results politicians would not spend hundreds of millions of dollars in a presidential campaign. Money spent in newspapers, radio, television, handbills, by good public relations people is never wasted. And since the meetings are community-wide, that broadens the appeal beyond a single church meeting, extending the outreach and increasing the potential greatly.

Place. A convenient suitable meeting place for the services on neutral ground will reach more people. No matter how much the meetings are promoted as cooperative, if the services are in a local church facility, they will be looked upon as that church's revival. A school auditorium, football stadium, civic center, community building, will give the meetings an area-wide image and bring in more churches. This neutral, non-sanctuary meeting place may also appeal to more folks who don't go to church or feel uncomfortable in church, and those are the people the meetings are trying to reach.

The meeting place is certainly critical to the outreach and that is critical to the potential.

Along with reviving Christians, reclaiming backsliders, regenerating sinners, there are other good things that come out of cooperative evangelistic meetings. Singing together, working together, praying together, Christians learn by experience that they agree on most things, may tolerate some things, and show love in all things. This relationship across various religious boundaries becomes the basis for future cooperation in common causes of vital interest to the entire evangelical community. That "oneness" in the early church flowed from the fact that "they continued steadfastly in the apostles' doctrine and *fellowship,* and in *breaking of bread* and in *prayers*...and all that believed were together...." (Acts 2:42-44).

This love for, and fellowship with, one another, displays the badge of Christian discipleship to an unbelieving world, who, because of what they have seen and heard, fussing, disagreement, dissension, division, in the image projected by so many churches, think that all Christians "put on the whole armor of God," go to church and fight with one another. This improved image will certainly enlarge the outreach and influence of the churches in general, and make them more effective at doing what Jesus said, "Let your light so shine before men that they may see your good works, and glorify your Father which is in heaven" (Matthew 5:16).

THE PROBLEMS

"With all this potential in mass evangelism, why haven't you spent your life in that area of ministry?" someone asks.

A simple question with a simple answer: cooperation and money, two insurmountable obstacles which must be overcome for such a ministry to be possible.

Cooperation – First Problem

Agur said, *There be four things which are little upon the earth, but they are exceeding wise… the locusts have no king, yet go they forth all of them in bands* (Proverbs 30:24, 27).

One locust is unnoticed, insignificant, and powerless. But a swarm! Hundreds of millions settle down for the night, like an army on bivouac planning an attack at sunrise. As the sun comes up and the air begins to warm, if they are not feeding, they take flight into the wind. The swarm is 100 miles long, four or five miles wide, so deep it blots out the sun which cannot pierce the thickness, covers 450-500 square miles, and moves like the shadow of death across the landscape for hundreds of miles, capable of eating and destroying the food supply of an entire nation in a matter of days. Trenches dug deep and wide can't stop them; they fill those and march over them. Fire fails. The mass is so great they fly into the fire and smother it, and the swarm moves on. Their strength and power is in their banding together by the billions.

Cooperation, the final point of the confused preacher's sermon on *Milking Bears,* from the text in Genesis 22, *...these eight Milcah did bear to Nahor...,* is an absolute in union meetings. The preacher said, "I guess it does say these eight milk-a-de-bear. Ain't no one man can milk a bear by hisself."

Ain't no one man, nor church, can have a cooperative meeting by 'hisself.'

The reason D. L. Moody insisted that the preachers get together for him to come to town was they were the key to the cooperation necessary for a united evangelistic effort. That has been an impossible task for a small-time evangelist with limited funds and no organization nor promotional staff. Did you ever try nailing Jell-O to the wall or loading a wheelbarrow with bullfrogs?

Let your imagination exaggerate the problem with the four men bringing their friend to Jesus in Mark 2. He was laid on a pallet with the four at the corners sharing the load. The guy at the left foot is a Baptist, "After we get him to Jesus, which one of these churches is he gonna join? I wouldn't want to put forth all this effort and my church not benefit from it."

The fellow at the right foot is a Methodist, "You know, what he really needs is a motorized wheelchair and the government will provide that, and then we should get some laws passed to equip all public places with ramps and doors for the handicapped."

On the right arm, a Charismatic, "We don't want him short-changed and not receive all the gifts. He needs to get in a real spiritual church."

That final preacher on the left arm is a Presbyterian, "Now, God decreed before the foundation of the world all things including that this man be a quadriplegic, and if He wants to do anything about it, He can do it without your help or mine. If he is one of the elect we won't have to bring him to Jesus. He'll go and get him."

It's not easy for them to put their sectarian thinking aside and simply bring the man to Jesus.

Since the imagination has already run beyond reason, we'll make all four of them Baptists. One of them says, "Okay, we'll get him in a Baptist church, but which one of these Baptist churches is he gonna join? He'll not really be in a church unless that church can trace its history back to John and the New Testament. If he's in the bride it'll have to be a Baptist church set in order by the real Baptists."

The next one says, "We certainly cannot allow him to go to one of these so-called Baptist churches which thinks he can deny the faith, commit apostasy, depart from Christ, and be lost. They believe in salvation by works and are not even saved."

A third guy, "We have to make sure he gets in a Baptist church with standards. He needs good religious rules and policemen to help him stay in line and not backslide."

The fourth preacher, "Check out the order of service, we don't want him exposed to the wrong kind of music."

Is a picture of the difficulty in getting preachers together coming into focus?

In June, 1959, during a cooperative effort in Rocky Mount, North Carolina, in the high school auditorium, some businessmen contributed money to pay for an hour's broadcast on Channel 9, WNCT, Greenville, North Carolina. The station agreed for a spot on Sunday afternoon. The men offered to raise any amount for an evening broadcast during prime time, but were arrogantly informed by the station manager that they preempted prime time for only two preachers, Billy Graham and

Oral Roberts, "and you are not either of them," he said. So he sold us Sunday afternoon.

Having very little experience in telecasting and preferring that it not be a one-man show, I went to a local Methodist pastor, who had a regular weekly television program, to seek his advice and assistance in our telecast, thinking he'd make a good emcee, introducing the music, announcing the meetings in the school auditorium, introducing the preacher, and helping direct the program.

His response was a bit shocking.

"I'm in the process of changing parishes," he said, "and I hope to get a promotion. To be identified with your meetings and the broadcast will be a negative in the bishop's mind and might keep me from getting the promotion and that new appointment."

Surprised that the association would affect his appointment, and even more surprised at his up-front, honest admission of self- interest, I pursued the matter no further.

Twenty years later, October, 1979, in the high school auditorium in Greenville, North Carolina, a group of local churches sponsored a series of meetings. The pastor of a large local Free Will Baptist Church refused to participate because the evangelist's son's hair was too long, and his lifestyle unacceptable to this pastor, although the son was 25 years old and not living at home.

Maybe my imagination didn't stray too far after all.

Along with the practical difficulties there are doctrinal differences that some cannot set aside. If the evangelist is not a Calvinist, at least a modified one believing in unconditional security, most Independent and Southern Baptists will not only not sponsor the meetings, they will not attend, even when the sermons do not identify the preacher's theological position.

A very successful meeting was in progress in the Fairmount Park Free Will Baptist Church, Norfolk, Virginia, February, 1958, with the house filled to capacity, four to five hundred each night and many responding to the invitation every night. A group of a dozen sailors from the Navigator's ministry, whose ship was in dock, was attending with great enthusiasm and compliments. At the door after service, they'd depart with, "See you tomorrow night."

And they did.

Never missed a night, until one night at the door their leader said to the evangelist, "Somebody said that you didn't believe in *Eternal Security*," with a tone of voice that indicated the 'somebody' was surely mistaken. Everybody who believed the Bible believed *Eternal Security*.

"I don't believe in unconditional security," I confessed. "I believe in conditional salvation from start to finish."

"But the Bible says..." he continued as he began to turn to John 10, knowing that surely I must have never read that passage about eternal life.

I stopped him and as politely as possible said, "For one full year I sat in Greek, Hebrew, and theology classes in graduate school, taught by extremely intelligent, educated professors who were Calvinists, and they never convinced me of their position. I don't think in five minutes in the door of the church, you'll be able to accomplish what they couldn't do every day in nine months. So, let's agree to disagree on this one theological issue, be friends, and continue to enjoy the meetings together."

They never came back. Nothing was said in a sermon that revealed the evangelist's position. Someone, who had not been to the meetings, never heard the preacher, in a negative critical manner had probably enlightened him about the "heresy" of conditional security, and closed the door to his mind on the subject, so he could not listen to that preacher anymore.

The plane was taxiing from the gate to the runway. Fastening a seat belt, I looked directly across the narrow aisle and thought, "Is that who I think it is?"

Hesitating to say anything for fear of being embarrassed by a false identification, I waited until we were airborne and he moved his briefcase. There in gold shining letters was a name that matched the face. It actually was Dr. R.G. Lee, renowned leader among Southern Baptists, former three-term President of the Convention, well-known author of several books, and famous pastor of Bellevue Baptist in Memphis, Tennessee. Acknowledging that I recognized him, I commented as to how I had enjoyed reading his sermons and complimented him on his knowledge of the English language, especially descriptive adjectives, and that I had heard him preach *Payday Someday* in the First Baptist Church in Nashville, when I was in college in the early 50s.

He enlightened me as to how many times he had preached that message, and that even though he had joined the society of the octogenarians, he was continuing a very full schedule of speaking engagements, specifically telling me how many times he preached the previous year, where he was coming from and where he was going to.

As the conversation moved along a little crack opened up for me to introduce myself and explain who I was and where I was headed…a full-time evangelist, had been since leaving college, and I was on my way to conduct a revival meeting in a Free Will Baptist church.

His response, "Well, maybe you can straighten them out on security!" left me speechless for a moment. On a plane, 30,000 feet in the air, across the aisle from a venerable Southern Baptist leader, was neither the place nor time to settle the question of eternal security.

"Yeah, maybe so," I said, changing the subject, leaving that can of worms unopened.

Afterwards, the thought that surfaced in my mind over and over again was that such a great, intelligent, spiritual man would honestly believe that the most important matter in a revival in a Free Will Baptist church was to convince them of the doctrine of eternal security.

In the fall of 1961, the pastor of an Independent Baptist church had scheduled a revival. A few weeks before the date, I finished a meeting on Sunday night, drove home after the service, arrived at 2:00 in the morning and found a letter from him cancelling the meeting. His two reasons were: my position on "eternal security" and my support of Mount Olive College.

At 3:00 a.m. I called him. "I just arrived home," I said, "and read your cancellation letter. The reasons have left me confused. In the first place, you understood my position on apostasy and the security question before we planned the meetings. It is, by the way, the same as Dr. Bob Jones Sr. and Jr." (He was very close with the Joneses and the university.)

"As to supporting Mount Olive College, the fact that I do not support the school is well known by all who know me and could be substantiated easily by a little investigating. If you think it best to call off the meeting, I'll not be offended nor inconvenienced. The schedule is filled and some churches are waiting for a possible cancellation. I'm just curious as to the real reason."

There was a long pause. The sound of his thinking could be heard in the silence.

He finally said, "Well, actually, Preacher, some of my Independent Baptist brethren are putting pressure on me not to have you preach in my church."

There was another pause. He was weighing the matter and came to this conclusion. "Oh, you come on, Preacher. It's none of their business."

"If it's putting you on the spot, don't worry over it."

"No, you keep it in your schedule. We're going to have the meetings."

And we did. It was well attended and very fruitful. He baptized several adult converts from the meeting, and we became good friends. Nine years later he was in a pastorate in South Carolina and invited me for another evangelistic campaign.

The experience simply adds evidence to the difficulty of "cooperative" evangelism.

Maybe those imaginary men in Mark 2 aren't so exaggerated after all.

Religion, education, money, and culture have erected walls that separate people into distinct groups, and built mountains that were too high to climb. Ministering in that environment for 60 years, it has been impossible for me to lay a foundation that would support cooperative or mass evangelism.

Money – Second Problem

About 3,000 years ago, a preacher, living on this third terrestrial planet in this solar system under the sun, looked at life as it appeared to be and said, ... *money answereth all things* (Ecclesiastes 10:19).

Here's another preacher three millenniums later, on the same planet under the same sun, living among descendants of that generation and saying, "I think he was right. Love may make the world go round, but money speeds it up and slows it down."

At the time of this writing, the winter of 2009-2010, the U.S. economy has stalled into a deep recession. The Federal Government has attached jumper cables to infuse one trillion five hundred billion, borrowed, printed paper dollars of financial energy in a desperate effort to jump-start that economy. That's one thousand five hundred billions, one million five hundred thousand millions, $1,500,000,000,000, a stack of $1,000 bills over 90 miles high. If the U.S. population is about 300 million, that's $5,000 for every man, woman, and child. That's money's answer to all things in the economic world.

In the 2008 presidential election, the winner spent over $711,000,000 and moved into the White House. The loser spent over $400,000,000 and went back to his Senate seat. In North Carolina the winner spent over $17,000,000 in the last four years, $8,000,000 through the primaries and $9,000,000 in the general election and moved into the governor's mansion. The loser spent more than $4,000,000 in the general election and moved to who knows where. That's money's answer to all things in the political world.

Is it necessary to bring up religion? Questionable methods of money raising, misuse of funds, lavish lifestyles, even criminal charges against so many big-time evangelistic ministries are evidence of the role money plays in modern evangelism. Not all such ministries have indulged in these questionable practices, yet in the honest, conservative, legitimate organizations, large amounts of money are needed for television, radio, cooperative campaigns, missions, etc.

Franklin Graham was in Greenville, North Carolina, September 27-28-29, 1998, in the football stadium at East Carolina University for a cooperative evangelistic campaign with a budget of just under one million dollars. If the attendance averaged 20,000 per night, to meet the budget the offering would need to be $15 per person, every man, woman, and child, for every service. In my ministry in over 50 years that has never happened and was not likely in the Graham meeting. A large portion of the budget must be raised from churches, businesses, and individuals along with free will offerings. Renting football stadiums, saturating the area with publicity, maintaining the organization necessary to plan and successfully bring to pass such a crusade takes money, large amounts of money which I have not been capable of raising, nor have I had any passion to try.

Speaking of big money, according to a recent news release, in 2008 Franklin Graham's compensation as CEO of Samaritan's Purse was $535,000, as CEO of Billy Graham Evangelistic Association, $669,000, totaling $1,204,000.

It's probably more pride than piety, but over these 58 years, we have never solicited funds through the mail, over the internet, nor in person to support a ministry of evangelism. There have never been any minimums set, expenses required, or financial demands for us to come for meetings, and there has never been a year when the total gross income from church love offerings reached $30,000, including the years that I preached almost 50 weeks. One year, 1984, it topped out at $29,503.

Maybe more should have been required of churches, possibly making it easier for other evangelists to follow. Right or wrong, the only way I could do the work was with no price on the ministry. No argument about cooperative evangelism being legitimate and many of those in it are honest, sincere preachers, and someone must be in the money-raising ministry since it is necessary for the Lord's work, the problem is that I couldn't do it. That put any large-scale cooperative evangelism beyond my reach, but freed me from frustration over finances.

So, on the earth under the sun money still talks in politics, economics, and religion, but not with the same volume. When money talks in church, it has a bad case of laryngitis.

In almost 60 years there have been few discussions and no serious disagreements about love offerings or revival remunerations.

On a Sunday evening in 1976, at the end of a series of meetings in Tidewater, Virginia, the pastor approached me in the vestibule with this explanation, "Since our church has become so large and the offerings so much, our board has decided that no evangelist needs that much money and has adopted a practice of paying an evangelist $500."

"That sounds generous enough," I responded. "But the offerings received each night were announced as revival offerings, so the people who gave assumed the money was for this revival."

"We'll use it for the next revival," he said.

"The problem is nobody understood the board's practice and no public announcement was made concerning the money. I'm only suggesting that the visitors and members who give should be told how revival money will be spent. If the plan is to raise a specific amount, then have a budget for the revival, $500 for the evangelist, $300 for advertising, $200 for musicians, utilities, building expense…, whatever. If the total budget is, say $1,500, make that clear to the congregation and when the offerings reach $1,500, take no more offerings. Otherwise some folks will think the evangelist received all of it and was overpaid. Let everybody know what's happening with the money. That way everything will be out in the open and no misunderstanding."

"Since you didn't understand our practice before you came, I'll talk to the board and we'll decide later," he said.

He walked away somewhat disturbed. I left, with no money, to await their decision.

A short time later, a brief letter came explaining how the offering had been allocated for musicians, advertisement, etc., and a check for $1,020 for the evangelist.

In answer I told the preacher that before I came for the meeting I had promised the Lord that whatever the love offering was, I'd give it back to his church school (At the time they operated a college.), and in order to put the contribution into two years for tax purposes, enclosed find a $500 check, and after January 1, there would be another $500. And there was.

That was my last meeting with that pastor and that church. Several years later a rather derogatory letter came, accusing me of lying about that offering and saying that I understood before I came that they paid $500 to evangelists, and they paid me my $500 as they did other evangelists and I had no right to be unhappy about the $500.

Oh the tricks that memory can play. How does a preacher forget receiving a $1,000 gift for his school and other details of the incident?

In a church in South Georgia, an area not known for being overly generous to evangelists, the pastor said after a couple of nights, "I guess you've noticed we're not receiving any offerings in the meetings."

"Hadn't thought about it," I said.

But after he mentioned it I did remember from previous meetings that it was customary to take up revival offerings in that particular church, which was not true of many churches. Some raised the money before the meetings. Some took it from the treasury. One or two raised the money by deacons on the ground before and after church, buttonholing men of the church and asking for their share of the money to finance the revival.

"We're taking no offerings because the last time you were here, the offering was more than they pay and they kept it. So I told them if they planned to pay a specific amount in the budget, we'd take it from regular church funds and pay that amount. But we weren't taking up love offerings and putting it in the bank. You'll not get as much as I'd like or as much as you would in a love offering, but I couldn't get them to give the love offering," he explained.

"Preacher, I'll be satisfied with whatever they give. But if you think the budgeted amount is not as generous as you want, give the people an opportunity to give if they so desire. During the preliminaries on Sunday night, last night of the meeting, you could say to the congregation, 'The church is paying this evangelist $200 for the week. If any of you want to give him something in addition to that, just put it in his hand as you leave.'"

After service, shaking hands at the door, as I bade farewell to everybody, money kept accumulating in my pocket. When we reached the parsonage the pastor could hardly wait to count that money. It was over $600.

Not long afterwards, he visited another revival, saw me, and his greeting was, "You got me fired."

Maybe he was joking. He did resign the church and move on.

Northport, Alabama, July 1956, was one of the most fruitful meetings of the '50s. The circumstances were such that with little effort it was an outstanding meeting. Some Southern Baptist churches were just coming out of a couple of great revivals with some of their best evangelists and those folks were excited. When word got around among them about our meetings, crowds began coming. During eight days I preached 13 times and every night the little church overflowed. The enthusiasm and response was evidence of a refreshing experience of revival.

The love offering was so large that the church board decided it was too much for an evangelist so they paid me a specific amount. When the matter came up at the church business meeting and people learned what had happened, they voted to send me that entire love offering. A little late, but the generosity of the people delivered the money to the evangelist.

Another meeting was scheduled and this time the board decided to take care of the matter ahead of time, so they passed a motion to pay all visiting evangelists a designated amount per service. In that meeting I preached 21 times in 12 days and the offerings were not enough to pay the per service amount for the 21 services, so they were forced to subsidize the meetings from the church treasury.

The third meeting, having learned from the second, the board voted to give me the offerings so they'd not need to take anything from the treasury. The offerings were more than the amount they voted to pay per service.

The pay policy was changed three times in three meetings so as not to pay the evangelist too much, and all three times he received more than their payment plan provided.

In 1992, Bill McCarty had gone to Ashland Free Will Baptist Church, Hayward, California, in an attempt to resurrect the dead. The building was closed. The yard had grown up and become a trash dump, and under trees and bushes in cardboard dwellings winos, alcoholics, drug addicts had declared squatter's rights. Bill cleared out the wine bottles, broken glass, hypodermic needles, cardboard and other home furnishings, but he had a difficult job evicting the tenants. They kept coming back and refurnishing the place. He and the police kept running them off and shipping out their furniture on a garbage truck.

When it was finally understood that there would be church services in the building most of them found some other place to sleep. New paint, inside and out, new blinds for the windows, lights outside and inside, and a new sign projected a new image that the church was back in business. Saturday they distributed handbills with an invitation to Easter Service, Sunday morning, April 19, followed by revival meetings through Friday, the 24th.

We had scheduled meetings in Sacramento, Fresno, and Stockton. Seeing as how we would already be in California, Bill asked if I'd consider preaching in a small re-opened church. He couldn't promise crowds, converts or cash, but the few folks needed to hear evangelistic preaching. So Bill and I stood in an open door in the warm spring sunshine of the Bay Area, looking as far as we could see down the street, waiting for someone to appear moving in our direction who might be coming to church, the church being at the end of the street beside the BART (Bay Area Rapid Transit) railroad tracks.

A family or two walked, a few more came in vehicles and with 15 or 20 we began revival that Easter morning. The house was never filled. Some visitors came from other churches. There were neither great crowds nor a community-shaking revival, which explains the shock on Friday night when Bill handed me the love offering check for $1,471.14.

"Where did all this money come from?"

"On Monday night, a visiting lady came with a woman from our church," he said. "She doesn't live in this community, came only one night, and said she would not be able to come back. At the door she asked me how she could make a contribution to your ministry. I suggested she could make a check to the church and we would include it in our gift to you for the meetings. She turned aside, wrote the check, handed it to me, commented about the preaching, and left. I looked at the check. It was for $1,000. That's where $1,000 of that offering came from."

In one way or another our personal, material needs have been more than supplied, never been confronted with a financial crisis, never solicited funds, never attempted to raise money for a ministerial budget, which also means there never was enough money to put together a large cooperative evangelistic organization.

With no organization, no public relations people, no one to go into areas and set up meetings, no full-time musicians, some, more or less cooperative meetings, grew from the grassroots concern of a pastor or several churches in a community.

Circumstances sometimes turned a local church revival into a community meeting. In the early '50s many churches were part-time, quarter-time, preaching one Sunday each month, half-time, two Sundays, first and third or second and fourth, with very few full-time churches with resident pastors and a full weekly schedule of activities. If a good revival was going on in the community, folks from all those part-time churches came, anxious to hear the preaching, responding with some fervor and zeal, spreading the word around, and crowds grew. There was not something to do at every church eight nights a week. They were not burned out and tired of listening to preaching. In most areas there had been a drought of evangelistic preaching for years. The fields were white, ripe for harvest, enlarging local church meetings to practical cooperative meetings with all the characteristics except organization and promotion.

THE PLACES
Elm Grove Free Will Baptist, Winterville, NC
Spring of 1953

One annual revival was the custom, but the pastor was so persistent the leadership agreed to allow him to use the new auditorium for a spring revival with the understanding it was not in the budget. Frank, the pastor, contacted me to preach six nights during spring break from college. The large auditorium, balcony, vestibule, and aisles, were filled to overflow every night with over 60 decisions and 50 baptisms.

From that, Frank and I became the closest of friends, and wherever he pastored until his death, we were together in revival services in: Johnston Union FWB; Hugo FWB; First FWB, Goldsboro; and beginning new churches, First FWB, Tarboro; Hope FWB, Scotland Neck; First FWB, Pinetops; West Duplin FWB, Warsaw; Faith FWB, Kinston; Faith FWB, Goldsboro; and the mission in Fremont, NC, where as an old retired preacher

Frank attempted to organize one more Free Will Baptist Church before he departed for heaven.

When Frank was young in the ministry, at a quarterly meeting he was appealing for funds for missions. The older leadership didn't like Frank's personality, preaching, or appeal and were against anything he was for. The way the story goes, in the heat of the debate, an old preacher, D. W. Alexander, stood and addressed his peers, "Men," he said, "you may revoke this man's credentials. You may take his church. But he'll find a street corner where he can preach, and in six months he will have organized a new one."

Every evangelist preaches for a circle of preachers and Frank was in my circle. We bumped heads only once, and that was not hard enough to bruise the relationship. Frank was at Faith Church, Goldsboro, which he started in addition to many other churches in eastern North Carolina, when some leadership conflict developed between him and a couple of deacons, sad but not unusual among strong-willed people, and a new church started, Victory. That's a great name for a church out of a church.

The folks at Victory invited me for revival. Before the dates came up, I met Frank, who was still chaffing under the disagreement with those who left, and he greeted me with, "I hear you're going to preach a meeting at Victory."

"They've invited," I said.

"Well, if you preach over there, you'll never preach for me again."

"Now, Frank. Whether I preach for you or not is your decision and we'll continue being friends whether or not you have me back in your church. There are many preachers who are my friends, in whose churches I've never preached. In the second place, I hope you have not used me in meetings over the years just because we were friends, but rather that you thought my preaching would help the church and reach the unsaved. Any meeting for a personal or political favor certainly has the wrong motive. In the third place, Frank, whether or not I preach in your church is your decision, but whether or not I preach in Victory is not your decision. That's my decision. You're trying to do to me what you would not allow any man to do to you, decide for you where you're going to preach. I wouldn't think of threatening you with where you could or could not preach."

He began to smile, broke out in laughter and said, "Oh, you're right. Go on and preach at Victory; I may attend the meeting. And count on coming back to Faith church."

Even after he retired at Faith and began the mission in Fremont, Frank and I were together in meetings several times. I was honored with the privilege of preaching the funeral of Frank Davenport, who started and organized more Free Will Baptist churches in eastern North Carolina, with little or no help from any mission board, than any other pastor, evangelist, or missionary in my generation.

First Free Will Baptist, Goldsboro, NC
Summer of 1951

Home from college after one year, working on the tenant farm during the day and preaching at night, I was in Goldsboro with a packed house every night. On Tuesday night Clarence Bowen, pastor of East Nashville Free Will Baptist, Nashville, Tennessee, visiting friends in the area, attended the meetings. Thirty people came forward that night (about 100 during the week). We needed help in counseling and praying with them, so I asked Brother Bowen. He gladly consented and went back to Nashville so excited that he asked me to conduct a meeting in his church during the following school year.

First Free Will Baptist, Greenville, NC
March, 1957

The church had not long progressed to full time. The meetings ran for two weeks, 16 services, with nightly attendance beyond the capacity of the auditorium. Sunday School rooms were opened, aisles and pulpit area packed, people coming from many churches in Pitt County and surrounding areas, many decisions, all the marks of a united evangelistic meeting, except the title.

Parkers Chapel Free Will Baptist, Greenville, NC
June, 1958

Billy, my brother, was serving Parkers Chapel as its first full-time pastor. The way that came about is an interesting little story in itself of how the church went full-time and Billy took a cut in pay.

Unusual circumstances laid the groundwork for this great meeting. A little girl, 10 or 12 years old, was converted, wanted to be baptized, but her father thought she was too young and refused to allow it. Soon thereafter, her body was found dead at the door of the outhouse, from what the medical examiner said was heart failure. Scores of people from that family and their friends and neighbors came to Jesus during that meeting. Crowds were large, response was great, and Billy baptized about 50.

Bethel Free Will Baptist, Kinston, NC
1968, 1969, 1971, 1972, 1979

Five times in 12 years with large crowds every time, we had meetings with David Paramore in Bethel Church, always with good cooperation from area churches,and large crowds. In one eight-day meeting, ten services, the attendance averaged over 900 per night and closed on Sunday night with above 1,100 people, the largest crowds in a local church revival in my 60 years of evangelism.

In addition to local church meetings which bore the marks of union meetings, there have been some planned, promoted cooperative meetings.

Flat River, Missouri
July, 1953

Several churches in the lead belt area rented a tent, erected it in the park, and invited the Gospeliers quartet to come for a two-week united effort. Sterling Tucker, a recent Bible College graduate and local preacher, planned and promoted the meetings. The Picirillis and Jacksons had just married that summer and were on sort of a working honeymoon. The fellowship was good. The work was difficult, with little evidence of much accomplished.

Pic and Tucker were called away in the middle of the meetings to go to South Carolina, Tucker for sickness in his wife's family, Pic to report to his draft board. Jackson, Waddell and Raper were left to work through the final week.

Several years later during a testimony meeting in Flat River First Church, a fellow said that he was converted in that tent meeting in the park. Maybe it wasn't totally fruitless. The Lord keeps better records on such matters than any of us.

High School Gymnasium, Winterville, NC
August, 1953

The Gospeliers quartet had been in Reedy Branch Free Will Baptist in June, and was invited back for a cooperative meeting in August, sponsored by several churches in the area. The previous meetings were a feeder to this one. It was August, no air conditioning, the crowds were large, the gym was hot. We sang, preached and sweated our suits wet every night. Even so the attendance and response were very good.

Tent in Park, Cordova, Alabama
June, 1954

Sponsored by the local Youth for Christ in an effort to reach young people, the meetings ran for one week. The "tent in the park" was neutral ground, hoping to attract some who would not go to a church. A young Wesleyan musician came to take charge of the music. Nothing earthshaking happened that moved the town, but there was good attendance and response from the teens.

Courthouse, Baxley, GA
August, 1954

The quartet was together again singing every night in the courthouse and on the street and on the radio every day. I was preaching. The meetings continued for two weeks after which the Baxley Free Will Baptist Church was organized. Brother C. D. Rentz planned the revival with the idea of organizing a church in Baxley.

Senior High School Auditorium, Rocky Mount, NC
June 15-27, 1959

There had been some successful local church meetings in Rocky Mount, so a group of businessmen came together to sponsor a two-week cooperative meeting, They rented the high school auditorium, brought in some musicians, purchased time for daily radio and an hour of TV time on the Greenville station, and spent some money in advertising and promoting. Meetings were well attended. Several Baptist churches participated.

Telecasts went without a hitch. Cystitis infection held me under the weather for one of the two weeks.

High School Auditorium, Durham, NC
April 17-24, 1960

Several fundamental churches in the Durham area every couple of years on a regular basis came together for an evangelistic meeting, rented the high school auditorium, brought in musicians and an evangelist, and spent enough promotional money for a successful effort. Thurlow Spur was the music man. There were services in several public high schools (That was before such were outlawed.), daily radio broadcasts, good attendance, and a fruitful meeting.

School Auditorium, Kinston, NC
May 29-June 4, 1961

Mt. Calvary Free Will Baptist, Hookerton, North Carolina, and a couple of Baptist churches in Kinston put this meeting together. David Paramore, pastor at Mt. Calvary, did most of the legwork. It was a good meeting. David came to Kinston soon afterwards to lead Bethel into becoming a great church.

Preaching Mission, Erwin, TN
March 12, 1962

This was an annual event sponsored by the ministerial association. There were only two services. One was in an auditorium, the other in First Free Will Baptist Church.

Community Building, Pikeville, NC
April 16-22, 1973

Johnny Howell and his insurance agency planned this cooperative effort, enlisting some town churches and Living Waters

Church near town. Nothing earthshaking or townshaking visibly happened, but it was a good meeting with several decisions.

School Auditorium, Perth, New Brunswick, Canada
April 2-13, 1975

This twelve-day meeting grew out of Wesleyan people and preachers who had participated in evangelistic meetings in towns along the St. John River south of Perth-Andover. The local Wesleyan Church took the initiative, sponsoring the meetings, furnishing musicians, and generally underwriting expenses. Attendance ran between 400 and 500 nightly with great response. As a result of these meetings, invitations came to conduct revivals in the Wesleyan churches in Halifax and Dartmouth, Nova Scotia.

During those meetings in Halifax, the pastor took us to Peggy's Cove on a stormy day, an unforgettable experience. An angry roaring ocean at war with the wind was sending 15 and 20 foot waves to attack the rock shoreline, crashing like thunder, then breaking into clouds of salty spray lifting over the rocks, and blown by the wind for half a mile, drenching the parking lot and everyone in it with fallout from the battle.

Small houses and cabins were holding to slick, wet, dark rock for dear life, evidently anchored in some unshakeable fashion to their rock foundation. People aren't so immoveable. Not being anchored, several are washed off the slippery rocks each year and some drown, in spite of the many warning signs. We listened to the roar, watched the waves, were soaked by the cloud, and were told that it was one of the most picturesque, photographed, canvas-painted places on the continent, a favorite spot and home for artists. Peggy's Cove painted its own picture in our memories. That picture has faded very little in 30 years.

Years later from the Nova Scotia revivals came meetings in Wesleyan churches in Myrtle Beach, South Carolina, and

Sanford, North Carolina, all resulting in a lasting friendship with many Wesleyan folks.

Bath School, Carleton County, New Brunswick, Canada
November 26-30, 1975

For about 14 years I had been preaching revivals in the Primitive Baptist churches in Carleton County with good attendance and response. This time the pastors decided to get together, combine their church efforts, rent school facilities and plan five days in each of three schools, Bath, Centreville, and Hartland. In morning services in various churches I preached a series on revivals in the Old Testament. In the evening, with about 500 people each night, there were evangelistic services. The interest and response were some of the most memorable in my ministry.

One Sunday morning I preached on the crucifixion in the First Baptist Church, Woodstock, New Brunswick. This church was a bit out of the area of the meetings and not participating. By the cool response to that message and overall unfriendliness, it was evident that they preferred not to be participants. But the general public in the towns where the churches were participating responded with great favor to the meetings.

Centreville School, Carleton County, New Brunswick, Canada
October 31 – November 4, 1975

From Hartland, through the world's longest covered bridge, across the St. John River, north on blacktop 103 about six miles, east four miles on 110, and there's a community, Centreville, New Brunswick. Or one may choose to go north on TransCanada and cross the river at Florenceville. In that school at Centreville the meetings continued five days. During my first meeting in Stickney, Ghernot Wheeler, known as the best gospel pianist in the area, played for the meetings. He owned and operated a general store in Centreville. Eska's China Shop, owned by Eska Buchanan, a longtime, close, dear friend, was there. The excitement in the meetings continued in Centreville.

Hartland School, Hartland, New Brunswick, Canada
November 5-9, 1975

The meetings climaxed and closed Sunday afternoon in Hartland, with a house filled. These area-wide meetings were as close to real cooperative evangelistic meetings as any in our ministry in over 60 years of preaching.

Several times in New Brunswick our meetings would begin in a local church, grow, move to a school, and close on Sunday afternoon. Most years the dates were the last of October into November, after potato harvest. More than one time on the closing Sunday from inside a cozy school auditorium, as the service was in progress, the first snow would begin to fall, turning all the attention away from the preacher to the sight of huge flakes of wet snow drifting softly past the large windows and beginning to stick to the trees, as if nature were saying it's time to finish these meetings and head south before you get snowed in for the winter.

One time after an eight-inch snow came overnight, we drove 100 miles the next day through a Christmas card. The road was clear, and on either side the spruce and fir trees, their boughs loaded with new fallen snow, bowed as we passed, or maybe they were weeping over the death of their children who had been cut down, wrapped, and corded by the side of the road, ready to be shipped away as Christmas trees in some large city.

The snow began again late in the afternoon forcing us to get off the road, sleep overnight, dig out the following morning, and continue heading south.

Freedom Hall, Johnson City, TN
July 20-27, 1975

With the most churches cooperating, more than 30, covering the largest area, Johnson City, Elizabethton, Erwin, Carter County, best work of coordination and promotion, largest budget for publicity and expenses, biggest facility for accommodating the meetings, more work with a choir, musicians, ushers, personal workers, etc., this became by far the largest evangelistic meeting of my ministry, opening on Sunday afternoon with over 3,000 in attendance, a 200 voice choir, the Gethsemane Quartet, and averaging over 2,000 per night through Friday, closing on Sunday afternoon, July 27.

Keith Kenemer served as coordinator, organizing, appointing committees, and raising funds to pay for the use of Freedom Hall before the services began. He helped get local choirs together with musicians for practice in preparation for the meetings. I preached in Central Free Will Baptist Church on Sunday morning before the meetings began and Eastside Free Will Baptist on the Sunday morning that the meetings ended in the afternoon. The joy of preaching to that many people and the excitement of those meetings lingers in memory with much gratitude to the Lord for the opportunity. Lest someone think money has anything to do with it, when the finance committee paid all the bills, there was some left, so they paid me $400.

School Gymnasium, Baxley, GA
June 20-26, 1976

The quartet was scheduled to be together again in Baxley, twenty-three years after those meetings in the courthouse. This time several churches came together, rented the gym, and Brother C.D. Rentz worked again promoting the effort. Problems developed in one of the leading churches undergirding the meeting. Families at odds, pastor caught in the middle, church split, a new one started, and the controversy almost destroyed interest in the meetings. So much so that the members of the quartet decided there was not enough support to merit the four fellows spending time and energy for the week.

Some folks, in spite of the problems, wanted the meeting. The gym had been secured, publicity material distributed, times set, and other plans made.

Without the quartet, the meetings were carried through. Attendance was less than great. For promotion on Friday night, Jane and Philip hosted the largest banana split in the state of Georgia, gallons of vanilla, chocolate, strawberry ice cream with bananas and toppings in a canoe.

Some decisions, mostly young people. Church trouble and lack of cooperation hindered the meeting from being what it could have been.

Football Stadium, Florence, SC
August 22 – 29, 1976

The following year, after the big meeting in Freedom Hall, the same team worked together in Florence, SC, in another cooperative effort. The pay was more, $1,550, although the attendance was less.

One of the most cooperative groups of Free Will Baptist pastors in the country is in the Florence area. Twenty-five or thirty meet for breakfast once a month just for fellowship and the joy of being together. Having heard about Johnson City, they decided to rent the local high school football stadium, work together and plan a united evangelistic campaign. For several years I had been in Florence almost every year in one of the churches in meetings with good attendance and response.

Keith Kenemer was enlisted again to help with the ground-work. Willie Justice, pastor of First Free Will Baptist, threw him-self with all his energy into it. Others joined in. A flatbed from an eighteen-wheeler became the stage platform and the stadium bleachers became seating for the congregation. About 500 per service attended. A policeman working security was converted and a few others.

On the closing Sunday afternoon a developing thunderstorm speeded things up somewhat. The storm in rolling heavy clouds like black smoke from a forest fire was rising up rapidly behind the crowd seated on the bleachers, invisible to them, but very vis-ible to those of us on the platform. Halfway through the sermon the wind shifted directions, picked up speed, and was behind that storm, blowing it directly toward the stadium. Thunder, lightning, and rain had not arrived but it was on its way, rid-ing the wind and gaining momentum by the minute. A few of the folks looking back through the wooded area of tall oak trees close behind the stands could see the darkness coming.

The sermon on *The Great White Throne Judgment* had a short last half, a shorter conclusion, an even shorter invitation, and a record-setting shorter benediction, with encouragement for everyone to seek shelter, as large drops of rain began falling from a sky now black overhead and rolling like smoke. The crowd dis-persed with the speed of fire ants when their nest is disturbed and everyone made it to cover before the bottom fell out. With that degree of excitement, the meetings came to an end.

Some experiences are memorialized by erecting marble monuments etched with unforgettable dates and events, good and bad. August, 1976, a day or two before the meetings were scheduled to begin in the stadium in Florence, two men walked into my study, introduced themselves, laid their badges on the desk, read me my Miranda rights, "You have a right to remain silent…etc.," and said, "We are IRS agents, understand we are not auditors, we are here to conduct a fraud investigation by reconstructing your income through a net worth audit. Would you mind answering a few questions?"

Fast forward eight or ten months, the income for 1973, 1974, 1975 having been reconstructed, and finding no fraud, the case was turned over to local auditors for resolution. The only question was the housing allowance. The house was debt free, but since the IRS used fair rental value on parsonages to collect Social Security Taxes, that seemed a fair figure and justifiable amount for housing.

Wrong.

"That's not the way it works," they said, "housing allowance must be spent on the house within the year that it is designated."

"Then, if I borrow money on the house and set up a monthly loan payment that can be housing?"

"Yes."

"That's great. The payment, which includes interest, will not be considered income, and the interest will be deductible as an itemized deduction, which means it will be nontaxable twice. That's a loss to the IRS."

"We know it. But that's the way it works."

The next day the local savings and loan had a new customer. In a few weeks a friend offered to sell to me a percentage owner-ship in some storage warehouses in Rocky Mount. The money borrowed on the house at 8% returned 15% for the next six years in the warehouses, and the 8% came off income tax twice. All as a result of that terrible experience with those IRS agents. Unquestionable evidence that it is wise not to evaluate the events of your life on the day they happen.

A Chinese fable goes something like this. A wealthy man owned a prize horse which ran away. His neighbors came to sym-pathize with him on his bad luck.

"How do you know it is bad?" he asked.

In two weeks that horse returned bringing with him a herd of 20 horses. His neighbors stopped by to rejoice with him and his good luck.

"How do you know it is good luck?"

His son, in an effort to ride one of those wild horses, fell off and broke both legs.

His neighbors sympathized with him and his bad luck.

"How do you know it is bad luck?"

While the son was laid up with broken legs the king conscripted all young healthy men for battle in a war. The boy was deferred.

His neighbors came to rejoice with him on the good luck.

And so on, and so on, and so on....

That day those fellows laid those badges on the desk, and read me my rights, I was terrified, and forced to push it to the back corner of my mind, and concentrate on what would probably be the largest evangelistic effort of the year. Looking back, that day forced me to make some financial decisions that proved to be most beneficial.

During the investigation the banker gave me some comic relief from the pressure. He saw me in the bank one day, and said, "Preacher, how are you doing?"

"I have a headache."

"Yeah, I met your headache yesterday," he said. "They were in here looking into your finances. Come in the office. Let me tell you about it.

"They came in, laid their badges on the desk, and asked to see your account records and your safety deposit box. I cooperated, until they asked to see your sons' savings accounts."

"'You're not authorized to see the sons' accounts,' I said.' Mr. Jackson gave you the right to see his. The sons have not given you that right.'

"'But his sons' accounts are a part of the family finances, and we can get authorization to see their accounts.'

"'I know that, but you don't have it.'

"So they departed, came back in a short while, laid their authorization on the desk, and demanded, 'Now, we want to see the sons' savings accounts.'"

"'They don't have any,' I said."

The agents didn't think it was funny.

But we did.

High School Auditorium, Sesser, IL
April 30 – May 5, 1978

Bear Point and Hazel Dell churches along with a couple of town churches sponsored the meeting. Attendance was good, but evangelistic outreach was limited.

Tabernacle, Portsmouth, OH
May 8-13, 1978

Calvin Evans, one of the best known pastor/evangelists in southern Ohio, was in charge of a camp meeting sponsored by the local association with services at the campground. The services were Monday through Saturday at the camp, Sunday morning at Union Free Will Baptist.

The meeting in the school in Sesser, IL, closed on Friday night. Monday driving across Kentucky on I-64 to get to Portsmouth, we were passing an old man driving a Mercury that was almost as old as he was, who decided to turn from the right lane of an interstate highway across the left lane through the grassy median to the other side of the highway, and go west instead of east. With no signal, no warning, he turned directly in front of us. Riding hard on the brakes, pulling left, I tried to miss him, but he kept coming left. With the horn blaring, brakes squealing, motor roaring, we crashed the right front into the driver's side of the Mercury, adding the sound of crumbling, twisting metal and breaking glass, knocking the old man and his car sideways through the grassy median into the westbound lane of I-64, crushing the right front quarter panel of the Cadillac, ripping the cables from the battery instantly cutting all electric power, shutting down the blaring horn, killing the engine, stopping the thumping windshield wipers in mid-cycle leaving them still against the glass...and silence, the deafening silence of a morgue. Motionless, speechless, like the frozen frame of a DVD movie when you hit the pause button, we sat with the sound of nothing...except the soft falling rain on the vinyl top, watching a hundred pieces of broken glass in slow motion slide on the water like lazy surfers down the windshield.

The Mercury was in the middle of the westbound lane, going the wrong way. A truck driver heard the horn, saw the accident, stopped and helped get the elderly man off the road. He was sitting in the car, stunned, bleeding from superficial cuts from flying glass, not critically hurt, but in danger of getting killed in the middle of that interstate.

The state patrolman said that he could not write a ticket because he didn't see the accident.

The truck driver said he would be glad to provide the details seeing as how he witnessed the whole thing.

The patrolman said that didn't matter. He still could not write a ticket because Kentucky had a no-fault insurance law.

A lingering suspicion says that the Kentucky law had nothing to do with it. The old man lived in that county and the Cadillac was from North Carolina, 500 miles away.

His insurance company totaled my car, paid half of what it was worth, and rented us a car for a week. That was the day I learned that plastic is the precious metal, not gold, and I didn't own any. The car rental company refused to rent me a car because I was so plastic poor that I didn't even have a little piece with all those numbers on it. They rented it to the insurance company.

Shaken up and bruised, saved by our seat belts from critical injury, we arrived in Portsmouth in time for the Monday service in the Tabernacle.

In May, 1981, in meetings at Sciotodale, OH, I was staying at Days Inn Motel. Early one morning on the way to walk a five-mile exercise route, it was necessary to drive to a convenient road, where there would be no competition with cars, 'cause in the game of chicken they always win.

Two eighteen-wheelers loaded with flour were parked on the edge of the access road while the drivers ate breakfast at Days Inn restaurant. Pulling out of the motel parking lot onto that access road, unable to see around the trucks, my almost new (less than 20,000 miles) 1979 Lincoln stuck its nose out two feet too far from behind those trucks and another old gentleman in an old car took $2,000 worth off the front end. Had it repaired and drove it 200,000 miles after that. Ohio is a dangerous place, and I drive through it with fear and trembling.

Lake City, SC
August 20-25, 1978

The meetings in the football stadium in Florence went so well, some Free Will Baptist churches south of Florence decided to rent the tabernacle of another denomination and plan an area-wide meeting for Lake City. Meetings were well attended, good cooperation and fellowship among pastors, but with limited evangelistic outreach.

Rose High School Gym, Greenville, NC
October 21-28, 1979

Pitt County, North Carolina, and the Greenville area is the home of more Free Will Baptists than most any other area of the country, dozens of churches, some of the larger, stronger churches in the denomination, making it apparently a most likely city for a cooperative, united evangelistic effort underwritten and sponsored by Free Will Baptists, except for that one huge obstacle – cooperation. So many differences, minor to some, major to others, make getting together almost impossible.

But in the fall of 1979, some of the pastors came together, planned and carried through with such an effort. Attendance was good, 500 on the beginning Sunday afternoon, and held at about 400 through the week, closing with 600 in the final Sunday afternoon service. One outstanding businessman was converted and has been actively involved in church as a leader for the past 30 years.

Not as successful as could have been with more participation by more pastors, but fruitful enough to make it worth the effort.

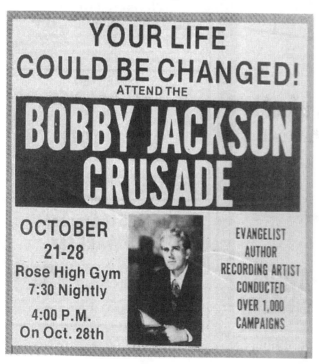

Coop meeting, October, 1979

Carleton County, New Brunswick, Canada
Bristol, November 12-17 .... Hartland, November 18-23, 1980

The previous meetings, in 1975, were so successful that five years later plans were made to do it again. Six days in the school at Bristol followed by six days in Hartland. Musicians were brought in to furnish good music, and 18 years of meetings up and down the St. John River in so many churches had spread a reputation for the evangelist. Many folks, who had attended and worked in other meetings for years, participated again, with 400 or 500 per service and good response. The closing on Sunday, November 23, was one of those that the first snow began falling during the afternoon service.

Liberty Association of Free Will Baptists
Friendship Church, Flomaton, AL
January 19-25, 1981

The meetings were held in a local church, but sponsored by the association. More like a camp meeting, with limited evangelistic potential.

School Auditorium, Erwin, TN
April 26-May 3, 1981

The meetings in Johnson City were so successful in 1975 that some pastors in the Erwin area got together for a similar effort on a smaller scale. Preached in the First Free Will Baptist Church on Sunday morning as meetings began, then Sunday night through Saturday in the auditorium, and closed Sunday morning and evening at Eastside, Elizabethton. Various local churches provided music and took turns directing the services. Good attendance and response. Less than Johnson City, but then there were fewer churches involved and a smaller town.

High School Auditorium, Edina, MO
April 1-7, 1985

This was the fourth series of meetings with the Assemblies of God church in Edina, having been there in 1971, 1975, 1982. The cooperation from the town was so exceptional in the three previous meetings that it was decided to make this one a united effort for all the churches in the town. The school auditorium was neutral ground, musicians were brought in and good publicity spread information about the services. Attendance and response exceeded any of the previous meetings. In every respect it was successful and fruitful in the town of Edina in northeastern Missouri.

Camp Meeting, Benton, IL
August 11-16, 1985

From Benton, Illinois east on Highway 14, ten miles toward McLeansboro, north on a blacktop road, past the Ketteman farm, Jane's home, another two miles is the Illinois Free Will Baptist Campground – *Camp Hope,* site of youth camps, retreats, and the annual adult camp. In the August heat, 1985, I preached at the adult camp meeting. Good attendance. House filled every night. Several responded to the invitation.

In July of 1957, 1959, 1964, I preached at their youth camp at the old location in West City across I-57 from Benton.

As a matter of fact, the record shows that I preached over 50 revival meetings in southern Illinois churches during the 60 years of my ministry.

In the fall of 1950, the most beautiful girl enrolled at Free Will Baptist Bible College, Nashville, TN, was from Ewing, IL. It was potential love at first sight and by December that potential had begun to be realized, so I was in Illinois during Christmas holidays visiting Jane, whose father, C. J. (Jack) Ketteman was pastoring a small church in Nason, an almost abandoned coal mining town with the mines closed and the people gone. Jack asked me to preach on Sunday morning. Ten minutes after the service ended he came to me and said, "The men just got together and decided we're beginning a revival meeting tonight with you doing the preaching."

For six months I had been speaking at youth rallies, in quartet services, and on Sundays, but this was the first revival meeting. My repertoire of three or four sermons had to be spread out over ten days of meetings, with the man who would two and one-half years later become my father-in-law, and for the remainder of his life the number one supporter of my ministry in southern Illinois.

During the winter of 1955 and 1956 we began services on Sunday night, December 25, 1955, Christmas Day, at Bakerville, about three miles south of Mt. Vernon on highway 37, continued through Wednesday night, January 4; skipped Thursday, Friday, and Saturday, moved to Waltonville, west about ten miles and picked up where we left off, continued for two full weeks ending on Sunday, January 22; from there to Ina, back on highway 37 six miles south of Bakerville, for two full weeks; only two days short of six weeks in three churches close enough in proximity to be one community.

Forty days, 44 services, six weeks of evangelistic meetings in sub-zero weather most of the time, with snow everywhere and some being added every six or seven days. During a snowstorm the church at Bakerville was packed to capacity. For the six weeks the crowds came, churches filled every night, scores of people converted, several families, mother, father, married children, in-laws, grandchildren. Some, who insisted on being baptized in the river instead of a baptistry, were baptized in the icy waters of the Big Muddy River. Some went to Bible College and into the ministry. Others became lifetime active members and leaders in area local churches.

No meeting has continued as long with as much success in my ministry as that one in Illinois in the winter of 1955 and 1956.

Many of those attending the camp meeting in 1985 brought with them memories of 1955. It was a great time of fellowship and reliving some wonderful times of the past, and enjoying the Lord's blessings in the present.

Central Conference of Free Will Baptists
Community Church, West Jefferson, OH
May 9-14, 1988

This was an annual event sponsored by the conference with services in one of their churches. More like a Bible Conference with limited evangelistic outreach. Therefore most of the messages were applicable to saint and sinner. Good attendance and interest.

First Free Will Baptist, Florence, SC
September 16-21, 1990

Danny Howell, pastor of First Free Will Baptist, Florence, SC, scheduled a week of meetings, decided to try a cooperative effort from a different angle and invited five churches from the area to participate. Each church would be responsible for one night of the week, Monday through Friday, bringing their choir with special music, supplying ushers, and that church's pastor would be in charge, directing the service, receiving the offering, introducing the speaker, with the same evangelist every night, using the same local church facilities but making the meetings community-wide in scope.

The effort was most successful, 400 to 500 every night, with good cooperation, fellowship and response. A short time after those meetings Danny was repairing a basketball goal in the gym, fell from the ladder, landed on his head, and died a few days later in the hospital. A good friend and fruitful pastor finished his day's work early and went home to rest.

Social Band Association, Pocahontas, AR
October 3 – 6, 1993

Calvin Evans was scheduled to preach for this cooperative effort sponsored by the local association, but Calvin became unable due to physical problems, so the committee chairman contacted me to fit it into my schedule and fill his place. In a community building in Hoxie, Arkansas, attendance was very good. On Sunday I preached in Sutton Free Will Baptist.

For two weeks, 16 services, I had been in Pocahontas, October 27 – November 9, 1958, and back for 12 days, 14 meetings, November 22 - December 3, 1961, with radio broadcasts every day, again April 15 – 21, 1985, for one week. So the 1993 meeting was a great time for touching base with old friends and making some new ones.

Chattahoochee Association, Butler, GA
March 21-26, 2004

The meetings were in Turners Chapel Free Will Baptist Church sponsored by the Association. Two years earlier, September 8-11, 2002, Sunday through Wednesday, we were in the local church with such good response to the meeting that Charles Clark, the pastor, planned another with the association participating. Charles, whose health had been deteriorating for several years, left to attend a much greater meeting with the Lord before the cooperative effort. Our meeting was good. His was great.

In addition to this list there were several youth camps, when I was young enough to keep the attention of that age group.

Benton, Illinois
July 23-30, 1957 – July 18-24, 1959 – July 20-31, 1964

Piney Woods, Woodlake, TX
August 12-17, 1957 – August 10-15, 1959 – August 19-23, 1963

South Carolina Youth, Cheraw, SC
August 8-20, 1960

West Fork, Bowie, TX
June 21-25, 1965

Youth Camp, Hartland, New Brunswick, Canada
July 7 – August 7, 1966

Are there any prospects for cooperative evangelistic meetings down the road? The road is short and the answer depends upon a group of pastors coming together with concern and interest and vision enough to work in the promotion of such a community-wide effort.

So we are back to where we began, facing the same obstacles. Keith Kenemer says that before both of us get too old to preach or sing, he would love to put together one more area-wide meeting, in which I would be overjoyed to preach.

So...maybe.

THE GOSPELIERS
By
Sackbut

After much discussion, the author finally agreed for me to write this chapter. The four fellows involved have grown old enough for the messenger boys whose responsibility it is to go into the memory vault, find stored information and deliver it to the mind, are moving slower, sometimes forgetting what they went after, other times not finding it at all. Their problem is not Alzheimer's, but more like that famous Albert Einstein train episode.

Albert Einstein was on a train going somewhere and misplaced his ticket. When the conductor came by collecting tickets, he said, "Oh! Dr. Einstein, don't fret over that ticket. You ride this train all the time. We know you. Forget about the ticket," and went on his way.

The conductor came back through and Einstein was down on the floor searching for that ticket.

"Dr. Einstein," he said, "I told you not to worry over that ticket. We know who you are."

The great scientist looked up at him and said, "I know who I am, too. But I don't know where I'm going."

They all know where they're going. They just don't remember why nor how to get there. They know what the refrigerator does. They don't remember why they went to it.

If their memories were sharp, it would still be impossible for any one of the four to objectively give an account of the events in their lives together during the past 50 years, since each one would color it as it appeared filtered through his subjective memory. I'm the only one, a part of the group, and apart from them, who can accurately tell the story. I've been with them almost from the beginning and will continue to the end. Fact is they never would have pitched a song in the right key without my help; sometimes they didn't with my help.

Battle between Sackbut and Train Whistle

In Bay Branch Church at Timmonsville, South Carolina, in a program representing the college, none of them had noticed that across the highway in front of the church was a mainline railroad track. As usual, I gave them the correct pitch. As they opened their mouths to hit that first note, a train near enough to shake the building sounded its whistle in a different key. Jackson started in the key of the whistle. Picirilli stuck with me. The other two were somewhere in between. Everybody laughed, and knowing they must try it again, I gave them that same pitch, and when the train whistle blew a second time, the house came down. By the time the laughter passed, so did the train. The third time was a charm, all in the right key but with a suppressed laugh just under the surface, they sang the song.

At times I was blamed for mistakes that are impossible for a pitch pipe to make. In the midst of a song as they reached the chorus where Waddell had a first tenor solo lead, he forgot it. Silence like a morgue hung over the congregation as the other three and the people waited, when it finally broke into Waddell's brain that he was supposed to be singing, knowing everybody would now realize someone had messed up, he looked at Picirilli and said, "Pic, you pitched it too high. Start over."

Pic and I pitched it in the same key, they started over, and anyone with enough musical ear to recognize the pitch had not been lowered, knew what happened.

Pitch pipes don't make mistakes. We're always right. We tell it like it is, so I'm telling the story.

The Beginning

Three eighteen-year-old fellows standing in the registration line at Free Will Baptist Bible College in the fall of 1950, bored at the length of that slow moving line, picked up on an old Southern Gospel tune, *Just a Little Talk with Jesus.* Two of them, Bobby Jackson and Eugene Waddell, had come from the same community, graduated from the same high school, sung together in school and out of school, before and after their conversion to Christ, in quartets, trios, duets, solos, and had been active in the youth revival movement that swept through eastern North Carolina.

The song began as a duet, until a third fellow, James Raper from Goldsboro, North Carolina, added the bass. The lead in the chorus made it impossible to sing *Little Talk* without a bass. What was left was tenor or baritone. Ray Turnage from Florence, South Carolina, was nearby and hearing the three, recognized the missing part and began with first tenor, Waddell switching to baritone. Thus was born, though maybe a bit malformed, a quartet.

The Freshmen

An official quartet was already working for the college, so these four sang at class functions, social gatherings, in the dorm, and the next time I saw them they were dressed in four blue turtleneck sweaters which identified them as a quartet, since they didn't look anything like a set of quadruplets. This was about the time I entered the picture. None of them had perfect pitch, no pianist was available for an accompanist, and somebody needed to get them started in the right key, even if they drifted flat during the song, which they did often enough to never ask me at the end of a song what key they finished in. Ignorance was bliss for them and their audience.

First Fundraiser

At the beginning of the second semester, early in 1951, the school planned to build an auditorium and needed $20,000. These boys were chosen to be sent on the road for three or four weeks with Henry "Pop" Melvin (Pop, the popular name he had chosen for himself.) the business manager, in an effort to raise enough funds to proceed with a concrete block auditorium. I made the trip, although not needed for every song, since Melvin played the piano, after a fashion, with that crooked arm cocked up on one side.

For advertising purposes on that fund-raising trip, Henry Melvin named the group the Freshman Quartet. Why didn't he think of the Four Freshmen? Other college quartets had used the name "Gospeliers" as they traveled for the school.

Sometime later, not far down the road, that official school name was stamped permanently on these four. No one realized at the time that all the former groups would disintegrate, come apart, pass away, but these four would be bound together with crazy glue that would hold them fast to each other for over 50 years and the name would stick and go with them. There had been other Gospeliers before them, but none would follow after them. The jerseys with that name would be retired. There'd not be another Gospeliers around the school in their lifetime.

Personnel Change

Soon after the tour, Turnage, out of necessity, hired on at a local pharmacy. They were not only paid nothing for the work on the road, but were charged room and board at the school while they were away, until they confronted Mr. Mac, the treasurer, who finally gave them credit for the food they didn't eat. Robert Picirilli had been singing with another school quartet, but the Gospeliers needed him and he was willing. Waddell switched to first tenor. Pic took baritone, Raper continued with bass, Jackson with the lead, bringing the permanent form to the group that continued over 50 years.

With Picirilli, an upperclassman who had traveled in promotion for the school and knew well the presentation of the program, on board, the four soon began going out with no official from the school accompanying them. That was when I really began to shine. I was the only musical instrument traveling with them, riding most of the time in Picirilli's coat pocket. I was finally a necessary member of the Gospeliers Quartet. Raper gave me the name "Sackbut" and it stuck.

Money

After a few trips some of the four found themselves in the position Turnage had faced, no income. The school wasn't paying them, so in a conference among themselves they weighed the possibilities: break up the group, look for weekend jobs, or approach the school about some remuneration for services on the weekend that would equal and take the place of jobs. The unanimous decision was to try the school first, since they enjoyed singing, traveling, and preaching.

Picirilli was appointed to approach the *powers that be* with their proposition. Four dollars per service seemed appropriate since that's what the school paid those who traveled in the summer. No one had been paid for going out during school term. Pic took the written request to Mr. McDonald, the treasurer, whose office was in the old Richland Apartment Building, and handed it to him. Mr. Mac was visibly upset, took the matter to Dr. Johnson, the college president, and the four were then called to a meeting with those two in Dr. Johnson's office in the Richland Building.

Picirilli explained that if there were not some way for the four to receive some pay for their services, it would be necessary to come off the road, get jobs on the weekend, and break up the group, which they would prefer not to do.

"Mercenary!" Johnson responded a little red in the face, implying that the guys had gone professional, singing for money. "Think you are the Blackwood Brothers."

Mr. Mac pitched in, "We don't have the money."

Pic said, "Well, that's the way it is, fellows. We might as well go and do what we have to do."

They had reached the door, when Johnson stopped them and said, "Wait a minute. Come back here. Sit down. How much do you want?"

"Four dollars per service," Picirilli said. "We figured that would give us about the same as other students are earning on weekend jobs. If we have a service on Friday or Saturday, two or three on Sunday, a total of four or five on the weekend, we would make $16 or $20, and that four dollar figure is what the school has paid summer groups."

Johnson looked at McDonald and said, "We can pay that."

Of course they could. The boys were bringing in hundreds in cash and pledges, plus student applications for enrollment. They couldn't afford not to pay it. And that's what they continued to pay probably for the next 20 years.

The Final Four

Practice makes perfect, not necessarily

Job Descriptions

Established as the paid, working quartet, the four lived on the road most weekends for the next four years, not only representing the school, but also turning the services into evangelistic meetings. In the beginning they alternated preaching, rotating around, but not long after the beginning, on the way to church Picirilli said to Jackson, "I don't want to preach tonight. Why don't you preach that same sermon that you preached last night? *Noah and the Flood*...Hebrews 11:7."

So he did.

The next night Waddell said, as they were getting dressed, "I don't want to preach tonight. Jackson, preach that same sermon again tonight, *Noah and the Flood*."

Next afternoon Raper said, "I don't feel like preaching tonight. Let's let Jackson do *The Flood* again."

They finally decided that this ritual was not necessary. They gave the preaching job to Jackson and divided up the rest of the service. Waddell led singing. Picirilli presented the college. Raper passed out pledge cards and took up offerings. With that order of service, they continued for years and I heard that sermon on *Noah and the Flood*, Hebrews 11:7, until I could have preached it myself...if I'd been a preacher, not a pitch pipe. I just sound a note so men can harmonize; come to think of it, so does the preacher. He sounds a note to bring men into harmony with God and with each other. I should have been a preacher, too late now. A little rust on my vocal cords creates hoarseness when I'm just pitching a song.

Midnight Train

In Cove City, North Carolina, as was their custom after service, the fellows paired off, Waddell and Raper, Picirilli and Jackson. When Waddell and Raper arrived at the home of Mrs. Annie Heath, after driving down a narrow dirt road in the dark and turning into the yard, they never noticed nor could they see the surroundings. After a brief bit of fellowship, they retired to a room in the front corner of the house, and were sound asleep in minutes.

About 2:00 the sound of a roaring train woke both of them. Waddell sat up in bed, looked out the window, and with astonishment said, "There's a train coming across that field, heading straight for this house. It's coming through this bedroom."

Since no two people experience exactly the same nightmare at the same time, it was no dream. Rattling, roaring, with that engine's headlight flashing in the bedroom as it circled like a giant searchlight, the train kept coming, aimed at that bedroom for a direct hit. No time to escape, so they waited for the crash, as the train went roaring down the track in front of the house, missed the bedroom by 20 feet, shook the entire house like an earthquake, sounded like a tornado, and didn't waken another sleeping soul in the house.

The others were like the man who lived by the tracks where a train passed every night at midnight. One night the train didn't pass. He jumped out of bed and said, "What was that?" Familiar noises don't disturb, they slept right through the train. The next morning Waddell and Raper were made aware of the railroad tracks, too bad they missed them the night before in the dark.

More Time to Loaf

Another time, another place, Waddell and Raper were left to spend Saturday night with an old couple possibly in their 80s. The last thing Pic told Raper was, "We have five meetings tomorrow, and the trip home to Nashville after that. The day's going to begin early and go all night. You and Waddell be ready at 8:00 a.m. We'll pick you up in this driveway at 8:00 sharp."

The boys were given the best, the couple's own bedroom in the front of the house. At 4:00 a.m. the bedroom door opened, letting in the old man who raised a window opening to the porch and began pulling in firewood to build a fire in the fireplace, saying, "Time to get up. The Old Lady's in the kitchen cooking breakfast."

Raper looked at the clock staring back at him saying, "4:00," turned over in the bed, pulled the covers over his head, thinking, "When he gets that fire going and gets out of here, I'm going back to sleep."

When the fire got going, the old man didn't. Pulling a chair beside the bed, he began talking and prodding, "Get dressed now, breakfast is about ready."

The fellows, forced out of bed, dressed, ate, shaved, and readied themselves for the day. There were no inside bathrooms, so Raper, after having been up for two hours or more went outside to find the outhouse. No outhouse was to be found, but in the darkness the shadow of a barn appeared. So he decided to go behind the barn, not knowing that the barn and farm animals were inside a fence made of barbed wire. In the dark he ran into that barbed wire fence. With a few scratches and the least possible damage to his clothes, he picked his way through the fence and after the behind-the-barn experience, went back through the same fence. If there was a gate it was lost in the dark.

The experience added a new dimension to the tale of the preacher who came to the closing point of his sermon and said, "Well folks, as the fat lady said when she crawled through the barbed wire fence, 'Just one more point and I'll be through.'"

Raper was now sympathetic with the fat lady.

To this day Raper declares that Picirilli set them up, as a prank, telling the old man to get them up at four in the morning and have them ready by six, knowing he wouldn't be there until eight, and they would have two hours to sit and wait. Pic has never denied it.

When he came back in the house, he asked the old man, "Why do you get up so early on Sunday morning when there seems to be no rush?"

"Just need more time to loaf," he said.

When Picirilli and Jackson pulled in the driveway at 8:00 a.m., Raper was standing in the yard, suitcase packed, coat hanging on a finger over his shoulder, ready to go. "Well, it's good to see you ready on time," Pic said.

"Oh, I've been ready. For over two hours I've been ready. I needed some extra time to loaf!"

Making a Record

The fall of 1951, Jackson was in revival at East Nashville, with the quartet singing every night, when someone suggested, "Make a record. Record some of these songs."

RCA was contacted about how to do that. They asked two questions. Number one: "Do you make your living singing concerts and traveling?"

If the answer to that was no, they didn't ask the second. No label would underwrite a recording for an unknown quartet attending college, but East Nashville Church did. With their backing, the fellows put four a cappella songs on two brittle, 78 RPM discs. Whatever the material was in those 78s, it was so fragile that dropped in a bowl of Jell-O they would have shattered. In promotional campaigns churches would break attendance records, and then get a laugh from breaking a record over the pastor's head. That ended with the coming of the flexible, vinyl material, which didn't break so easily.

Power in the Blood, It Is No Secret, I Know That My Redeemer Liveth, and *What a Savior* with Clarence Bowen, Pastor of East Nashville Free Will Baptist Church, quoting John 3:16 after the last verse, went into distribution. Enough money above cost came in to purchase four navy-blue, double-breasted, wool serge suits; finally they looked like a quartet, now all they needed was to sound like one.

A couple of years later in a classroom in the Sword Building, late at night so as not to be disturbed, came my opportunity to participate in a recording session. On an eight track reel-to-reel recorder, I kept them on pitch for 22 songs, all a cappella and with no purpose other than to be preserved for posterity. That tape was filed away, forgotten for 50 years, found by Raper, taken to Nashville where the songs were transferred to a CD, along with some others with accompaniment, and released for distribution, *For Ole Times Sake.*

In the early 1970s after a quartet revival at Liberty Free Will Baptist Church in Durham, North Carolina, the four went to Atlanta, Georgia, and at LeFevre Sound with the Goss Brothers as studio musicians, produced a full-length 12-song album, which moved well enough to reorder a couple of times. Some of these songs were added to the CD, which contains 29 with some duplicates, a cappella and with instrumental background. So goes the record-making history of the four.

Revivals in Winterville, NC

From 1951-1955, they continued to travel and do promotional work for the college, and I went along in Pic's pocket trying to keep them on key. The meetings in Reedy Branch, following Jackson's wedding, began Sunday morning without him. He took his time coming from Illinois, only 900 miles and it took him two days. From Monday through the week, closing on Sunday, Jackson preached, they sang, and the interest and response was such that preachers from other churches requested that they come back in August to the school gymnasium in Winterville, North Carolina.

Fishing / Slipping and Sliding

During that meeting the guys decided to make a one-day quick trip to the coast for a fishing excursion at Oriental, NC. Casting from the beach into the surf for puppy drum, blistering their bare feet in the hot sun, catching a few fish, the day passed so fast it was late before they realized there was barely time to make it back to Winterville for the service. Jackson drove his '51 Olds with slick tires that were to be replaced the next day with new rubber. Between New Bern and Greenville, he drove into a cloud burst, hit a one hundred-yard patch of asphalt on the concrete pavement, with water standing on it, and those slick tires hydroplaned.

The car skidded sideways in the middle of the road, picking up speed as it slid. Before the skid, it was running about 55 or 60 mph, sideways it felt like 80. With plenty of time to think, Jackson considered opening the door, getting out and allowing his sleeping passengers to continue their exciting ride without him. For a lot of reasons, that wasn't a good option. He remembered, "In a skid, turn into the skid, continue to accelerate, don't apply the brakes."

If the tires reconnect with the pavement, the car will right itself, pulling out of the skid. With no tread, those tires riding on the water never touched the asphalt, much less gripped the road. As the vehicle slid sideways down the road, gradually working its way toward the left berm and ditch, Picirilli, awakened by the strange ride, sat up in the backseat and said, "Take your foot off the gas, Jackson!"

He did, since there was no pulling out of this skid. Neither acceleration nor brakes were affecting the slide. As it reached the dirt shoulder of the highway, what brakes could not do, grass, dirt, and a road sign did. When the road sign hit the right front fender, creasing it like a folded piece of paper and flying across the ditch to get out of the car's way, it slowed the front for the back to pass it, bringing the car finally to rest with the right side in the ditch and facing the opposite direction from that which it should be going if it were to ever arrive in Winterville. Nobody moved. The silence was deafening, only the sound of pouring rain and an idling engine.

Someone broke the silence with the deep thought-provoking question, "What are we going to do now? We're stuck in the ditch."

Not too far away was a house, in the house a kind farmer, under his shelter a tractor, and in a few minutes he pulled the car from the ditch, the fender from the tire, and sent them on their way with no charge and no time to spare getting to that night's service.

Flying Bible

In the gym at 8:00 p.m. with no fans to stir the hot humid air, a crowd of people adding to the heat at about 50 watts per person, the temperature was approaching "yellowing heat," 90° to 110° in a curing barn, turning green tobacco leaves to a golden yellow, before the temperature was raised to 130° to dry the leaf, and gradually to 160° to dry the stem in that flue-curing process so familiar to the area.

There were hand fans which offered no solution, the more the folks fanned, the hotter they were, and the hotter they were the more they fanned. When the quartet finished singing and Jackson began preaching, their suits were already showing dark circles of sweat. From a stage five feet above a concrete floor, behind a small pulpit, Jackson preached in the increasing heat. With both hands dripping wet he reached for that red Bible someone gave him, because every young preacher needed a red Bible, picked it up with the left hand, switched over to the right, and in the process through those wet, slippery hands, the Bible slipped from the left, skidded through the right, sailed like a folded paper airplane 20 feet down and landed at the feet of a lady sitting in the front row of chairs.

She calmly retrieved it, delivered it back to the preacher at the edge of the stage, and said, "You missed me!"

"At least it was only the Bible," Jackson said. "Another evangelist preaching on the second coming of Christ, backed away from the pulpit, ran back and leaning on the pulpit quoting Jesus, he said, 'Behold, I come quickly' and in his excitement he forgot what came next. So he started over, same procedure…couldn't remember. The third time when he leaned on the pulpit saying, 'Behold, I come quickly,' he leaned too far, and the pulpit fell forward, dumping him in a lady's lap on the front row.

With nothing hurt but his pride, he stood, embarrassed, shook himself into shape and apologized to the lady, who responded with, 'Oh, no preacher, it's my fault. You warned me three times that you were coming and I didn't get out of your way.'

"All I did was throw the Bible," Jackson said, and went on with the sermon.

The next day Jackson bought that set of tires, closing the door after the horse was out, and gave the fender repair job to a local body shop who agreed to a fair price, since he was attending their meetings and an active member of one of the participating churches. The dent came out, fender shaped up, just a little different color from the rest of the car. The repairman never could figure that out since he had used exactly the same number of auto paint that was on the car originally.

Sometime later Jackson was at another body shop and the guy said, "Who painted your fender with enamel paint when the car is painted with lacquer?" He learned that enamel never matches lacquer and someone should pass that word along to his friend who fixed it.

During that summer Picirilli purchased a '52 Olds. After service at the gym one night, the two of them ran to the cars, cranked in a rush, and with the tires throwing a little gravel, pulled onto the highway from Winterville to Greenville, where they were staying at night. One passed the other and they immediately backed off to the speed limit. From the town of Winterville, the city cop came flying out of a parking lot, siren screaming and red light flashing. The two of them pulled off to the side to allow him to go by and catch whomever he was so desperately chasing, but to their surprise he didn't go by, he pulled in behind them with that light still flashing, got out of his car as they both exited theirs, asked to see driver's licenses, learned who they were and what they were doing in town, and with a friendly smile said, "You fellows aren't who I thought you were. I just knew I had a race on my hands between here and Greenville. No problem," he said, returning the licenses with best wishes for a good stay in Winterville.

Before the week was over, he showed up at the meeting.

Flat River, MO

Between Reedy Branch and Winterville meetings, the quartet met together in Flat River, Missouri, for a cooperative meeting under a tent in the park. Daily radio programs and meetings in the park for two weeks, practicing, singing, Jackson preaching, climbing the chat pile (a mountain of oversized granular rock pebbles taken as waste from the lead mines) at night after service in the moonlight, made for a busy two weeks, but not a very fruitful meeting.

Where's the Hospital

One night after church, Waddell took a local girl for a ride. (She didn't realize it but that car ride would never develop into a life-long, permanent relationship. Waddell was going to marry Leah. Everybody seemed to know that except the girls who followed him back to college every fall.) Being in unfamiliar territory they lost their way. (That's how he tells it.) However, he knew where he was spending the nights during the meetings in relation to the local hospital, so when he spied a policeman sitting in his parked patrol car, Waddell rolled down the window and asked him how to get to the hospital.

The policeman picked up on the situation quickly, a young man and woman, late at night anxiously looking for the hospital.

"Just follow me," he said, and with siren whining, red light flashing, at high speed, he led them to the hospital. As Waddell pulled into the parking lot behind him, the policeman waved an encouraging farewell, wished them luck, turned around and drove away, figuring Waddell didn't need any further help getting her into the emergency room, and he didn't. He sat bewildered for a few minutes, geographically pulled himself together, and drove her home, explaining to everyone the reason for the late hour, and they believed him. No one could make up a story like that.

Those meetings ended with no great success. The love offering was divided four ways. As the accompanist I never shared in that. Each member of the quartet received $37 for 2,000 miles travel and two weeks work. Soon after, however, at Memorial Free Will Baptist Church in Baxley, Georgia, for one week, two services each day, they were given $500, $125 each, and in 1953, that was big money.

Memorial Church, Baxley

Memorial was the place that the tale was told, true or untrue, I don't know. As a pitch pipe, not being involved, I can't testify. It is true that Jane Jackson and Clara Picirilli were newly pregnant with Stephen and Jean who were born the same day, April 5, 1954, Stephen a few hours before Jean. The story is a good tale, even if a fable. During a morning service, one of the women, nauseated with morning sickness left the service. There were no inside restrooms and as she turned the corner to go behind the church, she met the other one coming around the other corner. Maybe that was the morning the two babies decided to come out into this glorious world on the same day. That part is true.

Detroit

On one of those weekend excursions in 1953 or 1954, we made a promotional journey to Detroit, by "we" I mean me and the quartet. I was indispensable at the time to pitch those songs in the right key, so I rode along in George Lee's pocket. George took Pic's place during that senior year when Pic was away in graduate school. I only participated in the singing, not the extra-curricular activities.

We left Nashville on Friday morning in order to make a service Friday night, plus one on Saturday night, Sunday morning, and Sunday night. Arriving in Detroit on time, finding a public telephone, Jackson called Bill Mishler, pastor of Philadelphia Free

Will Baptist Church (another Philadelphia, not in Pennslyvania) and said, "We're here."

"We who?...Where?" was the surprised response.

"The Gospeliers Quartet from Bible College, here for the weekend of services, and at a pay phone near the church."

"That's next weekend," said the bewildered preacher. "You're a week early."

Someone in scheduling at the college must have set his clock forward one week. Daylight savings time is one thing, but a full week forward is another.

"Can't come back next week," Jackson said. "So what should we do with the mistake?"

"Come on to my house, we'll work out something."

The decision was to stay for services on Sunday and maybe put one together for Saturday night. Billy Graham was in town. The pastor planned to attend, so the quartet went along on Friday night. To prevent Saturday from being a total waste, someone suggested they tour Ford Motor Company's plant and see how cars were made. Graham had said Friday night that putting a Cadillac hood ornament on a Ford didn't make it a Cadillac, to illustrate that stamping a Christian symbol on a man didn't make him a Christian. "There must be a change of heart," he said.

They went to see what made a Ford.

Touring Ford Plant

When they arrived at the plant, the Graham Team, Cliff Barrows, Grady Wilson, Beverly Shea, all except Billy, showed up at the same time and followed them through the plant. After all were introduced, those fellows were extremely friendly, however, they never invited the guys to sing that night at the crusade and that's just as well, since they already had a service planned for about 30 people.

That automated assembly line was unbelievable, fascinating, watching parts come together by conveyor from everywhere, meet at one point on line, resulting in a car finished to the exact specifications of a pre-ordered vehicle, and rolling them off that line faster than one per minute.

The process began with ingots of steel melted into red-hot liquid form in large vats with an iron grid catwalk over and around the vats for touring groups to venture near enough to feel the intense heat.

Standing over that liquid fire, one of the fellows asked the guide, "What would happen if a man fell into that boiling steel?"

"A worker did," he said. "And when his body hit the red stuff, he didn't feel a thing, a puff of white vapor from the evaporating water in a human body quickly formed a little cloud above the boiling steel, leaving no evidence that anything had ever dropped in the pot. They removed a small block of metal from that batch, stamped his name and a date on it, had a funeral and buried it."

As they walked away, one of the quartet fellows suggested that it resembled the lake of fire in Revelation, except that fire never consumes its victims.

Vulcan, Birmingham

In Birmingham, Alabama, a similar, horrible picture had already been painted in flaming color, on the canvas of their minds and hung in the hall of memory. To conduct a Youth Rally in Cordova, Alabama, in a small auditorium in City Hall on a Saturday night, the four made the trip from Nashville, arriving in time to change clothes, rush to the service, sing, and Jackson preach. Afterwards, being Saturday night, 10:00 o'clock, and no place to go, plus the fact they had never been to Birmingham, which was only about 50 miles southeast, the possibility of a flying trip came up, was agreed upon, and away they went.

The main tourist attraction in Birmingham was the Vulcan, a gigantic iron statue standing atop Red Mountain, just off Highway 31, a little southeast of downtown, overlooking the Pittsburgh of the south, second largest steel producing city in the U. S., situated in the midst of rich deposits of coal, iron ore, and limestone, the three natural elements necessary for steel production. The iron Vulcan statue stands 56 feet high, second only to the Statue of Liberty as the largest metallic statue in the country, representing the Roman god of fire, who also was a blacksmith for the gods, making the scepter for Jupiter, the breastplate for Hercules, the arrows for Apollo and Diana, thus becoming the patron of blacksmiths and all iron, steel, and metal workers, a fitting symbol to stand on a mountaintop and watch over Birmingham, since most of the people worked in coal mines, iron-ore mines, or steel mills.

One resident commented that his folks were in the iron and steel business, "My Mama ironed all day and my Daddy stole all night," he said, a little different business, but indirectly related.

Steel Mill

At midnight the quartet was at the top of the Vulcan tower, singing, and listening to the tower add the reverb, the mix, and amplification to the a cappella harmony, a great sound, when one of them looked over the city and was stunned by a fire.

"The whole city's on fire," he said. Birmingham was evidently going up in flames, and everybody is drawn to a big fire like lead to a magnet, moth to a flame.

Down the tower, over a short distance to the fire faster than legally possible, they arrived at a viaduct overlooking a steel mill. The steel-making process begins with iron ore and limestone in a blast furnace turning out pig iron. Pig iron was named for the ingots or pigs, into which it was poured. Pig iron and limestone are mixed in a furnace, heated to about 3,000° Fahrenheit, which melts the limestone to form slag that rises to the top as foam, bringing the impurities with it. What they saw was the slag overflowing those open hearth furnaces, running like liquid fire, more fluid than lava from a volcano, and about 3,000°, into an open pond.

Feeling the heat and watching the flow of fire, Picirilli said, "That sure looks like Hell, doesn't it?"

An experience Jackson used for several years to introduce a sermon on the subject.

Back to Cordova in the early hours of Sunday morning, two services the next day, and the drive back to Nashville on Sunday night in time to make class at 8:00 a.m. on Monday, a typical weekend.

The Wedding

The womanless wedding, the shotgun wedding, and the hillbilly wedding as comedy routines, when done well, for years have entertained audiences roaring with laughter at the slapstick comedy. Reality is sometimes more entertaining than the unreal. Truth is funnier than fiction, especially when it is mixed with a little fiction, which is very likely when the source of truth is a seventy-five-year-old memory that has a tendency to add detail and color to make the picture more vivid and interesting.

The quartet was scheduled for a short weekend in southern Illinois, Saturday night, two or three Sunday services, and then back to Nashville on Sunday night. Leaving in the afternoon, driving over five hours, put them in the area an hour before service time at Hazel Dell Free Will Baptist Church, Sesser, Illinois. Not in Sesser, but in the country near Sesser on the edge of what is now Rend Lake. Deep shaft coal mining had created caverns of emptiness underneath the church resulting in cave-ins in the area and damage to the building. With repairs and underpinning, it was a beautiful little country church.

The fellows went directly to the church, since they needed that hour to change from their traveling clothes to quartet suits. To their surprise, four or five cars were already in the parking lot. They flattered themselves with the thought, "These folks really enjoy quartet singing, and came early to get good seats before the crowd arrives." With a suitcase in one hand, a suit dangling from a hanger in the other, they entered the vestibule and were stopped in their tracks by the realization that a wedding was about to take place. Quietly and as inconspicuously as four guys with suitcases could be, they slipped inside and took a back seat as uninvited guests.

A dozen folks had gathered in front of the communion table and were evidently discussing the ceremony in low mumbling voices. When the preacher came in a side door, everyone went silent and slowly took seats about six pews behind the front row. The old preacher, dressed in a clean wrinkled white shirt with arm bands above the elbows which shortened and puffed the sleeves, buttoned to the top but with no tie, dark trousers held up by striped suspenders, took charge.

Standing in front of the communion table, he broke the silence, "Where is the boy getting married?"

A tall, lanky kid, late teens, dressed in a farm boy's best for a trip to town on Saturday afternoon, stood.

"Well, come forward," the preacher insisted.

He stood before the minister, who sent out a second request, "Does he have a best boyfriend in the house? If so, come and stand with him."

A second fellow, hesitating for a moment responded. The two now stood facing the preacher.

"The girl who is marrying this boy, come forward."

A pretty little girl dressed in blue jeans, nervously chewing gum with a giggly smile, looked back at her friends, and made her way to the front.

"Will her best girlfriend come and stand with her?"

The three of four girls looked at each other as if trying to decide which one was the bride's best friend. Three of them nodded at the fourth whom they selected for the part and watched her leave them and journey slowly to the front.

With the wedding party in place, the officiating minister spoke briefly about biblical marriage, and began the ceremony.

Attempting to read the vows from his marriage manual, he stumbled, started over, held the book closer, but in the dim light was unable to see the print, so about halfway through, he stopped, went back to the beginning and started over. The couple went through the first vows a second time. Starting over didn't increase the light, which was located on the pulpit ten feet behind him, nor improve his eyesight, as he held the book closer. At his age he had probably lost the ability to read close print, which blurred the vows even more, so he gave up. Seeing as how he was too far from the light, he left the four standing in front of the communion table and went to the pulpit to start over a third time.

Through the first two new beginnings these four uninvited guests had restrained themselves, only allowing a smile to force its way to their faces as they refused to look at each other. But when he made his way to the pulpit and began to ask the couple to "repeat after me" for the third time, Waddell lost it. Spitting and coughing to cover his uncontrollable laughter, he left the wedding. The others calmed themselves and listened to the preacher finish the ceremony, pronounce the couple man and wife, tell the boy to kiss the girl, and dismiss the audience of eight, all of whom left, including the preacher. Not one remained for the quartet service, which was a bit discouraging. If they had stayed it would have doubled the attendance.

The wedding added new meaning to the bonds of matrimony. Having repeated those vows three times this couple was really bound, making a divorce nigh impossible, since the Bible says "a threefold cord is not quickly broken" (Ecc. 5:12).

For the quartet it was just another weekend, three services on Sunday, six-hour drive, three hours sleep and class at eight on Monday morning. George had taken the baritone job in Pic's place. I rode in his pocket and slept in his desk drawer until the next weekend. Their music classes couldn't teach a pitch pipe anything, so I skipped class all week.

Singing in the Ryman

Wally Fowler and his Oak Ridge Quartet sponsored an all night singing one Friday night each month at the Ryman Auditorium, the Grand Ole Opry House, with the top quartets, Blackwood Brothers, Hovie Lister and the Statesmen, and other leading Southern Gospel groups. The thought of attempting to get on that program went through the Gospeliers minds, but didn't linger long, assured that the school would frown upon such a venture. One day, with the "no harm in trying" attitude, they approached the powers-that-be with the possibility of going to Wally's singing. When they asked Ralph Lightsey, the Dean, for permission, it was denied and then in an offhanded way, Lightsey, without thinking it through, offered what he knew was an impossible condition.

"It would be different," he said, "if you were going there to sing!"

He probably wished, later, that he hadn't said that. When George Lee learned of this (no one knows how), knowing Wally from having sung with the All American Quartet and moving in those circles, he called Wally, told him about the Gospeliers, recommended them, and that they would like to sing on his all night program. To the surprise of all, Wally obliged, extended the invitation, and Lightsey couldn't back down. So off they went to the Ryman with George to introduce them to Wally. Frank Sexton accompanied them at the piano.

The fellows met Wally backstage while another group was singing. George introduced them, four preachers, friends in college, preparing for the ministry, and traveling for the school. Wally said they were on the program to sing two songs right before the brief intermission before they went on the air over WSM for an hour broadcast.

Waiting in the wings, anticipating a spot on the program and just before intermission, the door opened. Wally introduced them to sing one song, *All Hail the Power*, the anthem arrangement. The enthusiastic response from the crowd brought Wally back with the request, "Sing another one, and hang around. We'll use you on the radio broadcast." And he did. They sang two more over WSM.

Wally insisted that they make a return engagement, after all they sang free. Those other groups were expensive, $500 per night, and in the '50s that was big money.

Backstage the Blackwoods were friendly, asking about their ministry and their plans to preach. Bill Lyles, the bass, talked to them extensively about the work and asked where they found that arrangement of *All Hail the Power*.

"In the Broadman Hymnal," he learned to his surprise.

The Blackwoods were real entertainers who performed well that night. James was the master of ceremonies when R.W. crossed the stage with an accordion case that belonged to a trio. James asked, "Where are you going?"

"I'm taking this case to court."

In a moment R.W. came back across the stage without the case.

"What happened?"

"I lost the case."

Another moment R.W. came dragging a stepladder across the stage.

"Now what?" James asked.

"I'm taking that case to a higher court."

Added to their stage presence was the fact that they were the leading Southern Gospel quartet and filled the auditorium on the nights they sang. A short time after that night, Bill Lyles, bass, and R.W.Blackwood, baritone were killed in the crash of their private plane, with R.W. as the pilot.

The Statesmen were also on that Friday program. Those two quartets always drew large crowds. The fellows sang with them in the Ryman, never answered Wally's invitation to return, but added the experience to their memory bank.

One other time they went back to the Ryman for a rally to raise funds for the Nashville City Rescue Mission. Dr. Charles Fuller was the invited guest speaker. The quartet, this time with George Lee singing baritone in Picirilli's place, who was away at Bob Jones University in graduate school, and with Frank Sexton playing piano, so I didn't go along (no pitch pipe needed), sang two of the songs from the *Old Fashioned Revival Hour* quartet's repertory to accommodate Dr. Fuller, founder and speaker on that radio program for many years on Sunday afternoon, thinking he would recognize the songs and appreciate the effort at honoring his ministry.

The fellows must not have done them well. Dr. Fuller seemed unappreciative, unfriendly, aloof, and could not lower himself even to be nice, much less complimentary. Maybe the guys were young, brash, expecting too much, but the experience was disappointing. Some people, especially religious greats, are too important to be approachable.

Cuba

During the summer of 1954, each went his own way. Waddell, Raper, and Jackson graduated from Free Will Baptist Bible College with plans to continue their education in graduate school, Waddell at Columbia Bible College, Columbia, SC, Raper and Jackson at Bob Jones University, Greenville, SC, where Picirilli already was.

Waddell married Leah Nichols; Jackson met up with them in Baxley, Georgia. They went to Cuba, while Jane and the baby took a very unpleasant train ride to Illinois. Jackson and the Waddells drove to Key West, parked the car in a church lot, caught a small puddle-hopper for Havana, rode in a wild taxi with a lunatic driver from Havana to Pinar del Rio, met the Willeys and with them, the three traveled, preached, and sang around Pinar for two weeks, sleeping in the Cedars of Lebanon school dorms at night, eating white rice, then yellow rice, then brown rice, then white rice again (*Variety is the spice of rice!* Arroz con pollo without the pollo. No chicken had even waded through the water that rice was cooked in.) and living like Cubans. The Willeys said it was to introduce them to the rough life of a missionary who was sleeping in the big house on a comfortable bed, eating bacon and eggs.

An interesting discussion between Leah and Mrs. Willey concerning long hair for girls made the air a little tense for a short time. Mrs. Willey told Leah, who had cut her hair, that the girls in Cuba took the scriptures literally and that it was a shame for a woman to cut her hair.

Leah asked, "What about the feet washing in John 13?"

"Oh! Some things are a matter of interpretation," she said. Being CMA background, feet washing was not a conviction of the Willeys.

So Leah simply said, "Yes, some application of the scriptures is a matter of interpretation."

The subject of hair never came up again.

Fidel Castro was in the mountains with his revolutionary forces attempting to overthrow Batista. Soldiers were everywhere. Waddell snapped some pictures from a bus window, which brought the bus to an abrupt stop for soldiers to board and take the film from his camera. They didn't take the camera, just the film. Brother Willey was pro-Castro, and so confident that his famous quote was "If Castro is a communist, I'll eat my hat."

Later when he prayed with some of the many men Castro executed before firing squads, he didn't eat his hat, but he did eat his words, and they gave him indigestion.

The two weeks in Cuba were profitable for the two young preachers, riding in the back of a truck in the rain, walking miles into the mountains with no drinking water, feasting on a barbecued pig after the chickens had first choice and pecked his eyes out as he hung near the ground before he was cooked. They'd been living on rice, and that pig was delicious.

Courthouse, Baxley, GA

When the little missionary trip was finished, they flew back to Key West, found a nice restaurant, ordered the largest fried chicken dinner on the menu, specified no rice, drove from there back to Baxley, Georgia, and began a revival meeting with the quartet in the courthouse, after which the Baxley Free Will Baptist Church was organized. On the radio every day and in the courthouse at night the fellows sang, Jackson preached.

In 2004, the Baxley Church promoted a 50th Anniversary celebration and invited the quartet to come back for the occasion. Two drove from Nashville, two from North Carolina with their wives, and now the quartet had a fifth member, Pic's daughter, Jean Lewis, who flew from Nashville to accompany them on the piano. Over the years, I, the pitch pipe, sackbut, was their only accompanist, until the Picirillis reared a daughter, the oldest of five, who not only became an accomplished musician, but by listening to the album made in Atlanta, could duplicate Larry Goss and make that piano sound like it did in the studio. From then on she became the piano accompanist for the quartet, leaving me, the sackbut, to be put out to pasture, not disposed of, since in every concert for old times' sake and nostalgia or simply to give a sample of what once was, I was dragged out of Pic's pocket, introduced to the crowd with no great applause, and asked to sound a "G," pitching *Heartaches* for them to sing a cappella, with close, good harmony.

Honestly, the harmony wasn't as close, nor the sound as good as it was before their voices grew weaker, and it took more wind for me to produce the pitch and Pic had to produce the wind, and Jackson's tendency to go south was no longer a tendency, but a regular drift downward into flat country. The piano covered so much that once didn't need covering, so Jean became a permanent part of the Gospeliers.

They all met Saturday afternoon at the church, practiced for a couple of hours, went out for supper ("Dutch," they learned at the cash register.), went various directions for the night, and assembled Sunday for Sunday School, morning worship, afternoon celebration, singing and preaching in each service.

When all was finished, the treasurer handed each one of the four a check for $100 to cover all their expenses and remuneration for the weekend, with nothing to pay for Jean's plane ticket. The four, feeling responsible for Jean, divided their $400 with her to help on the tickets, leaving each one of them $50 for the trip. So it really is true, "The more things change the more they stay the same." They left Flat River 51 years earlier with $37 each for two weeks and expenses. The time had shortened by 12 days, and offerings increased by $13.

This account is not meant to be an example of mistreatment. That was possibly all the church could do. The fellows in the quartet were comfortable in semi-retirement, and could have gone to Georgia for nothing. It is only to say that things are as they were and will continue to be.

During the five years the quartet traveled for the college, 90% of the time they ate and slept in the homes of church people, saving the expense of motels and restaurants, and hoping to make friends for the school by becoming friends with grass roots supporters. Breaking down barriers and making good impressions were part of the job representing the school. The few times they were blessed to get a motel room with the privacy and convenience were highlights along the journey.

You Can't Get There From Here

There were times everything turned upside down and the reverse happened. At the evening meal before service in eastern North Carolina, conversation was light and everyone had taken his turn at a little humor, when the old man of the house decided it was his turn. He began the old joke, "You can't get there from here"…except he told it in the first person. He asked directions of some farmer beside the road who told him, "Go about a mile, turn left…no that won't get you there…" and so on, until he is finally told, "Mr., you just can't get there from here."

The fellows had heard the tale over and over, but the old man's first person account was really funny, and he mistook the laughter for a genuine response to his story and thought it went over so well that he would tell it again. This second time through it was hilarious. The guys were laughing uncontrollably by the time he finished.

When he started the third time, there was an explosion, like an actor or comedian with a mouthful of water faking a spontaneous explosion of laughter, spitting and spraying everything within a radius of ten feet. Jackson's mouth was full of little green English peas when that laughter mechanism ignited a no-fake spontaneous explosion. He caught most of them in his napkin, including those that blew out through his nose. By the time the host had finished his third telling of the tale and the volcanic eruption had blown the lid off and released all that pressurized energy, the atmosphere was calm. They finished the meal and the old man was certain he had wasted his life farming. He should have been a comedian.

Specs with no Lenses

Raper's effort to make conversation and create a little levity sometimes fell flat. At breakfast one morning he was reading the paper through spectacle frames with no lenses. He worked at it until he got the attention of the man of the house, showed him the glasses, commented about how much better he could read with them, but the man never noticed there were no lenses.

Raper went a step further, put the frames on the man, handed him a paper, asked if the print was clearer, and the man responded, "Yes, I believe it is," not yet aware there were no lenses in them. Somehow Raper had to get the little joke across without telling the guy, "There are no lenses in those frames."

Looking at the frames on the man, Raper said, "Those lenses are a little dirty, I'll clean them for you. That'll make things clearer."

With a handkerchief he wiped over the empty frames, poking his finger through the space where a lens wasn't, touching the man's eye, and saying, "There, that should make it clearer."

"Yes, that did help some," the man said.

Now what does Raper do? Tell the man he is stupid and there are no lenses in that frame, embarrassing both of them? Not a chance. He takes back his lensless glasses, puts them in his pocket, drops the subject, wonders why that guy never saw there were no lenses in those frames, and nobody laughs, except the other three at Raper.

While in graduate school in Greenville, SC, Raper pastored the Free Will Baptist Church in Arcadia. Many revivals in which they sang and Jackson preached were in churches pastored by a quartet member, and so it was at Arcadia. The four worked in the small town for a week, visiting every house on every street, telling folks about the singing and preaching, and at the end of the week not a person had attended the meetings as a result of their hard work. As has been true through the years, they continued to sing and preach every night to those who did come.

Not a Cecil B. DeMille Production

When Waddell pastored First Free Will Baptist in Portsmouth, VA, in 1958, the quartet was there for the closing weekend. A man from Norfolk with an 8mm black and white camera suggested that they produce a film of one of the services. Arrangements were made for Sunday afternoon. The quartet sang. Jackson preached on *Death* in ten-minute segments, since that was the length of a roll of film and having only one camera it was necessary to stop, wait for the cameraman to reload, and begin again where the previous roll stopped. The camera was fixed in one position. To get variety and close-up shots he preached the last point second and the second point third, making continuity next to impossible. At the time it was a special venture, long before the technology of color, video, DVD, computers, digital, etc.

Pop's Barn

The sophomore year in college was different for three members of the quartet. Raper, Waddell, and Jackson, due to overcrowded dorms, were moved to a barn/garage on the Melvin property, two blocks from the main campus. "Pop's Barn" was converted to an apartment upstairs with two makeshift dorm rooms under that. Waddell and Raper bedded down in an oversized closet, large enough for one stack of bunk beds and a dresser. If two walked in, it was necessary to back out. Only one could turn around. The closet was off the end of a 10 x 15 room with two stacks of bunk beds.

In this room Jackson cohabited with three older fellows, one a chicken farmer from Arkansas, another a strange, zealous preacher from Michigan, who came to school driving an old Studebaker with loud speakers mounted on top, over which he did street preaching as he drove along city streets, and a man from Georgia who left his wife and five children at home and fought homesickness as he struggled to go back to school from which he had departed many years before.

The Chicken Farmer

The chicken farmer came to Nashville driving a large flatbed farm truck with a load of commodities to subsidize the school grocery budget, parked the truck in a single lane of Richland Avenue in front of the dining hall, blocking traffic until the police came and insisted he move the truck.

He must have been better at growing chickens than another Arkansas farmer who bought 300 little chickens at the hatchery, took them to the farm, and then returned in a few days saying that the chickens died. He bought 300 more with the same results.

On the third trip, the man at the hatchery said, "I don't understand about these chickens. They are perfectly healthy when they leave here. Why are they dying?"

"I can't figure it," said the farmer, "I'm planting them six inches deep and watering them real good."

This farmer had been more successful and adopted some of the chickens' lifestyle. His biological time clock was set with the chickens. He retired every night about eight and rose in the morning at four. At the lavatory in the little room, he brushed his teeth, like the sound of a steel brush on concrete, washed his face, shaved, coughed up the chicken feathers that had accumulated in his lungs over the years, and by 5:00 a.m. was sweeping that tar paper covering the concrete floor, cleaning the room and stirring dust while the other three tried to sleep.

That continued for only a short while, as the roommates saw to it that he didn't go to sleep at 8:00, forcing him to stay up until 10:30. He learned to sleep until 6:30. They reset his biological clock, which must have frustrated the chickens when he returned to the farm.

Man from Michigan

The Michigan fellow was blessed or cursed with an unusual sensitivity to the Spirit's leadership. At breakfast time, alone in his Studebaker, he would sit at the intersection where he should turn right to get to the dining hall on the main campus, and mumble to himself, "I wonder which way the Lord is leading me to turn?"

Rain or shine, cold or hot, snow or sleet, he never offered the roommates a ride from the barn to the campus. A few times in the rain, they crowded into the car ahead of him, without asking.

One Monday morning in the wee hours between midnight and daybreak, the quartet returned from a weekend of services, and finding the Studebaker unlocked, Raper, Waddell, and Jackson pushed it down one street, around the corner, and parked it on another street. When the poor guy came looking for his car the next morning, he couldn't remember where he had left it. He walked to the dining hall for breakfast, searched over the main campus, and was puzzled as to how he lost the car.

Later in the day, someone told him that they saw a Studebaker like his, loud speakers and all, parked on another street a block away. He located the car, but continued wondering when and why he had parked it on that street. The fellows left it with him as one of life's unsolvable mysteries.

That year in a makeshift dorm was uncomfortable, inconvenient, and unforgettable.

Scattered / Not Separated

When the four finished graduate school, each went his own way to a separate ministry. Picirilli spent his life back at the alma mater, teaching, writing, and in administration. Waddell went to the pastorate for several years, then to the Foreign Missions Department for many years of effective promotion. Raper spent a parenthetical portion of his life at the children's home in Greeneville, TN, and on each side of that, the pastorate. Jackson stayed with evangelism for over 55 years.

Never drifting very far apart, the four stayed close and continued singing in revivals, at denominational functions, college get-togethers, and local churches for over 50 years with never a slight fracture in their fellowship.

When the Free Will Baptists gathered a large group of singers in Nashville to make a video, the quartet took part with interviews and *Peace in the Valley*, except this time, as a few others in later years, one's voice was away on vacation with laryngitis, so Michael Waddell, Eugene's son, sang the first tenor while Waddell held a mike and pretended.

At Trinity Free Will Baptist in Greenville, NC, Philip Jackson, Bobby's son, filled in the baritone for Picirilli, who couldn't be there because of glaucoma surgery. At least once a year for most years, they were together: Cofer's Chapel (Nashville, TN), Bay Branch (Timmonsville, SC), Horse Branch (Turbeville, SC), First FWB (Elizabethton, TN), etc.

New Brunswick / Prince Edward Island

They visited the Free Will Baptist churches in New Brunswick, Canada, preached and sang at a retreat in June and July of 1995, accompanied by the wives and Jane's sister, Catherine. They made a whirlwind visit to Prince Edward Island, so the women could see the geographical setting for *Anne of Green Gables*, the beaches, and the beautiful wild flowers. The men saw the Island and the large ferry boat which ferried them and their cars across the Northumberland Strait from New Brunswick to Prince Edward Island before the bridge was finished.

Where Do They Go From Here?

All of them are now in their mid-70s, and their get-togethers have been reduced to a once-a-year reunion at Chimney Rock, NC, in a beautiful, comfortable vacation house owned by James Earl's brother, Burkett Raper, to sit on the screened-in back porch, watch and listen to the clear, cold mountain water rush over the rocks in the Little Rocky River, visit the wonderful world of nostalgia, thinking and talking about those things in the past worth remembering, and the joy of having lives filled with such things.

Since they're not singing anymore, they don't need me, the sackbut. They have been gracious and kind to me, and not thrown me out. I have simply retired to Pic's pocket staying ready and available should the occasion ever arise to try singing again.

Current events that creep into their conversation, often concern everybody's physical condition, doctors' visits, medication, etc. Waddell, Raper, and Jackson have had prostate cancer; Waddell's cancer recently returned with critical physical problems.

Picirilli and Jackson have glaucoma, leaving them like the horse the Mexican sold to the Texan. As the Texan examined the animal, the Mexican kept telling him, "He no look so good."

To which the Texan replied, "He looks fine to me."

So he bought the horse. The next day, very upset, he came bringing the horse back and said, "Man, this horse is almost blind."

The Mexican said, "I toll ya. He no look so good!"

Jackson and Picirilli "no look so good," don't see too well. Some pots of artificial red flowers, along the outside edge of the screened-in porch of the house at Chimney Rock, not only fooled the hummingbirds which kept moving quickly from one pot to the next, they left Picirilli wondering why that hummingbird never found any of those beautiful flowers satisfying.

Hearing also is a problem. Waddell has an aid but doesn't wear it. Raper's hearing is a little dull. Jackson is almost deaf. Picirilli must constantly remind everybody to speak up so Jackson can hear you. He's like the old man with the new hearing aid who said to his friend, "Man, that's the best hearing aid I've ever had. It cost me $5,000."

His friend said, "What kind is it?"

The old man looked at his watch and said, "4:15."

An old couple was sitting on the porch during a summer evening, and the wind was blowing. She said, "It's windy."

"No, it's not, it's Thursday," he said.

"I'm thirsty, too," she said, "I'll get us some water."

That's where Jackson is, needs a hearing aid, doesn't want to wear one because it doesn't sound right, creating a problem for everybody else.

Late in the Game

A speaker at a minister's conference used the analogy of an airplane flight to illustrate one's life in the ministry. A flight plan is filed before takeoff, but during the flight it becomes necessary sometimes to make a correction in order to stay on course. It's too late for these guys to make a mid-flight correction. It's time to get the landing gear down, and make sure it's locked in position.

Realizing they're playing the game after the two-minute warning, trying to get out of bounds to stop the clock, they enjoy reliving where they've been and what they've done, with little thought to where they're going and what they're going to do.

Now and then the conversation will drift to the time when it will be a trio, then a duet, then a solo, then silence. In this world, silence, but maybe they will be singing on a different level, music of a different kind. If there are quartets in heaven, they'll enjoy trying their hand at it together again. The old repertoire will be outdated, not fitting to sing anymore. The poetic promises of *Peace in the Valley, In My Father's House, We'll Soon Be Done, We Shall Rise*, will have been fulfilled with reality.

They could continue to sing Jackson's favorite hymn,

> *There is a fountain filled with blood*
> *Drawn from Immanuel's veins;*
> *And sinners, plunged beneath that flood,*
> *Lose all their guilty stains.*

if the fifth verse is true:

> *When this poor lisping, stammering tongue*
> *Lies silent in the grave,*
> *Then in a nobler, sweeter song,*
> *I'll sing Thy power to save.*

William Cowper (1731-1800)

There will be a new song, maybe four-part harmony. The sound will be absolutely perfect and beautiful, in a land beyond discord. Being a pitch pipe, I certainly won't be needed then. No one will have to sound an A. Everybody will have perfect pitch.

The years have been such a joy tagging along with these guys, if it were possible I'd like it to continue forever. I don't read anything in the Bible about sackbuts in Heaven; trumpets, harps, maybe percussion that sounds like thunder. Then I bear no similarity to my ancestors anyway. The biblical sackbut was something like a triangular stringed instrument, forerunner of the harp. The medieval sackbut was a wind instrument which produced different notes by a slide, maybe the beginning of the trombone.

Here I am a little round black pitch pipe. Maybe I could claim kin to the biblical sackbut, and say evolution produced the change. Or, maybe I could get in by grace with no lineage or kin of any kind. Dives didn't make it, and he was a descendent of Abraham. Evidently pedigree doesn't have much to do with it. So maybe I'll tag along with the four fellows I've learned to love over these 50 years.

Jackson agreed, with no argument, that any memoirs must include his experiences with those three, Waddell, Raper, and Picirilli, whose relationship has been more harmonious over the years than their a cappella music. Otherwise a great chapter of his life would be missing.

Seniors

Later

Eugene died October 21, 2007. The three of us, Pic, Raper, and I continue to meet at Chimney Rock. It's not the same. Without Gene's wit, humor, and tenor voice, there is no quartet. Three quarts will never make a gallon. With no first tenor we're not only not a quartet, we're not a trio, not even a duet, so we don't sing anymore. Maybe tomorrow or the day after....

Still Later...

Pic now has prostate cancer. He thought 75% was a maximum possibility and then he grew old enough to join the other three.

Jackson finally has hearing aids, one in each ear, to the relief of everybody.

Sackbut in Retirement

DAY AFTER TOMORROW

If this were a play with a Freytag form there would be a long portion of "rising action,"a climax, a short section of "falling action," followed by a quick resolution, denouement, and the END. This is not a play. There is no climax, no falling action, and no end.

The search for tomorrow in the crystal ball was futile, forcing the search elsewhere. The future must be out there. Where? And how do we find it? The answer is in the One Who lives outside of time, dwelt in it for a few years, went from it back into forever, and never changed through it all. The One Who is, and always will be, what He has always been – Jesus, the Christ, the same yesterday, today, and forever (Hebrews 13:8).

Without faith in this Christ and hope in His promise, tomorrow is an anticipated repeat of a miserable yesterday.

Lady Macbeth, in her memorable summation of the futility of life and certainty of death, put it like this,

Tomorrow, and tomorrow, and tomorrow,
Creeps in this petty pace from day to day,
To the last syllable of recorded time;

And all our yesterdays have lighted fools
The way to dusty death.
Lady Macbeth…Macbeth. Act V, Sc.5

In the resurrection chapter of the Bible Paul concluded, "If in this life only we have hope in Christ, we are of all men most miserable" (I Corinthians 15:19).

But our hope is not in this life only and when He shines the light of revelation into the dark room of the future, it lights up a most beautiful world of splendor, glory and brilliance in Revelation, chapter 21. The wonder of it exceeds our most fantastic dreams and imagination, and to that world there is no end. Life goes on … and on….

Through the periscope of faith we can see around the curve and over the hill from here to the end. There is going to be a very happy ending, and knowing that helps to live through the pressure of the mess in the middle.

Saturday Matinee

When I was a boy, now and then on Saturday Daddy hitched two mules to a wagon and went three miles to town, Fremont, NC, allowing me to tag along. He went to get flour, sugar, coffee, the essentials, from the landlord's store. I went to see Ken Maynard, Bob Steele, Tom Mix, Johnny Mack Brown, Lash LaRue and Hopalong Cassidy whup all the bad people in the world, and save every little western town from being overrun by villains who were always easily identified by their black hats. Those weren't singing cowboys like Gene Autry and Roy Rogers, they were heroes who rode in from nowhere, and could ride faster, shoot straighter, fight harder than any man who ever wore a black hat.

As the wagon made its way down Main Street, passing in front of the theater it dropped off one passenger, who for a dime disappeared into that little dark hole-in-the-wall, not to reappear until the wagon was leaving town. The lady in the glass cage with a round hole in it slipped a ticket under the glass in exchange for a dime. Past the doorman, who took the ticket, I stepped into total darkness, sat in a few laps, walked on some feet, found an empty seat and relaxed, until my attention was turned to the screen.

The most beautiful girl in all the world was tied on a log at the sawmill. The saw was whining its way rapidly through that log, headed for the beautiful girl to make two halves of her in short order. The hero was bound hand and foot in a shack that was engulfed in flames. The villain was escaping with all of the town's money because the dumb stupid sheriff didn't know how to ride a horse. My blood pressure was rising and heartbeat increasing as I sat frozen, holding my breath. The burning shack exploded and out came the hero, one second before the blast. (He hadn't even lost his white hat.) On a horse that would make "Man o' War" ashamed of himself, he reached the sawmill just as the saw touched the first hair on that girl's head, stopped the saw, untied the girl, took a shortcut to catch the bank robber (Heroes always knew a shortcut.), brought him back to the dumb stupid sheriff, kissed his horse, said goodbye to the pretty girl, and rode off into the sunset.

Since I came in at the climax of the feature, I saw the end first, followed by the beginning. In fact, I saw all of it through two or three times during the afternoon.

It was the second time through and we were back at the saw-mill where the girl was on the log. In the meantime a new kid had just arrived, taken the seat next to me, and was about to have a nervous breakdown. Calm and relaxed, I looked at him and said, "Take it easy. Don't get all lathered up over this. She's not going to get cut in two by that saw, and he's not going to burn up in that shack. I've already seen it." I knew enough to know that it always ended the same way every time.

Two fellows were watching a cowboy movie. The hero was riding at top speed down a narrow trail. The first guy said to the second, "When he goes around that rock at the bend and under that tree, I'll betcha five dollars that limb will knock his hat off."

"You're on."

Round the rock, under the tree, the limb knocked his hat off.

"You win," the second one said. "Here's your five dollars."

"No, you keep your five dollars. I'd already seen it before."

"Oh, go on and take the five dollars," he said. "I've seen it three times before, and I thought that fool had learned where that limb was by now, and he wouldn't hit it again."

Knowing the end from the beginning helps to live through the pressure and problems of the present. Sometimes it seems that in the drama of human history we are about where the girl is on the log at the sawmill. Don't have a nervous breakdown over it. There really is going to be a happy ending.

Jesus has prepared a place. He referred to it as *my Father's house*. David called it *the house of the Lord*. "Home" seems a most fitting designation for the place.

The Boll Weevil

In the '40s, cotton farmers waged a yearly war with the boll weevil over the cotton crop. When the weevil punctured a square, which is the bud before the blossom before the boll, the square fell off. When he stuck his nose in the boll he destroyed the lock of cotton in that section of the boll. The boll weevil was just trying to find a place to lay his eggs to raise his family, which was destroying the cotton that the farmer needed to raise his family. That struggle for survival was a never-ending battle. Most of the time, the boll weevil won.

We mopped cotton with poisoned molasses seeping through small holes in the bottom of a syrup bucket, soaking attached cloth rag strips. Swinging a bucket in each hand, I mopped two rows at a time with that sticky, dripping mixture. The weevils drank it, grew fat, and used it as an aphrodisiac. The black, bitter, strong molasses came in square five-gallon tin cans and was not fit, nor meant, for human consumption. But after all the weevils were fed, we stirred fatback grease, instead of arsenic, into what was leftover and ate it. The grease changed the color to brown, cut the bitterness and made it possible to swallow the stuff.

The weevils thrived on it and were determined to settle in the cotton fields of Wayne County, North Carolina. A little ditty that originated somewhere by somebody over 100 years ago gives expression to that warfare. Here is the Jackson version put together from bits of memory scattered around in his brain:

"The boll weevil 'am a little black bug, come from Mexico, they say.

He come all the way to Texas just lookin' for a place to stay,
Lookin' for a home...lookin' for a home.
"The first time I saw the boll weevil he was sittin' on a square,
The next time I saw the boll weevil he had all his family der.
Lookin' for a home, just lookin' for a home.
"The missus said to the farmer, 'Now isn't that a mess,
That weevil done made a nest in my old cotton dress!'
Lookin' for a home, he's just lookin' for a home.
"The farmer said to his missus, 'Well whatta ya think o' that?
That weevil gone and made a nest in my best Sunday hat!'
He's lookin' for a home...just lookin' for a home."

The people of God have this in common with the boll weevil. They are pilgrims passing through this world "lookin' for a home."

If Jesus doesn't come to get me very soon, tomorrow I'll pass through the other door which leads from here to there, Death.

That's the door through which so many of my family and friends have already passed.

The Leah Waddell Story

Eugene Waddell and Leah Nichols fell in love while in elementary school, but put off marriage until he graduated from college in 1954. In fact, they postponed the wedding for a few weeks beyond schedule, due to a problem created by a jealous widow in the community. Leah was decorating the church when a black widow hiding in the flowers bit her. At the very time she was to have been saying "I do" and "I will" she was lying in the hospital recuperating from a spider bite. They married anyway, as soon as she was able.

Four babies came along in about five years, two, not twins, were born in the same calendar year. He pastored Bay Branch, Timmonsville, SC, First Free Will Baptist, Portsmouth, VA, and in 1960 was in Garner, NC.

Christmas eve, 1960, we were in Illinois for the holidays with the Kettemans. Gene called me from Rex Hospital in Raleigh with a broken heart and said, "Bobby, Leah's gonna die."

"Are you sure?"

"The doctor just told me that she will live about a year."

For the first six months there were no symptoms that the rapidly growing breast cancer was advancing on the offense with plans to take her life. By January, 1962, it was evident she was dying. Death is so cruel and inconsiderate. He gave no thought to the fact that the young pastor needed her for his ministry. He turned a deaf ear to the cry of four little children begging him not to take their mother away.

On my way to Nashville for the Bible Conference in the spring of 1962, I stopped by to see her, knowing she would die in a few days. When we returned she was gone with Jesus, and Gene asked me to speak at her funeral. The message was an acrostic listing some of Leah's personal attributes, Loving, Energetic, Able, and Happy. That sermon was the most difficult of my 60 years preaching.

The nurse who cared for Leah during her last few days gave me this account of her death. She loved to sing, and her favorite was "I'd Rather Have Jesus." The nurse said that Leah asked Gene to set her up in bed, sit beside her and sing with her. When the two of them began to sing the nurse was so overcome with emotion she left the room, closed the door, and didn't allow anyone to go in for a few minutes. They finished, but Leah continued singing, until under pain-killing sedatives she drifted into unconciousness, entrusted her four babies and husband to Jesus for Him to take care of them, left a cancer-ravaged, lifeless body, and with a big smile on her face and a song in her heart went to wherever Jesus is.

Being with Jesus is what will make it Heaven. In 1972, I wrote and recorded a song that says it like this:

"There is a world beyond the stars of wondrous beauty,
The streets are gold, so I am told, and joys in store.
The gates are pearl, the jewels rare,
Yet all I want when I go there
To see His face, to be with Him
Forevermore."

"There are no clouds in Heaven's sky to cast a shadow,
A river clear, and friends so dear, I'll see I know.
The jasper walls no thrill will be
For there His beauty I shall see.
His fellowship means more to me
I'll be with Him."

"To be with Him will make eternity worth living,

To be with Him will be my everlasting joy,
To be with Christ, who gave His life because He loves me,
I ask no more when life is o'er
To be with Him."

Eugene Waddell, My Friend

Gene and I were diagnosed with aggressive prostate cancer at about the same time in 1995. On the Gleason scale his was an eight, mine a nine. The treatment was the same, a prostatectomy. Removal of the gland lowered my PSA, prostate-specific antigen, to 0.0. Prostate-specific antigen is a molecular substance produced only by the cells in the prostate gland and when it rises rapidly it signifies that cancer cells are probably present and active. With the gland gone, if any of this antigen shows up in the blood it is being produced by prostate cancer cells which have moved outside the gland and taken up residence at some other place in the body. His never dropped to an absolute zero, indicating that the cells had probably escaped the gland.

For five years the cancer in both of us remained under control. Then my PSA moved to 0.3, his to 3.0. Each of us received thirty-some radiation treatments on the immediate area where the gland had been, hoping the cells were contained in that area. My PSA dropped back to 0.0, and has remained there for the past ten years. Gene's continued to rise to 4, 6, 8. The cells were multiplying and spreading. He went on Lupron shots to rid the body of all testosterone, the food supply of prostate cancer cells. Removing the source of sustenance limits their multiplying so rapidly.

For about four years the Lupron worked and kept the cancer from spreading. Then the cells made adjustments, went on the offense, and began multiplying and invading other parts of his body. His PSA continued rising. A bone scan revealed spots in the hip, the back, the shoulder, and on the skull.

A chemotherapy treatment, along with his being allergic to morphine, almost killed him. So the decision was made to treat the infected places with spot radiation and use pain killers, excluding morphine, to relieve his suffering and make him as comfortable as possible.

When the Gospeliers' chapter of this project was written nobody knew who would be the first to leave and break up the quartet. By January, 2007, that question was clearly answered. In Waddell's case the cancer with aggressive vengeance was determined to take his physical life. The medical question was no longer whether or not he would live, but how long.

The quartet, with his family and many friends gathered at Cofer's Chapel Church in Nashville for a special Eugene Waddell Day on Sunday, July 22, 2007. Eugene's hair had come out, uprooted by the chemo. He apologized for his appearance, said he was having a bad hair day. Gene sat in a chair for our last public performance. We sang "Where Could I Go?", and when he sang his solo verse, "Life here is grand with friends I love so dear. We get along in sweet accord. But when I face the chilling hand of death, where could I go but to the Lord?," backing him up was difficult for the other three of us. We had sung the song hundreds of times but never with death so near and the reality so personal. Waddell was dying.

For several years the quartet and wives met at Chimney Rock, North Carolina, during the first week of October for a time of vacationing, visiting, reminiscing, and enjoying being together. In the fall of 2007, it was evident Waddell would not be able to make the trip. He was rapidly losing the war with the cancer.

We met together for a few days at Waddell's home, shared memories of our good times, laughed at so many things we had experienced together, expressed our love for each other and what it had meant individually to be a part of the group for over 50 years.

The hospice workers insisted that we sing a song. We agreed to try. Our signature song, "Peace in the Valley," and our a cappella arrangement of "Heartaches," seemed most fitting at the time. Waddell was weak, but for a couple of songs his tenor came through loud and clear. At the end of the three days, when we separated, everyone understood that our next meeting would be at Gene's funeral, and it was. Three weeks later on October 23rd in Cofer's Chapel Free Will Baptist Church, Raper, Picirilli, and I gave testimony to the life of R. Eugene Waddell and our relationship with a wonderful friend from 1950 to October 21, 2007.

Gene was my best friend for 69 years, beginning in 1938 in the first grade at Nahunta School, Wayne County, North Carolina. Such a friendship must not end with a few years on the earth. Some day, some where, just as I did that day at Nahunta after having been separated for eight years, I'll walk up behind him and say, "Hi, I'm Bobby Jackson. We used to be friends." He'll turn, smile, and say, "Oh, I remember you." And it will be as if no time has transpired at all.

Mabel Ketteman's Miracle
September 2, 1902 – November 25, 1991

Mabel Ketteman, Jane's eighty-nine-year-old mother, having lost the fight with colon cancer, was dying at her home in Benton, Illinois, under hospice care. She was in and out of consciousness for several days as she prepared for her departure. Jane was with her and gives this account of her deathbed testimony:

On Tuesday, November 18, 1991, about 11 a.m., after four or five days of not being able to see or speak, and only able to occasionally swallow a medicine dropper's worth of water with great difficulty (four hard swallows for each dropper-full), Mother began sipping water more easily and opened her eyes brightly. She started speaking and smiling.

As Catherine, Daddy, Gene Outland and I stood by her bed, she said, "I want to tell you my miracle. God has given me a miracle. Praise His name."

With such adoration she would whisper, "Precious Lamb. Oh, Precious Lamb. <u>I have seen the LORD!</u> It was wonderful. I can't tell you how wonderful. Praise His name. Precious, precious Lamb.... I am so happy."

Then she said, "I tried to tell you before, but couldn't get the words out. I told you, 'You won't believe what I've seen.'" Indeed she had. She had very weakly said those words a few days earlier, and we thought perhaps her medication had caused her to say it.

Her face was radiant, her eyes bright. She would not let go of her joy. She stayed awake almost all day and all night apparently enraptured by His presence. No matter that she had not been able to eat for four days. She had meat to eat that we knew not of. No matter that her body was only a skeleton of her former beauty. No matter that we might be afraid of hurting her frail arms and legs as we turned her with the sheet.

I would say, "Mother, do you hurt anywhere?" She would calmly answer, "Oh, no. I'm so happy."

Later, I asked, "Mother, what did the Lord look like?"

Her reply, "Well...that's what everyone wants to know."

Besides being able to see the Lord, she had also been given the privilege of telling us about it. She wanted desperately for us who love her to be able to know the joy she was experiencing. She had prayed and asked the Lord to make her able to give us her message. As she was telling us about it, she would pause and say, "Lord, give me the strength. Lord, give me the strength to tell it."

And HE DID! She wanted us to be comforted as she was. She would say, "How many more miles, Lord? How many more miles?"

Catherine said, "I don't think it's many more, Mother."

She knew we would tell others and it would affect their lives. Sometime later I was making reference to her miracle, and she said, "I figured the word would get around."

And indeed it will. We who heard her have told it many times already, and will continue to tell it as long as we live. HE is really there when we need Him.

All my life I've quoted Psalm 23, but never had I experienced, "Yea, though I walk through the valley of the shadow of death, I will fear no evil, for thou art with me; thy rod and thy staff they comfort me." We who were with her during those last days became acutely aware of this comfort.

She had previously told one of her visitors that she was just WAITING on the Lord. I quoted to her, "Mother, 'They that wait upon the Lord shall renew their strength. They shall mount up with wings as eagles; they shall *run* and not be weary; and they shall walk … and not faint'" (Isaiah 40:31).

Praise His name!

Mother, who couldn't even lift her hand or turn her head, who lay completely helpless in a cancer-ravaged body, has been given her wings and soared away with Him, where she can even run and not be tired.

What a blessed, blessed gift the Lord has permitted her to share with us.

Mother walked through the valley of the shadow of death for another week after she told us of her happiness in seeing the Lord. It was hard to see her body deteriorate during those days, but precious because we knew she was with Him.

"*Precious* in the eyes of the Lord is the death of His saints" (Psalm 116:15).

My Little Brother, Billy

In 1997, my younger brother Billy left here and went there.

In February, Billy was visiting in a revival in New Hope Free Will Baptist Church in Jacksonville, NC, where I was preaching. "Bud," he said, "my tongue is so thick I can hardly preach. I sound like a drunk, and my throat is so swollen it's difficult to swallow. The doctor's treating me for a sore throat, but it isn't getting any better."

"You'd better find a throat specialist and let him diagnose the problem."

A few weeks later he was in the University Hospital at Chapel Hill, NC, for the removal of a massive, fast-growing squamous cell carcinoma in his neck and throat, a tumor the size of a tennis ball, another, a ping pong ball. To replace the mass removed from inside the neck, a large graft of skin, blood vessels, and nerves taken from his arm was grafted in its place. The extensive surgery took over 20 hours. The twenty-some hours of anesthesia was more than Billy could get over. He woke only to a dreamy state, drifted back to sleep, heart stopped for no one knew how long, was resuscitated, but remained brain dead, with only enough activity in the brainstem to keep the heart and lungs functioning for another week or so, and on March 2, 1997, went home. Had he lived here, preaching would have been very difficult, or impossible. His labor was finished. He preached in his church on Sunday before going for the surgery. No one realized those were his last sermons.

The following tribute, written by the older brother, was published in *Contact* magazine in May, 1997:

Billy entered this world little. He was born prematurely, weighing about two pounds. In July 1934, there were no hospital nurseries or incubators for such babies. Mother placed the little fellow on a pillow before an open fire in the fireplace to keep him warm. Billy was dealt a poor hand to begin this game.

When he was four, one Saturday morning in February, he watched Mother go away in a car to die in an automobile wreck. That left two little boys, seven and four, without a mother.

A stepmother came along within a year. She was only 16. The following ten years would be years of struggle, extremely hard work and serious abuse.

Life as sharecroppers was abuse enough. Labor began when the child was young. It was long and difficult. Daddy believed in working only half- a-day, and it didn't matter which 12 hours that was.

There was also abuse at home. Today, these little boys would be removed from the home. When Billy was six the stepmother beat him with a stick, leaving blue bruised streaks across his back.

There was no lingering hatred or bitterness in Billy. He loved her. As a young man he tried to help materially. He always stayed in touch. When she died, Billy wept and said, "She was the only mother I ever knew."

Billy began school still a bit premature. He missed many days and was asked to repeat grade two.

In the fall of 1949, Billy was 14, the older brother 17. It was early Sunday morning. The two were in the cornfield pulling soybeans, stalk and all, to feed to the hogs. The older had given his heart to the Lord the night before and told Billy about the experience.

Billy looked across that row of beans, with tears in those big eyes and said, "You mean you've become a Christian and would go to Heaven if you died?" As best he understood, his brother assured Billy he was serious.

Billy responded, "Then I want to be a Christian and go to Heaven when I die."

The two of them knelt in the field between rows of corn and beans. With no Bible, no preacher, no knowledge of scripture verses, only faith that the Lord who received one the night before would receive the other, if he gave himself to Him. Billy gave himself to God in the cornfield; that changed the rest of his life.

Within a year the older went away to college and Billy began preaching. Billy had no money. He would hitchhike to churches and youth meetings. Some nights when he could not get home, he would stop and sleep under the shelter of a tobacco barn.

Conflict continued at home. One day when he was 17, he finally walked away from the troubled home and didn't go back.

For a short time Billy lived, worked and attended school around New Bern, North Carolina. During this time he met and married Shirley Gaskins. He called on that older brother for the wedding.

In the fall of 1953, he entered Free Will Baptist Bible College in Nashville, Tennessee. Billy worked 40 hours a week at H. G. Hill's grocery store for 50 cents an hour, and tried to carry a load at college. During that time the school gave minus quality points for failing a subject.

Billy got behind in quality points and never was able to make them up. When time came to graduate, he had enough hours but lacked quality points. Meanwhile, the school had changed the system, no longer giving minus points.

Under the new system he could have made it, but there was no grandfather clause in the change. While he possibly could have taken more hours and obtained the necessary points, it just didn't seem that important to Billy. No doubt he could have obtained a degree by correspondence, but degrees never were his main pursuit.

He went away to become pastor to "little" churches. In some of those churches, he had a very fruitful ministry. One half-time church approached Billy about preaching two Sundays per month. He told them that he would preach every Sunday and take pay ($50 per week) for two Sundays. He would preach the other two for no pay, accepting whatever offering came in. They agreed.

After a month or so, the men of the church noticed those off-Sunday offerings were a bit more than $50, so they changed their policy to pay the preacher $50 every Sunday and put the extra money in the treasury. So the pastor took a cut in pay and the church went full-time. Billy's pastoral package was $50 per week.

In one revival in that church, there were over 60 people saved. Billy baptized about 50.

Billy worked with his hands to subsidize his ministry during all those early years. With boundless energy and no lazy bone in his body, he worked.

In Augusta, Georgia, he attempted to build a mission church. There his third child was born, a total diabetic. Some clause in small print in his health insurance policy gave the company an out from paying the exorbitant medical bills. Billy operated a taxi service and service stations to pay off that debt while he continued trying to build the church.

Billy wanted to build a big church for Jesus. He didn't understand why he worked tirelessly, lived a morally clean life, tried to preach the gospel as best he understood it, and never built a large church. It may be that the solution to his puzzle is in understanding the Lord's measure of "big" and "little."

With his debts paid, Billy left Augusta. Two years later he landed in Jacksonville, North Carolina. There he would spend the last 18 years of his ministry. The work prospered and the church grew, but then leveled off at 150 to 200 in attendance. Not a big church as men measure churches.

A pastor appreciation service one evening became emotionally moving as people gave witness to Billy's service among them. A black lady stood, with tears trickling down, and told of the night when "Brother Billy" came to sit all night with her family and sick child. Another told of an accident and that when he arrived at the emergency room "Brother Billy" was already there and stayed with him through the terrible ordeal.

Billy built and ministered to one of the few, maybe the only, truly racially integrated churches among Free Will Baptists.

Billy was one of that large group of preachers who serve with little recognition. They are always at the National Association. They never serve on a committee or board. They seldom, if ever, speak on the floor. They are part of the whole. He did preach once at a Tuesday Bible Conference.

This world never noticed. While he was dying in the hospital at Chapel Hill, North Carolina, his wife had difficulty with motel accommodations. Tar Heel basketball fans got priority. There will be no streets nor buildings named after Billy.

In the kingdom of God, that's a different matter. No one can say where the servants' places are. Jesus made it clear that the greatest are those who are servants.

The "little" children are big in His kingdom. He turns things upside down; the first are last and the last are first. It may be in that world, the older brother will be Billy's little brother.

In a small part of this world, Billy was important. To the boys and girls in the Children's Home at Turbeville, South Carolina, Billy was a great man. A few years ago at Christmas, he and his church bought and personally delivered to each child his own new bicycle.

To those people he loved and ministered to in their times of trouble and sorrow, "Brother Billy" was very important. To all of them my little brother Billy was a Big, Big man.

So many Sunday mornings Billy got up early to go to the house of the Lord and prepare for the services. On March 2, 1997, Sunday morning at about 6:00 a.m., Billy rose up early to go to the Lord's house, the one David referred to in Psalm 23, not to prepare, but to dwell with the Lord in His house forever.

Three Days to Home

The cooperative meeting in Durham closed Sunday, April 24, 1960. I was scheduled to begin at Johnston Union FWB Church on Highway 70 between Smithfield and Raleigh on Monday. The route from Greenville went through Eureka, a one-stop-light village on Highway 222 between Fremont and Stantonsburg. Daddy was janitor/ custodian, at the small one-through-twelve school in Eureka. On my way I dropped in to see him. He was sweeping floors.

"How are you doing?" I asked. "Working hard?"

"I ain't doing so good," he said. "My feet hurt so bad I can't walk. My legs ache and when I get down, I can't get up again. I'm weak as water."

He raised his trouser legs, and from the split skin about his swollen ankles bloody water was draining into his shoes.

"Man, you are sick," I said. "Something is terribly wrong. You need to go to a doctor."

His face grimaced with pain, lips began to tremble, "I don't have any money to go to a doctor," he said.

"Then lay down that broom. Get in my car. We're going to find a doctor."

In Goldsboro, I checked him into the hospital, found a Dr. Sasser listed in the phone book, requested that he examine my father, promised to pay him, and went to preach the opening revival service.

The next day the doctor said, "Preacher, your dad has nephritis. The nephrons which filter the blood in the kidneys have shriveled and died. The BUN count in his body is over 200. In a healthy body it's about 15. If we can't get it down the poison will do critical damage to his vital organs."

At the hospital, I told Daddy that he was really sick. His kidneys were not functioning. The doctor would do what he could.

On Wednesday I checked back with the doctor. "Doc," I said, "I'm supposed to close this meeting on Sunday night, fly to St. Louis to begin on Monday. So I need to know where things stand with my father."

"He's not going to get well. That count is over 600 and it's not coming down."

"What do you think will happen?"

"By Friday the tissue in the lungs will begin to break down. They'll start filling with fluid. It's like drowning a few drops at a time, takes about three days for them to fill. I'd say he'll probably die Monday afternoon."

By Daddy's bed in the hospital, I told him what the doctor said. I said, "Daddy, I'm not going to St. Louis Monday. You're going to die on Monday. We'll have your funeral Wednesday in the little Antioch Church. I'll get Gene Waddell to preach it, if that's all right with you. He's a good friend. I'll fly to St. Louis on Saturday and start that revival Sunday."

Some folks object. "You shouldn't have told him," they say.

If I had only three days to live and anybody knew that, I'd like to know it.

"I have to go preach," I said. "And you may be unconscious when I get back. So I must ask you: Are things right between you and the Lord? Where will you be next Wednesday when we are having your funeral?"

"Son," he said, "If the Lord's ready for me to come to be with Him, I'm the most ready I've ever been in my whole life."

What do you say to a man who has three days left on earth? I read John 14:1-6 to him, prayed, and went away to preach.

The meetings closed Sunday night. I was by Daddy's bed at 7:00 Monday morning. One of the most solemn, serious days of my life was that Monday standing alone all day watching him die, wiping perspiration from his hot unconscious brow, moistening his dry cracked lips with a cool wet cloth, listening to the rattling fluid rising in his lungs, watching his chest rise and fall with each breath becoming more shallow and farther apart, thinking he would not breathe again when the pause was so long, until at about 7:00 p.m. the pause became permanent.

What made the day so soul-searching and serious was when I closed my eyes to pray, the brain hit the fast forward button and the scene changed. I was the father on the bed. My son was standing by the bed, watching his daddy die, swallowing a lump in his throat, holding a tear in his eye forbidding it to trickle down his cheek, wiping my face with a cool rag.

That day is 50 years closer than it was in 1960. The fast forward button moves time only slightly. My turn is next in the family. I asked the Lord that day to help me die by what I had preached through the years, to bring peace and joy in the face of death, and make me a good testimony. If He would, I'd like to be conscious long enough to say to Jane and the boys, "Good night, I love you, I'll see you tomorrow," close my eyes and open them in the presence of Jesus.

Like Abraham the people of God are sojourners, pilgrims, wanderers, looking for a city whose builder and maker is God. If Jesus tarries a few more years, my wandering will end when death separates me from the only house I have ever known.

Paul put it like this, "…whilst we are at home in the body, we are absent from the Lord…we are willing rather to be absent from the body, and to be present with the Lord" (II Corinthians 5:6, 8). So for a little while the body and I will be separated. It will be embalmed, dressed for the occasion, placed in a casket, in a vault, in the ground, in the community of the dead, with a gray granite stone engraved with the vital statistics, born –died, with the dash indicating the duration between the two, marking the spot. That stone will be the only hard evidence that I ever lived on this planet.

No one has ever said it better than the old bespectacled printer himself, when he was a young man:

"The body of Benjamin Franklin, Printer
Like the Cover of an Old Book,
Its Contents torn Out,
And Stript of its Lettering and Gilding
Lies Here, Food for the Worms,
But the Work itself shall not be Lost
For it will, as he Believes, Appear once More
In a New and More Perfect Edition
Revised and Corrected
By the Author."

(Benjamin Franklin, born January 6, 1706, died April 17, 1790)

Through the process of decay and decomposition the earth will recycle the body, turning it back to dust from which it came and leaving no physical evidence that I was ever here, until the alchemy of the resurrection changes the earthly to the heavenly, the mortal to the immortal, the corruptible to the incorruptible, the natural to the spiritual, the non-glorious to the glorious.

While the earth is recycling the body, I will be with Jesus and that will be Heaven.

So, in a few years news will spread, not far and wide, but here and there, among friends and folks who have heard him preach during the past 60 years, that Bobby Jackson is dead. Hang this little epitaph over the casket:

"He is not here.
He has vacated the house,

Exited the building,
Left the premises,
Gone home with Jesus."

"…and I will dwell in the house of the Lord for ever" (Psalm 23: 6).

The future is forever, tomorrow and the day after.

The end of Chapter One…………

"The Best Laid Plans…"

Stephen will not watch his father die, the father lived too long and Stephen died too soon. Saturday, September 7, 2013, at 8:00 p.m., Gisella, Stephen's wife, called. I ran across the street and found him lying face down on the floor of his bedroom. Jane and I tried desperately to administer CPR, but he was gone. With no apparent symptoms, he died from "hypertensive heart disease" according to the death certificate.

On Saturday, September 21, friends from California, Alabama, Arizona, Connecticut, New York, and Tennessee, along with those from North Carolina, gathered in Greenville for a memorial service, with regrets from those in London, Barcelona, Milan, and Turin who were kept away by the distance.

Without saying good-bye Stephen went away to see Jesus, leaving Gisella, Isabel (his 12 year old daughter), and the rest of us with a great void in our lives. He was 59.

A TRIBUTE TO STEPHEN
by
Philip

How do you write an obituary for a great writer? When he's put so many words and thoughts into so many paragraphs that express his essence, what else can be written? With that, apologies are made to Stephen for any inadequacy and also blame given him for making this so difficult. Never let this obituary or any obituary take the place of any life ever lived. Only let it spur a eulogy within us of the amazing, wonderful ways he touched our lives and left this world a better place.

Stephen was born in Nashville, TN on April 5, 1954. From before he could remember, his life was filled with travels and adventure. As the son of Evangelist Bobby Jackson, he traveled across this country from state to state, town to town, and revival meeting to revival meeting. From this amazing upbringing, he learned to love people, tolerate some people, respect people's rights, and always be a help to people. He settled in Greenville, NC, beginning 1st grade in 1960 and graduating from JH Rose High School in 1972. This was just the beginning of a life that was constantly looking for more knowledge, sharing it and teaching it when he could in any way possible to anyone who would sit and listen.

Stephen attended numerous colleges and universities including the University of Perugia, Italy, receiving degrees from NYU and ECU. His education began in the field of music, but quickly changed to creative writing. An award-winning playwright, Stephen had many works performed in NYC during his early career. After several years living in Brooklyn, Stephen spent time traveling in Europe and fell in love with Italy and ultimately fell completely in love with Gisella Verando whom he married in 1999. After the birth of his daughter Isabel Jane in 2001, Stephen moved with his family back to Greenville where he settled. Proficient in the Italian language, Stephen spent his final years as one of the most sought after Italian-English translators, translating many books, articles, and more for publication.

Stephen died suddenly on September 7, 2013. He will be deeply missed by all who knew him and also by a world of people that never got to know him. It is a joy to know that the imprints of his writing and the footprints he left in the lives of those he touched will live on forever.

The Writer
Stephen Rand Jackson
1954-2013

APPENDIX

The Circuit

As a general rule, pastors control pulpits. Therefore, evangelists who work in revivals and evangelistic meetings in local churches don't preach for congregations, committees, or people. They preach for pastors–not all pastors, but a circle of pastors. To this, the record is clear evidence, showing that we had meetings 10, 12, 15 times in the same churches and with the same pastors. The circle was not very large considering the 2,500 churches in the National Association. It grew from a very small group in 1955 to a number large enough to keep two full years booked ahead. For some time we were making the schedule for the third year down the road.

Retirement and death are now shrinking the circle every year. Not long ago I said to a pastor with whom I was working, "The invitations for meetings have always come from a circle of preachers, and my circle is dying on me."

"You're not coming back here no more," he said.

"I didn't say I was killing 'em. I just said they were dying."

Many of those for whom I preached meetings have finished their work and are resting with the Lord.

Controversy has also removed some from the circle. Several churches in North Carolina where I had meetings from the beginning of the church to its establishment as a strong large church are now closed to my ministry by pastors with whom there have been disagreements. Church members still ask why I don't come in revivals anymore. I tell them that the pastor and I just have not been able to get together. It's best left that way. It would be impossible for a pastor and evangelist to work together in an atmosphere so charged with electrical disagreements that each was waiting for lightning to strike. Neither needs to be put under that kind of pressure.

When invited to have lunch with me, one of those who is now outside the circle said, "Bobby Jackson and I don't agree on enough to have anything to talk about."

It was probably meant to be facetious and exaggerated, but sometimes a man jokingly speaks his heart.

One church with a beautiful new building in a great location, which was begun as a denominational mission with the investment of money in property, buildings, and ministry, was closed to me by a new preacher who took the church out of the denomination to Independent Baptist without refunding a dime of the original group's investment. His nasty letter informed me that I would not be allowed to preach in his pulpit anymore because I remained a member of the National Association of Free Will Baptists, who tolerated "hermeneutical liberal amillennialists."

The reply that he received went something like this, "Preacher, we not only disagree on those hermeneutical amillennialists, we disagree on a simple more basic matter like ethics and morals. You stole a church."

There's been no further communication.

With every general rule there are exceptions. In the early '50s some churches were part-time, half-time two Sundays per month, quarter-time one Sunday. The preacher lived out of the community, came, preached, went home, and exercised very little pastoral leadership. The church or Sunday School under the leadership of strong laymen planned revivals. Some meetings the pastor never attended.

When some of these churches went full-time, strong laymen continued to have more influence than the pastor and were involved in the choice of an evangelist. In one of them, I returned for several meetings about every two years. At the close of one of those, they were in the process of finding a new pastor. When the men asked me to come back in two years, my question was, "Suppose your new preacher doesn't want me to come?"

The leader smiled, "Then we'll fire him and get another pastor."

All laughed. I returned and there never was a problem with any of their pastors. Those laymen are now dead, and I have not been back in several years.

There are exceptions, and exceptions to the exceptions concerning part-time churches. In northeast Mississippi, Brother M. L. Hollis pastored five or six churches at one time. In fact, he organized most of them. When I was with him in revivals, we started early Sunday morning, raced from one appointment to the next like in a Darlington 500 making pit stops, and preached in four or five churches every Sunday.

I would finish the sermon, close the service, rush through a side door where he was waiting in the car with the engine running, and jump in with the car moving. We'd scratch gravel, fly to the next meeting, arrive as they were singing the last verse of the last song, go directly to the pulpit, and preach again. The Lord knows I don't need that schedule at this time of my life.

The purpose for listing the total revival offerings from churches is not to plead poverty, nor imply that the Lord has not met our needs, nor to manifest envy of those who have received much larger incomes over the years in other areas of ministry, but rather to give some indication as to why there were, to my knowledge, no full-time evangelists (men living solely on the income from evangelistic work) among Free Will Baptists in 1950. There have been a few in and out for various periods of time over the last 60 years, and there is not a long line of applicants waiting now for the job. As a movement we have not yet shown enough concern for evangelism to support full-time evangelists whose work is needed and Biblical. Not yesterday. Not today. Maybe tomorrow.

Reducing the circle in a man's old age may be the Lord's way of reducing the load on his back, and his heart.

In the beginning not knowing what was down the road, or where it would lead, I told the Lord that wherever the doors opened for me to preach, I would go and preach, never making a decision based on the size of the church, nor the pay.

The record shows there were times of 10 and 12 weeks, three months of closing on Sunday, starting on Monday, a few days' break and another 10 or 12 weeks, and some of those were two services per day. An old man, approaching 80, even in good health would find that schedule beyond his reach.

The promise to the Lord to go into the open doors is still intact. He doesn't open as many and I'm happy and satisfied to go into those that He opens.

THE RECORD

THE RECORD

1955

6/3-12	HighlandPk	Detroit, MI
6/13-19	DawsonGr	Scotland Neck, NC
6 /21-7/2	First FWB	Miami, FL
7/4-9	ChristianHl	Rochelle, GA
7/1-17	FWB	Vernon, AL
7/17-23	Pearce Ch.	Amory, MS
7/24-29	Fawn Gr.	Fulton, MS
7/31-8/ 6	Philadel'	Folkston, GA
8/7-13	Bethel	Baxley, GA
8/14-20	FWB	ValleyFalls, SC
8/27-9/3	Edgewd	Tarboro, NC
9/3-10	FWB	Tarboro, NC
9/10-23	SherronAc	Durham, NC
25-10/ 6	FWB	Thom'tod, GA
10/9-23	Calvary	Durham, NC
23-11/5	FWB	Smithfield, NC
11/6-13	Hollis Ch	Columbus, MS
11/13-20	FWB	Fulton, MS
12/2-18	FWB	Nason, IL
25-1/4	B'rville	Bakerville, IL

1956

1/8-22	FWB	Waltonv'le, IL
1/22-2/5	FWB	Ina, IL
2/14-20	FWB	Leeds, AL
2/22– 3/4	FWB	ThomastonG
3/4-11	Ozias	Pearson, GA
3/11-18	Unity	Jacksonville, FL
3/19-24	Oak Gr.	NewtonGr, NC
3/25-4/1	Prospect	Erwin, NC
4/8-15	FWB	PineBluff, AR
4/18-29	Arcadia	Arcadia, SC
4/29-5/6	Bay Br.	Timonsvle, SC
5/7– 6/12	Tee's Ch.	Smithfield, NC
6/13–19	Grace	Greenville, NC
6/20-26	FWB	Baxley, GA
5/27-6/2	Fawn Gr.	Fulton, MS
6/3-10	FWB	E.Tupelo, MS
6/11-17	DawsonGr	Scotland Neck, NC
6/17-22	Friendship	Midlesex, NC
6/25-7/1	FWB	Red Bay, AL
7/2-8	FWB	Leeds, AL
7/9-12	NAFWB	Huntingt'n, WV
7/15-21	FWB	Fulton, MS
7/22-29	FWB	Northport, AL
7/29-8/5	First FWB	Columbus, MS
8/6-12	Harmony	LakButler, FL
8/13-22	FWB	Chipley, FL
8/26-9 2	Pine Level	Alma, GA
9/2-8	Ebenezer	Glenville, GA
9/9-15	St. Mary's	Kenly, NC
9/16-23	FWB	Tarboro, NC
30-10/6	FWB	Warwick, VA
10/7-21	Edgemont	Durham, NC

10/22-28	Bay Br.	Timonsvle, SC
11/4-11	Casey Ch.	Goldsboro, NC
18-12/2	Blue Point	Cisne, IL
12/2-16	First FWB	MtVernon, IL
Total Offerings: $4,817		

1957

1/6–20	Bethel FW	Roxanna, IL
1/21–30	Webbs Pr.	Ewing, IL
2/10–20	FWB	Bakervile, IL
24-3/10	First FWB	Portsmouth, VA
3/11- 24	Prospectfwb	Erwin, NC
3/24-4/6	First FWB	Greenville, NC
4/7-14	FWB	Manning, SC
4/14-21	First FWB	Albany, GA
4/22-5/5	Unity FWB	Jack'ville, FL
5/2-18	Hope FWB	Scotland Neck, NC
5/9- 25	Hugo FWB	Kinston, NC
5/26-31	Faith FWB	Kinston, NC
6/2-9	FWB	E. Tupelo, MS
6/10-16	BethelFWB	Marvel, AL
6/8-23	FWB	PineLevel, NC
7/3-14	FWB	Northport, AL
7/15-18	PreachNAL	Birm'ham, AL
7/23-30	Youth Cam	Benton, IL
31-8/11	First FWB	Columbus, MS
8/12-17	Piney Wds.	Woodlake, TX
8/25-9/1	FWB	Warwick, VA
9/2-14	FWB	Lowell, NC
9/8-29	First FWB	Goldsboro, NC
30-10/6	FWB	Arcadia, SC
10/7-13	Watery Br.	Stant'burg, NC
10/13-20	FWB	Belhaven, NC
10/20-26	Westside F	Johnsonvile, SC
10/27-3	White Oak	Bailey, NC
11/3-10	St. Delight	Louisburg, NC
20-12/8	First FWB	Monett, MO
Total Offerings: $4,607		

1958

1/26-2/1	Hyde Park	Norfolk, VA
2/2-9	FairmontPk	Norfolk, VA
2/10-16	FWB	Beaufort, NC
2/7-23	First FWB	Rocky Mt., NC
2/24-3/9	First FWB	Portsm'th, VA
3/10-21	FWB	Maury, NC
3/23-27	FWBBC	Nashville, TN
3/30-12	First FWB	Greenville, NC
4/13-20	FWB	Manning, SC
4/21-5/4	Hope FWB	Scotland Neck, NC
5/6-18	Philadelphia	Detroit, MI
5/9 -25	Hugo FWB	Kinston, NC
5/25-6/1	Faith FWB	Kinston, NC
6/1-8	Parkers Ch.	Greenville, NC

6/9–15	FWB	Selma, NC
6/16–29	First FWB	Raleigh, NC
7/7–10	NAFWB	St. Louis, MO
7/13-25	First FWB	Darlington, SC
7/28-8/3	FWB	Iola, TX
8/4–10	Fellowship	Bryan, TX
8/1–16	Piney Wds.	Woodlake, TX
8/7–23	Good Hope	Henderson, TX
8/25-31	Midway	Moultrie, GA
9/1–7	First FWB	Savannah, GA
9/8–14	FWB	Lowell, NC
9/15- 21	FWB	Mt. Holly, NC
9/22-28	Fellowship	Washington, NC
9/28-4	GumSwamp	Greenville, NC
10/7- 19	First FWB	Drumright, OK
10/20-26	First FWB	Bryan, TX
27-11/9	First FWB	Pocahontas, AR
11/16-29	White Oak	Bailey, NC
30-12/7	Bay Branch	Timmonsvile, SC
28-1/11	Grace FWB	Greenville, NC

Total Offerings: $4,763

1959

1/25 –2/7	Maranatha	Greenville, NC
2/8–15	Parkers Ch	Greenville, NC
2 /16–3/1	First FWB	Houston, TX
3/2–15	FWB	Cushing, OK
3/16–22	St. Delight	Louisburg, NC
3/25–4/3	First FWB	JohnsonCity, IL
4/5–12	FairmontPk	Norfolk, VA
4/15–26	FWB,	Beaufort, NC
4/27–5/6	Westside	Johnson'lle, SC
5/7–17	Beulah	Pamplico, SC
5/18–31	Pleasant Gr	Erwin, NC
6/1–13	AspenGrov	Fountain, NC
6/15–27	CoopCamp	Rocky Mt, NC
6/28-7/5	Dawson	Scotland Neck, NC
	Grove	
7/6–12	Duplin Gr.	Aurora, NC
7/13–15	NAFWB	Asheville, NC
7/18–24	YouthCam	Benton, IL
7/26–8/2	FWB	Cordova, AL
8/3–9	First FWB	Dallas, TX
8/10–15	PineWood	Woodlake, TX
8/16–23	Good Hope	Henderson, TX
8/24-30	Evergreen	Iola, TX
9/6-20	First FWB	Miami, FL
28-10/3	Rosebud	Wilson, NC
10/7-18	Bethel	Roxanna, IL
19-11/1	Fulton Un.	Delta, OH
11/8-14	FWB	Vanceboro, NC
11/15-28	Rock Sprs.	Bailey, NC
12-13	FWB	Fredricktn, MO

Total Offerings: $4,978

1960

1/6 – 10	Webbs Pr.	Ewing, IL
1/17- 24	FWB	Grifton, NC
1/5-2/7	Parkers Ch.	Greenville, NC
2/ 8-14	Mt. Calvary	Hookerton, NC
2/15- 28	First FWB	Darlington, SC
3/1- 13	PineyGrove	Kenly, NC

3/14- 20	Ruths Ch.	New Bern, NC
3/21-3/3	FWB	Beaufort, NC
4/10-17	FWB	Selma, NC
4/17- 24	CoopCap'n	Durham, NC
4/25-5/1	JohnsonUni	Smithfield, NC
5/2	Father died	
5/8 – 15	Southside	St. Louis, MO
5/16- 25	First FWB	Berkley, MO
5/29 -6/5	PleasatVi'w	Mt. Vernon, IL
6/8-19	Milbournie	Wilson, NC
7/3-13	FWB	Wilmington, NC
7/17- 24	Hope FWB	Scotland Neck, NC
7/27-8/7	FWB	Northport, AL
8/8 – 20	YouthCamp	South Carolina
8/22-28	MalachisCh	Columbia, NC
8/29-9/4	Tippetts Ch.	Clayton, NC
9/5 – 11	Prospect F	Erwin, NC
9/14-25	First FWB	Florence, SC
26-10/2	First FWB	Albany, GA
10 5-16	First FWB	Portsmouth, VA
10/17- 23	Everetts Ch.	Clayton, NC
10/4-30	SharonBapt	Wilson, NC
30-11/6	FWB	Smithfield, NC
11/7 – 13	Sherron Acr	Durham, NC
11/16- 27	First FWB	Lake Charles, LA
28-12/4	Unity FWB	Jacksonville, FL
12/5 – 14	FWB	Stacy, NC
12/8 – 25	FWB	Waltonville, IL
12/25-1/6	FWB	Nason, IL

Total Offerings: $5,408

1961

1/18 – 29	FWB	Rock'gham, NC
1/30-2/5	FWB	Grifton, NC
2/6 – 12	FWB	Plymouth, NC
2/13- 26	Mt. Calvary	Hookerton, NC
3/1- 12	Ruths Ch.	New Bern, NC
3/13-19	White Oak	Bladnboro, NC
3/20 -4/2	First FWB	Morehead, NC
4/9 – 16	Cedar Grov	Rober'ville, NC
4/16 – 22	FWB	Williamston, NC
4/23-30	St. Delight	Louisburg, NC
5/1 – 7	Shady Grov	Durham, NC
5/8 – 14	Bay Branch	Timonsville, SC
5/15- 21	FWB	Baxley, GA
5/22 – 28	FWB	Brunswick, GA
5/29 -6/4	CoopC'pain	Kinston, NC
6/5 – 11	Aspen Gr.	Fountain, NC
6/12 – 18	JohnsonUn	Smithfield, NC
6/19 – 25	Powatan	Clayton, NC
6/26 -7/2	Bible Bapt.	Norfolk, VA
7/3 – 9	First FWB	Newport News, VA
7/0 – 13	NAFWB	Norfolk, VA
7/16 – 23	SulphurSpg	Samantha, AL
7/24 – 30	First FWB	Dothan, AL
8/2 – 13	First FWB	Columbus, MS
8/14 – 20	Fellowship	Flat River, MO
8/22 – 27	FWB	Columbia, SC
9/3 – 10	FWB	NLimerick, ME
9/10 – 13	FWB	Linneus, ME
9/4 – 17	Baptist	ERandolph, VT
9/17 – 22	CommBapt	Twin Mt., NH

9/24 – 29	First FWB	Littleton, NH
10/1 – 8	Edgemont	Durham, NC
10/9 – 15	Southside	Darlington, SC
10/16-22	St. Pauls	Elizabeth City, NC
10/22-29	Taberncle	Wilson, NC
11/5 – 19	FWB	Garner, NC
22-12/3	First FWB	Pocahontas, AR
12/4 – 10	Cherryvale	Sumter, SC
12/11-17	Hope FWB	Scotland Neck, NC
12/25-31	New Hope	Ina, IL

Total Offerings: $4,963

1962

1/15-21	Faith FWB	Goldsboro, NC
1/22-28	FWB	Swananoa, NC
1/9-2/4	Mt.Calvary	Hookerton, NC
2/5-11	TippettsCh.	Clayton, NC
2/2-18	Funeral Ch.	Louisburg, NC
2/21-3/4	White Oak	Bailey, NC
3/5-10	Oak Grove	Elm City, NC
3/11-12	Mission	Erwin, TN
3/8-25	Central	Royal Oak, MI
3/26-4/1	First FWB	Greenville, NC
4/11-22	First FWB	Beaufort, NC
4/3-29	Dublin Gr.	Aurora, NC
4/30-5/3	First FWB	E. Rock'ham, NC
5/14-20	GraceFWB	Greenville, NC
5/1-27	FWB	Cheraw, SC
5/28-6/3	FWB	Cove City, NC
6/6-17	FWBMis'n	Jacksonville, FL
6/18-24	SatillaFWB	Hazelhurst, GA
6/25-7/1	Friendship	Ashland City, TN
7/2-8	New Hope	Joelton, TN
7/9-12	NAFWB	Nashville, TN
7/16-29	FWB	Stacy, NC
7/30-8/5	Bible Bapt	Norfolk, VA
8/7-19	First FWB	Jesup, GA
8/22-9/2	Woodale	Knoxville, TN
9/10-16	FWB	Elizabeth City, NC
9/17-23	HortonHht	Nashville, TN
26-10/7	First FWB	Albany, GA
10/10-21	Fellowship	Durham, NC
24-11/4	First FWB	Florence, AL
11/7-18	Fellowship	Flat River, MO
25-12/2	First FWB	Jacksonville, NC
12/3-9	Palmetto	Vanceboro, NC

Total Offerings: $4,817

1963

1/14-20	Enfield FW	Enfield, NC
1/1-2/3	First FWB	Jacksonville, NC
2/3-10	Phildelphia	Folkston, GA
2/3- 24	Ruths Ch.	NewBern, NC
2/25-3/3	First FWB	Sylacauga, AL
3/3- 10	FWB	Northport, AL
3/13-24	Maranatha	Greenville, NC
3/5-4/7	FWB	Swannanoa, NC
4/4-21	FWB	Bristow, OK
4/21-28	FWB	Drumright, OK
4/28-5/5	Lewis Ave.	Tulsa, OK
5/6-12	Oak Grove	Elm City, NC

5/13-19	Southside	Darlington, SC
5/20- 26	FWB	Lowell, NC
6/3- 9	FWB	Linneus, ME
6/10-16	FWB	Limmerik, ME
616 -23	Primitive Baptists	Stickney, NB, Can.
6/24- 30	FWB	Littleton, NH
7/1-7	FWB	Twin Mt., NH
7/8- 14	FWB	Millville, NB
7/15-18	NAFWB	Detroit, MI
7/1-28	SulphurSpr	Samantha, AL
7/29-8/4	FWB	Pine Bluff, AR
8/5-11	First FWB	Dallas, TX
8/2-18	FWB Assn.	FortWorth, TX
8/9-23	PineyWod	Woodlake, TX
9/2-15	Ben Ave.	Kannapolis, NC
9/6- 22	Hope FWB	Scotland Neck, NC
9/23- 29	Joy FWB	Tarboro, NC
30-10/6	Goshen	N.Belmont, NC
10/7-13	BayBranch	Timonsville, SC
10/14-20	Hazel Park	Hazel Park, MI
23-11/3	Calvary F	Durham, NC
11/4 -10	Gum Sprgs	Winfield, NC
11/11-17	Ensley	Birm'ham, AL
18- 24	FWB	Charleston, SC
25-12/ 1	PleasanAcr	New Bern, NC
12/2- 8	ShallalyRd	Norfolk, VA

Total Offerings: $6,277

1964

12/26-1/3	Hazel Dell	Sesser, IL
1/12 -26	Bethel	Kinston, NC
1/27-2/2	Okefnoke	Waycross, GA
2/3-9	Calvary	Enfield, NC
2/10-16	First FWB	Savannah, GA
2/17- 23	Fellowship	Micro, NC
2/24-3/1	Emmanuel	Jacksonville, NC
3/2- 8	MtCalvary	Hookerton, NC
3/9-18	First FWB	Elizabethton, TN
3/23- 29	First FWB	Gastonia, NC
3/30-4/5	W. Calvary	Smithfield, NC
4/12-19	First FWB	Thomastn, GA
4/22-5/3	FWB	Garner, NC
5/6-17	FWB	Ahoskie, NC
5/19-31	Philadlphia	Folkston, GA
6/3-14	ShallalyRd.	Norfolk, VA
6/15- 21	First FWB	Columbia, SC
29-7/12	FWB	BumpusMl, TN
7/13-16	NAFWB	KansasCty, MO
7/20-31	Youth C.	Benton, IL
8/3-9	FWB	Blakely, GA
8/10-16	PlesantHill	Vienna, GA
8/17-23	First FWB	Jesup, GA
8/24-30	FWB	Brunswick, GA
9/9-20	Southside	Darlington, SC
9/21-27	Prospect	Erwin, NC
10/1-11	First FWB	Houston, TX
10/12-25	First FWB	Miami, FL
11/1-8	Prim Bapt.	Stickney, NB
11/8-15	PrimBapt.	Bristol, NB, Can.
11/15-22	PrimBapt.	Holmesville, NB

11/22-29	PrimBapt.	Lerwick, NB,
1,8,15	RosedaleP.	Woodstock, NB
12/ 6-13	FWB	Greensboro, NC
12/14-19	Imman'l B.	Edenton, NC
12/27-31	Harmony F	WFrankfort, IL
Total Offerings: $5,966		

1965

1/6-17	Faith FWB	Goldsboro, NC
1/18-27	Bethel	Kinston, NC
2/1-7	First FWB	Morehead, NC
2/8-14	Westconet	Jacksonville, FL
2/15-21	Parkers Ch	Greenville, NC
2/22-28	GardenCty	Whelersb'g, OH
3/1-7	Mt. Olive	Plymouth, NC
3/10-21	First FWB	Erwin, TN
3/24-4/4	PleasantAc	New Bern, NC
4/11-18	Westside F	Johns'ville, SC
4/19-5/2	First FWB	Anderson, IN
5/3-9	Bethany	Norfolk, VA
5/10-16	First FWB	Richmond, VA
5/21-23	Maranatha	Greenville, NC
5/24-30	FWB	Charleston, SC
6/13-20	First FWB	Dallas, TX
6/21-25	Youth Cam	Bowie, TX
6/27-7/4	Westside	Midland, TX
7/5-10	FWB Miss.	Monterey, MEX
7/12-15	NAFWB	Raleigh, NC
7/18-25	SulphurSpr	Samantha, AL
7/26-8/1	First FWB	Panama City, FL
8/2-8	Ensley	Birm'ham, AL
8/9-15	Gum Spgs.	Winfield, AL
8/16-22	Cedar Crk.	Hartselle, AL
8/23-29	Immanuel	Jacksonville, FL
9/1-12	First FWB	Spartanbg, SC
9/13-19	FWB	Thomastn, GA
26-10/6	Grace FWB	Arnold, MO
10/7-12	Bear Point	Sesser, IL
10/18-24	Fellowship	Micro, NC
10/25-31	First FWB	Washington, NC
11/1-7	FWB	Buckatuna, MS
11/8-14	Fellowship	Richton, MS
11/15-21	Grace FWB	Greenville, NC
11/22-28	Hope FWB	Scotland Neck, NC
29-12/5	Fellowship	Durham, NC
12/6-12	Trinity	LaGrange, NC
Total Offerings: $7,303		

1966

1/5-16	First FWB	Grensboro, NC
1/24-30	Calvary	Georgeton, SC
31-2/6	FWB	Cramerton, NC
2/8-13	Mt. Olive	Plymouth, NC
2/14-20	Brookwood	Fayetteville, NC
2/21-26	Marnatha	Greenville, NC
2/27	Grace	Greenville, NC
3/2-13	Trinity	Phoenix, AZ
3/21-27	First FWB	Phoenix, AZ
28-4/3	FWB	Hobbs, NM
4/7	FWBBC	Nashville, TN
4/11-17	Central	Norton, VA
22-5/1	First FWB	Columbia, SC

5/5-15	First FWB	Ahoskie, NC
5/16-22	Emanuel	Jacksonville, NC
5/23-29	Colinswod	Portsmoth, VA
6/12-19	Baptist	Harington, ME
6/20-26	PrimBapt.	Holmsville, NB
26-7/6	United B.	J'town, NB
7/7-17	Y'th Camp	Hartland, NB
7/17-24	PrimBapt.	Stickney, NB
7/24-31	PrimBapt	Bristol, NB
31-8/7	RosedaleP.	Woodstock, NB,
7/10, 17,	STJohn	Hartland, NB
24,31 8/7	Camp	
	Tabernacle	
6,7,8	Radio	Woodstk, NB
8/17-21	2nd FWB	Ashland, KY
9/7-18	Southside	Darlington, SC
21-10/2	FWB	Brunswick, GA
10/9-16	Antioch	Pikeville, NC
10/16-23	Faith FWB	Goldsboro, NC
10/24-30	Fairm't Pk	Norfolk, VA
11/7-13	Westcont	Jacksonville, FL
11/16-18	FWBBC	Nashville, TN
11/14-20	Woodbin	Nashville, TN
11/21-27	Mizpah	Washington, NC
28-12/4	FWB	Donelson, TN
12/5-11	WhiteOak	Bailey, NC
Total Offerings: $6,117		

1967

1/9-15	First FWB	Charleston, SC
1/18-29	Joy FWB	Tarboro, NC
1/30-2/5	Trinity	Nashville, TN
2/6-2	First FWB	Florence, SC
2/13-19	First FWB	Grifton, NC
2/20-26	Liberty	Durham, NC
2/27-3/5	Mt.Calvry	Hookerton, NC
3/6-12	Grace	Rocky Mt., NC
3/15-26	CofersCh.	Nashville, TN
4/9-16	First FWB	Winfield, AL
4/17-23	TippetsCh	Clayton, NC
4/26-5/7	First FWB	Berkley, MO
5/15-21	Calvary	Jacksonville, NC
5/22-28	First FWB	Newport News, VA
6/2	Maranath	Greenvile, NC
6/11-18	Westside	Midland, TX
6/19-28	First FWB	Houston, TX
6/30-7/2	S.Houston	Houston, TX
7/1	Qtly Meet	Bryan, TX
7/4-9	First FWB	Panama City, FL
7/10-13	NAFWB	Jacksonville, FL
7/16-23	SulphrSpr	Samantha, AL
7/24-30	Unity	Sylacauga, AL
7/31-8/6	First FWB	Ensley, AL
8/7-13	FWB	Buckatuna, MS
8/14-20	GumSprgs	Brilliant, AL
8/21-27	Felowship	Richton, MS
9/3	Marnatha	Greenville, NC
9/6-17	First FWB	Spartanbg, SC
9/18-24	Brookwod	Fayeteville, NC
9/2-10/1	First FWB	Greensboro, NC
10/2-8	Bethany	Norfolk, VA
10/16-22	First FWB	Eastman, GA

10/23-29	First FWB	Canton, NC
11/6-12	Calvary	Georgetown, SC
11/13-19	FWB M.	Florence, SC
11/20-26	Hope	Scotland Neck, NC
17-12/3	Mt.Calvry	Hookerton, NC
12/4-10	Calvary	Enfield, NC
12/11-17	Hilltop	Fuquay, NC
Total Offerings: $8,090		

1968

1/8-14	First FWB	Pamplico, SC
1/15-21	FWB	Clinton, NC
1/28-2/4	Bethel	Kinston, NC
2/5-11	First FWB	Ocala, FL
2/12-18	WindsrPk	Cheraw, SC
2/19-25	Trinity	LaGrange, NC
2/26-3/3	St.Delight	Louisburg, NC
3/4-10	ComunitB	Mattoon, IL
3/11-17	First FWB	Decatur, IL
3/18-24	Marnatha	Greenvile, NC
3/25-31	FirstFWB	Raleigh, NC
4/1-7	Felowship	Durham, NC
4/14-21	MemBapt	Ahoskie, NC
24-5/ 5	FirstBible	NewCastle, IN
5/6-12	Trinity	Nashville, TN
5/15-19	FirstFWB	Grifton, NC
5/20-26	FirstFWB	Darlington, SC
5/20-26	TV	Florence, SC
6/9-16	First FWB	Tucson, AZ
6/17-23	Northside	Phoenix, AZ
7/7-14	FirstFWB	Denver, CO
7/15-18	NAFWB	Okla.City, OK
7/22-28	Heads	CedarHill, TN
7/29-8/4	LoyalChpl	Columbia, TN
8/25-9/1	First FWB	Dothan, AL
9/9-15	Southside	Darlington, SC
9/16-22	Grace	Rocky Mount, NC
9/23-29	First FWB	Brunswck, GA
30-10/6	Phildlphia	Folkston, GA
10/7-13	Colnswod	Portsmth, VA
10/14-20	Mizpah	Washington, NC
10/21-27	First FWB	Elizabetht, TN
28-11/3	Bloss	Arlington, VA
11/7-9	BibleClub	Greenville, NC
11/11-17	First FWB	Charleston, SC
11/18-24	First FWB	Florence, SC
12/2-8	Friendshp	Wilmington, NC
12/25-31	Bakerville	Bakerville, IL
Total Offerings: $8,191		

1969

1/19	RuthsChpl	NewBern, NC
1/20/26	Victory	Gldsboro, NC
1/27-2/2	First FWB	Miami, FL
2/9	Grace	Greenville, NC
2/14- 16	Mt.Calvry	Hookertn, NC
2/17- 23	Trinity	Greenville, NC
2/24-3/2	First FWB	Greensboro, NC
3/10-16	Comunity	Rockingham, NC
3/17- 23	Comunity	Weldon, NC
3/24- 30	First FWB	Florence, SC
3/31-4/6	Woodbine	Nashville, TN

4/13- 20	First FWB	Winfield, AL
4/ 28-5/4	Victory	Kan.City, MO
5/5-11	Central	Kan.City, MO
5/12-18	Marnatha	Greenville, NC
5/19- 25	First FWB	Columbia, SC
6/8-15	Hilltop	Fuquay, NC
6/16- 25	Liberty	Ayden, NC
6/ 29	Trinity	Greenville, NC
7/7- 13	First FWB	Louisa, KY
7/14- 17	NAFWB	St. Louis, MO
7/20- 27	SulphrSpr	Samantha, AL
7/28-8/3	FWB	Fulton, MS
8/11- 17	Eastside	Tuscalosa, AL
8/18- 24	GumSprgs	Brilliant, AL
8/25- 31	Fellowshp	Richton, MS
9/8-14	UnionChpl	Chocownity, NC
9/15- 21	Prospect	Erwin, NC
9/22- 28	S'thside	Suffolk, VA
9/29- 10/5	Bethel	Kinston, NC
10/6 – 12	First FWB	Eastman, GA
10/13-19	LibertyCh	Macon, GA
10/20-26	Unity	Smithfield, NC
27-11/2	BiblFWB	Florence, SC
11/ 3- 9	Trinity	LaGrange, NC
11/10-16	First FWB	NewportN, VA
11/17-23	ParkersCh	Greenville, NC
11/24-30	Calvary	Georgetn, SC
12/1 -7	First FWB	Winter Haven, FL
12/ 8-14	Mt.Calvry	Hookerton, NC
Total Offerings: $9,229		

1970

1/5 -11	First FWB	RockyMt. NC
1/12-18	First FWB	Mt.Vernon, IL
1/19-25	First FWB	Waltonville, IL
1/26-2/1	FaithFWB	Goldsboro, NC
2/2-8	First FWB	Kingstree, SC
2/9-15	PleasantA	New Bern, NC
2/16-22	First FWB	Spartanburg, SC
3/1-8	First FWB	Beaufort, NC
3/ 8-15	First FWB	Jack'ville, NC
3/16-18	FWBBC	Nashville, TN
3/23-29	BayBrnch	Timonsvile, SC
3/30-4/5	Heads	Cedar Hill, TN
4/6-12	Peace	Wilson, NC
4/13-19	BibleChch	NewCastle, IN
4/27-5/3	FairmotPk	Norfolk, VA
5/4-10	FWB	Owasso, OK
5/11-17	First FWB	Berkeley, MO
5/18- 24	Mission	Warsaw, NC
5/25-29	First FWB	Garner, NC
6/8-14	First FWB	Ocala, FL
6/15- 21	New Zion	Headland, AL
6/22- 26	Y'thCamp	PineyWds, TX
6/27- 28	G'dHope	Hendersn, TX
6/29-7/5	First FWB	Houston, TX
7/13-16	NAFWB	Fresno, CA

7/19- 26	First FWB	Buena Pk, CA
8/ 2-7	FaithFWB	SanAntonio, TX
8/9-16	First FWB	Dothan, AL
8/17-23	Mt.Plesnt	Montevalo, AL
8/24-30	First FWB	Albany, GA
9/5-6	Grace	Greenville, NC
9/7-13	Palm'toCh	Vanceboro, NC
9/14-20	Southside	Darlington, SC
9/21-27	First FWB	Brunswick, GA
28-10/4	First FWB	Morehead, NC
10/5- 11	Colinswod	Portsmouth, VA
10/12-18	Central	RoyalOak, MI
10/19-25	Friendship	Wilmington, NC
11/1-8	Bethel	Roxana, IL
11/9-15	First FWB	Florence, SC
11/16-22	Northside	Charleston, SC
11/23-29	WCalvary	Smithfield, NC
12/6-13	LakevewB	Roanoke Rpds, NC
12/27	First FWB	Mt.Vernon, IL
Total Offerings:		
$12,520		

1971

1/4-10	Emanuel	Jack'ville, NC
1/11-17	Unity	Smithfield, NC
1/18-24	Cheryvale	Sumter, SC
1/25-31	First FWB	Charleston, SC
2/7-12	FaithFWB	Rockingham, NC
2/14-24	First FWB	Kirksville, MO
3/1-7	Liberty	Durham, NC
3/8 -14	Comunity	Weldon, NC
3/21-28	First FWB	Winfield, AL
3/294/4	First FWB	Roxboro, NC
4/ 5-11	St.Delight	Louisburg, NC
4/12-18	CMA	Lima, OH
4/23-25	Belvoir	Greenville, NC
4/26-5/2	First FWB	Monett, MO
5/3- 9	Victory F	Kan.City, MO
5/10-16	Bethel	Kinston, NC
5/17- 23	Okef'noke	Waycross, GA
5/24- 30	Bethany	Hazlhurst, GA
5/31-6/6	Joy FWB	Tarboro, NC
6/7-13	First FWB	Amory, MS
6/14-20	Hilltop	Fuquay, NC
6/27-7/4	Harmony	WFrankfort, IL
7/4-11	FWB	Bakerville, IL
7/12-15	NAFWB	Nashville, TN
	Asst. Mod	
7/18-25	SulphurSp	Samantha, AL
7/26-8/1	First FWB	Jonesboro, AR
8/2- 8	Spr'gfield	Vernon, AL
8/9-15	Eastside F	Tuscaloosa, AL
8/16-22	Shiloh	Atmore, AL
8/30-9/5	TippettCh	Clayton, NC
9/6-12	SylvanPk.	Nashville, TN
9/8-9	FWBBC	Nashville, TN
9/13-19	Prospect F	Erwin, NC
9/20-26	First FWB	Rocky Mt., NC
27-10/3	BibleFWB	Florence, SC
10/4-10	CalvaryB.	Goldsb'roNC
23-11/7	PrimBapts	Bristol, NB, Can.
11/10-14	Assembly	Edina, MO

11/15-21	Marnatha	Greenville, NC
11/22-28	Immanuel	Winterville, NC
29-12/5	First FWB	Kingstree, SC
12/8-17	FWB	Cove City, NC
12/27-31	Salem	Mt.Vernon, IL
Total Offerings:		
$11,268		

1972

1/3- 9	W. Duplin	Warsaw, NC
1/10-16	First FWB	Selma, AL
117-23	First FWB	Decatur, GA
1/24 -30	W.Calvary	Smithfield, NC
2/2-6	Trinity	Greenville, NC
2/7-13	ColonalHt	Clinton, NC
2/14-20	FWB	Lyons, GA
2/21-17	Ebenezer	Glennville, GA
3/5	Grace	Greenville, NC
3/6 -12	CofersChp	Nashville, TN
3/20-26	First FWB	Grifton, NC
3/27-4/2	BayBranch	Timonsvill, SC
4/3- 9	Peace FW	Wilson, NC
4/10-16	Fellowship	Durham, NC
4/17- 23	Capitol	LittleRock, AR
4/24- 30	Grace	Rocky Mt., NC
5/1- 7	First FWB	Owasso, OK
5/8 -14	First FWB	Claremor, OK
5/15-21	Faith FWB	Goldsboro, NC
5/22-28	Bethel FW	Festus, MO
6/11-18	Bible	NewCastle, IN
6/21-30	Oakwood	Woodl'wn, TN
7/2 -7	Y'th Camp	PineyWds, TX
7/ 8 -14	NAFWB	Ft. Worth, TX
	Ass'tMod.	
7/16-23	Heads	Cedar Hill, TN
7/24- 30	First FWB	Elizabethton, TN
31-8/ 6	Olivet	Guthrie, KY
8/7-13	Fellowship	Richton, MS
8/14-21	New Zion	Headland, AL
28-9/3	Shady Gr.	Clarksville, TN
9/10-17	Bethel	Kinston, NC
25-10/1	Randall	Memphis, TN
10/2 -8	CollegeLks	Fayetteville, NC
10/9-13	First FWB	Wilson, NC
10/15	Bethel	Newport News, VA
1016- 22	FWB	Mullins, SC
10/23-29	Lebanon	Effingham, SC
30-11/5	HorseBh	Turbeville, SC
11/6- 12	Bethel	Roxana, IL
12/13-19	First FWB	Decatur, IL
12/20-26	Belvoir	Greenville, NC
27-12/3	FWB	Cedar Springs, GA
12/4 -10	Immanuel	Winterville, NC
12/13-17	Faith FWB	Cary, NC
12/26-31	First FWB	Waltonville, IL
Total Offerings:		
$14,153		

1973

1/15- 21	Victory	Goldsboro, NC
1/22- 28	Cheryvale	Sumter, SC
1/29-2/4	Unity	Smithfield, NC

2/5-11	W'tconett	Jacksonville, FL
2/14-18	Emanuel	Jacksonville, NC
2/19- 25	First FWB	Roxboro, NC
2/26-3/4	Felowship	Micro, NC
3/ 5-11	Friendship	Wilmington, NC
3/12-18	Comunity	Weldon, NC
3/25-4/1	FairmontP	Norfolk, VA
4/ 4- 8	Hope	Scotland Neck, NC
4/ 9-15	First FWB	Newport News, VA
4/16- 22	CoopCpgn	Pikeville, NC
4/23- 29	First FWB	Columbia, NC
4/30-5/6	Liberty	Durham, NC
5/11- 13	Trinity	Greenville, NC
5/14- 20	Cavanaug	FortSmith, AR
5/27	Grace	Greenville, NC
5/28 -6/3	Liberty	Marion, NC
6/7-9	Bethel	Kinston, NC
6/11-17	First FWB	Carthage, TX
6/18-24	First FWB	Houston, TX
6/25-7/1	First FWB	Tuscon, AZ
7/6-12	NAFWB	Macon, GA
	Ass'tMod.	
7/15- 20	Bethel	Marvel, AL
7/22- 29	Bellview	Colquitt GA
7/30-8/5	Appleton	Castlberry, AL
8/6-12	First FWB	Dothan, AL
8/13-19	First FWB	Albany, GA
8/24-26	Lakeview	High Point, NC
9/2	Grace	Greenville, NC
9/3 -9	Mt. Olive	Guin, AL
9/10-16	RuthsCh.	NewBern, NC
9/17-23	First FWB	Jacksonville, NC
9/ 27- 30	ColonalHg	Clinton, NC
10/1 -7	FaithFWB	Rockingham, NC
10/8- 14	St. Delight	Louisburg, NC
10/15-21	Eastside	Elizabetht, TN
10/22-28	Bethel	Newport News, VA
29-11/4	WhiteOak	Bailey, NC
11/5- 11	FaithCMA	NewBrem, OH
11/17-18	Belvoir	Belvoir, NC
11/19-25	First FWB	Dover, NC
26-12/3	FWB	Mullins, SC
12/5 -9	Felowship	Dunn, NC
12/12-16	First FWB	Dublin, GA
12/26-30	First FWB	Waltonville, IL
Total Offerings:		
$13,492		

1974

1/6	Grace	Greenville, NC
1/7-13	W. Duplin	Warsaw, NC
1/14-20	Okef'noke	Waycross, GA
1/21-27	First FWB	Sanford, NC
1/28-2/3	Bible FWB	Florence, SC
2/4-10	First FWB	RockyMt, NC
2/11-17	First FWB	Swananoa, NC
2/21-23	SandyCrk	Louisburg, NC
2/25-3/3	Hilltop	TravRest, SC
3/4-10	Mt.Moria	Ethelsville, AL
3/11-17	ForestGr.	Knoxville, TN
3/24	Grace	Greenville, NC
3/25-31	OakviewB	Rocky Mount, NC

4/1-7	Hilltop	Fuquay, NC
4/8-14	First FWB	Amory, MS
4/15-21	Trinity	LaGrange, NC
4/22-28	First FWB	Lebanon, MO
4/29-5/5	Evangel	Joplin, MO
5/13-19	Victory	Kan.City, MO
5/20-26	Northside	Charleston, IL
5/27-6/2	Faith FWB	Kinston, NC
6/9	Grace	Greenville, NC
6/10-16	ThomasM	Hunt'ton, WV
6/26-30	Felowship	Durham, NC
7/1-7	First FWB	Greensboro, NC
7/12-18	NAFWB	Wichita, KS
7/21	Bethel	Kinston, NC
7/22-28	FWB	Richton, MS
7/29-8/4	Eastside	Tuscaloosa, AL
8/11	WebbsPra	Ewing, IL
8/12-18	Bethl'hem	Ashland City, TN
8/19-25	FWB	Decatur, GA
8/25-31	TippetsCh	Clayton, NC
9/1	Temple	Greenville, NC
9/2-8	Comunity	Ayden, NC
9/9-15	SatteCom	Nitro, WV
9/16-22	CalvyCMA	Lima, OH
9/23-27	BeulahCh	Wake Forest, NC
9/29	Temple	Greenville, NC
9/30-6	Grace	RockyMt, NC
10/7-13	SpenceRd	Okla. City, OK
10/14-20	CapitolHill	Okla.City, OK
10/23-27	Ogeechee	Miller, GA
10/28-3	Victory	Goldsboro, NC
11/4-10	FWB	Lyons, GA
11/11-17	FWB	CoveCity, NC
11/18-24	First FWB	Jesup, GA
12/4	Bethel	Kinston, NC
12/4-11	First FWB	Kingstree, SC
12/20-21	Bible Club	Burnsville, NC
Total Offerings:		
$13,362		

1975

1/2-5	FWB	Grimesland, NC
1/6-12	HowardGr	Cotonwood, AL
1/15-19	First FWB	Berkeley, MO
1/22-26	StoneyCrk	Goldsboro, NC
1/27-2/2	First FWB	Blakely, GA
2/5-9	BayBr'nch	Timonsvile, SC
2/10-16	First FWB	Florence, SC
2/17-23	Liv'gW'ter	Pikeville, NC
2/24-3/2	First FWB	Donelson, TN
3/3-9	Belvoir	Greenville, NC
3/10-16	Woodbine	Nashville, TN
3/17-23	Black Jack	Greenville, NC
3/24-30	First FWB	JohnsnCty, TN
4/2-13	Wesleyan	Perth, NB, Can
4/16-20	First FWB	Florence, SC
4/21-27	Fellowship	Durham, NC
4/28-5/4	Ebenezer	Glennville, GA
5/5 -11	Baptist	Mildred, NC
5/12- 18	Victory	Wnatche, WA
5/19- 24	DoverBpts	Dover, NC
5/28-6/1	Mission	Farmville, NC

6/2 -8	Mt.Calvry	Hookertn, NC
6/9-15	First FWB	Decatur, AL
6/16- 22	FWB	CedarSprg, GA
6/23- 29	Morrison	Kingsport, TN
7/6 -10	First FWB	Chipley, FL
7/13- 17	NAFWB	Dayton, OH
7/20 -27	CoopMtg.	JohnsonCt, TN
7/28-8/3	First FWB	Stanley, NC
8/4-10	Appleton	Castlberry, AL
8/11-17	New Zion	Headland, AL
8/18-24	Shiloh	Atmore, AL
8/25-31	TippettCh	Clayton, NC
9/1-7	Sydney	Belhaven, NC
9/8-14	First FWB	Savannah, GA
9/22-28	First FWB	Farmington, MO
9/29-5	Cavanaug	Ft. Smith, AR
10/6-12	First FWB	Chesterfield, IN
10/13-19	Tabernacl	Dover, NC
10/26-9	Carleton County	Bath, NB, Can
10/26-30	First FWB	Bristol, NB, Can
10/31-4	Centervile	Cent'ville, NB, Can
11/5-9	Hartland	Hartland, NB, Can
11/12-16	HamocSpr	Donldsnvl, GA
11/17-23	First FWB	WinterHvn, FL
11/24-28	JohnstnU	Smithfield, NC
12/3-7	Assembly	Edina, MO
12/8-14	FWB	Mullins, SC
Total Offerings:		
$19,584		

1976

1/1-4	PenderCh	Tarboro, NC
1/5-11	Friendship	Wilminggtn, NC
1/12-18	W. Duplin	Warsaw, NC
1/19-25	Cheryvale	Sumter, SC
1/26-2/1	Hope	Scotland Neck, NC
2/1-7	Unity	Smithfield, NC
2/9-15	First FWB	Rocky Mt, NC
2/16-22	First FWB	Beaufort, NC
2/23-29	HorsBrnch	Turbeville, SC
3/1-7	ShadyGr.	Durham, NC
3/8-14	Liberty	Durham, NC
3/15-21	First FWB	Conway, AR
3/22-28	PearceCh	Smithville, MS
3/29-4/4	Fairm'tPk	Norfolk, VA
4/12-18	Hilltop	Fuquay, NC
4/19-25	BlossMem	Arlington, VA
4/26-5/2	BibleChur	NewCastle, IN
5/3-9	Bethel	Roxana, IL
5/11-16	Emanuel	Jacksonville, NC
5/17-23	Lighthous	Siler City, NC
5/24-30	FaithFWB	Cary, NC
6/7	Temple	Greenville, NC
6/8-13	S.Highlan	MuscleShl, AL
6/20-26	CoopMtg	Baxley, GA, co
7/4-8	SulphurSp	Samantha, AL
7/10-11	Plean'tHill	Norman, OK
7/11-15	NAFWB	Tulsa, OK
7/15-16	Grace	Bixby, OK
7/19-25	Goodsprg	PleasantV, TN
7/26-8/1	Bethel	Marvel, AL

8/7-15	Pr. Baptist	Holmesville, NB
8/22-29	CoopCpgn	Florence, SC
9/5-10	First FWB	Springfiel, TN
9/12-17	ColegeLke	Fayetteville, NC
9/19-24	First FWB	Richmond, VA
26-10/1	First FWB	Thomastn, GA
10/3-8	First FWB	Columbia, SC
10/10-15	St. Delight	Louisbrg, NC
10/25-31	Mac'dona	SpringHope, NC
11/1-7	FaithCMA	NewBrmn, OH
11/8-14	First FWB	Swananoa, NC
11/24-28	FWB	Weldon, NC
29-12/5	Grace	Arnold, MO
12/8-12	FWB	Olive Br, IL
12/13-15	HamocSpr	Donaldsonville, GA
12/16-19	First FWB	Raleigh, NC
Total Offerings:		
$18,926		

1977

1/2-9	First FWB	Sikeston, MO
1/12-16	KendalAcr	Sanford, NC
1/17-23	E. Tupelo	Tupelo, MS
1/31-2/6	FWB	Athens, GA
2/7-13	First FWB	Swainsboro, GA
2/14-20	First FWB	Statesboro, GA
2/21-27	FWB	Lyons, GA
2/28-3/6	Liv'gWtrs	Pikeville, NC
3/9-13	Macedoni	Millport, AL
3/20-27	Bethany	Norfolk, VA
3/30-4/3	Hilltop	Traveler Rs, SC
4/4-10	First FWB	Inman, SC
4/11-17	First FWB	Greenville, SC
4/18-24	Cofers Ch	Nashville, TN
4/25-5/1	Colinswod	Portsmouth, VA
5/2-8	First FWB	Pamplico, SC
5/9-15	Liberty	Manning, SC
5/23-29	Eastside	Elizabethton, TN
6/8-12	Cherryval	Sumter, SC
6/15-19	SheratnPk	Greensboro, NC
6/20-26	Wildwood	Wilson, NC
6/29-7/3	FWB	Farmville, NC
7/16-21	NAFWB Elect mod	Detroit, MI
7/24-29	HowadsGr	Cotonwood, AL
7/31-8/5	Victory	Columbus, MS
8/7-12	Eastside F	Tuscaloosa, AL
8/18-21	PleasatUn	Fuquay, NC
8/24-28	FaithFWB	Darlington, SC
8/29-9/4	CedarGr.	Wiliamston, NC
9/5-11	BibleFWB	Florence, SC
9/11-18	CatawSpg	Fuquay, NC
9/13-18	WakeAca	Fuquay, NC
9/19-25	Twin City	Nitro, WV
26-10/2	PenderCh	Tarboro, NC
10/3-9	First FWB	Morehead City, NC
10/10-16	First FWB	Springfiel, OH
10/20-23	First FWB	Conroe, TX
10/24-30	Eastside	Houston, TX
31-11/6	First FWB	Houston, TX
11/7-13	Felowship	Bryan, TX
11/14-20	Bayshore	Baycliff, TX

29-12/4	First FWB	Jesup, GA
12/7-11	First FWB	Roxboro, NC
12/18	Hilltop	Fuquay, NC
12/25-28	First FWB	Waltonville, IL
Total Offerings: $14,879		

1978

1/6	Temple	Greenville, NC
1/9-15	BayBrnch	Timonsvile, SC
1/16-22	First FWB	Florence, SC
1/23-29	First FWB	Beaufort, NC
1/30-2/5	Trinity	LaGrange, NC
2/12-17	First FWB	Chesterfield, IN
2/19	FWB	Russelville, AR
2/20-26	Cavanaug	Ft. Smith, AR
2/27-3/1	First FWB	Guin, AL
3/6-12	First FWB	Ahoskie, NC
3/19-22	CardinalV	Jacksonville, NC
3/23-25	First FWB	Swansboro, NC
3/26-31	Grace	Greenville, NC
4/3-9	CedarCrek	Hartselle, AL
4/10-16	CanahChp	Erwin, TN
4/19-23	Felowship	Dunn, NC
4/30-5/5	Coop.Mtg	Sesser, IL
5/8-13	Tabernacl	Portsmouth, OH
5/15-21	W. Wayne	Wayne, MI
21-5/24	Trinity	Ypsilanti, MI
5/29-6/4	Felowship	Wilson, NC
6/5-11	SulphurSp	Samantha, AL
6/12-18	Peace	Spartanburg, SC
6/19-25	HamocSpr	Donalsonville, GA
6/28-7/1	Liv'gWatrs	Pikeville, NC
7/8-12	Appleton	Castlbery, AL
7/14-20	NAFWB	Kansas City, MO
7/23-28	First FWB	Flomaton, AL
7/30-8/4	Shiloh	Atmore, AL
8/6-11	New Zion	Headland, AL
8/13-18	Corinth	MidlandCy, AL
8/20-25	CoopMtg	Lake City, SC
8/28-9/3	TippettCh	Clayton, NC
9/5-10	PleasanAc	NewBern, NC
9/11-17	FaithBapt	Sumter, SC
9/17-22	First FWB	Stanley, NC
9/24-29	First FWB	Charleston, SC
10/1-6	First FWB	Cookeville, TN
10/8	Union	Wheelersburg, OH
10/9-15	CaseysCh	Goldsboro, NC
10/18-22	Mt. Olive	Plymouth, NC
10/30	Bethel	Kinston, NC
11/3-12	Wesleyan	Perth, NB, Can
11/14-19	Wesleyan	Halifax, NS, Can
11/21-26	Wesleyan	Dartm'th, NS
12/7-10	Lakeview	High Point, NC
12/17	Hilltop	Fuquay, NC
12/24	WebbsPr.	Ewing, IL
Total Offerings: $19,198		

1979

1/7-10	CollegLak	Fayetteville, NC
1/15-21	W. Duplin	Warsaw, NC
1/22-28	Liberty	Durham, NC
1/29-2/4	Tabernacl	Kinston, NC
2/5-11	First FWB	Rocky Mt, NC
2/12-18	ShadyGrv	Durham, NC
2/19-25	Cheryvale	Sumter, SC
2/26-3/4	HorseBra	Turbeville, NC
3/12-18	JefersnRd	Sumter, SC
3/26-4/1	First FWB	Conway, AR
4/2-8	Assembly	Edina, MO
4/9-15	Victory	Wenatchee, WA
4/16-22	First FWB	Berkeley, MO
4/29-5/2	First FWB	Swansboro, NC
5/3-6	Faith	Maysville, NC
5/7-13	Hilltop	Fuquay, NC
5/19	NCStateA	NC
5/20-27	First FWB	Jacksonville, NC
5/30-6/3	First FWB	Malden, MO
6/3-10	First FWB	Sikeston, MO
6/11-17	First FWB	Winter Haven, FL
6/27-7/1	Lighthous	Siler City, NC
7/11	FaithFWB	Goldsboro, NC
7/13-19	NAFWB	Charlotte, NC
7/22-27	PearceCh	Smithville, MS
7/29-8/3	First FWB	Swainsboro, GA
8/12-17	First FWB	Thomaston, GA
8/19-24	Midway	Moultrie, GA
8/26-31	Satilla	Hazelhurst, GA
9/10-16	Grace	Bixby, OK
9/17-23	FaithFWB	Milan, IL
9/24-30	FWB	Kistler, WV
10/1-7	UnionCha	Chocowinity, NC
10/8-14	S.Highlan	Muscle Shoals, AL
10/15-19	St. Delight	Louisburg, NC
10/21-28	CoopMtg	Greenville, NC
29-11/4	Faith FWB	Cary, NC
11/12-18	First FWB	Dayton, OH
25-12/2	Bethel	Kinston, NC
12/5-12	W.Calvary	Smithfield, NC
Total Offerings: $19,753		

1980

1/4	CollegeLk	Fayeteville, NC
1/21-27	First FWB	Beaufort, NC
1/28-2/3	Faith FWB	Goldsboro, NC
2/4-10	FWB	Mullins, SC
2/11-17	First FWB	Kingstree, SC
2/18-24	SprgGrove	Jesup, GA
2/27-3/2	Hilltop	Travelers Rest, SC
3/3-9	Macedoni	Millport, AL
3/9	CofersChp	Nashville, TN
3/10-13	FWBBC	Nashville, TN
3/16-23	Colinswod	Portsmouth, VA
3/31-4/6	First FWB	Benton, IL
4/7-13	First FWB	Greenville, SC
4/14-20	HearonCir	Spartanburg, SC
4/21-27	Sheratnpk	Greensboro, NC
4/28-5/4	Peace	Washington, NC
5/11-16	Woodale	Knoxville, TN
5/18-23	First FWB	Columbia, SC
5/26-6/1	Emanuel	Washington, NC
6/16-22	Sherwood	El Sobrante, CA
6/23-29	Capitol	Sacramento, CA
7/2-6	Northside	Stockton, CA
7/7-13	First FWB	Buena Pk, CA

7/14-17	VillageCha	Ceres, CA
7/18-24	NAFWB	Anaheim, CA
7/27-8/1	HowardGr	Cotonwood, AL
8/3-8	Liberty	Vernon, AL
8/10-15	First FWB	Jesus, GA
8/20-31	Heritage	Columbus, OH
9/1-7	OttersCrk	Fountain, NC
9/8-14	Bethel	Newport News, VA
9/15-21	First FWB	Inman, SC
9/22-28	PenderCh	Tarboro, NC
29-10/5	First FWB	Poteau, OK
10/6-12	First FWB	Pryor, OK
10/20-26	FWB	Chatanooga, TN
27-11/2	Trinity	LaGrange, NC
11/3-9	Central	Hunt'ton, WV
11/12-17	CoopMtg	Bristol, NB, Can
11/18-23	CoopMtg	Hartland, NB, Can
30-12/7	FWB	Stacy, NC
12/10-14	FloodsChp	Bailey, NC

Total Offerings: $22,632

1981

1/4	ColegeLak	Fayeteville, NC
1/12-18	OpenBible	Valdosta, GA
1/19-25	Friendship	Flomaton, AL
1/26-2/1	First FWB	Flomaton, AL
2/2-8	Tabernacl	Kinston, NC
2/16-22	FWB	Swainsboro, GA
2/23-3/1	Felowship	Florence, SC
3/2-8	Grace	Rocky Mt, NC
3/9-15	First FWB	Farmington, MO
3/16-22	First FWB	Russelville, AR
3/23-29	First FWB	Batesville, AR
4/5-10	Peace	Wilson, NC
4/12-17	FWB	Emporia, KS
4/19-24	FWB	Salina, KS
4/26-5/3	CoopMtg	Erwin, TN
5/11-17	FWB	Sciotodal, OH
5/18-24	Morrison	Kingsport, TN
5/25-31	W. Green	Mosheim, TN
6/1-7	FWB	Pamplico, SC
6/8-14	First FWB	Vernon, AL
6/15-21	First FWB	Bainbrdge, GA
6/22-28	First FWB	Athens, GA
7/12-16	Heritage	Columbus, OH
7/17-23	NAFWB	Louisville, KY
7/26-31	First FWB	Jasper, AL
7/2-7	SulphurSp	Samantha, AL
8/9-14	Corinth	MidlandCt, AL
8/16-21	FWB	Tallahasee, FL
8/31-9/6	TippettCh	Clayton, NC
9/7-13	Liberty	Durham, NC
9/14-20	RuthsCha	NewBern, NC
9/21-27	Shiloh	Atmore, AL
28-10/4	Felowship	Dunn, NC
10/5-11	FWB	Rocky Mt, NC
10/12-18	FaithBapt.	Sumter, SC
26-11/1	Lebanon F	Effingham, SC
11/2-8	Temple	Greenville, NC
11/9-15	CardinalVl	Jacksonville, NC
11/16-22	Felowship	Bryan, TX
29-12/2	Floyds	Nichols, SC

12/3-6	Immanuel	Durham, NC
12/11-13	Lakeview	High Point, NC

Total Offerings: $22,534

1982

1/10	CollegeLk	Fayetteville, NC
1/17	Felowship	Durham, NC
1/18-24	Faith FWB	Maysville, NC
1/25-31	Mission	Princeton, NC
2/1-7	Cheryvale	Sumter, SC
2/8-14	Midway	Moultrie, GA
2/15-21	First FWB	Albany, GA
2/28	Temple	Greenville, NC
3/1-7	Hilltop	Fuquay, NC
3/14-19	KendalAcr	Sanford, NC
3/22-28	Pleas'tV'ly	Warren, AR
3/29-4/4	First FWB	Conway, AR
4/5-11	Assembly	Edina, MO
4/12-18	First FWB	Tucson, AZ
4/25	Temple	Greenville, NC
4/26-5/2	OakGrove	Durham, NC
5/10-16	Calvary	Fenton, MO
5/17-23	Gr'ge Hall	Marion, IL
5/24-30	St. John	Goldsboro, NC
6/7-13	First FWB	Johnson City, TN
6/14-20	RockyPass	Marion, NC
6/21-27	Lifegate F	Belhaven, NC
7/16-22	NAFWB	Ft. Worth, TX
7/25-30	Shiloh	Gordo, AL
8/1-6	Liberty	Vernon, AL
8/15	Bethel	Kinston, NC
8/16-22	FWB	Great Bridge, VA
8/23-29	FWB	Swansboro, NC
9/8-12	Felowship	Durham, NC
9/13-17	Eastside	Dothan, AL
9/19	Temple	Greenville, NC
9/20-26	ForestGrv	Knoxville, TN
27-10/3	FWB	Kistler, WV
10/4-10	W Calvary	Smithfield, NC
10/11-17	First FWB	Russelville, AL
13,20,27	ChristnSc	Florence, AL
10/18-24	JonesChp	Florence, AL
10/25-31	SHighland	Muscle Shoals, AL
11/8-14	Faith FWB	Cary, NC
11/15-21	First FWB	Dayton, OH
29-12/5	First FWB	Red Bay, AL

Total Offerings: $20,868

1983

1/2	Immanuel	Durham, NC
1/3-9	FWB	Mt. Olive, NC
1/10-16	First FWB	Beaufort, NC
1/24-30	W. Duplin	Warsaw, NC
2/6	ColegeLke	Fayetevile, NC
2/7-9	Min'tConf	Dothan, AL
2/13-16	Victory	Goldsboro, NC
2/20	Trinity	LaGrange, NC
2/21-27	Wildwood	Wilson, NC
3/2-6	First FWB	Donelson, TN
3/7-13	BlueSprgs	Kansas City, MO
3/14-20	DeepCrk	Midville, GA
3/21-27	Unity	Greenville, NC

3/28-4/3	SprgGrove	Jesup, GA
4/4-10	Calvary F	Georgetown, SC
4/11-17	First FWB	Greenville, SC
4/18-24	SheratnPk	Grensboro, NC
4/25-5/1	Comunity	Weldon, NC
5/2-8	FWB	Limestone, TN
5/9-15	Philadlpha	Folkston, GA
5/16-22	Emanuel	Sharpsbg, NC
5/25	Temple	Greenville, NC
5/29	Temple	Greenville, NC
6/1-5	FWB	VA Beach, VA
6/6-12	PenderCh	Tarboro, NC
6/13-9	FWB	Chatanoga, TN
6/20-26	Central	Huntington, WV
6/27-7/3	BayBrnch	Timonsville, SC
7/10-13	First FWB	Springfield, OH
7/15-21	NAFWB	Columbus, OH
7/24-29	HowardGr	Cotonwod, AL
8/7-12	Macedoni	Millport, AL
8/14-19	SandyAcr	Columbia, NC
8/28-9/4	FWB	Baldwin Pk, CA
9/6-11	Harmony	Fresno, CA
9/12	FWB	Clovis, CA
9/14-18	VillageCh	Ceres, CA
9/20-25	Capitol	Sacramento, CA
9/25-27	Sherwood	El Sobrante, CA
28-10/2	First FWB	Concord, CA
10/9	Temple	Greenville, NC
10/16-19	Twin City	Nitro, WV
10/24-30	Cavanaug	Fort Smith, AR
31-11/6	First FWB	Poteau, OK
11/7-13	Grace	Broken Arrow, OK
11/14-20	W. Tulsa	Tulsa, OK
11/27-30	Grace	Rocky Mt, NC
12/1-4	WhiteOak	Bladenbor, NC
Total Offerings: $24,296		

1984

1/1	Fellowship	Durham, NC
1/8-11	HopeFWB	Scotland Neck, NC
1/12-15	Tabernacl	Kinston, NC
1/16-22	Victory	Andrews, SC
1/23-29	Laurel	Charlotte, NC
1/30-2/5	Peace	Spartanburg, SC
2/6-12	HorseBrnh	Turbeville, SC
2/20-26	First FWB	Winter Haven, FL
2/27-3/2	HopeFWB	Plymouth, NC
3/4-7	Corinth	Dunn, NC
3/12-18	MadisnAv	Tulsa, OK
3/19-25	Fellowship	Flat River, MO
3/25	First FWB	Flat River, MO
3/26-4/1	First FWB	Farm'ton, MO
4/2-8	First FWB	Mt Grove, MO
4/9-15	First FWB	Rusellville, AR
4/18	Temple F	Greenville, NC
4/22-27	Peace	Wilson, NC
4/29-5/4	St. Johns	Goldsboro, NC
5/6-11	First FWB	Tucson, AZ
5/14-20	Providenc	Hampton, VA
5/21-27	Fellowship	Greenville, NC
5/30-6/3	FWB	Columbia, SC
6/3-10	FWB	Pamplico, SC

6/11-17	First FWB	Vernon, AL
6/18-24	FWB	Bainbridge, GA
6/25-7/1	FaithFWB	Maysville, NC
7/13-19	NAFWB	Little Rock, AR
7/22-27	SulphurSp	Samantha, AL
7/29-8/3	First FWB	Jasper, AL
8/5-10	Shiloh	Atmore, AL
8/12-17	SoulsHrbr	Pensacola, FL
8/20-26	FWB	Garner, NC
8/27-9/2	Colnialhgt	Clinton, NC
9/7-11	Hyde Park	Norfolk, VA
9/17-23	ValeyForg	Elizabethton, TN
9/24-30	First FWB	Bristol, VA
10/1-7	FaithFWB	Washington, NC
10/8-12	Christian	Pink Hill, NC
10/15-21	FWB	Emporia, KS
31-11/4	Emmanuel	Washington, NC
11/10	Quarterly	TN
11/7-11	W.Greene	Mosheim, TN
11/12-18	Red Hill F	Marshall, NC
11/25-28	Antioch	New Bern, NC
29-12/2	FaithFWB	NewBern, NC
12/2	Temple	Greenville, NC
12/9-12	Floyds	Nichols, SC
12/30	Fellowship	Durham, NC
Total Offerings: $29,503		

1985

1/6-9	FWB	Swansboro, NC
1/10-13	Liv'gWatrs	Pikeville, NC
1/14-20	First FWB	Richmond, VA
1/20-27	Heritage	Wiliamsburg, VA
1/30-2/3	Corinth	Dunn, NC
2/4-10	Cherryval	Sumter, SC
2/10-13	Westside	Johnsonville, SC
2/17-20	Victory	Goldsboro, NC
2/21-24	First FWB	Ahoskie, NC
2/14-27	Unity	Greenville, NC
3/4-10	First FWB	Conway, AR
3/10-11	Pleas'tVly	Warren, AR
3/18-24	FWB	Grenbrier, AR
4/1-7	CoopMtg	Edina, MO
4/8-14	Trinity	Bridgeton, MO
4/15-21	First FWB	Pocahntas, AR
4/24-28	Calvary	Fenton, MO
5/5	Temple	Greenville, NC
5/6-12	RockyPass	Marion, NC
5/15	Temple	Greenville, NC
5/19-22	Antioch	Pikeville, NC
5/26-29	Comunity	Florence, SC
6/9-14	Appleton	Castlbery, AL
6/16-19	First FWB	Washington, NC
6/23	Five Pts.	Wash'ton, NC
6/24-30	Cedar Hill	Asheville, NC
7/7	Bethel	Kinston, NC
7/19-25	NAFWB preached	Nashville, TN
7/28-8/2	Shiloh	Gordo, AL
8/4-9	Liberty	Vernon, AL
8/11-16	CampMtg	Benton, IL
8/18-23	Bethel	Mablevale, AL
9/1-6	Emanuel F	Washington, NC

9/9-15	Cross	Iola, TX
9/16-22	First FWB	Johnson City, IL
9/23-29	First FWB	Ina, IL
30-10/6	Loudendal	Charleston, WV
10/7-13	Peace	Washington, NC
10/14-20	First FWB	Russelville, AL
10/21-27	GraysChp	Florence, AL
27-11/3	S.Highl'd	Muscle Shoals, AL
11/4-10	First FWB	Morehead, NC
11/11-17	W.Wayne	Wayne, MI
12/1	Bethel	Kinston, NC
12/8-11	Bethel	S. Roxana, IL
12/12-15	First FWB	Mt.Vernon, IL
12/22	Gethsmne	Wilson, NC

Total Offerings: $23,533

1986

1/5	Felowship	Durham, NC
1/6-12	Fellowship	Dunn, NC
1/17-19	HopeFWB	Scotland Neck, NC
2/2-5	First FWB	Tucson, AZ
2/10-16	Capitol	Sacramento, CA
2/17-23	Victory	Wenatchee, WA
3/2-7	First FWB	Bristol, VA
3/10-16	Deep Crk	Midville, GA
3/16-23	SprgGrove	Jesup, GA
3/31-4/6	First FWB	Farm'ton, MO
4/7-13	First FWB	Greenville, SC
4/20	Trinity	Greenville, NC
4/21-27	Calvary	Georgtown, SC
4/27-5/4	ChlstnHgt	Charleston, SC
5/5-11	SheratnPk	Grensboro, NC
5/12-18	Phildelpha	Folkston, GA
5/20-25	VandraSpr	Garner, NC
6/1	Bethel	Kinston, NC
6/3-8	Laurel	Charlotte, NC
6/9-15	FWB	Mullins, SC
6/16-22	FWB	Grifton, NC
7/6	Temple	Greenville, NC
7/18-24	NAFWB	Tulsa, OK
7/19-20	FWB	Enid, OK
7/27-8/1	HowardGr	Cotonwood, AL
8/3-8	FWB	Northport, AL
8/10-15	FWB	Belk, AL
7/17-21	Grace	Greenville, NC
8/24	Faith FWB	Kinston, NC
8/25-31	Red Hill	Marshall, NC
9/7-10	First FWB	Checotah, OK
9/11-14	Bethany	Tulsa, OK
9/15-19	Comunity	Weldon, NC
9/21-26	Faith FWB	Washington, NC
9/28	UnionGrv	Fremont, NC
29-10/5	Victory	Auburndle, FL
10/6-12	BayBranch	Timonsville, SC
10/15-19	Corinth	Dunn, NC
10/20-26	FWB	Limeston, TN
11/2-5	Cavanaug	Ft. Smith, AR
11/6-9	FWB	Drumright, OK
11/12-16	Heritage	Fredricksburg, VA
11/17-23	Unity FWB	Smithfield, NC
12/7-10	FWB	Bakerville, IL

Total Offerings: $25,417

1987

1/4	Felowship	Durham, NC
1/11-16	Haven	Raleigh, NC
1/25-30	CardinlVlg	Jacksonville, NC
2/8-13	DoubleBr	Unadilla, GA
2/16-22	St. Johns	Goldsboro, NC
3/1-6	Heritage	Phoenix, AZ
3/8-11	Victory	Goldsboro, NC
3/15-19	Black Jack	Greenville, NC
3/22-27	Oak Park	Pine Bluff, AR
3/29-4/3	First FWB	Mt.Grove, MO
4/5-10	Pleas'tHm	Mt.Grove, MO
4/12-17	FWB	Decatur, AL
4/19	GardnCty	Detroit, MI
4/26-5/1	Calvary	Conway, AR
5/3-6	First FWB	Russelville, AR
5/13-17	Faith FWB	Maysville, NC
5/24-27	Providenc	Hampton, VA
5/31-6/3	Faith FWB	Kinston, NC
6/7-12	Bethel	Brilliant, AL
6/14-19	First FWB	Thomaston, GA
6/21-24	FWB	Bainbrdge, GA
6/28	Bethel	Kinston, NC
6/29-7/5	WhiteOak	Bladnboro, NC
7/12	Temple	Greenville, NC
7/17-23	NAFWB 10th, last year mod	Birmingham, AL
7/23-25	FWB	Northport, AL
7/16-31	SulphurSp	Samantha, AL
8/2-7	First FWB	Russelville, AL
8/9	GraceDed.	Greenville, NC
8/12-16	Fairview	Marion, NC
7/17-23	RockyPass	Marion, NC
8/30-9/4	CanahChp	Erwin, TN
9/21-25	Goshen	Belmont, NC
27-10/2	First FWB	BatonRge, LA
10/4-7	First FWB	Flomaton, AL
10/8-11	Friendship	Flomaton, AL
10/25-30	Shiloh	Atmore, AL
11/1-4	UnionChp	Jacksonville, NC
11/8-15	FWB	Waipahu, HI
11/22-25	PenderCh	Tarboro, NC
12/6-9	W. Green	Mosheim, TN
12/10-13	Peace	Moristown, TN

Total Offerings: $24,491

1988

1/3	Fellowshp	Durham, NC
1/10-15	RuthsChp	NewBern, NC
1/17	Temple	Greenville, NC
1/24-29	First FWB	Savannah, GA
2/1-7	Cheryvale	Sumter, SC
2/15-21	United	Bryan, TX
2/22-28	PinePrairi	Huntsville, TX
3/7-13	PleasantV	Warren, AR
3/14-20	Felker	Valiant, OK
3/21-27	First FWB	Conway, AR
3/28-4/3	Trinity	Bridgeton, MO
4/10-15	Hyde Park	Norfolk, VA
4/17-20	Grace	Greenville, NC
4/21-23	Heritage	Fremont, NC

4/24-29	First FWB	Ahoskie, NC
5/1	Mt.Calvry	Hookertn, NC
5/2-8	FWB	Rol'gPraire, IN
5/9-14	FWB	W.Jeffersn, OH
5/15	FWB	Urbana, OH
5/22-25	Satilla	Hazelhrst, GA
5/29-6/1	First FWB	Tarboro, NC
6/5-8	Immanuel	Durham, NC
6/12-15	Hazel Dell	Sesser, IL
6/16-19	FWB	O'Fallon, MO
6/26-7/1	FWB	Swansboro, NC
7/10-13	FWB	Carthage, MO
7/17-21	NAFWB	Kansas City, MO
7/24-29	Cross	Iola, TX
7/31-8/4	GoodHpe	Henderson, TX
8/7-12	Liberty	Vernon, AL
8/21-26	ZephyrHill	Asheville, NC
8/28-9/2	Felowship	Micro, NC
9/4-7	WhiteOak	Bailey, NC
9/11-14	First FWB	Benton, IL
9/15-18	FWB	Waltonville, IL
9/19-25	E.Nashvile	Nashville, TN
9/28	Temple	Greenville, NC
10/2-9	Philadelp	Detroit, MI
10/9-16	First FWB	Pontiac, MI
10/23-27	Sherw'dF	New Bern, NC
30-11/4	CardinalVi	Jacksonville, NC
11/6-9	Liberty	Gainesville, GA
11/13-18	Meadwbr	Black Mt., NC
11/20-23	First FWB	Washington, NC
27-12/2	Heritage	Fredricksburg, VA
12/4-7	Hope	Scotland Neck, NC
Total Offerings: $24,096		

1989

1/8	Felowship	Durham, NC
8/9-15	Liberty	Marion, NC
1/23-29	JnWesley	Hartsville, SC
1/30-2/5	Tabernacl	Kinston, NC
2/19-24	First FWB	Henderson, TX
2/26-3/3	Eastside	Batesville, AR
3/5-10	Mt.Bethel	Rose Bud, AR
3/13-16	FWBBC	Nashville, TN
3/19-22	WhiteOak	Macon, GA
3/23-26	DeepCr'k	Midville, GA
4/2-7	First FWB	Johnson City, TN
4/9-14	Felowship	Kingsport, TN
4/16-21	First FWB	Bristol, VA
4/23-28	Heritage	Fremont, NC
4/30-5/5	Capitol	Sacramento, CA
5/7-12	VillageCh	Ceres, CA
5/14-17	Harmony	Fresno, CA
5/18-19	CASt.Mtg	CA
5/28-6/2	GoodNew	Richmond, VA
6/7-11	St. Johns	Goldsboro, NC
6/12-18	FWB	Mullins, SC
6/21-25	Comunity	Jacksonville, NC
7/9	Temple	Greenville, NC
7/16-20	NAFWB	Tampa, FL
7/21-23	SuwneeSp	Live Oak, FL
7/30-8/2	Friendship	Jacksonville, FL
8/3-6	PineyGrov	Bristol, GA

8/13-18	Eastside	Dothan, AL
8/21-27	Red Hill	Marshall, NC
9/5-10	Pleas'tAcr	NewBern, NC
9/11-17	SheratnPk	Grensboro, NC
9/17-22	First FWB	Greenville, SC
10/1-6	FWB	Bakerville, IL
10/8-13	FWB	Wheeling, WV
10/22-25	FWB	Garner, NC
11/5-10	CharleHgt	Charleston, SC
11/12-16	Peace	Morristwn, TN
11/19-21	Cavanaug	Ft. Smith, AR
11/24-29	HorseBrch	Turbeville, SC
12/3	First FWB	Richmond, VA
12/10	Temple	Greenville, NC
Total Offerings: $25,352		

1990

1/7	Felowship	Durham, NC
1/8-14	WhiteOak	Bladnboro, NC
1/21-24	BibleChch	Florence, SC
1/28-2/4	RuthsChp	NewBern, NC
2/5-11	Liberty	Orangeberg, SC
2/18-23	Bethel	Brilliant, AL
2/25-3/3	Friendship	Flomaton, AL
3/4	First FWB	Flomaton, AL
3/5-11	First FWB	Houston, TX
3/12-18	FWB	Tallahasee, FL
3/21	Temple	Greenville, NC
3/25-30	First FWB	Pamplico, SC
4/1-6	Liberty F	Ayden, NC
4/15-18	First FWB	Checotah, OK
4/22-27	PleastHm	MtGrove, MO
4/29-5/4	Beacon	Kan.City, MO
5/9-13	Providenc	Hampton, VA
5/20	FWB	Urbana, OH
5/20-23	FWB	Woodstock, OH
5/27-6/1	Felowship	Newland, NC
6/3	Temple	Greenville, NC
6/10-15	SulphurSp	Samantha.AL
6/17	Bethel	Cullman, AL
7/8	Heritage	Phoenix, AZ
7/12	Heritage	Phoenix, AZ
7/15-19	NAFWB	Phoenix, AZ
8/5-10	Fairview	Marion, NC
8/12-17	FaithFWB	Birmgham, AL
8/18-24	Shiloh	Atmore, AL
8/26-29	Felowship	Micro, NC
9/9-14	CoopMtg	Florence, SC
9/16-19	Prospect	Dunn, NC
9/23-28	AirportRd.	Allentown, PA
30-10/5	BayBrnch	Timonsvile, SC
10/7	Bethel	Kinston, NC
10/8-10	St. Delight	Ormondsville, NC
10/14-19	First FWB	Muntn Gr, MO
10/21-26	First FWB	Decatur, IL
28-11/2	Crossroad	Effingham, IL
11/4-9	Bethel	S. Roxana, IL
11/11-16	Liberty	Ayden, NC
11/18-21	First FWB	Richmond, VA
11/23-25	HorseBrch	Turbeville, SC
12/9	First FWB	Washington, NC
12/23	Temple	Greenville, NC

Total Offerings: $24,255

1991

1/6	Felowship	Durham, NC
1/21-25	FWB	Swansboro, NC
2/2-8	Memorial	Baxley, GA
2/11-17	Cheryvale	Sumter, SC
3/4-10	Felker	Valiant, OK
3/11-17	FWB	Carthage, MO
3/18-19	FWBConf	Frederktw, MO
3/25	Temple	Greenville, NC
3/31-4/3	Hyde Park	Norfolk, VA
4/7-12	Heritage	Fredriksburg, VA
4/14-19	Trinity	LaGrange, NC
4/21-24	First FWB	Beaufort, NC
4/29-5/5	FaithFWB	Darlington, SC
5/6-12	Liberty	Marion, NC
5/19	FaithFWB	Kinston, NC
5/20-26	Bethlehm	Ashland City, TN
5/27-6/2	First FWB	Conway, AR
6/9-14	FWB	Stacy, NC
6/23-26	Gethsmne	Wilson, NC
7/10-14	Victory	Wilmingtn, NC
7/21-25	NAFWB	Charleston, WV
8/4-9	Liberty	Vernon, AL
8/11-16	Comunity	Corinth, MS
8/18-23	GoodHpe	Hendersn, TX
8/25-28	First FWB	Morehead, NC
9/1-5	FWB	Knightdale, NC
9/8-11	FWB	Garner, NC
9/15-18	W'stconet	Jacksonville, FL
9/19-22	Immanuel	Jacksonville, FL
10/6-13	Jn Wesley	Hartsville, SC
10/14-18	FaithFWB	Kinston, NC
10/20-23	ShadyGrv	Durham, NC
30-11/3	FWB	Bristol, NB, Can
11/4-10	Lansdown	Bath, NB, Can
11/18-24	Liberty	Ayden, NC
11/29	Gethsemn	Wilson, NC
12/1-6	Sydney	Belhaven, NC
12/8-11	FaithFWB	Darlington, SC
12/22	Temple	Greenville, NC
12/29	Temple	Greenville, NC

Total Offerings: $20,961

1992

1/5	Felowship	Durham, NC
1/6 -12	WhiteOak	Bladnboro, NC
1/19-22	Emanuel	Jacksonville, FL
1/26-31	W. Duplin	Warsaw, NC
2/1-6	Tabernacl	Kinston, NC
2/9-14	Liberty	Orangeburg, SC
2/23	CardnalVg	Jacksonville, NC
2/24-3/1	Felowship	Manning, SC
3/11-12	FWBBC	Nashville, TN
3/15-20	Pleas'tAcr	NewBern, NC
3/22-27	First FWB	Greenville, SC
4/6 -12	PineyGrov	Bristol, GA
4/19-24	Ashland	Hayward, CA
4/26-29	Capitol	Sacramento, CA
5/3 -6	Harmony	Fresno, CA
5/9	CCC,grad	Fresno, CA

5/10-15	FWB	Clovis, CA
5/17-20	FWB	Stockton, CA
5/24-29	Heritage	Fremont, NC
5/29	Immanuel	Durham, NC
5/31-6/3	OakGrove	Durham, NC
6/8 -12	Bethel	Brilliant, AL
6/14-19	SulphurSp	Samantha, AL
6/21-26	First FWB	Tuscloosa, AL
6/28	Riverdale	Atlanta, GA
7/12-15	FWB	DeGraff, OH
7/19-23	NAFWB	Indianapolis, IN
8/2- 7	CenterPnt	Birmingham, AL
8/16-21	First FWB	Pontiac, MI
8/23-28	Mt.Calvry	Marion, NC
8/30-9/2	Southside	Hickory, NC
9/6	Temple	Greenville, NC
9/8 -13	UnitedBpt	Nitro, WV
9/14-20	SheratnPk	Greensboro, NC
27-10/2	Northside	Charleston, IL
10/4- 9	FWB	Bakerville, IL
10/11-12	First FWB	Elizabethton, TN
10/18-21	FaithFWB	Kinston, NC
10/25-30	Beacon	Kansas City, MO
11/1- 6	First FWB	O'Fallon, MO
11/8-13	Parkway	Sedalia, MO
11/15-20	OakGrove	Oakland, IL
11/24	Thanksgv	Greenville, NC
12/27	CedarChp	Greenville, NC

Total Offerings: $26,092

1993

1/3	Felowship	Durham, NC
1/17-20	Emanuel	Jacksonville, NC
1/24-31	RuthsChp	NewBern, NC
2/7-12	First FWB	Flomaton, AL
2/21-24	Hope	Scotland Neck, NC
2/28-3/5	FWB	Pamplico, SC
3/7-12	First FWB	Glennville, GA
3/14-19	WhiteOak	Bailey, NC
3/28-4/2	Bethel	Rose Bud, AR
4/4-9	FWB	Fordland, MO
4/11-13	First FWB	Checotah, OK
4/14-16	Grace	BroknArw, OK
4/18	Cavanaug	Ft. Smith, AR
4/26-5/2	ColonalHg	Clinton, NC
5/3-9	Liberty	Marion, NC
5/24-30	Liberty	Manning, SC
6/6-9	Memorial	Baxley, GA
6/13	Emanuel	Washington, NC
6/21-27	Crossroad	Wentzville, MO
7/18-22	NAFWB	Louisville, KY
8/1	CedarChp	Greenville, NC
8/2-8	Harmony	LakeButler, FL
8/9-15	GoodHpe	Hendersn, TX
8/22-27	First FWB	Stanley, NC
9/5	Marantha	Greenville, NC
9/12-17	Bethel	S. Roxana, IL
9/19-24	First FWB	Decatur, IL
26-10/1	First FWB	Farmington, MO
10/3-6	CoopMtg	Walnut Ridge, AR
10/10-13	Providenc	Hampton, VA
10/17-22	Red Hill	Marshall, NC

10/24-29	Blue Point	Cisne, IL
31-11/3	Crossroad	Effingham, IL
11/7-12	BayBrnch	Timonsvile, SC
11/14-17	FaithFWB	Kinston, NC
12/12	Peace	Washington, NC
12/19	Emanuel	Washington, NC
Total Offerings: $21,826		

1994

1/2	Felowship	Durham, NC
1/3-9	WhiteOak	Bladenboro, NC
1/16-21	W. Duplin	Warsaw, NC
1/23	CedarChp	Greenville, NC
1/26	CedarChp	Greenville, NC
1/30	Immanuel	Durham, NC
1/31-2/6	Cheryvale	Sumter, SC
2/14-20	JnWesley	Hartsville, SC
2/27-3/2	FWB	Ontario, CA
3/3-6	FWB	Baldwin Pk, CA
3/7-13	FWB	Chula Vista, CA
3/29-4/1	Ephesus	Chocowinity, NC
4/3-6	Hope	Scotland Neck, NC
4/10-15	Heritage	Fredricksburg, VA
4/24-25	Friendship	Myrtle Beach, SC
4/27-5/1	Faith FWB	Darlington, SC
5/2-8	FWB	Madison, AL
5/13-15	First FWB	Columbia, SC
5/16-22	Col'nalHgt	Clinton, NC
5/23-27	FWB	Carthage, MO
5/29	St. Johns	Goldsboro, NC
6/5-10	Bethel	Brilliant, AL
6/12-17	SulphurSp	Samantha, AL
6/19-24	First FWB	Tuscaloosa, AL
6/26	Liberty	Gainesvile, GA
7/3	Trinity	Greenville, NC
7/17-21	NAFWB	LittleRock, AR
7/31-8/5	Shiloh	Atmore, AL
8/7-12	CenterPnt	Birmingham, AL
8/14	Trinity	Greenville, NC
8/21-26	First FWB	Pontiac, MI
8/28-31	GardnCty	Detroit, MI
9/11-16	First FWB	Elizabethton, TN
9/18-21	FWB	DeGraff, OH
9/25-30	ArnoldVw	Creal Springs, IL
10/2-7	First FWB	Florence, AL
10/9-12	CedarChp	Greenville, NC
10/16-21	Parkway	Sedalia, MO
10/23-28	First FWB	McAllister, OK
11/6-11	Lebanon	Effingham, SC
11/13-20	S'ernMth	Aynor, SC
11/21-25	St. Delight	New Bern, NC
11/27-2	Mission	Dunbar, WV
12/4	Shnandoa	Rocky Mt, NC
Total Offerings: $25,725		

1995

1/1	Bethel	Kinston, NC
1/1	Peace	Washington, NC
1/8	Felowship	Durham, NC
1/15	Immanuel	Durham, NC
1/22-25	Southside	Darlington, SC
1/29-2/3	Appleton	Castlberry, AL

2/5-10	Friendship	Flomaton, AL
2/12-15	Chiquapin	Trenton, NC
2/16-19	ChristianC	Comfort, NC
2/19-24	Tabernacl	Kinston, NC
2/26	Heritage	Bethel, NC
2/27-3/5	FWB	Mullins, SC
3/6-12	FaithBapt.	Sumter, SC
3/19-22	Peace	Granite City, IL
3/26-29	Shnandoa	Rocky Mt, NC
4/2-5	Grace	Concord, CA
4/9-12	Capitol	Sacramento, CA
4/16-23	FWB	Fairfield, CA
4/23	FWB	Hayward, CA
4/30-5/5	First FWB	Conway, AR
5/8-14	Liberty	Marion, NC
5/15-21	Liberty	Manning, SC
5/28-31	Hamlet	Rockingham, NC
6/4-7	Memorial	Baxley, GA
6/11	FWB	Belvoir, NC
6/23-7/2	FWB	Hartland, NB, Can
7/9-12	BibleFWB	Darlington, SC
7/16-20	NAFWB	Charlotte, NC
7/30-8/6	Red Hill	Marshall, NC
8/13-18	FWB	Madison, AL
8/20-25	Mt.Plesnt	Montevalo, AL
9/17-22	SheratnPk	Grensboro, NC
9/24-28	UnionGrv	Fremont, NC
10/1-6	FWB	Bakerville, IL
10/25-27	SheratnPk	Greensboro, NC
29-11/1	FWB	Reidsville, NC
11/5-19	FWB	Holmesville, NB
11/26-1	Beacon	Farmville, NC
Total Offerings: $27,469		

1996

1/8-14	WhiteOak	Bladnboro, NC
1/15-17	RuthsChp	New Bern, NC
2/18-21	CardnalVil	Jacksonville, NC
3/3-6	FWB	Carthage, MO
3/7-10	NT'ntFWB	Neosho, MO
3/17-20	Crossroad	Pontiac, MI
3/21	Trinity	Greenville, NC
3/24	Trinity	Greenville, NC
3/25-29	UnionChp	Jacksonville, NC
3/1-3	ChrtianCh	Pink Hill, NC
4/7-10	Providenc	Hampton, VA
4/21-25	PeaceChp	Washington, NC
4/28-5/1	Chnquapn	Trenton, NC
5/2-3	Christian	Comfort, NC
5/5-10	First FWB	Greenville, SC
5/13-19	Philadelp	Folkston, GA
5/16	Methodist	Leesville, SC
6/2-7	Bethel	Brilliant, AL
6/9-14	SulphurSp	Samantha, AL
6/14-18	RockSprgs	Clarksville, TN
7/7-12	FWB	Hendersonville, TN
7/21-25	NAFWB	Ft. Worth, TX
8/4-9	CenterPnt	Birmingham, AL
8/18-23	First FWB	Fayette, AL
9/8-13	FWB	Checotah, OK
9/14-19	First FWB	Decatur, IL
9/22-26	FWB	Fairfield, CA

29-10/2	Harmony	Fresno, CA
10/3-6	FWB	Clovis, CA
10/13-18	BayBrnch	Timonsville, SC
10/20-25	PineyGrve	Albertson, NC
10/27-30	FWB	DeGraff, OH
11/10-15	Hamlet	Rockingham, NC
11/17-22	First FWB	Florence, SC
12/1	Shnandoa	Rocky Mt, NC
12/8-13	JnWesley	Hartsville, SC
12/12	Emanuel	Hartsville, SC
12/31	FWB	Grimesland, NC

Total Offerings: $24,768

1997

1/5	Felowship	Durham, NC
1/12	Emanuel	Hartsville, SC
1/15	Mission	Zebulon, NC
1/19-23	New Hope	Jacksonville, NC
1/27-2/2	Cheryvale	Sumter, SC
2/3 -9	FaithBapt	Sumter, SC
2/23	Heritage	Phoenix, AZ
3/2 -7	Shnandoa	Rocky Mt, NC
3/9-12	Hope	Scotland Neck, NC
3/16-20	FWB	Fairfield, Ca
3/23-26	Capitol	Sacrmento, CA
3/27-30	Grace	Concord, NC
4/6-9	Eastside	Dothan, AL
4/13-18	Heritage	Fredricksburg, VA
4/20-24	First FWB	Winterville, NC
4/27-30	Chnquapn	Trenton, NC
5/1 -2	ChristianC	Comfort, NC
5/4 -7	First FWB	Urbana, OH
5/11-16	N Home	Appleton, AL
5/18-23	FWB	Grimesland, NC
5/25-29	Methodist	Hahira, GA
6/8 -11	Memorial	Baxley, GA
6/15-20	Red Hill	Marshall, NC
7/20-24	NAFWB	Cincinnati, OH
8/10-14	FWB	Madison, AL
8/17-22	MtPlesant	Montevalo, AL
8/24-28	Bethel	MontevaloAL
9/14-17	Cedar Hill	Asheville, NC
9/21-25	Sydney	Belhaven, NC
28-10/3	First FWB	Jacksonville, NC
10/ 5-8	UnionChp	Jacksonville, NC
10/10-17	CardinalVi	Jacksonville, NC
10/19-24	FWB	Fordland, MO
10/26	Bethel	Kinston, NC
11/2 -5	Grace	Broken Arrow, OK
11/9-16	FWB	Ozark, AR
12/14	Chnquapn	Trenton, NC

Total Offerings: $27,062

1998

1/4	Felowship	Durham, NC
1/5-11	WhiteOak	Bladnboro, NC
1/18-23	Ruth'sChp	NewBern, NC
2/1	FaithFWB	Bridgeton, NC
2/22	CedarChp	Greenville, NC
3/1-4	Friendship	Pink Hill, NC
3/8-13	FWB	Nason, IL
3/22-27	Zion Hill	Waycross, GA

3/29-4/3	SpringGrv	Jesup, GA
4/5-8	Hamlet	Rockingham, NC
4/6-10	First FWB	Richmond, VA
4/12-15	First FWB	Greenville, SC
4/19-22	Providenc	Hampton, VA
5/24-29	Methodist	Hahira, GA
6/7-11	FWB	Verona, NC
6/14-19	SulphurSp	Samantha, AL
6/21-24	First FWB	Jesup, GA
7/12	FWB	Cramerton, NC
7/15	CedarChp	Greenville, NC
7/19	Mt.Calvry	Hookertn, NC
7/26-8/2	Red Hill	Marshall, NC
8/16-19	FWB	Conway, AR
8/23-28	Calvary	Georgtwn, SC
9/13-16	HarperRd.	Joelton, TN
9/14-16	School	Pleasant View, TN
9/20-25	SheratnPk	Greensboro, NC
9/27-30	FWB	DeGraff, OH
10/4	Emanuel	LaGrange, NC
10/11-16	BayBrnch	Timonsville, SC
10/18-23	Hope	Plymouth, NC
11/2-8	FWB	Holmsvill, NB, Can
11/9-15	FWB	Bristol, NB, Can
11/29	CedarChp	Greenville, NC
12/6-10	CedarChp	Greenville, NC
12/13	First FWB	Beaufort, NC
12/27	CedarChp	Greenville, NC

Total Offerings: $23,331

1999

1/3	Immanuel	Durham, NC
1/24-27	Bethany	Timonsville, SC
1/31	First FWB	Beaufort, NC
3/7-10	FWB	Carthage, MO
3/11-14	NewTesta	Neosho, MO
3/21-24	Charity	Zebulon, NC
3/28-31	SpringGrv	Jesup, GA
4/4-9	FWB	Grimesland, NC
4/18-23	FWB	Bakerville, IL
4/25-28	First FWB	JohnsnCity IL
5/2-5	Chnquapn	Trenton, NC
5/16-19	Crossroad	Wake Forest, NC
5/22	First FWB	Beaufort, NC
6/13-18	First FWB	Inman, SC
7/18-22	NAFWB	Atlanta, GA
7/27-30	Memorial	Baxley, GA
8/1-6	Mt.Pleast	Montvalo, AL
8/8-12	FWB	Madison, AL
8/15-18	SouthPark	Huntsville, AL
8/29	NewBegin	Wilson, NC
9/26-29	Hamlet F	Rockingham, NC
10/3-8	FWB	Pamplico, SC
10/24-27	FWB	DeGraff, OH
11/7-10	Liberty	Gainesville, GA
11/14-17	Mt. Tabor	Creswell, NC
11/21	Shenando	RockyMt.,NC
11/28-1	AllenChpl	Batesville,AR
12/2-5	BallewsCh	Grubbs, AR
12/26	Grace	Greenville, NC

Total Offerings: $20,949

2000

1/3-9	WhiteOak	BladnbroNC
2/6-9	Southside	DarlingtnSC
2/20-25	Calvary	HollywodFL
3/4-5	CofersCp	NashvilleTN
3/12-15	FWB	Fairfield, CA
3/19-23	Capitol	Sacramento, CA
3/26	Mt.Calvay	Hookerton, NC
3/27-4/2	Riverside	Harrells, NC
4/5-9	First FWB	GreenvillSC
4/13-28	Heritage	Fredricksburg, VA
5/7-12	First FWB	Monett,MO
5/14-19	Temple	Darlingtn,SC
5/21-24	HopeFW	Scotl'dNkNC
5/28-6/2	Crossroad	WakeFrstNC
6/12-18	SulphurSp	SamanthaAl
7/16-21	Mt. Tabor	Creswell,NC
7/22	ArnonBap	Elm City, NC
7/23	CardinalV	Jacksonville, NC
7/30-8/6	Red Hill	Marshall,NC
8/13	Hyde Park	Norfolk, VA
8/20	CardinalV	Jacksonville, NC
9/10-15	FaithBapt	Sumter, SC
9/17-20	ElwoodLn	Kanapolis,NC
9/24-25	Chnquapn	Trenton, NC
10/2-6	Mt.Calvry	WhitevilleNC
10/8-11	BlackRivr	Andrews, SC
10/15-18	FWB	DeGraff, OH
19-11/1	Lebanon	Effingham, SC
11/5-8	First FWB	Tarboro, NC
11/12-15	Hyde Park	Norfolk, VA
29 12/3	Ballews	Grubbs, AR
12/31	Macripine	Maclesf'ldNC
12/31	FWB	Grimesl'd,NC

Total Offerings: $26,526

2001

1/14-19	RuthsChp	New Bern, NC
1/28	FWB	Grimesl'dNC
2/5-11	Cheryvale	Sumter, SC
3/18	Providenc	Hampton,VA
3/26-4/1	Riverside	Harrells, NC
4/8-12	Emanuel	LaGrange,NC
4/22	Trinity	Greenville, NC
5/13	Chnquapn	Trenton, NC
5/20-23	FWB	Colquitt, GA
5/24-27	NewSalm	Colquitt, GA
6/3	Temple	Greenville, NC
7/15	Trinity	Greenville, NC
7/29-8/3	LtleBrnCk	Boonville,MS
8/5	KendallAc	Sanford, NC
8/15	Chnquapn	Trenton, NC
9/23-26	First FWB	Benton, IL
30-10/3	FWB	DeGraff, OH
10/7-10	Mt.Calvry	Hookert'nNC
10/14-19	Jn Wesley	Hartsville, SC
10/28-1	Red Hill	Marshall, NC
11/11-16	SheratnPk	Greensb'oNC
11/18	Shnandoa	Rocky Mt, NC

Total Offerings: $14,556

2002

12/1-1/6	Comunity	Weldon, NC
1/7-13	WhiteOak	Bladenboro, NC
2/3-5	FaithWesl	Myrtle Beach, SC
3/10-13	FWB	Carthage, MO
3/14-17	NewTesta	Neosho, MO
3/31-4/5	Riverside	Harrells, NC
4/14-17	FWB	Hendersonville, TN
4/28-5/2	BritishChp	Ayden, NC
5/6	CedarChp	Greenville, NC
5/6-12	Comunity	Weldon, NC
5/13-17	FWB	Verona, NC
6/2	Trinity	Greenville, NC
6/23	Maranath	Greenville, NC
6/30	KendallAc	Sanford, NC
7/21-25	NAFWB	Memphis, TN
8/2-4	BayBrnch	Timonsville, SC
8/11-14	Mt.Bethel	Weverville, NC
8/18	Red Hill	Marshall, NC
8/25-28	FWB	DeGraff, OH
9/8-11	TurnersCh	Butler, GA
9/15	W. Duplin	Warsaw, NC
9/18	Trinity	Greenville, NC
9/22-15	Southside	Darlington, SC
10/13-17	Wesleyan	Sanford, NC
10/20-23	Lighthous	Belvoir, NC
10/27	Trinity	Greenville, NC
11/3-8	Lebanon	Effingham, SC
11/10	Heritage	Bethel, NC
12/8	Heritage	Bethel, NC

Total Offerings: $13,905

2003

1/ 19	DanielsCh	Wilson, NC
2/ 9-12	SpringGrv	Jesup, GA
2/23- 26	Sherwood	El Sobrante, CA
2/27	FWB	Fairfield, CA
3/2- 5	Capitol	Sacramento, CA
3/10-13	CfFWBBC	Nashville, TN
3/16-19	First FWB	Tarboro, NC
3/ 23-26	FaithFWB	Darlington, SC
3/30-4/3	Riverside	Harrells, NC
4/6-10	Heritage	Fredricksburg, VA
4/13-18	First FWB	Tuckerman, AR
4/20-24	Red Hill	Marshall, NC
5/18-21	Immanuel	Durham, NC
5/25	Chnquapn	Trenton, NC
5/30-6/1	First FWB	Columbia, SC
7/16	Trinity	Greenville, NC
7/20-24	NAFWB	Tampa, FL
8/3- 6	First FWB	Madison, AL
8/24	Chnquapn	Trenton, NC
8/24-27	FWB	DeGraff, OH
8/31	CedarChp	Greenville, NC
9/14-19	CampMtg	Benton, IL
9/28	Mranatha	Greenville, NC
10/5-10	Jn Wesley	Hartsville, SC
11/2- 7	FWB	Holmesville, NB, Can
11/9-12	FWB	Plaster Rk, NB, Can
11/13-16	FWB	Up Brightn, NB, Can
11/23	Heritage	Bethel, NC

12/28	First FWB	Beaufort, NC

Total Offerings: $20,232

2004

1/12-18	Cheryvale	Sumter, SC
2/ 8	SheratnPk	Greensboro, NC
2/22-27	Ch.of God	Manteca, CA
2/29-3/3	Capitol	Sacramento, CA
3/21-26	Coop Mtg	Butler, GA
3/28-4/2	Riverside	Harrells, NC
4/4-7	Prospect	JohnsnvillSC
4/18-21	First FWB	Tarboro, NC
5/9-12	Red Hill	Marshall, NC
6/20	Grace	Rocky Mt, NC
7/14,18,	Trinity FWB	Greenville, NC
21, 8/1		
8/22	First FWB	Baxley, GA
8/23-29	WhiteOak	Bladenboro, NC
9/12-16	WateryBr	Eureka, NC
9/19-24	SheratnPk	Greensboro, NC
10/3 -6	FaithFWB	Darlington, SC
10/17-22	FWB	Lyons, GA
31-11/3	First FWB	Darlington, SC
11/28	CedarChp	Greenville, NC

Total Offerings: $14,056

2005

1/ 9	OakGrove	Durham, NC
1/26	FWB	Belvoir, NC
2/13	CedarChpl	Greenville, NC
2/20, 23	Trinity	Greenville, NC
4/17-22	Rivermont	Kinston, NC
4/24 27,1	CapitFWB	Sacramento, C
5/11	Trinity	Greenville, NC
5/22	Chnquapn	Trenton, NC
6/ 5	FWB	Belvoir, NC
6/ 26	Red Hill	Marshall, NC
7/ 3	First FWB	Mt.Vernon, IL
7/11	SheratnPk	Greensboro, NC
7/17- 21	NAFWB	Louisville, KY
9/4	Trinity	Greenville, NC
10/16-19	Red Hill	Marshall, NC
10/23	CardinalVi	Jacksonville, NC
10/23-26	Immanuel	Winterville, NC
10/30	Mt.Calvry	Hookerton, NC
11/ 6	WhiteOak	Bailey, NC
11/6-9	FWB	Pamplico, SC
11/13-16	First FWB	Tarboro, NC

Total Offerings: $9,517

2006

1/8	Trinity	Greenville, NC
1/15-16	Hyde Park	Norfolk, VA
2/5-8	Capitol	Sacramento, CA
2/12-15	Sherwood	El Sobrante, CA
4/9-12	IndianSpr	Seven Springs, NC
4/16-19	OakGrove	Elm City, NC
4/ 20	CardinalVi	Jacksonville, NC
4/23-26	Felowship	Micro, NC
5/3	CardinalVi	Jacksonville, NC
5/7, 14	Mt.Calvry	Hookerton, NC
5/21	Trinity	Greenville, NC

5/21	Heritage	Bethel, NC
6/4-7	Wildwood	Wilson, NC
7/16-20	NAFWB	Birmingham, AL
8/20	Peace	Washington, NC
9/3 -6	Mt. Elon	Pamplico, SC
9/10-13	NewTesta	Vinton, VA
9/17	W. Duplin	Warsaw, NC
9/18-20	Min.Rtrt	AlbemarleNC
9/24	Marantha	Greenville, NC
9/25-28	Sydney	Belhaven, NC
10/1	Immanuel	Durham, NC
10/15-18	Red Hill F	Marshall, NC
10/22	W.Calvary	Smithfield, NC
29-11/1	GrantsCpl	Seven Springs, NC
11/2	Heritage	Bethel, NC
11/19	FWB	Grifton, NC
11/21	CedarChp	Greenville, NC
11/26	FWB	Belvoir, NC

Total Offerings: $15,676

2007

1/21	Heritage	Phoenix, AZ
2/5	Temple	Greenville, NC
2/25	Shenando	RockyMt. NC
3/4	Emanuel	Washingtn NC
3/18-21	FWB	Carthage, MO
3/23-25	Jones Chp	Neosho, MO
4/1 -4	NewHom	Colquitt, GA
4/15-18	ColnialHg	Clinton, NC
4/22-25	Peace	Washington, NC
4/29-5/2	Cedar Chp	Greenville, NC
5/8- 9	Ruths Chp	New Bern, NC
5/ 9	Trinity	Greenville, NC
5/23	Beulah	Pamplico, SC
5/23	FWB	Belvoir, NC
6/10	Maccripin	Macclesfield, NC
7/15-18	Roari'gCk	Newland, NC
7/23-29	SpringHill	Albany, GA
8/8	FWB	Belvoir, NC
8/19-22	FaithFWB	Washington, NC
9/2- 5	Friendship	Myrtle Beach, SC
9/16-22	Union	Wheelersburg, OH
9/23	Bloom	Wheelersburg, OH
9/23	Harrison	Wheelersburg, OH
10/7	OakGrove	Durham, NC
10/8-12	Calvary	Durham, NC
10/24,28	Red Hill F	Marshall, NC
11/4	Calvary F	Durham, NC
11/11	DanielCp	Wilson, NC
11/11	Wildwood	Wilson, NC
11/18	Trinity	Greenville, NC
11/25-28	Chnquapn	Trenton, NC
12/30	First FWB	Tarboro, NC

Total Offerings: $18,396

2008

1/27	Trinity	Greenville, NC
2/20-27	Capitol	Sacramento, CA
3/ 1	CardinalV	Jacksonville, NC
3/ 9 -14	LowC'ny	Charleston, SC
3/16-19	W.Calvay	Smithfield, NC
4/4 -5	CarBibleI	Pine Level, NC

4/9-11	IndianSpg	Seven Springs, NC
4/20-23	First FWB	Florence, AL
4/27-30	Rivermont	Kinston, NC
5/25	Chnquapn	Trenton, NC
7/21-8/1	SpringHill	Albany, GA
9/17-21	Grace	Louisa, VA
28-10/1	Beacon	Farmville, NC
10/4	HortonRd.	Durham, NC
10/5	FWB	Shelby, NC
10/12-17	KgsCrosd	Falkland, NC
10/19-23	VandoraS	Garner, NC
10/26-29	FWB	Virginia Beach, VA
11/2 -5	WhiteOak	Bladenboro, NC
11/9-14	Bethany	Timonsville, SC
11/16	Williamsb	Kingstree, SC
Nov. 26	CedarChp	Greenville, NC
12/8	First FWB	Tarboro, NC

Total Offerings: $17,998

2009

1/4	OakGrove	Durham, NC
1/11	CalvryBib	Wiliamston, NC
1/22-23	SC Conf	Johnsonville, SC
2/1	Trinity	Greenville, NC
3/17-20	Liberty	Manning, SC
4/5	Trinity	Greenville, NC
4/19-22	CedarGrv	Wiliamston, NC
4/26-29	Unity	Smithfield, NC
5/3 -6	Peace	Florence, SC
6/28-7/1	Hilltop	Travelers Rest, SC
7/12	CalvaryBl	Wiliamston, NC
7/18	Trinity	Greenville, NC
7/26-31	SpringHill	Albany, GA
8/30	Red Hill	Marshall, NC
9/16-20	Grace	Louisa, VA
10/4	Immanuel	Durham, NC
10/12-16	White Hill	Aurora, NC
10/18	CedarGro	Elm City, NC
11/1a.m.	ColonialH	Clinton, NC
11/1 - 4	OakGrove	Vanceboro, NC
12/27	First FWB	Tarboro, NC

Total Offerings: $13,950

Bobby and Jane Jackson have lived in Greenville, NC, since 1957.
The boys, Stephen and Philip, with their families also live in Greenville.
The grandchildren and great grandchildren are not far away.

Made in the USA
Charleston, SC
04 February 2014